The New Testament in Context

The New Testament in Context

A Literary and Theological Textbook

V. George Shillington

t & t clark

Published by T&T Clark

A Continuum imprint

The Tower Building, 11 York Road, London SE1 7NX
80 Maiden Lane, Suite 704, New York, NY 10038

www.continuumbooks.com

British Library Cataloguing-in-Publication Data
A catalogue record for this book is available from the British Library

ISBN-13: HB: 978-0-567-03404-5
             PB: 978-0-567-03405-2
ISBN-10: HB: 0-567-03404-6
             PB: 0-567-03405-4

Typeset by Newgen Imaging Systems Pvt Ltd, Chennai, India
Printed and bound in Great Britain by MPG Books Ltd, Bodmin, Cornwall

For Grace
arkei moi

Contents

viii Contents

Acknowledgements

The seer of Revelation, exiled on an island, wrote his visions of things to come in relative isolation. I, on the other hand, was surrounded by a crowd of witnesses who kept urging me forward to complete the writing of this volume. I cannot acknowledge all of them here. Some were closer to the project than others, and deserve more recognition than these few words afford. I refer to the nine members in a graduate seminar dealing with the New Testament at Canadian Mennonite University: Dale Friesen, Anton Froese, Deborah Funk, Jesse Hofer, Henry Klassen, David Kruse, Al McBurney, Melinda Pearce and Karen Schellenberg. They all agreed to read the first draft of the manuscript and offer constructive comments in time for the final draft. I cannot begin to thank them enough for working through the material with me. I especially need to recognize the detailed work of David Kruse, who rightly prides himself as proofreader and style critic. Some of the smoother sentences in the text owe their existence to David.

A special thanks to a talented undergraduate student, Eric Matyas, who tested the manuscript in an introductory course at the University of Winnipeg, and came back with helpful corrections and suggestions. To all of these I owe a debt of gratitude.

Then there were friends who did not read a word of my work, but their daily contribution at morning coffee by way of encouragement to persevere to completion was no less useful. To Joe Nocita and Stephen Rosenfield, good friends, please accept this word of appreciation and thanks.

A word of gratitude also goes to the editors of T & T Clark International, Continuum International Publishing Group. I could not ask for a better team of professionals.

My son, Ralph, kept sending instant messages from Ottawa, and making phone calls to enquire how the work was coming. Ralph is an ever present source of encouragement and involvement in my endeavours. My other son, Brad, is more of a listener, and for that I am very grateful.

Grace, so easily taken for granted, is a wellspring of understanding and constancy. I cannot thank her enough for allowing me so much time in the study and in the library. To her I dedicate the book.

Finally, I wish to acknowledge the lasting influence of an outstanding New Testament scholar, E. P. Sanders, on my life and work. Over 30 years ago I learned from him the discipline of reading texts on their own terms and in their own context. I shall be forever grateful.

Abbreviations

The following abbreviations for biblical books follow the order used in most English Bible translations:

Scripture

Gen.	Genesis
Exod.	Exodus
Lev.	Leviticus
Num.	Numbers
Deut.	Deuteronomy
Josh.	Joshua
Judg.	Judges
Sam.	Samuel (1 and 2)
Kgs	Kings (1 and 2)
Chron.	Chronicles (1 and 2)
Neh.	Nehemiah
Ps.	Psalms
Prov.	Proverbs
Eccl.	Ecclesiastes
Isa.	Isaiah
Jer.	Jeremiah
Lam.	Lamentations
Ezek.	Ezekiel
Dan.	Daniel
Hos.	Hosea
Obad.	Obadiah
Jon.	Jonah
Hab.	Habakkuk
Zeph.	Zephaniah
Hag.	Haggai
Zech.	Zechariah
Mal.	Malachi
Macc.	Maccabees
Mt.	The Gospel according to Matthew
Mk	The Gospel according to Mark
Lk.	The Gospel according to Luke
Jn	The Gospel according to John
Acts	The Acts of the Apostles
Rom.	Romans
Cor.	Corinthians (1 and 2)

Gal.	Galatians
Eph.	Ephesians
Phil.	Philippians
Col.	Colossians
Thess.	Thessalonians (1 and 2)
Tim.	Timothy (1 and 2)
Tit.	Titus
Phlm.	Philemon
Heb.	Hebrews
Pet.	Peter (1 and 2)
Rev.	Revelation
Jn	Epistle of John

Ancient sources

Annals	Tacitus, *The Annals*
Ant.	Josephus, *Antiquities of the Jews*
Claud.	Suetonius, *Lives of the Caesars*, 'Claudius'
EH	Eusebius, *Ecclesiastical History*
Geog.	Strabo, *Geography*
Politics	Aristotle, *Politics*
War.	Josephus, *Wars of the Jews*

Introduction

Fifty university students filled the classroom assigned for the course. Others were put on a waiting list. This popular entry level course promised to introduce students to the literature of the Bible. Thirteen weeks were devoted to the Hebrew Bible in English, and thirteen weeks to the Greek New Testament in English. The latter was my assignment. In the first 'get acquainted' class one young man asked candidly.

> I have not read any part of the Bible in my life, and I am not religious. Am I at a disadvantage in this course?

One might think he would be. Other students around him were talking about their religious background in church or synagogue or mosque. He had no such thing to talk about. Yet here he was, registered in a university course about the Bible, not having read any part of it to that point.

The young man was encouraged to stay with the course. He had met the university requirement, after all. He might even have an advantage of not having his reading of the texts controlled by a particular tradition or system of doctrine. He finished the course successfully.

1. Purpose of the book

Why give this story about a student taking a Bible course at a university? Simple. This book is designed for such a student, and for any other person interested in exploring the multi-textured literature of the New Testament in the context in which it was first written and received. The purpose is not merely to inform readers about the books of the New Testament, but to invite them inside the literary rooms, each one furnished and decorated in keeping with its shape and function.

Context is emphasized throughout, and for good reason. Texts do not yield interpretive fruit when plucked from the native soil in which they were rooted. Being an 'introduction', however, this book can do only so much eliciting of relevant social history in connection with the reading of the texts. Awareness of the relevance of context for inquiring into the various textures of texts is an important step towards further investigations.

Unlike many standard 'historical introductions' to the New Testament that lay out multiple factors about the different books, this one leads the reader inside the various texts, there to discover the literary and theological textures that make New Testament what it is. Historical elements relevant to the reading of the texts become integral to the discursive discovery of the internal features. The hope is that students will be drawn into trying their hand and mind at deciphering the sense and significance implicit in a given text, and to do so authentically.

For many people, Christians in particular, the New Testament is a resource for spiritual and moral guidance through life. Discussions in the 12 chapters that follow should enhance, rather than detract from that endeavour. A scholarly approach to reading sacred texts is often seen as threatening to a life of faith. And there is some validity to that perception. Biblical scholarship, by definition, inquires into matters of history, culture, religion, ideology, literature, etc. in relation to the various documents of the New Testament, without predetermining the outcome of the inquiry. As a result, some of the findings come into conflict with long-standing, traditional ways of reading the same texts. The purpose of this book is not to pit a scholarly reading of the texts against a traditional faith reading, but to invite charitable dialogue between reading partners in pursuit of truth and justice and love.

The New Testament is a library of early Christian literature, not a very large library, but a library of 27 documents nonetheless. Like any library, the documents can be catalogued according to their kind, or genre, and according to subject, title, author and date. Part of the aim of this work on the New Testament library is to carry out a reading according to the catalogue: gospels read as gospels, letters as letters, apocalypse as apocalypse, etc. In that way, the texts are more likely to yield their treasures without too much damage being done to them in the process.

2. Method and program

The writing of this book was not undertaken with the scholarly guild in view, except, of course, for those, like myself, in search of suitable textbooks as resource for courses on the New Testament. Moreover, footnotes/endnotes are non-existent. A few resources are indicated here and there inside brackets in the body of the discussion in connection with particular points drawn from those sources. Debated issues (of which there are many in New Testament studies) are recognized, and a position taken without too much intrusion of the debate into the flow of thought in relation to the text under review. If a student wishes to pursue a subject/text further, resources listed in the Bibliography are plentiful and up to date. Insofar as it is assumed that the book will be used in the English speaking world, resources in other languages have been omitted from the Bibliography, except in English translation.

One of the features important to the use of the book is that of 'Further related reading' listed at the end of each of the 12 succeeding chapters. Its function is to encourage students to pursue relevant research beyond the material of the chapter. A few books are recommended, with a pointer to consult commentaries listed in the Bibliography for additional insight into specific texts.

Even though the New Testament was written in Greek, most students taking the course are not likely to have facility in that language. Thus, Greek words and phrases do not appear in the flow of the discussion, but are referenced in transliterated form in brackets for those with some Greek language skill, and an interest in knowing which words lie behind the key texts in translation. Texts are woven into the discussion frequently, yet not intrusively, in an attempt to keep the focus where it belongs: on the primary text under interpretation. The chosen translation is from the New Revised Standard Version (NRSV), except for a few places where I translate, and other places where I compare the NRSV with other translations. The choice of the NRSV is not arbitrary. Its aim is to render the Greek as literally as possible, while communicating as clearly as necessary. In addition, the NRSV uses gender-inclusive language where the intent is male and female in the human family. The English spelling in the NRSV is the American form.

To aid in focusing significant ideas for review, certain words and phrases within paragraphs are highlighted. The operative word here is 'review'. There is no substitute for reading a whole discussion on a given topic or text. But a quick review of material is often needed, especially if the reader expects to be examined on the material at some point.

The next 12 chapters follow a certain logic, outlined as follows.

Chapter 2 describes and illustrates a socio-rhetorical and theological approach to reading biblical texts. The emphasis is on 'texts and their contexts'. The intent is to give students some help in carrying out an interpretation of a particular text with a degree of confidence. Competence is expected to grow.

Chapter 3 sketches the larger world within which the texts of the New Testament came into being, and in which also they were first received and read.

Chapter 4 introduces readers to the two principal figures, Jesus and Paul, who reside prominently in the texture of the various texts, and whose powerful influence on the history of Christianity is indisputable. A comparison between the two historical figures sets the stage for a discussion of the literature in which they are inscribed.

Chapter 5 surveys the whole library of the 27 documents, with special emphasis on the role of genre in seeking to understand the inner workings of the text.

Chapter 6 attempts to set forth the Synoptic Problem and solutions to date, but with an eye to the literary and theological quality of each of the three gospels: Mark, Matthew and Luke.

Chapter 7 is devoted to evaluating the contribution of the Fourth Gospel and the Johannine Epistles to the development of Christian thought and community.

Chapter 8 is likewise dedicated to one document, the Acts of the Apostles. The aim is not to reconstruct a history of the first 20 years of the church, using Acts as a source, but to explore narratives that reflect critical moments in the development of the primitive Christian movement on its way to becoming a recognizable religion in the Roman world.

Chapter 9 opens a gateway into the sphere of Paul's missionary work, especially his letter-writing. Emphasis is placed on the urban character of his congregations. A narrative picture of the cities in which the congregations lived out their new faith helps in understanding Paul's responses to the situations that arose in his absence.

Chapter 10 is the longest chapter in the book, understandably so. Paul was the most prodigious contributor to the New Testament. The discussion explores the arguments in each of the letters, with a tentative extrapolation of Paul's prevailing thought offered up at the end.

Chapter 11 deals with letters under Paul's name, but appear to have come from a time and situation that post-dates Paul's mission in the fifties CE. A portrait of a later 'Paul' emerges, and with it a different situation in the life of the churches represented.

Chapter 12 engages texts not under Paul's name, more general in nature, reflecting situations in the life of the second and third generation of the church's life in the world.

Chapter 13 peers inside the apocalyptic vision of John (Revelation) for clues in the narrative drama about the difficult life and times facing the seven churches of Asia Minor under the shadow of the imperial rule of Rome.

The Appendices at the end are intended for quick reference to Emperors, Herodian dynasty, Philosophers, and corresponding dates, all pertaining to the macro-context of the New Testament. Another appendix indicates the need to recognize the role of 'textual criticism' in doing New Testament studies.

It is hoped that the book will serve both students and instructors in the quest to understand the literature of the New Testament that has shaped Christian communities, institutions and causes world-wide through 20 centuries of history.

2 No Text is an Island: Laying Claim to the New Testament

The lead title of this chapter is an obvious allusion to John Donne's *Meditation XVII*: 'No man is an island, entire of itself; every man is a piece of the continent, a part of the main; if a clod be washed away by the sea, Europe is the less . . . ; any man's death diminishes me, because I am involved in mankind.' By analogy, no text of the New Testament is entire of itself, unrelated to the complex world out of which it emerged, and within which in turn it found a place.

Moreover, those who lay claim to the New Testament, whether their interest is faith-based or otherwise, can expect to find within the literary *texture* of the various texts distinctive threads of the cultural fabric embedded in the texts. Nor can the cultural aspects be rendered inoperative in favour of some distillation of truth or meaning. Meaning derived from a literary text of the New Testament is invariably linked to a larger socio-cultural network, an understanding of which is indispensable to the project of mediating meaning arising from the reading of the texts.

1. Multi-layered literature in a pluralistic collection

One may gather already from the opening two paragraphs that a study of the New Testament involves much more than the mere selection and memorization of favourite texts. No doubt these short texts without context help sustain faith for the individuals using them thus. But imagine how much richer the 'favourite texts' would be, given an authentic context. A study of the New Testament involves, among other things, grasping contexts that facilitate the understanding of the particular text under review.

The body of literature in the New Testament is multi-layered. One layer may be historical, another social and cultural, another religious, another rhetorical. All of the layers together make the text what it is. An identification of the layers in relation to one another paves the way for an authentic production of meaning arising out of the reading of the text.

But the smaller texts of the New Testament, such as a parable of Jesus or an argument of Paul, are not disparate literary pieces. Each of the smaller units resides within a *document*. The document as a whole is a text. That is, the document has a point to make, an implied purpose for its existence as a whole document. The letter to the Romans, for example, has an aim quite different from that of the Epistle of James. In short, the collection of documents that make up the New Testament differ from one another. Each one arose out of a different situation in life, a different context, and calls for investigation in keeping with that setting in life.

As such, the documents that make up the New Testament are a pluralistic collection. The tone and texture of James is quite different from that of Galatians. The vision and vocabulary of the Gospel of John is quite different from those of Mark. This recognition of a pluralistic New Testament may not sit well with some faith-communities. But the fact remains, not all books of the New Testament tell exactly the same story in exactly the same way. For example, the story of the Apostle Paul's escape through a window in a wall in Damascus is told in two sources written by different hands at different times: in Acts 9, Paul's persecutors are Jewish; in 2 Corinthians 11 they are Gentile. The pluralism that constitutes the New Testament, rather than diminishing its gift, enriches it. Similarly, plurality exists within the Christian Church, each branch claiming its right to be heard on its own terms among the other voices.

2. Biblical texts are value-laden vehicles

Whatever else may be said of the biblical texts we read, this much is self-evident: biblical texts carry values. Valuing is given by virtue of being born into the human family. We humans make choices. And the reason we do is because we value one course of thought and action over another. That notion of valuing, of judging and deciding, is simply who we are. By such mental and emotional activity we form communities that share the same values.

But the values we carry with us through life are not just ours by virtue of our having the unique human capacity to make judgements. Most of our values are learned, and lodged in the mind for future decision-making. Many values are inherited from family, church, society, nation, and hemisphere. Of course, they can and do change as we move through life-in-history.

It should not be at all surprising, then, to find the texts of the New Testament to be value-laden. Sometimes the values embedded in the texts do not square with our own. Is it really a shame in our time and place for a woman to cut her hair? Is it really against 'nature' in our culture for a man to have long hair? (1 Cor. 11). Values implicit in the text of 1 Corinthians 11 were real to Paul and his community at Corinth. But they are, one might say, foreign to us in our western culture in the twenty-first century. Values reside within a particular society, history and community. They do not transfer directly and statically to another society, history and community. They translate. By 'translating' values I mean the *dynamism of change* that history forces upon us. Static transfer of values is meaningless. To be authentic, they have to go through a revaluing process, and in that sense they become new in the different setting. The new values are not bad and the old ones good; nor the old ones bad and the new ones good. They are values commensurate with the time and place and situation in life. Every generation has to work out for itself a new set of values that mesh meaningfully with the cultural configuration of the time.

All of this means that the texts we read in the New Testament, laden as they are with norms that seem so outdated to our modern sensibilities, call for *mediation*. They are otherwise foreign to our way of thinking. But we can be in conversation with the texts. Texts prompt questions. Ancient texts prompt a multitude of questions as we read them. When the relevant questions come to mind in our encounter with the elements of the text, we are driven to do research, to answer the questions the text puts to our minds.

Research helps make the unknowns of the text known. Still the operation of making an unknown known rests with ourselves as reasonable and responsible readers. Research simply enhances insight, which then enables us to make sense of the formal features of the text before our eyes. 'Making sense' does not mean arriving inevitably at certainty. It means, rather, that more light is shed on the issues to the end that higher probability may be reached.

3. Human readers are intention-driven beings

So far the focus has been largely on the context of the texts of the New Testament. On the other side of the desk is the reader, or reading community. Unlike the texts, the living readers are not fixed forms, but *dynamic thinkers* making sense of things in their world. If the readers of a text happen to be historians or archaeologists their intention is to figure out how the historical allusions in the texts of the New Testament square with the findings elsewhere on the same subject area. It is not that these readers are trying to prove the truth of the Bible against archaeology, or vice versa. Their reading is simply for the purpose of gathering as much literary and artefactual evidence as possible to be able to write a responsible history of a given time and place and people and events.

But if the readers of the text are people whose faith is rooted in the biblical texts, their pursuit is not primarily historical or geographical or social. Their primary intention in reading is towards spiritual and theological confirmation and enrichment. That does not make their reading right or wrong. Their aim in reading the texts is simply different from that of the historian. And the reading of people of faith, based on New Testament texts, needs to be added to the findings of all the other kinds of readers. At the same time, it is very possible that the lens of an uncritical believer will not see beyond the elements that foster her or his particular faith. Where that is the case, the reading becomes truncated, in need of others to fill in some gaps. Faith-readers do well to seek out the insights of the *critical historian* as much as the historian needs the insight of the faith-based reader. One is in search of the fabric of faith in the New Testament, while the other is in search of historical truth. The two, biblical faith and historical truth, are sometimes seen as incompatible factors, like oil and water, but they are not necessarily. They can become compatible partners.

4. What is texture?

The English word 'text' derives from an old Latin word *textus*, which means basically 'a weave', as in a garment. The English word 'texture', on the other hand, is generally used in relation to matters other than texts. We speak of the texture of certain food dishes, or the finish of a wall, instead of being smooth, as textured. Traditionally texts are said to have grammar and syntax. But when a text with grammar and syntax becomes literature we recognize a quality that lifts the text out of the level of the mundane. Such a literary text lives on, is passed from community to community, and from generation to generation. In conjunction with its grammar and syntax, such a text has texture that produces *an effect* in the minds of the readers. That now leads to the question: What makes up the texture of texts?

i. Rhetoric

Of all that could be said of great texts, such as those of the New Testament, rhetoric stands out. Rhetoric is not something contrived by modern literary critics. It is as old as the first public speech ever made by a leader of people to persuade them to adopt one course over another. Rhetoric was taught in the schools of ancient Athens and Rome. The instructional works of Cicero (106–43 BCE) and Quintilian (35–100 CE) bear witness.

Rhetoric is the careful construction of words for oratory or literature for the purpose of *persuading* an audience or readership to change their thinking or behaving or feeling in the direction dictated by the form of address. A particular turn of phrase, an inflection in the voice, a question that calls for only one answer are all part of rhetorical speech. The effect is lasting, memorable. Take the single phrase, 'I have a dream', for example. Most American people would think immediately of the powerful speech of Martin Luther King Jr. delivered in 1963 in front of the Lincoln Memorial in Washington DC. The repetition of that phrase at key junctures in the speech is itself rhetorical. It invites the audience to join King in his dream for the equality of all the people of the United States, regardless of the colour of their skin. The fact that the speech was delivered where it was, 'five score years' after Lincoln signed the Emancipation Declaration, shaped the texture of King's speech, giving it rhetorical currency.

Just as King's 'I have a dream' speech is laced with multiple images – geographical, biblical, social, racial, repeated phrasing, personal, opening and closing markers – so also the texts of the New Testament.

ii. Internal elements large and small

What better way to discover the elements that make up the texture of texts than to illustrate from a text of the New Testament: 1 Corinthians 9.3-18, set out here in full for easy reference, will serve the purpose. The socio-rhetorical approach expounded in the discussion that follows should serve as a model for the interpretation of other units of text (*pericopae*) in the New Testament.

---

1 Corinthians 9.3-18

3 This is my defense to those who would examine me. 4 Do we not have *the right* to our food and drink? 5 Do we not have *the right* to be accompanied by a believing wife, as do the other apostles and the brothers of the Lord and Cephas? 6 Or is it only Barnabas and I who have *no right* to refrain from working for a living? 7 Who at any time pays the expenses for doing military service? Who plants a vineyard and does not eat any of its fruit? Or who tends a flock and does not get any of its milk? 8 Do I say this on human authority? Does not the law also say the same? 9 For it is written in the law of Moses, 'You shall not muzzle an ox while it is treading out the grain.' Is it for oxen that God is concerned? 10 Or does he not speak entirely for our sake? It was indeed written for our sake, for whoever plows should plow in hope and whoever threshes should thresh in hope of a share in the crop. 11 If we have sown spiritual good among you, is it too much if we reap your material benefits? 12 If others share this *right*ful claim on you, do not we still more? Nevertheless, we have not made use of *this right*, but we endure anything rather than put an obstacle in the way of the gospel of Christ. 13 Do you not know that those who are employed in the temple service get their food from the temple, and those who serve at the altar share in what is sacrificed on the altar? 14 In the same way, the Lord commanded that those who proclaim the gospel should get their living by the gospel. 15 But I have made no use of any of *these rights*, nor am I writing this so that they may be applied in my case. Indeed, I would rather die than that – no one will deprive me of my ground for boasting! 16 If I proclaim the gospel, this gives me no ground for boasting, for an obligation is laid on me, and woe to me if I do not proclaim the gospel! 17 For if I do this of my own will, I have a reward; but if not of my own will, I am entrusted with a commission. 18 What then is my reward? Just this: that in my proclamation I may make the gospel free of charge, so as not to make full use of *my rights* in the gospel.

---

a. Opening and closing

Verse 3 *opens* the argument, marking it as Paul's defence of himself and his behaviour, not a defence of the gospel as such. The rhetoric will therefore aim at persuading the Corinthians that his behaviour neither belittles them, nor reduces his apostolic status. The argument *closes* with a concluding statement at verse 18: 'I . . . make the gospel free of charge, so as not to make full use of my rights in the gospel.'

From a later letter of Paul to the same group (2 Cor. 11.7-12), we learn that the Corinthians were offended at Paul for refusing their financial support. They were beginning to conclude (1) that he did not like them, and (2) that he must be inferior to other apostles who did take money from them for their missionary service. The same issue is addressed in this earlier letter to the Corinthians, at 1 Cor. 9.3-18.

b. The choice and configuration of words

A tell-tale sign of a theme running through a text is the *repetition* of a word or phrase. In this text the 'right' to take money comes through no less than seven times. But the repetition of the phrase is not empty, merely for the sake of repetition. With each occurrence comes nuance, or progression. In verses 4 and 5 'the right' is stated. In verse 6 the question is, do Barnabas and I have 'no right'? This is followed by 'rightful claim' (v. 12a), 'this right' (v. 12b), 'these rights' (v. 15), and finally 'my rights in the gospel' (v. 18).

Much of the texture of this text consists of *questions*. The questions are not for inquiry, but are structured in a way that the answer is so obvious as not to need an audible or written reply. There are no less than 14 such questions in this brief text. The response is implied in the way the question is framed, with each implied response furthering the case for Paul's defence in the minds of his readers. For example: 'Do we not have the right to our food and drink? (v. 4). Who tends a flock and does not get any of its milk?' (v. 7). The answers are indisputable: Yes, Paul and his friends have the right to food and drink; no one tends a flock without getting its milk.

Opposition is often part of the texture of a rhetorical text. In this text, a certain opposition is implied between Paul and his congregation(s) at Corinth, on the one hand, and between Paul and other apostles on the other. The believing community at Corinth owes its existence to him (vv. 11-12), not to the other apostles. The others make use of their right to have their wives accompany them on their missionary travels (v. 5), whereas Paul does not.

The texture of texts such as this one will often have *characterization*. In this case Paul is the principal character, and does not hesitate to characterize himself to make his case. He is not one to boast inappropriately, but does boast of his right to refuse money for his apostolic service (vv. 15-16). By contrast, other apostles such as Cephas (Peter) make full use of their rights, even to the extent of an added expense of bringing along a wife (v. 5). By bringing these items into the text, Paul favourably compares his apostolic character to theirs. They are self-assured of their apostleship, and use their rights to the full. Paul declines his right to financial support from the Corinthians, which makes him more honourable, not less so.

Human *feelings* often become part of the rhetorical texture of a text as well. They could be feelings of anger, joy, sorrow, pain, hunger, loneliness, grief, etc. In our sample text there are two human feelings textured into the fabric of Paul's text: hunger and sex. Repeatedly, the feeling of being deprived of food and drink appears (vv. 4, 7, 13). When such feelings are evoked in the text, it tends to generate sympathy in the minds of the readers. Sexual desire is also part of human experience. Other apostles have their sexual desires satisfied by having their wives with them as they travel. Paul, on the other hand, has overcome his sexual feelings out of commitment to his call and mission (v. 5; cf. 1 Cor. 7.7-9). Again, the textured feeling of sexual desire unfulfilled evokes sympathy from his audience, who likewise share Paul's human needs.

c. *Historical allusions*

Although there are few historical references in the illustrated text, it is important to note that texts often carry historical allusions as part of the rhetorical texture. Sometimes the allusions are deliberately used for effect, and at other times they enter as though unconsciously. Two elements in Paul's text qualify as historical. One is the figure of Moses (v. 9), a man believed to be a significant figure in the inauguration of the nation of ancient Israel. More than that, mention of the Law of Moses makes connection with the historical people of Judaea and the Diaspora who live by that Law. Another historical figure is 'the Lord' (v. 5b, 14), namely Jesus crucified and raised in Judaea. Jesus was recognized as the inaugurator of the new movement now openly operative in the Roman world. Paul cites 'the Lord' as historical authority for his argument. Both of these historical realities – Moses and Israel, Jesus and the church – are textured into Paul's text to advance his case about his 'right' to financial support, and also his right to decline such support from the Corinthians.

d. Intertexture

Explicit citation of an authoritative text, while part of intertexture, should not be viewed as the sum total of the phenomenon. Simply put, intertexture means the incorporation of existing texts into the texture of the 'new' text. A cited text takes on a new dimension, sometimes well beyond the original sense. That is true in the illustrated text from 1 Corinthians 9. Paul cites no less an authority than the Torah (Law) of Moses to underwrite his case for the apostolic right of support for his ministry from those to whom he ministers: 'You shall not muzzle an ox while it is treading out the grain' comes from Deuteronomy 25.4. The wording is almost exactly the same in Paul's text.

But the text from Deuteronomy is *rhetorically exploited* in Paul's text, to the extent that the new sense is stretched well beyond the original sense in the original regulation, which prohibited the muzzling of working animals on the threshing floor. The animals should be allowed to eat as they work. But in Paul's mind and hand the intended sense of the text had nothing to do with the 'rights' of animals, but with the rights of ministers of Christ. 'Is it for oxen that God is concerned?' Paul asks rhetorically (v. 9b). Actually, his audience could answer the wrong way in this case: 'it looks as though God is concerned about oxen, Paul'. So Paul short-circuits that response promptly: 'Or does he not speak entirely for our sake? It was indeed written for our sake' (v. 10). Moreover, the text of Deuteronomy is merged with Paul's new text, and thus takes on a new sense.

Sometimes a biblical text is *echoed* in a New Testament text. The echo may be loud or modulated. The echoing, so called, flows out of a reservoir of knowledge of the texts in the mind of the author, on the one hand, and a keen interpretive sense on the other. Numerous examples of the 'echoing' of texts could be cited. Readers should become aware of the presence of echoed texts in the 'new' texts, and thus enhance understanding in the process of interpretation.

Intertexture involves not only the incorporation of existing text material into the 'new' text, but also the inclusion of material from oral tradition. In our model text from 1 Corinthians 9, Paul draws in a saying of Jesus from the early tradition – orally transmitted material – to advance his argument further: 'those who proclaim the gospel should get their living by the gospel' (Cf. Lk. 10.7; 1 Tim. 5.18).

Social and religious texture comes into texts invariably. In the illustrated text Paul is aware of shepherds and their flocks of goats or sheep. The rule is that those who tend a flock are allowed to drink the milk from the animals (v. 7). In Paul's socio-political world also, military service was common knowledge. His rhetorical question at verse 7 elicits the practice of the Roman authorities in paying the soldiers for their service to the Empire. All of this material is social texture made to serve another function in the construction of the new text. The same is true of religious texture. Ancient societies were predominantly religious. Temples were plentiful in every city, Corinth being a prime example. Paul knows about a rule of temple practice, and textures the practice into his letter to the Corinthians: priests who administer the offerings of the people in worship take a cut for themselves (v. 13). Paul then applies the commonly understood religious rule for priests in a temple to himself as an apostle of Christ. He has the right to an offering from his congregations. Thus the temple practice is transformed into a texture about the rights of an apostle to physical, monetary support from the congregations. This weaving of social/religious practice into the texture of a text, such as 1 Corinthians 9, is rightly called intertexture, not merely illustrative material.

e. Ideology

All great speeches and great literature are laced with ideology. Ideology may be described loosely as uncritically held ideas that govern the way a cultural group of people think and live. A text or speech may challenge people to live up to the standard of an ideology already espoused. Or it may call for a revision of the ideology. The speech of Martin Luther King Jr., noted above, challenged the American people, especially white Anglo-Americans, to put into practice the ideology enshrined in the Constitution of the United States, that 'all [people] are created equal'. This ideology in practice means that all human beings, whatever their individual or group differences, have equal right to the resources, equal opportunity in the workplace, and are equally deserving of respect.

Religious belief systems are essentially ideological, in that the religious ideas govern life and thought. The same is true for sociological ideas. For example, in the ancient world of the New Testament, society was governed by a system of honour and shame. Group dynamics were important, just as membership in a community was vital for the well-being of the individual. A person was always at risk of losing status by one stroke of fate or another: loss of family, land, health, freedom, etc. The loss could quickly bring shame to the person, which could lead to the exclusion of the individual member.

As an apostle of Jesus Christ, Paul belonged to a group of Apostles that had the honour and respect of the people to whom they ministered. A mark of the honour due to an apostle was the gift of money for service in the apostolic ministry. When Paul refused to accept money from the Corinthians, whatever his reason, he ran the risk of losing their respect, and hence his honour as a member of the group of Apostles. His strongly worded, and somewhat contrived, rhetoric in 1 Corinthians 9 bespeaks an ideology of honour/shame with which he and his readers would have been quite familiar. If he had the right to receive financial support for his ministry, why would he not exercise the right? The answer toward which he argues in 1 Corinthians 9.3-18 is that he wants to make the gospel 'free of charge' to the Corinthians. This may win him honour among the Corinthians for the time being, but the issue surfaces again in the second part of 2 Corinthians (10-13) written at a later date.

As an aside, Corinth was one of the richest cities to which Paul brought the gospel of Jesus the Christ. Why he did not accept financial support from the members of the church in that city is puzzling, especially so since he accepted support from the poorer churches of Macedonia to the north (see 2 Cor. 8-9).

One more matter calls for attention before drawing this discussion to a close: the role of communities that received the documents of the New Testament in different situations in life, starting with the first recipients. Reading communities interpret as they read, and do so out of their life-experience. Respect for the role of interpreting communities through history brings forward the theological side of the study of the New Testament, which is itself characteristically theological.

5. The role of reading communities through the ages

New Testament texts do not 'speak' for themselves. Readers invariably *interpret* what they read in an attempt to understand, in order to act responsibly.

One thing about New Testament texts is beyond dispute: they are *religious* and *theological*. They are religious in that they depict rituals, symbols and language related to a faith experience shared in a particular human community. They are theological in that they depict a particular God-consciousness that governs life and thought in the given community and world. From the first century to the present time, the communities that received the texts of the New Testament were formed by the interpretation of those texts for their time and place and situation. Each community interpreted the texts as relevant to their personal and communal life. Moreover, it is useful for every new generation of interpreters to give attention to the interpretations that have gone before. The exercise can only enhance self-understanding. But it is also incumbent on every generation to interpret in keeping with its own time and situation in life and history. Authenticity matters above all.

Giving due diligence to interpretations from other communities, past and present, does not mean a wholesale, uncritical takeover of those interpretations. Every generation, and every community-setting, will produce an interpretation commensurate with its needs and cultural expectation of the time. In this sense, then, interpretations are not determinate. Not fixed. An authentic interpretation for one community is not then set in stone for all other communities to memorize and enshrine. Interpretation is dynamic and open, *shaping* the community within which it is executed, and also being *shaped by* the community. Both of these dynamisms, shaping and being shaped by interpretation, go hand in hand, and should do so consciously.

Interpretation that is handed down – i.e. tradition – however valuable it may be, is subject to being reshaped and revalued. Theological interpretation is not like cookie-cutting, the same with each new cut. Interpretation is dynamic, edifying and relevant. Perhaps an example from the history of the interpretation of Paul will help illuminate the point.

Martin Luther (1483–1546 CE) was a German priest in the Roman Catholic Church. He sought to reform some of the doctrines and practices of his church. In the process he returned to the Scriptures afresh, and interpreted them in accordance with his current self-understanding. He was particularly interested in Paul's letters. His reading of Paul, among the other Scriptures, led him to two principal convictions: (1) authority for doing theology and ethics rests on the Scriptures alone (*sola scriptura*); (2) the heart of Paul's theology, and thence all Christian theology, is that a person is justified by faith in Christ alone (*sola fide*) apart from works of Law. Luther's preaching and writing during the sixteenth-century Reformation wielded a powerful influence on succeeding generations of interpreters. Those in the Protestant tradition especially adopted Luther's understanding of Paul as positively representative of Paul's understanding of himself. Followers of Luther were convinced, for example, that Paul believed it impossible to obey the Law God gave to Moses, even though that Law required obedience. From that interpretive stance then came the notion that people 'in Christ' are still sinners, struggling constantly to do right but never attaining right-eousness because of the power of sin in the flesh that remains with the Christian (Rom. 7. 7-25).

In 1977, E. P. Sanders challenged the Lutheran interpretation of Paul's understanding of the Jewish Law on the one hand, and of imputed right-eousness on the other. The struggle epitomized in Romans 7 is not about the struggle of a believer 'in Christ', but about the futile struggle of the human being under the power of Sin 'in Adam'. The 'I' (*ego*) of Romans 7 is the 'I' of every human being caught in the plight of sin and death, apart from the grace of Christ to save. Moreover, a person of faith in Christ is put right before God, incorporated into the community of Christ, and enabled to live in accordance with 'the law of Christ' (Gal. 6.2). Paul did not believe it was impossible for him to keep the Jewish Law; as a Jewish person he believed salvation was by the electing-grace of God; the Law 'was added because of transgressions' (Gal. 3.19).

This new interpretation of Paul – otherwise called 'the new perspective' on Paul – puts quite a different spin on the Lutheran interpretation of Paul's letters, and no less on the notion that Judaism is a 'works-righteousness' religion. If being transferred 'into Christ' means being put right with God, and empowered for doing good, then Christians may soon stop calling themselves 'sinners' who are merely 'declared righteous', while they remain under the power of Sin. The 'new perspective' may lead Christians to think of themselves as 'saints' rather than sinners. Paul had no hesitation in call-ing his faithful converts 'saints'. They were, after all, 'in Christ', empowered by the Spirit to 'fulfill the law of Christ' (Gal. 6.2). (A fuller treatment of these subjects comes up in Chapter 10).

This one example of how a community of readers shaped the interpreta-tion of Paul's letters, and were themselves shaped in the process, illustrates the role of reading communities in the ongoing work of doing theology.

6. Conclusion: self-appropriation

Two insights emerge from the exploration of this chapter. First, no text is an island, and second, no interpreter of texts is an island. Texts of the New Testament were written in a social context to people enmeshed in that context, but written also to break new ground. Capturing carefully the *con-text* and *texture* of the texts puts a rein on immediate interpretation, which is often alien to the intended sense of the texts. Texts call for mediation.

Interpreters, in addition to being well aware of the particular context and texture of the texts, have to be aware of themselves. In one very important sense every human interpreter within every human community operates with the same set of instruments. The instruments are inherent in the human make-up. They are, in brief, the capacity *to understand reasonably*, and the will *to act responsibly.*

Interlaced with these two classic human abilities for interpretation are all the cultural and social conventions received from parents, society, religion, government, language, work, recreation, and anything else that makes cultural beings who they are in life and thought. This was true for the writers of the texts, as also for the interpreters of the texts. Being conscious of our own consciousness as reasonable and responsible human beings on the one hand, and as particular persons within a social and cultural environment on the other, may be called *self-appropriation.* This above all is the centrepiece for authentic interpretation of the New Testament.

Further related reading

Of the plethora of books on methods for the interpretation of biblical texts, the following few should help the beginning student develop understanding and skill for the interpretive challenge:

Vernon K. Robbins (1996a) explains in some detail how the socio-rhetorical approach works, *Exploring the Texture of Texts.* Trinity Press International.

Steve Moyise (2004) provides a splendid overview of modern and postmodern approaches to biblical interpretation currently in vogue, *Introduction to Biblical Studies.* Second Edition. T & T Clark International.

John H. Hayes, and Carl R. Holladay (2007) have updated their helpful guide to reading biblical texts, although their chapter on new approaches lacks depth and conviction, *Biblical Exegesis: A Beginner's Handbook.* Third Edition. Westminster/John Knox.

An incisive discussion of underdetermined theological interpretation is set forth by Stephen Fowl (1998), *Engaging Scripture.* Blackwell.

Ben F. Meyer's (1994) work on critical realist hermeneutics is worth the effort to read, *Reality and Illusion in New Testament Scholarship: A Primer in Critical Realist Hermeneutics.* Liturgical.

3 The Mainland: Macro-context

Context is multiplex. One aspect would be the context of a small text within a larger text. The illustrative text of 1 Corinthians 9. 3-18, used in the last chapter, sits within a whole letter to the Corinthians, and even beyond that, within the two letters Paul addressed to the same congregation. This is the immediate literary context of a text.

Another aspect of context is social and cultural. Such matters as dress, food, the difference between rural and urban people, recreation and sports, honour codes, sickness and health, all enter into the meaning of life, which in turn ends up embedded in the texture of texts. The socio-cultural context is therefore important for understanding latent assumptions embedded in texts.

In addition, there is a larger context, often imposed from an outside power on people in their particular social way of life. The effects of such overarching categories can be both positive and negative. If the negative side becomes too aggravating for the people where they live, they may revolt.

Revolution has on occasion worked in favour of the people, but very often it does not. The issue is usually one of power and privilege, over against an oppressed and marginalized class.

1. Empire

The reality of 'empire' was *present and pervasive* among the people in the times and places of the events recorded in the New Testament, including the 'event' of writing the documents. In this section the intent is not to provide an analysis of the policies and practices of the various Roman Emperors during New Testament times. Students interested in gaining further insight about the emperors can check the names and dates in Appendix I, and carry out research as they see fit.

The purpose here, rather, is to understand the principle of empire as it applies to the occupied peoples living within smaller national and territorial boundaries. *Imperialism*, however promising the rhetoric coming from its prime movers, is the wielding of power over people without their consent. Moreover, whatever its benefits, imperialist power tends to become oppressive for the occupied peoples.

Alexander the Great of Macedon (356–323 BCE) spent twelve years leading his army eastward from Macedonia in a tireless conquest of territories as far east as India. He took over the Old Persian realm, including Anatolia, Syria, Judaea, Mesopotamia and Egypt. His takeover of all the territories brought with it not only his political will, but also Greek ideology that he had espoused in his youth from such giant thinkers as Aristotle. Alexander believed the world would be well served by Greek language and philosophy. Thus began a process of Hellenization (*hellenè*, 'Greek') in which the Greek language and patterns of thought and social behaviour were imposed on the conquered people. Alexander chose Egypt as the place to build a city in his own honour, named after him, Alexandria. That city thereafter became one of the great centres of learning in the world, noted especially for its library in which collections of documents from the various conquered cultures were catalogued.

Hellenization affected many of the conquered peoples, and nowhere more profoundly than in Judaea. After Alexander's death, the empire was divided up and apportioned to the rule of generals, who then formed dynasties. One such dynasty, under the name Antiochus, ruled in Syria from a city called by the name of the dynasty, *Antioch*. From there the ruler controlled the eastern Mediterranean seaboard, including Judaea. In the second century BCE, Antiochus IV came to power (*c.* 175–164 BCE), and ruled with a heavy hand. His honorific title was Epiphanies ('enlightener'). He imposed the culture of Hellenism on the people of his realm, much to the chagrin of the Israelite people of Judaea. Judaeans loyal to their faith resisted the strong Hellenistic influence that threatened their Jewish way of life. One family in particular, going under the name Maccabeus ('hammerer'), led a resistance movement against the tyranny of Antiochus IV. Judas Maccabaeus and his brothers gathered around them a band of fighters who smashed Hellenistic icons dotted throughout the land of Judaea. Their subversive activity brought upon them the wrath of Antiochus Epiphanies. He took control of the Temple of Jerusalem, turning it into a place of pagan sacrifice and worship, and forbade Jewish religious practice anywhere in the land.

Eventually the *Maccabees* led a successful assault on the occupied Temple, rededicated it to the worship of the Jewish God, and gained Jewish independence for Judaea, which lasted for about 100 years (164–63 BCE; see 1 Macc. 1.1–10.25). The Hasmonaean dynasty of priest-kings, established in the wake of the Maccabaean Revolt, came to an end with the invasion of the Roman armies under Pompey in 63 BCE. But the memory of the Maccabaean resistance lingered in the tradition of the Judaeans during Roman occupation, and doubtless spurred other groups of Zealots to resist the foreign rule of Rome on their land and culture.

The Roman Empire, having extended its arms from England to India and around the Mediterranean basin, promised peace and security to the occupied peoples, especially under the long reign of Caesar Augustus (Octavian). *Pax Romana* – 'Roman peace' – meant essentially limited expansion in favour of strengthening the lands already under the control of Rome. Good *roads* connected the Empire, providing greater access to cities scattered here and there throughout the realm. For example, because roads provided easier access between major centres, Paul could readily make travel plans to go from Corinth in Greece to Rome in Italy, and from there to Spain (Rom. 15.22-24). Good roads also enhanced *commerce* throughout the Empire.

But the peace and security came at a heavy price. Huge *armies*, called the Roman legions, meant *conscription* of soldiers from among the occupied peoples. The soldiers then made their presence felt in provinces such as Palestine. If Roman soldiers asked for anything from the occupied people, they could not be refused without serious repercussion. This attitude of occupation may lie behind the saying of Jesus in his instruction to his followers: 'If anyone strikes you on the cheek, offer the other also; and from anyone who takes away your coat do not withhold even your shirt. Give to everyone who asks from you; and if anyone takes away your goods, do not ask for them again' (Lk. 6.29-30). In other words, resisting Roman authority has no hope of success. John the Baptizer in the Gospel of Luke instructs the soldiers in Judaea who came to him for advice: 'be satisfied with your wages' (Lk. 3.14). Organizing some form of strike action for higher wages from Rome would be futile.

Among the most oppressive aspects of imperialist occupation of people was *taxation*. Roman roads, cities, military, etc. came at a high price. People in a *traditional land* like Palestine understood having to pay taxes to support their social and religious life in the land. Judaean Palestine was largely populated by Jewish residents. The Temple of Jerusalem was their historic and traditional shrine. They made pilgrimages to their centre of worship, and brought with them offerings of various kinds. The Temple system at the time of Jesus and Paul was large and its functions elaborate. Taxes, based on the old tithe system of Torah (Law), provided the means of maintaining the priestly function. The people supported the Temple because it was theirs, situated in their land and serviced by their priests. But taxation by the Romans was another matter. The occupied peoples reaped little direct benefit from such taxation. Furthermore, the Roman taxes exacted from the Judaeans were going to support pagan deities. And there was no escaping Roman taxation in Judaean Palestine, or anywhere else in the occupied provinces.

The Gospel of Luke recounts a *census* decreed by Caesar Augustus, taken at the time of Jesus' birth (Lk. 2.1-5). The census was not simply an innocuous move to satisfy the statisticians in Rome. It had a much more pragmatic function. The census let the Roman authorities know who the eligible taxpayers were, and where they lived. And it provided information about potential soldiers for the imperialist army, or for any other service in the regime, such as the collecting of taxes.

Imperialist taxation required a retinue of *collectors*. These people were allowed to take a certain commission for their work. More than a few Jewish residents of Judaea succumbed to the offer of money from the job that violated their religious tradition. From an orthodox Jewish perspective, the job of collecting taxes from the Jewish people in support of the Roman system was abhorrent. It is puzzling, on the surface, why Jesus, himself an observant Jewish resident of Galilee, would befriend the despised tax collectors, despised because they were *deviants* from the Law, thus 'sinners'. But Jesus probably saw many villagers of Galilee lose their plot of ground and end up in destitution. Others may have turned to tax collection as a means of survival. The Jewish tax collector in the Lukan parable of Jesus is not overjoyed about his job that has made him 'the sinner' in front of the Temple precincts (Lk. 18.10-13). All he can do in the parable is to ask God for mercy. Jesus, standing in for God in the parable, pronounces the 'sinner' justified for asking thus.

Revolts against the occupying forces in Palestine, as elsewhere in the Empire, led to a spiral of violence with no relief from the burden of taxation. Yet revolts continued to break out, especially in the province of Palestine. The most strident offensive launched against Rome in Palestine in the period of the New Testament happened in 66 CE. The war lasted four years. In the end the revolutionaries failed. General Titus and his legion marched into Jerusalem in 70 CE and destroyed everything the Jewish people held dear. Titus and his soldiers ravaged houses and shops, killing any who stood in their way. Thousands lost their lives in the 4-year war, and especially in the final onslaught on the city. To crown his forceful put-down of the revolution in Judaea, Titus and his army burned down the magnificent Temple that Herod the Great had built some 90 years earlier. (See Appendix II). The people of the city and surrounding area were scattered far and wide. Many were forced into slavery, a legal institution at the time of New Testament.

Herod's mighty fortresses also fell. The story of the fall of *Masada* is now well known. The group of zealot Jewish fighters had fled to that fortress in the desert for safety. But the Roman army succeeded in scaling up the rock fortress. When the soldiers had reached the top they found every occupant of the site dead, having killed themselves rather than suffer the shame of death at the hands of Romans. Even the sectarian community of Judaeans at *Qumran* on the northwest corner of the Dead Sea was not spared. Fortunately, the leaders of the Qumran covenanters were astute enough to hide their treasured scrolls in caves high up in the rock face. The Dead Sea Scrolls, though somewhat damaged by time, have survived for 2000 years and are now available for study.

2. Politics

It should go without saying that national and imperial existence is inevitably political. Politics are not in themselves evil. The word comes from the Greek word *polis*, usually translated 'city'. An urban centre was always the seat of political power, a place of concentrated population, institutions identified with buildings, specialization, education, etc. By contrast, an ancient village community was the place of peasants, day labourers, etc.

Awareness of the difference between an ancient agrarian society and a modern industrial society helps in locating the intended sense in many of the texts of the New Testament. In the modern western/northern world, 95 per cent of the people live in urban centres. In the ancient world, by contrast, about 95 per cent of the population were rural with little or no political power. The rural setting in that world was not one of mega-agriculture as it is today – e.g. three family members are able to manage 6,000 acres of grain on the Canadian prairies, or a barn of 40,000 pigs, or a milking parlour serving 500 dairy cows.

The ancient world of the New Testament was *agrarian*, made up mostly of a peasant class. A peasant family had a small plot of land from which they garnered a subsistence level of life. Often they found themselves in debt to elite overlords living mostly in cities. If the peasants could not pay off their debts, they were forced to forfeit their plot and become either day labourers or tenant farmers serving the wealthy land owners. This situation most likely informed the line in the model prayer of Jesus, 'forgive us our debts' (Mt. 6.12; cf. Lk. 11.4).

In short, political power in the ancient world was located in the *polis*, not in the village. The bigger and better the city the greater the political power. The city of Rome was a classic example. Politicians and architects of that city built into its matrix symbols representative of imperial power. Rome became a magnet in the world. Many people wanted to live there and be part of the glory. Or, if they could not live there, they might visit the city to have it to say they belonged somehow to its grandeur. But even in a city like Rome, the power rested with the elite few. The ruler at the top, surrounded by his cabinet and senate, had ultimate power.

Other cities in the Empire likewise had their own power structures, but not apart from the power of imperial Rome. The ideology of Empire would not allow it. Jerusalem is a prime example. Even when Herod the Great managed to have himself appointed 'King of the Judaeans', his rule as king had to resonate with the policy and program of Rome. Herod incorporated into his building projects magnificent symbols of power, but his rule still required the stamp of Rome coupled with the trust of the Jewish leaders. To conjoin both sides, Herod adopted the Jewish religion while accommodating himself to Rome.

One of Herod's greatest *building achievements* was the construction of the harbour city of Caesarea on the Mediterranean coast. He made it into a strong political centre of power, having one of his principal residences there. He named the city Caesarea in honour of Augustus (Octavian) Caesar. Herod's political moves, such as this, helped gain him favour with the Emperor.

On the Judaean side of his reign, Herod had to do his best to avert an uprising. He won favour with the Jewish leaders in Jerusalem when he promised to build them *a temple* in the manner and size and magnificence of Solomon's temple. He made good on his promise. He had his labourers and stone masons quarry huge stones, cut them on location and then haul them to Jerusalem where the stone masons built them into an elaborate sanctuary, second to none in the world of the day. When the peasant Galilaean disciples of Jesus looked across the Kidron valley from the Mount of Olives they could not help but marvel at the sight: 'Look, Teacher, what large stones and what large buildings!' The response of Jesus to their vision of the impressive power symbolized in the 'large' Herodian masonry was revolutionary and ominous: 'Do you see these great buildings? Not one stone will be left here upon another; all will be thrown down' (Mk 13.1-2).

Even though Herod I built the magnificent Temple of Jerusalem, the Jewish priests ran the religious operation. The Temple was not merely a benign shrine that people visited for spiritual nurture. It was itself a political power house subject to intrigue and collusion, like any religious-political institution of the kind. The office of high priest was a position of power. Without the high priest and his priestly assistants in the Temple, the Jewish Law could not be fulfilled. The priests, together with the Jewish lawyers, made up the court system for the people of Judaean Palestine. That in itself granted a profound sense of political power to the Temple priesthood over the ordinary Jewish people in Palestine. The question was always about how much power the high priest could have in an occupied country. The situation was tenuous and constantly in danger of becoming corrupt.

For example, the *appointment of the High Priest* was not by a general election of the Jewish people, but by the approval of the representative of Rome. If the high priest was found to be in any way antagonistic to the Roman occupation of the land he could not be trusted to uphold the Roman jurisprudence that overshadowed the Law of the Jewish people. Some of the Jewish population resented this kind of interference in Jewish politics and religion. They saw the Roman-appointed high priest of Jerusalem as a puppet of the Roman Emperor and his minions. In reaction they withdrew from the political fray centred in that city. The best example of this political-religious withdrawal from the Jerusalem hierarchy is that of the Qumran Covenanters mentioned above. From the community scrolls they left behind, we learn about their sharp critique of the priesthood of Jerusalem. They call the high priest evil. He colludes with those who violate the Law of the Lord. The covenanters concluded that the Jewish priests of Jerusalem were complicit in oppressive Roman politics and pagan Greek culture by their unholy alliance.

Traces of this attitude of Qumran can be found also in Jesus of the Gospels. However, instead of withdrawing from the politics centred in Jerusalem, Jesus of Galilee entered the city and Temple and confronted the ones who ran the system. That fact is one of the best critically attested in the Jesus tradition. Such confrontation from a peasant Galilaean rabbi from the despised village of Nazareth could not go unchecked. Here is how the record reads: 'Then [Jesus and his followers] came to Jerusalem. And [Jesus] entered the temple and began to drive out those who were selling and those who were buying in the temple, and he overturned the tables of the money changers and the seats of those who sold doves; and he would not allow anyone to carry anything through the temple. He was teaching and saying, "Is it not written, My house shall be called a house of prayer for all the nations? But you have made it a den of robbers"' (Mk 11.15-18). The action and word of Jesus were revolutionary. They challenged the Temple system and its officials that enjoyed the blessing of Rome. Reaction was swift. The powers resident in the Temple were obliged to eliminate any sign of insurrection. And according to the gospel record, that is exactly what they did: 'When the chief priests and the lawyers heard it, they kept looking for a way to kill him.' Within a week of that episode in the Temple Jesus was executed by decree of the Roman prefect, Pilate.

Much more could be written about the *political matrix* of the New Testament. Suffice it to say that the politics of the time show up in one form or another in the various literatures. Luke and Acts, both books written by the same hand, appear to be mediating between the new 'Christian' movement and the powers of the Empire. Roman officials come through in Luke-Acts as the protectors of Christians who mean Rome no harm. That sentiment appears especially in texts depicting Paul's trial in a Jewish court in Caesarea and Jerusalem (see Acts 25). The governors present at the trial sanction Paul's appeal to be heard in the highest court in Rome.

Paul earlier, in his own letter to the Roman believers in Jesus, instructed them to 'be subject to the governing authorities; for there is no authority except from God, and those authorities that exist have been instituted by God' (Rom. 13.1). An argument could be made from this comment that Paul is here being somewhat subversive of Roman rule: ultimate authority is with God; all other authority is derived from God; the derived authority must be for the good of the people; therefore, if people do good the government will be their friend. If this can be regarded as a critique of the rule of the current Emperor (probably Nero, 54–68 CE), it is heavily veiled. The statement seems, rather, to suggest that resistance against Rome is destined to failure:

> Whoever resists authority resists what God has appointed, and those who resist will incur judgment. For rulers are not a terror to good conduct, but to bad. Do you wish to have no fear of the authority? Then do what is good, and you will receive its approval; for [the government] is God's servant for your good. But if you do what is wrong, you should be afraid, for the authority does not bear the sword in vain! It is the servant of God to execute wrath on the wrongdoer. (Rom. 13.1-4)

History has proven that the Emperor, Nero, not long after the time of Paul's writing Romans (57–58 CE) became ambitious and cruel. He persecuted many of the Jewish sect called 'Christians', throwing some of them to the lions while he watched their suffering with glee. He even blamed the great fire of Rome (64 CE) on this group, a fire that destroyed about two-thirds of the city structures.

3. Geography

Politics and geography intertwine, especially within an empire. When the imperial army of Rome conquered the various peoples, they also occupied the land from which the people gleaned a living. *Land claims* were important to the ancient people, as they are today. Borders marked off one land mass from the next. And by so doing the people who laid claim to the land within the border identified themselves in relation to their land that gave them livelihood. Within those borders also the people set up their symbols that defined who they were at the deepest level.

Mountains were charged with meaning as the people acted out their faith in connection with the particular topography. *Mountains* were seen as holy places, some more holy than others. Revelation of God's goodness and provision happened on the 'high places' of the land. Moses received the Law of the Lord on Mount Sinai (Exod. 19.3). Elijah called down fire from heaven to consume the pagan sacrifices of Ba'al on Mount Carmel (1 Kgs 18.19). Jesus delivered his provocative discourse on a Mountain (Mt. 5-7). His disciples went to a mountain in Galilee to meet the resurrected Jesus (Mt. 28.16). But the most sacred of all mountains was that of Zion in Jerusalem on which the central sanctuary stood, the high and holy place from which forgiveness and salvation flowed to the worshippers.

Within the border also were *waterways*. These too were gift to the inhabitants. Water was a symbol of life, and life-giving. Not only was it good for drinking and cleansing, but also for the irrigation of crops. In Palestine the River Jordan was almost sacred, if not altogether so. The story in the Hebrew Bible about Naaman, a Syrian army general who had leprosy, illustrates the point. He came to the Israelite prophet, Elisha, to be healed. Elisha told him to wash seven times in the Jordan River. Naaman was angry. The Jordan River was not nearly as big and powerful as the rivers of Syria. Why should he wash in the insignificant Jordan? (2 Kgs 5.9-15). Answer: because the river Jordan runs through the prophet's land of Israel.

The Lake of Galilee was yet another water resource within the border of the land of Palestine. The Lake provided fish protein for the population, and the people knew the value of that resource. Being part of the territory within the border, the water of Galilee was also a gift from God for life and health.

Moreover, the bordered land that provided food and water was not just neutral soil and rock and H_2O like any other. The land – with its mountains and valleys, its rivers and lakes, its cities and shrines – was sacred earth, a gift from the God of the people. In that sense land meant *salvation*. Ancient people, especially the Hebraic people, did not think in purely spiritual terms when they thought and spoke of salvation. Being 'saved' for them meant that they not 'go down to the pit', to borrow the Psalmist's language (e.g. Ps. 28.1). The land provided food and drink and well-being. God had given the land, making it sacred earth in the mind of the inhabitants.

Within the border that marked out the territory that once belonged to historic Israel, there were other borders. The area to the north called Galilee had its own distinct character. It was the farthest removed from the Holy City and Temple. Its population was mixed ethnically between Jewish and Gentile. From numerous pig bones found among artefacts in different sites, archaeologists believe a good number of non-Jewish people occupied the Galilee. *Observant Jewish people* would not have owned pigs. The major cities of Galilee also show many signs of Hellenistic (Greek) influence.

The excavated city of Sepphorus, about 30 kilometres west of the Lake of Galilee, built by Herod Antipas, shows signs of strong Hellenistic influence in it architecture and structures. The city of Tiberias on the Lake of Galilee likewise was non-Jewish in character. It is noteworthy that the Gospel record does not portray Jesus ever having entered either of these important cities of Lower Galilee. The Jewish people of Galilee, even though surrounded by Gentiles and Hellenistic influence, were nevertheless faithful to their central shrine and city in the south, Jerusalem. There was doubtless some tension between Jewish Galilaeans and the religious elite of Jerusalem. Jewish pilgrims from Galilee were obliged to buy their offerings for the temple on site in Jerusalem to ensure that the offerings were without blemish. The priests charged for the service. The protest of Jesus of Galilee in the Temple court (mentioned above) may well have something to do with this priestly practice, which tended to privilege the Jerusalem residents over the poorer Galilaeans.

Also within the border of Palestine was *Samaria* in the centre. The population was largely made up of descendents who could trace their heritage to the northern Kingdom of Israel that had been taken captive by the Assyrians in the eighth century BCE. Their sacred mountain was Gerizim, not Jerusalem. Witness the dialogue of the Jewish Jesus with the woman of Samaritan background. 'You [Samaritans] worship what you do not know', Jesus said to her. 'We [Judaeans] worship what we know, for salvation is from the [Judaeans]' (Jn 4.22). The Judaeans, whether living in the area of Judaea or Galilee, despised the Samaritans and their territory in the centre of the land. From a Jewish perspective, the Samaritans had profaned the Law of Moses, which made Samaritans worse than Gentiles who did not have the Law.

A similar scenario could be adduced for any of the other national/ provincial identities within the Roman Empire. But the geography of each was nonetheless different from the others. *Greece*, for example, had its mountains, the highest being Olympus at 2,904 metres. Likewise rivers and lakes, all of which took on symbolic/mythic meaning for the people who used them for sustaining life. And Greece had its sacred shrines in abundance, the most prominent, perhaps, being the Parthenon of the goddess Athena. Built in the fifth century BCE, its pillars and floors remain to this day atop the Acropolis in the city of Athens.

Greece, like Palestine, had borders within borders. To the north was Macedonia. Residents of Attica to the south, with the celebrated Athens at the centre, distinguished themselves from the Macedonians. The Apostle Paul, for example, describes the Macedonian congregations as poorer in comparison to their richer counterparts to the south in the region of the city of Corinth (2 Cor. 8 and 9). Moreover, geography in the ancient cultures was tied in with economics, class, politics and religion.

4. Religions

Ancient societies were religious. The notion of a secular society seems not to have occurred to very many people, even less the notion of a secular-sacred dichotomy, as though part of one's life in society could be lived outside the sphere of religion. The religions of the people intertwined with all aspects of life.

The religion of *Judaism* was centred in Judaea, more specifically in the Temple of Jerusalem where sacrifices and prayers were offered to the one God of Israel. By the end of the Hasmonaean rule, Judaism in Palestine consisted of four schools of thought identified in the writings of the Jewish historian, Josephus (e.g. *War.* 2.119-166): (1) *Pharisees* devoted themselves to understanding and teaching the Law that had guided the people through Exile and Restoration to their land. Their Scriptures included all the books recognized today as the Hebrew Bible, and their theology developed accordingly. (2) *Sadducees* were the priestly party, devoted particularly to the Temple and its service. They acknowledged the five scrolls of the Law as authoritative, and developed their theology accordingly. From this party came the High Priest, who exercised significant control over the lives of the Jewish people. (3) *Essenes* are mentioned in Josephus also as a party within Palestinian Judaism that withdrew from the political religion, which they saw as an untenable compromise between the High Priest and the pagan overlords. Their ascetic stance is evident in the writings of the Dead Sea community at Qumran. (4) *Zealots* were more politically motivated, believing that the God of Israel expected them to defend the faith and its symbols, especially the Temple, from external incursions. Zealots seem to have taken their cue from the success of the Maccabees (*Ant.* 18.23).

Not all Jewish people of Palestine belonged to one or another of the parties. The majority were content to live within their ethnic and cultural heritage of Israel without membership in a specific sect. They were referred to as 'people of the land', perhaps distinguishing them from 'people of the Law'. Pharisees, keen on having the Law observed by all Jewish people, committed themselves to teaching the Law to as many people as possible. Synagogues ('local congregations') became the places where the Law was taught widely through homily, singing and prayers.

Many of the non-Jewish religions of the Graeco-Roman world were *local*. The gods or goddesses of a particular people-group were named locally, as in the goddess Athena after whom the city of Athens was named. There were elaborate *rituals* associated with the deities, many of whom were part of a fertility cult. Fecundity was deemed to be the product of powers beyond the ordinary world of human life. Crops of the earth were bountiful after rain from heaven. Ba'al worship, identified in the Hebrew Bible and in Ugaritic texts, was a fertility religion. The god Ba'al rode on the clouds and poured the rain into 'mother earth' from whence came the crops. Gods like Ba'al had to be appeased with offerings and rituals.

Judaism was not without its own forms of fertility mythology and ritual. The seven-day Festival of Booths (*Sukkot*) ordained in Leviticus 23.42, and further described in the *Mishnah* (e.g. Sukkah 4-5), celebrated the gathering of the harvest at the beginning of the Jewish New Year. The priestly ritual of lighting lamps during the drawing of water from the brook Siloah (or Siloam), and then pouring the water over the altar along with wine, celebrated the fruitfulness of the land that the Lord had given. The festival was a time of great rejoicing. The Gospel of John also alludes to the *Sukkot* ritual as the setting in which Jesus invites anyone who is thirsty to come to him and drink 'living water' (Jn 7.37-38).

Some Gentile cults had 'temple prostitutes', as they are often called disparagingly. But they were religious figures, ordained as symbols of the life-giving power of the universe. Blood likewise was seen as a symbol of life in many of the mythraic religions. Priests in some cults were dedicated by having the blood of a slaughtered bull fall through a lattice over the designated candidate. The blood-drenched figure would then emerge qualified for the task of bringing the life-gifts of the gods to the people under his charge.

The symbol of blood figures prominently in Judaism and Christianity. Jewish Law required the blood of a bullock and a goat to be sprinkled on the 'mercy seat' of the Temple on the annual Day of Atonement for the removal of sin from the covenant community (Lev. 16.14-15). In early Christianity the wine of communion symbolized the blood of the new covenant instituted by the death of Jesus (1 Cor. 11.25; Lk. 22.20). It was also believed that 'the blood of Jesus [God's] Son cleanses . . . from all sin' (1 Jn 1.7; cf. Heb. 9.13-14; Rom. 3.25).

Some religions of Egypt and Mesopotamia in the first century were quite sophisticated, probably influenced by Greek philosophy. Religious leaders sought to accommodate their religious systems of belief to the philosophic understanding of the origin of the universe. Salvation came to the worshippers by their *spiritual knowledge* of Creator God who is spirit and truth (cf. Jn 4.23-4). This form of religious thought – often called 'Gnostic' – entered both Judaism and Christianity in some parts of the Roman world as these two religions encountered the great schools of philosophy. In short, religion, in one form or another, was a massive fact of ancient societies. Any reading of the New Testament that does not take into account trace elements of the surrounding religions in the tapestry of New Testament texts has short-changed the understanding of those texts.

5. Philosophy

In the period of the New Testament – first century CE – philosophy had reached a high watermark. For five hundred years thinkers had set themselves the task of figuring out the nature and origin of the universe, and the meaning of life within that vast domain. One philosopher built on the work of another in an ever-widening spectrum of speculation and argument about the nature of things. *Athens* was a principal centre of speculative thought, but other cities, such as *Alexandria* in Egypt, were homes to some of the great minds of the time.

This is not the place to enter into detailed discussion of the various philosophies of the time. A synopsis of the major contributors can be found in Appendix III, and in the sources listed below. For now it is important to point out that the New Testament writings bear the marks of various philosophical schools present in the Graeco-Roman world of the day. Any attempt to understand the theological aspects of the texts of the New Testament apart from the philosophical contexts of the time, which the texts reflect variously, would be misguided. The influence of the thinkers in the Greek world was pervasive and unavoidable, even if a New Testament writer disagreed with one philosophy or another.

The writers of the documents of the New Testament were subject to the philosophical findings, and adapted them consciously or unconsciously to their own understanding of God and Jesus and the new Christian movement. For example, the Prologue to the Gospel of John (Jn 1.1-18) exhibits unmistakable signs of contact with *logos* philosophies circulating at the time. From Thales to Plato to Aristotle, all the way down to Plotinus in Egypt, the doctrine of the *logos* (reason, intellect, mind) inhabiting the universe had been hammered out this way and that. Behind the whole cosmos is one transcendent principle and power, which the Prologue of John calls *Theos* (God). The influence of *logos* philosophy is clearly evident. But the Fourth Evangelist adapts it to his Christian confession and understanding in relation to Jesus. Perhaps the most provocative and paradoxical statement appearing in the literature of the time comes at John 1.14: 'And the *logos* became flesh and lived among us, and we have seen the glory thereof, the glory as of a father's only son, full of grace and truth.' Here the first transcendent Principle is personified as 'father' and the effulgent *logos* as 'son'. The relationship between the two is one of generation, not creation.

Awareness of philosophies abounding at the time of the New Testament is indispensable in mediating the sense and significance in the texture of New Testament texts.

6. Conclusion: macro-context enhances understanding

Far from being an extraneous scholarly pursuit, a study of the context of the texts of the New Testament makes for responsible interpretation. Of course, there are those who would argue today that the elements and structure of a text should be allowed to provide their own terms of reference for understanding: meaning is produced by the encounter with the texts. On the other hand, just as a psychiatrist would ask questions about a client's social, cultural, familial setting in order to understand what is going on in the client's mind and behaviour, so also questions need to be put to a text concerning the factors that underwrite its story.

Without relevant knowledge of the common sense of the embedded terms of reference in the texts of the New Testament, a veil lies over their intended sense. A grasp of context helps remove the veil. Contexts can never be separated from texts without leaving gaps in understanding. Does it matter who Samaritans were in the eyes of the Judaeans when reading the parable of Jesus in Luke 10? Yes it does matter. The power of the parable lies in the juxtaposition of loaded terms in the texture of the parable drawn from that particular setting.

The purpose of this chapter was modest: (1) to make readers of the New Testament aware of assumptions encoded in the texts they read, and (2) to encourage a hunt for the sources of those assumptions in pursuit of better understanding.

Further related reading

C. K. Barrett (1995) provides original sources in English representative of various religious, philosophical and political contexts related to the study of the New Testament in his *New Testament Background: Writings from Ancient Greece and the Roman Empire*. HarperSanFrancisco.

For the significance of geography, Walter Brueggemann's (2002) Second Edition of *The Land: Place as Gift, Promise, and Challenge in Biblical Faith*, Augsburg Fortress, offers stunning insight into the role of 'place' in religious self-definition.

A user-friendly, concise and reliable introduction to philosophy at the time of the New Testament is that of Julia Annas' (2000) *Ancient Philosophy: A Very Short Introduction*, Oxford University.

The matter of imperialism is dealt with admirably by Richard Horsley (1997) in his *Paul and Empire: Religion and Power in Roman Imperial Society*. Trinity Press International.

Lawrence E. Toombs' (1960) little book paints a concise, clear and scholarly picture of the situation in Judaea leading up to the time of Jesus: *The Threshold of Christianity: Between the Testaments*. Westminster.

Palestine at the time of Jesus.

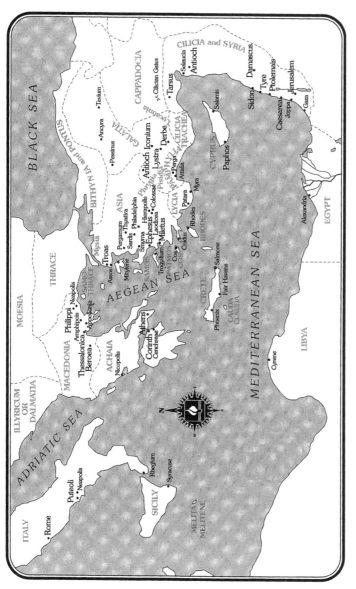

Early Christian movement in the Roman Empire.

4 Two Principal Figures: Jesus and Paul

The New Testament relates stories about historical figures, places and events, and links the historical with the religious and the spiritual. One does not exist without the other in the New Testament. Two figures come to prominence in the writings: Jesus and Paul.

Modern historical inquiry is characteristically critical; i.e. researchers make judgements of truth and fact. Historical critics rely on reason and empirical evidence. They do not allow Christian doctrine to impede the investigation so as to determine the outcome. For example, a modernist doctrine of 'the inerrancy of Scripture', coupled with the doctrine that 'all Scripture is of one mind', effectively militates against the possibility of inconsistency or inaccuracy in matters of history or science in a biblical text. For this reason, among others, many Christians view modern New Testament scholarship with suspicion, fearing the erosion of faith.

But even faith-based reading of the New Testament must deal with perceived inconsistency from one place to another within the New Testament.

The usual solution is to harmonize the disparate statements by positing something not in the text, or by proposing two or more events. The account of Jesus' act in clearing the Temple court is a case in point. The story is carried by all four Gospels. The first three Gospels have it at the end of Jesus' ministry (Mt. 21.12-13; Mk 11.15-17; Lk. 19.45-46.), whereas John places the event at the beginning of the ministry (Jn 2.14-16). A harmonizing approach makes two clearings of the Temple, one at the beginning of the ministry and one at the end. Yet not one of the Gospels gives any indication that there were two such events in the Temple. The conclusion about two acts in the Temple court, strictly speaking, is extra-biblical fabrication, the product of a modernist doctrine that requires complete consistency on all matters historical in the New Testament. Why not be content to let the Fourth Evangelist put the story of Jesus' action in the Temple at the beginning of his Gospel for theological and/or literary reasons? The first readers of the Gospel of John by itself would not have found two such events in their reading. Furthermore, the historical likelihood of two subversive acts of Jesus in the Temple, separated by three years, would be hard to fathom!

This is not the place to take this discussion further, except to say that any doctrine of the inspiration of Scripture that blocks the pursuit of truth is a false doctrine. The purpose of raising the issue here is to alert readers to the nature of doing a 'critical' study of historical figures and events appearing in the New Testament of the Christian religion. That word 'critical' requires some clarification. Briefly put, a 'critical' investigation is one in which judgements are made based on evidence in the data. All such judgments are subject to revision when further evidence comes to light, or when other interpreters see something previously overlooked.

If the investigation is to yield *historical* fruit, the outcome cannot be predetermined by a system of doctrine, however satisfying the system may be to the community of faith that espouses it. With these few pointers in place, we may proceed to sketch the two principal figures of the New Testament from the available data.

Two events stand out in the New Testament. They are, chronologically, (1) the emerging of a new messianic Jewish sect within the Roman occupied province of Palestine at about 30 CE, and (2) the extension of that movement into the Gentile world in the second half of the first century CE. Two figures are closely identified with the two events: a man named *Ièsous* (Jesus) from the village of Nazareth in Galilee with the first, and a man named *Paulos* (Paul) from the city of Tarsus in Cilicia with the second.

1. Different sources

Archaeology has contributed significantly to an understanding of the times of these two figures, but without documentary sources historical investigation would be seriously hampered. Archaeological artefacts, while valuable, scarcely capture the living personality of the people in the way literary evidence is qualified to do. In the case of both Jesus and Paul the documents of the New Testament are essential sources of evidence available for the project.

But the sources related to the two figures are not of the same character. Those for Jesus were written by persons *other than Jesus* some 40 to 60 years *after his death*, and therefore also after the extension of the Jesus-movement into the Gentile world. The sources are the Four Gospels of the New Testament, along with other non-biblical materials, of which there are many. The primary sources for the figure of Paul, on the other hand, are from *his own mind and hand*, written in his own time and situation. Seven letters under Paul's name in the New Testament are undeniably the product of the Apostle (1 Thessalonians, 1 and 2 Corinthians, Galatians, Philippians, Philemon and Romans). These letters express his deep convictions and aspirations first hand. The Acts of the Apostles, even though it highlights the massive contribution of Paul, was written by someone other than Paul many years after Paul's death. Similarly, some epistles under Paul's name, but probably not written by him, paint a picture of him in connection with congregations and situations that post-date him. More on this matter in Chapter 11.

An important issue in dealing with the historical Jesus and the historical Paul is one of methodology in relation to the sources of information. The Four Gospels, which are the main sources about Jesus, were written out of a new context that included a developed understanding of the significance of the person and work of Jesus. Post-Easter reflections on the historical figure of Jesus led to faith convictions and confessional statements about him. These in turn were mixed in with the other historical data. The title 'Christos' (Messiah/Christ), for example, came to be synonymous with the name Jesus, and remains so to this day. But at the time of the historical Jesus that was not the case, or at least not to the extent that the later church adopted and used the title 'Christ'. Furthermore, the message that Jesus had preached in Jewish Palestine was adapted and applied to very different circumstances and people in the Gentile settings outside Palestine.

When the Gospels were written all of these situations in life were brought to bear in their composition. Each of the gospel writers wrote out of a particular situation in life, and with a particular purpose in writing the story in the form of *a gospel*. Even if it could be proven that the anonymous gospel writers were eyewitnesses of the historical Jesus, devoted to his teaching, much had happened to them over the years in their new circumstances and experiences. Their post-Easter contemplation on the earthly Jesus could hardly be expected to be equal to their pre-Easter experience of the man of Galilee. Adoration of Jesus as the Christ indwelling the new Spirit-filled communities of faith produced a value-added narration of the events.

However, the writers were probably not eyewitnesses. They were more likely second (or in some cases third) generation 'Christians' who inherited an oral tradition about Jesus from the 'eyewitnesses and ministers of the word' (Lk. 1.1-4), and from some written sources. The resulting gospels thus document the theological significance of the person and work of Jesus for the purpose of encouraging and edifying the communities that bear his name and Spirit after his crucifixion and resurrection.

This is not to blame the sources. The available sources are what we have, and what we have are gospel documents that give accounts of the historical figure of Jesus from the perspective of a developed theological confession of his significance as Messiah/Christ, Lord, Son of God. The job of the historical investigator is to read the sources carefully, sifting through the mixture of material responsibly to find an image (or images) of the historical figure of Jesus of Nazareth in Galilee and Jerusalem. Any statement of the image is tentative, to be sure. New evidence enhances insight, yielding a cumulative result. But the figure of Jesus remains to be rediscovered anew.

As indicated already, the sources for the figure of Paul are of two kinds: first hand and second hand. First hand sources of a historical person are those written by that person. They represent an unmediated account of the writer's thought and action. Of course, these first-hand sources do not tell everything there is to know about the writer. But they do present the writer's own understanding of the matters discussed. If Paul wrote about having been pursued out of Damascus by agents of a Gentile governor, his testimony has currency (2 Cor. 11.32; cf. Acts 9.22-25). How could he mistake the people who were seeking his life? When he tells of receiving the forty lashes less one on five occasions from Jewish leaders, we have good reason to believe there were five occasions, and that the ones who lashed him were Jewish (2 Cor. 11.24). These experiences one would be inclined to remember in detail. The fact that the details are woven effectively into powerful rhetoric does not disqualify them as first-hand historical data.

Paul of Acts is another matter. There Paul's person and activity are presented second-hand. The Acts of the Apostles was written years after the narrated events, and years after the death of Paul. There was a *Pauline tradition* to be sure, and Acts drank from that well freely. Yet Acts shows little sign of knowing *the letters* of Paul. They may not have been collected and available to the writer of Acts at the time of writing. Some have argued, indeed, that the publication of Acts was a catalyst for the collecting and publication of the letters of Paul. But the writer of Acts had his own agenda for Paul. Acts avers Paul's membership in the party of the Pharisees, his observance of the Jewish Torah (Law), devotion to the Temple, and allegiance to his nation, Israel (Acts 21.24; 23.6; 24.10-21; 25.8; 26.4-5). In Paul's letters, however, he presents himself as one who adopted a rather radical interpretation of the Jewish Law, having taken on the 'law of Christ' by means of the life-giving Spirit (Phil. 3.3-7; Gal. 3.13; 6.2; Rom. 8.2).

So much for the sources from which to trace the two principal figures of the New Testament. It remains now to highlight results of scholarly investigation to date.

2. Locating Jesus

Numerous scholars over the last century have attempted to locate the 'real Jesus' behind the sources, using the sources to do so. The result is a mixed blessing. Mixed in that each description of Jesus of Galilee does not quite agree with those that have gone before it. An endless parade of 'lives' of Jesus had come to the fore by the end of the nineteenth century. Then came Albert Schweitzer's *The Quest of the Historical Jesus* in 1906 (in German; English translation 1910). Schweitzer, sceptical of the nineteenth century models of the historical figure of Jesus, believed that the quest could not fully capture the historical figure in his own time and place. Nor would such a discovery be admirable if it were possible. Jesus must come into the present in the form of mystical experience. Schweitzer's much quoted last paragraph of his famous book sums up lyrically the results of his study of those who searched for the historical figure of Jesus during the nineteenth century:

> [Jesus] comes to us as One unknown, without a name, as of old, by the lakeside, He came to those men who knew Him not. He speaks to us the same word: 'Follow thou me!' and sets us to the tasks which He has to fulfil for our time. He commands. And to those who obey Him, whether they be wise or

simple, He will reveal Himself in the toils, the conflicts, the sufferings which
they shall pass through in His fellowship, and, as an ineffable mystery, they
shall learn in their own experience Who He is. (Schweitzer, 1910, p. 403)

For Schweitzer, Jesus was a preacher of a failed apocalyptic vision. What
Jesus had thought would happen did not happen. In any case, Schweitzer's
work brought to a halt the endless flow of positivist reconstructions of
Jesus of history using the gospel sources. In the aftermath of Schweitzer's
work, scholars such as Rudolf Bultmann and Martin Debelius, using form
criticism and redaction-criticism, carried out studies in the Gospels as
documents of the Church. Their efforts opened the way to a new quest under
different terms of reference.

In the years following World War I a revival of 'the quest' developed
under new terms and conditions. Scholars of the second quest, so-called,
exercised considerable restraint in their reconstructions of Jesus. Martin
Debelius, Rudolf Bultmann, Joachim Jeremias and C. H. Dodd pioneered
the search of the gospels for layers of tradition, with an eye to the earliest
layers in the redacted materials from which to construct their vision of the
historical figure of Jesus. Bultmann and Debelius were more sceptical about
the possibility of recovering a true historical picture of Jesus of Nazareth.

The third quest – often identified with the Jesus Seminar – emphasized
the Jewish character and context of Jesus of Galilee. An important part of
the work of making Jesus known is to search the relevant *Jewish sources* that
shed light on the Palestine of Jesus time. Any rediscovery of Jesus should
include Judaism rediscovered. In that milieu one would likely find Jesus
in ministry. The third quest, beginning in the 1970s, has had many contributors, among them John Dominic Crossan, E. P. Sanders, Raymond E. Brown,
Bruce Chilton, Paula Fredriksen, Geza Vermes, N. T. Wright and Sean Freyne.
The contribution of each of these merits a much more comprehensive
review than this chapter allows.

The work of E. P. Sanders in his *Jesus and Judaism* is one of the most
incisive, in my opinion. In that volume Sanders examines carefully the con-
tributions that preceded his own, at the same time analysing the primary
sources in search of the thought and action of Jesus in the midst of the
Judaism of his time and place. Sanders opens his discussion with what he
calls 'the evidence which is most secure', which points to several facts that
can be 'known beyond doubt'. He identifies eight:

1. Jesus was baptized by John the Baptist
2. Jesus was a Galilaean who preached and healed.

3. Jesus called disciples and spoke of there being twelve.
4. Jesus confined his activity to Israel.
5. Jesus engaged in a controversy about the temple.
6. Jesus was crucified outside Jerusalem by the Roman authorities.
7. After his death Jesus' followers continued as an identifiable movement.
8. At least some Jews persecuted at least parts of the new movement (Gal. 1.13, 22; Phil. 3.6), and it appears that this persecution endured at least to a time near the end of Paul's career (2 Cor. 11.24; Gal. 5.11; 6.12; cf. Mt. 23.34; 10.17). (Sanders 1985, pp. 10–11)

I would be inclined to add another 'fact' to Sanders' list, or combine it somehow with the eight: Jesus was an *observant Jewish teacher/rabbi* who challenged unjust practices in his social-religious setting in Palestine. This fact seems to be as secure as any in the sources, and should be articulated along with the others.

Around these bedrock aspects of Jesus' career multiple features could be discussed: the nature of the controversies he had with his contemporaries; his use of parables and other sayings; his commensality, especially his choice of table company; the Roman occupation; the plight of peasants, widows, and the destitute. A multifaceted image of Jesus emerges from a disciplined reading of the available evidence. Thus, Jesus of history does not come to us as One unknown, without a name, but as One always becoming known. It is the job of good scholarship to bring more and more light to bear on the subject, and by so doing make remaining unknowns about Jesus known.

3. Locating Paul

No responsible scholar doubts the existence of the historical person of Paul. We have his own writings from which to garner insight into his character and mission. And we have the secondary sources, such as Acts, which verify the person and work of the man that went by the name Paul. Using both sources, we can state some *irrefutable facts* about Paul and his work:

1. Paul was born into a Jewish family who lived outside Palestine, probably in the city of Tarsus in Cilicia (Phil. 3.5-6; Acts 21.39).
2. Paul was educated in Torah (Jewish Law), possibly under the tutelage of Rabbi Gamaliel of Jerusalem (Gal. 1.14; Acts 22.3).
3. Paul became a member of the influential Jewish group known as Pharisees – 'separated ones' (Phil. 3.5; cf. Acts 23.6).
4. Paul persecuted some members of a group of Jewish believers in Jesus who had been crucified and resurrected, probably because of their faith claim that Jesus was

Messiah/Christ, and/or because their new faith had led to a new interpretation of Torah (Gal. 1.13; Phil 3.6; Acts 8.1).

5. Paul knew and used the Greek translation of the Hebrew Bible called the Septuagint (abbreviated LXX). He quoted abundantly from this Bible in his letters.

6. Paul had an epiphany in which he accepted Jesus as Messiah/Christ, Son of God, and therein experienced a call to spread the good word about Jesus among Gentiles (Gal. 1.15-17; Acts 9.3-20; 22.6-15; 26.12-20).

7. Paul wrote letters to congregations of believers in Jesus Messiah, of which seven are extant in the New Testament and indisputably written by him.

8. Paul continued to affirm his status within Judaism as valid, even though his new status 'in Jesus the Christ' had led to a new understanding as to how the Law should be appropriated among Gentiles (Rom. 9.1-3; Gal. 3.10-21; cf. Acts 15.1-30).

These bare points hardly do justice to the complex figure that was Paul the Apostle of Jesus Christ of the first century CE. Nevertheless, their singling out and their acknowledgement is important for the interpretation of Paul's thought as it comes through in his letters. For Christians, it would be all too easy to read Paul as a modern convert out of Judaism to Christianity. The religion known now as Christianity did not exist in the first century. To be sure the name of that religion comes from the title 'Christ', which appears repeatedly in Paul's writings. But his understanding of the title was a Jewish understanding. He had not separated himself from his heritage of faith, or from his Jewish kinfolk. The 'newness of life' (Rom. 6.4) that he experienced was that of knowing Jesus crucified and raised as the authentic Jewish Messiah, now available to the whole world. How else is it possible to explain his statement about receiving the forty lashes less one (Deut. 25.3)? He had to show up at the synagogue as a Jewish worshipper to receive that punishment. Presumably, Paul's reinterpretation of the Law, and his notion of a crucified Jewish Messiah, were perceived as deviation from orthodox Jewish understanding and practice.

The matter of *Paul's thought* has been the subject of much discussion from the time of his preaching until now. In recent years numerous volumes have appeared, dealing with his eschatology (end-time), soteriology (salvation), pneumatology (the Spirit), ecclesiology (church/community), ethics and not least his view of the Law. And there is no sign of an end to the outpouring of books and articles about Paul. His view of the Jewish Law is perhaps the most difficult to understand. He wrote so many different things about it in his letters! (See the conclusion to Chapter 10 for more on Paul's thought).

According to Jewish tradition, God revealed *the Law* to Moses. Paul seems not to have given up that belief when he received his call in relation to

Jesus Christ. But this new relationship to Christ, and especially his new work as missionary to the Gentiles in the name of Christ, led him to an appropriation of the Law more radical than any other in circulation at the time. In particular, he did not require of his Gentile converts the covenant sign of circumcision for inclusion in the fellowship and worship in the new community. Nor did he call for Sabbath observance, or attention to kosher regulations, all of which were commanded of members of the covenant of Israel. Even so, Paul maintained 'the law is holy, and the commandment is holy and just and good' (Rom. 7.12). In virtually the same breath he disregards the demands of this same holy and good Law: 'Now we are discharged from the law, dead to that which held us captive, so that we are slaves not under the old written code but in the new life of the Spirit' (Rom. 7.6). No wonder the subject of the Law in Paul's thought has been debated this way and that. This brief sketch of the great Apostle must suffice for the present. More details will accrue from the discussion of his letters in Chapter 10.

4. Jesus and Paul: a very brief comparison

Paul, most likely, did not know Jesus in the flesh. If he had contact with Jesus of history he kept it out of his writings, as did the writer of the Acts of the Apostles. Paul was clearly not one of Jesus' disciples in Palestine, nor was he present at the crucifixion of Jesus in Jerusalem. One would expect him to have made that fact known had he been there. Paul came to faith in Jesus as the Christ some time – about one or two years – after the disciples had experienced Jesus' resurrected. Moreover, any knowledge Paul had of Jesus of history came out of the Jesus-tradition that the disciples had handed down.

What is remarkable and puzzling is the fact that Paul makes so little reference to the historical figure of Jesus: his parents, baptism, sayings, miracles, controversies, etc. He alludes to only a very few sayings (1 Cor. 7.10; 9.14; 11.24-25; 1 Thess. 4.15). He does say that Jesus was 'born of a woman, born under the law' (Gal. 4.4), and that he was betrayed at night (1 Cor. 11.23). Otherwise, Paul seems not to have needed much data about Jesus of history to accomplish his mission to the Gentiles. Central to Paul's preaching was the death of Jesus by crucifixion and his subsequent resurrection by the power of God (1 Cor. 1.18-24; 15.3-5). But a comparison can still be made between the two historical figures, and that to good advantage. A full-blown discussion would require an entire volume!

(1) They shared the same *religious heritage*: Judaism. An argument could be made that the Judaism of Jesus was Palestinian, whereas the Judaism of Paul was Hellenistic (Greek-oriented). True enough, Jesus was Jewish and lived in Palestine. His particular understanding from his setting would not have been precisely that of Paul. But the jury is still out on the question of Paul's particular brand of Judaism. He was a member of the party of the Pharisees whose home base was Jerusalem, but Paul was also steeped in Greek language and culture. Jesus lived in Galilee, which had its own share of Hellenistic culture. Still, Paul was a resident in the Diaspora. Was the Jewish religion the same in the Diaspora as in Palestine? E. P. Sanders' search of Jewish sources discovered a 'common pattern of religion: covenantal nomism'. He then identified the shape of *covenantal nomism* summarily as having eight essential elements: '(1) God has chosen Israel and (2) given the law. The law implies both (3) God's promise to maintain the election and (4) the requirement to obey. (5) God rewards obedience and punishes transgression. (6) The law provides for means of atonement, and atonement results in (7) maintenance or re-establishment of the covenantal relationship. (8) All those who are maintained in the covenant by obedience, atonement and God's mercy belong to the group which will be saved. An important interpretation of the first and last points is that election and ultimately salvation are considered to be by God's mercy rather than human achievement' (Sanders 1977, p. 422).

Of course, Sanders' view of *the religion of Judaism* in the Graeco-Roman period has had its critics. Some say covenantal nomism is too neat to be altogether true. Judaism was more diverse than the pattern portrays. Others consider covenantal nomism too plastic to be of real service in understanding the variegated nature of Judaism of the period. This much is true at the end of the day: Sanders sparked a new perspective on the character of Judaism. It was not a works-righteousness religion as most Protestant theologians had been saying for years. Merits were not the means of salvation. Election by God's mercy was paramount. Obedience to the Law was the mark of gratitude for the gift of God. Sanders' 1977 work (*Paul and Palestinian Judaism*) was a watershed for both Judaic and Pauline studies. There can be little doubt that the religion of both Jesus of Palestine and Paul of the Diaspora was in all essentials the same. But Paul's mission to the Gentiles was bound to lead to a reinterpretation of the Jewish Law with respect to their inclusion in the community of Christ.

(2) The *geography* of each was different. Life in Palestinian Galilee, as noted already, had its own distinctive atmosphere. Galilee had always been part of the 'holy land' of promise. Jesus lived in that part of the holy land, and witnessed peasants around him suffering from poverty, debt, and in more than a few cases destitution. To the south of the 'holy land' stood the Temple in Jerusalem, central symbol of God's gift of life and salvation to his elect people. But the Temple of the Gospels seems to have been indifferent to a penniless widow who threw her last small coin into the Temple treasury (Mk 12.42), or to a parabolic victim on the roadside (Lk. 10.30-35). The geography of Jesus coloured his attitude towards his religion based on the gift of the 'holy land' of promise on which the Temple stood. His experience led him to tell parable stories against servants of the Temple.

Paul did not share the same experience of living within the borders of the land of promise as stated in the Law. He was daily in the streets and shops of Gentile people, and thought little about the land under his feet as having anything to do with salvation. To be sure, he knew the Law concerning the land of promise. But he did not live there. He probably did not speak the traditional language (Aramaic/Hebrew) that had become entrenched with the notion of the gift of the law and the land. Outside of Palestine, Paul was a Jewish man of the world. He travelled widely, being able to converse with Gentile and Jewish persons alike. The temples he passed by every day were 'pagan'. His place of worship was the Diaspora synagogue. He doubtless made pilgrimages to the Temple in Jerusalem. Both the Temple and the city of Jerusalem were magnetic for all observant Jewish people of the Roman world. But pilgrims like Paul returned to their non-Jewish land after the holy days in Jerusalem.

(3) Paul was a man of *the city*. Jesus was *rural*, his home set in the hamlet of Nazareth in Galilee. Jesus focused his ministry on village communities like Capernaum and Nain. The Gospels picture Jesus entering only one city of importance, his own 'holy city' in Judaea. Even there his critique of the Jewish hierarchy was stern. Paul, on the other hand, frequented cities in addition to Jerusalem. Probably born in Tarsus of Cilicia, he grew up in a city known for its commerce and high culture. He would have been familiar with the games and the dramas in the theatre. Tarsus was situated on a main thoroughfare that connected cities along the north Mediterranean. Paul had easy access to those cities and seems not to have had misgivings about

visiting them. His mission in the name of Jesus focused mainly on urban populations.

Jesus, on the other hand, seems to have distrusted the two principal Hellenistic cities in his area of Lower Galilee – if one can judge from the silence of the Gospels. He lived very near to the magnificent Hellenistic city of Sepphorus, and not far from Tiberias. One can only guess that his observant Jewish orientation restricted his interest in visiting cities founded on Hellenistic cultural ideology. Even the Gospel record of his journey into Upper Galilee does not have him actually enter the city of Caesarea Philippi, but rather the 'villages' in the vicinity of the city (Mk 8.7), or the 'district' in which the city stood (Mt. 16.13), not the city proper.

(4) The *extent of the ministry* of Jesus was limited to Palestine, particularly Galilee. The three Synoptic Gospels (Matthew, Mark and Luke) record only one journey south to Jerusalem on the occasion of a Passover. The bulk of his ministry was confined to Galilaean Jewish village communities. His focus on his own Jewish people seems to have been deliberate. Once he went outside the boundary of his own Jewish 'holy land', but not very far. The region of Tyre and Sidon was a short distance north from Galilee on the coast. In that region he met a Canaanite (Gentile) woman who wanted him to heal her daughter. Jesus did so, but with some reluctance. 'I was sent only to the lost sheep of the house of Israel,' he said to her (Matt 15.21-28). Paul, by contrast, was called to bring the good news of God's grace to Gentiles, which he did without reluctance (Gal. 2.2-9). He would, of course, have spoken to Jewish people the same word, but his call and mission were directed to people precisely like the Canaanite woman whose daughter was sick.

(5) It is said with good reason that Jesus believed in the *restoration of Israel*. His baptism in Jordan at the hands of John the baptizer was not a sign of repentance for transgressions. As the water through which the ancient Hebrews passed to possess the land of promise, the Jordan River had become important in the long tradition of Israel. It is quite possible that the inaugural event of that first crossing by the Hebrews was being re-enacted in a way by Jesus' going down again into the Jordan waters. Israel was about to be reborn. The shackles that were depriving the trustees of the land were about to be broken. Freedom was on the way. It is a live possibility. Or what about the calling of the Twelve men? The symbolism is unmistakable. The twelve sons of the patriarch, Jacob, constituted the

founding forebears of the nation of Israel. With Jesus and his Twelve followers, Israel was coming into newness of life.

Paul considered himself a member of that elect nation of Israel, and looked forward to the inclusion of 'all Israel' in the last great ingathering in the Day of the Lord. But Paul's vision for Israel included the 'full number of the Gentiles' (Rom. 11.25-26). His horizon took in the whole world known to him. The basis of inclusion was the same for all: faith in the faithful Son of God, the crucified and resurrected Jesus. What happened to Jesus – crucifixion and resurrection – affected Paul's vista. Jesus' followers experienced the Spirit after Easter. All of this was at the heart of Paul's proclamation, without bounds and without prejudice. It was a proclamation that did not need a doctrine of the land to be effectual; neither did it need the Temple to make salvation possible. Even some traditional requirements of the Law were set aside to accommodate the incorporation of Gentile believers into community-life in the Spirit of the resurrected Jesus.

Paul's was a gospel without borders. His preaching had the power to break down walls that had divided humanity along socio-cultural lines. In Paul's vision of a 'new humanity' (Eph. 2.15), already under way in his experience, 'there is no longer Jew or Greek, there is no longer slave or free, there is no longer male and female; for all of you are one in Christ Jesus' (Gal. 3.28).

5. Resulting Christianity

The question has been asked: Who founded Christianity, Jesus or Paul? The answer may seem obvious at first blush: Jesus was the founder of Christianity. Paul was his faithful advocate, nothing more. But there is more to it than that.

There can be no doubt that Paul saw a connection between his mission to the Gentile world and the witness of Jesus in Jewish Palestine. The death of Jesus was particularly important in Paul's preaching. But the ministry of Jesus within the borders of Jewish Palestine was not tailored for successful expansion into Gentile territory. For example, there is nothing in the record about the preaching of Jesus to suggest that he had abandoned circumcision as a mark of inclusion in covenant relation with God. Nor is there anything to suggest that he had set aside the kosher food regulations of the Law. (The narrative comment in Mk 7.19 that Jesus 'declared all foods clean' almost certainly came out of the experience of the mission of Paul). Even the Sabbath was not abandoned by Jesus, the controversies in the Gospels notwithstanding. All of these were the very things that kept Gentiles at arm's length. Inclusion in the covenant with Israel required that these *markers* be observed.

Paul set them aside for *the incorporation of the Gentiles*. He ran into serious conflict with his Jewish peers for doing so. But he prevailed in his mission. Even more striking was Paul's ability to *preach Jesus* without any significant use of *the preaching of Jesus*. Paul's message focused on the kind of death Jesus died, and then pointed to the hand of God in using that act for the salvation of humankind. By the time of Paul's mission some creedal formulas had already crystallized. He had received them and passed them on in his own preaching. The formula in 1 Corinthians 15.3–5 is a prime example: 'that Christ died for our sins in accordance with the scriptures/ that he was buried/that he was raised on the third day in accordance with the scriptures/that he appeared to Cephas, then to the twelve'.

In short, Paul opened the door of the Israelite covenant very wide in his effort to gather in the Gentiles. The openness, at the same time, tended to alienate his orthodox Jewish counterparts. What possible catalyst could lead to setting aside the very things that identify the elect people of God? Paul had one answer: Jesus Christ crucified (1 Cor. 1.23). God used that critical act to inaugurate a new age, or 'new creation' (2 Cor. 5.17), through the resurrection of the crucified One. With the dawning of the new came a corresponding understanding of the role of the Law. Observing its requirements was not a means of salvation. God's grace had always been the way of salvation. And the Messiah of God became the end-time agent through whom the grace of God had come to the Gentiles. This thinking occupied Paul in mission.

Regardless of Paul's deep desire to unite historic Israel with the believing Gentiles of his mission, his free interpretation of the Jewish Law drove a wedge between his churches and the synagogues. With the passing of time that wedge was driven deeper, giving rise to Christianity separated from its parent religion of Judaism.

6. Judaism reconstituted

Before the end of the first century CE, Judaism had lost its central symbol, the *Temple of Jerusalem*. But Judaism prevailed against great odds. The Roman authorities allowed the Jewish rabbis to relocate in the city of Jamnia in the old Philistine territory of Gaza. There they *studied the Law* diligently, making adjustments in their understanding of life without the Temple and the sacrifices. They drafted articles of faith that set in motion the dynamism that would lead to the world religion known as Rabbinic Judaism. Its leaders and congregants set themselves apart from the emerging Christianity, which began to do likewise with respect to Judaism. By the end of the second century the two had all but parted company. Theological border lines were drawn between the two religions. Name-calling was not unheard of on both sides. Then came the fourth century, and with it the rise to power of Emperor Constantine, who had converted to Christianity. The Church gained ascendency it had not known to the same extent before. Elaborate centres of worship were erected. Liturgy developed. The once Jewish Jesus from the village of Nazareth became the lofty central symbol of Christianity enshrined in cathedrals across Europe, and eventually around the world.

Meanwhile, Jewish people suffered at the hands of the Christian hierarchy and also laity, even though Christians owed their faith-existence to the Jewish people and the Jewish Jesus. There are now signs in this post-holocaust world that Jewish and Christian people can not only live together with mutual respect, but also learn from each other for mutual enrichment.

Further related reading

Books on Jesus and on Paul are myriad, but not many to date compare the religion and culture of the two figures in one volume. These few should help develop the points outlined in this chapter:

From Jesus to Paul (1984) is a collection of articles by a number of eminent scholars, edited by Peter Richardson and John C. Hurd in honour of Francis W. Beare. They examine important aspects of the Jesus–Paul debate, but fall short of a proper comparison between the two historical figures.

Paula Fredriksen (1988) traces 'images of Jesus' in the early Christian traditions embedded in the Gospels and Paul's letters.

Martin Hengel (1983) explores the development of Christology in the 20 years *Between Jesus and Paul*, SCM. His chapter on the geography of Palestine is illuminating.

Victor Paul Furnish's (1993) little book, *Jesus according to Paul*, Cambridge, deals with the question of Paul's relation to Jesus as evidenced in his letters.

From the long list of books on each of the two principal figures of the New Testament I select one per figure as reliable and accessible: Sean Freyne (2005), *Jesus, a Jewish Galilaean*, T & T Clark International; and the very readable and ever popular Samuel Sandmel (1979), *The Genius of Paul: A Study in History*. Fortress.

New Testament Literature: An Overview **5**

Consideration of the 'world' in which the literature of the New Testament took shape, however indispensible, is no substitute for a disciplined exploration of the literature itself. A literary text is not like a grocery list, which is transient. When it serves its momentary function it is thrown away. A newspaper is a notch or two higher than a grocery list. Libraries do store newspapers for later reference to bits of information. Yet in the hands of everyday people who pick up the newspaper out of a box, or from their mailbox, its usefulness is short-lived. Another newspaper comes the next day, and renders the previous one obsolete. Neither grocery lists nor newspapers qualify as 'literature'.

Literature, as I am using the term, has lasting value. People who know and appreciate texts that are known as 'literature' return to those texts repeatedly. And with every fresh read comes nuanced appreciation. Literature is like that. The other day I heard a person say (unwittingly) in public speech that he had heard another preacher refer to the love of God as 'the hound of heaven'. The speaker thought the other preacher coined the phrase! Little did he know that the great poem by that title represented the work of Francis Thompson a century ago. I was driven to look at the poem afresh after hearing the speaker, and found there images I had let slip out of my vision. 'The Hound of Heaven' was, and is, literature. It comes into speeches, and calls the reader back again and again for deeper reflection, for clearer vision, for greater understanding.

Whatever else may be said of the documents of the New Testament, they are literature, not merely writings for the support of church dogma. People who know the great literatures of the world cannot escape the richness of its texture, the variety of its imagery, the majesty of its claims. Its characters can paint pictures that stay in readers' minds through life:

> Consider the lilies of the field, how they grow; they neither toil nor spin, yet I tell you, even Solomon in all his glory was not clothed like one of these. (Jesus in Mt. 6.28-29)

> My soul magnifies the Lord, and my spirit rejoices in God my Savior, for he has looked with favor on the lowliness of his servant.

> Surely, from now on all generations will call me blessed; for the Mighty

> One has done great things for me, and holy is his name.

> His mercy is for those who fear him from generation to generation. He has shown strength with his arm; he has scattered the proud in the thoughts of their hearts.

> He has brought down the powerful from their thrones, and lifted up the lowly;

> he has filled the hungry with good things, and sent the rich away empty.

> He has helped his servant Israel, in remembrance of his mercy, according to the promise he made to our ancestors, to Abraham and to his descendants forever. (Mary in Lk. 1.46-55)

> [The Lord] said to me, 'My grace is sufficient for you, for power is made perfect in weakness'. So, I will boast all the more gladly of my weaknesses, so that the power of Christ may dwell in me. Therefore I am content with weaknesses, insults, hardships, persecutions, and calamities for the sake of Christ; for whenever I am weak, then I am strong. (Paul in 2 Cor. 12.9-10)

These are neither items on a grocery list, nor news flashes in a daily paper. These are extracts from the literary treasury that is the New Testament. And it is in treating the writings as literature that we gain a wholesome appreciation for their existence on our shelves, in our minds and in our activity. Saying things about the theological nature of the texts, without actually reading the literary quality of the texts, is superficial and unwarranted. However highly sophisticated the 'doctrine of Scripture' as applied to the

New Testament, it should not be allowed to impede the literary reading of the respective texts.

The purpose of this chapter is to give a brief overview of the literature of the New Testament. In so doing, the later study of the various parts will not be in isolation from the larger literary configuration.

1. Canon and chronology

We begin with canon and chronology to help clarify the relationship between the two in approaching the literature of the New Testament.

'Canon' is a Greek term first used in the late fourth century to identify the documents of the New Testament as we now have it. Bishop Athanasius of Alexandria in Egypt wrote an Easter Letter in 367 CE, usually called his 39th Festal Letter, in which he listed 27 documents that the churches should recognize as authorized for public worship. The *list* he called *kanòn*. This Greek word means essentially a 'rule' or 'standard'. The list of books then became the 'rule' of faith and practice for members of the Church, and thus authoritative.

But the New Testament canon was not just a list of acceptable books for public reading. The list had a particular order of priority. In some sense the canon is arranged logically. It would hardly be reasonable to put the book of Revelation, dealing with 'last things', first on the list. Nor would it be logical to put Paul's writings at the top of the list, ahead of those that account for Jesus of Paul's gospel. In the end, though, the way the books are ordered should be referred to as 'canonical', not simply logical. Canonical ordering is both theological and chronological. Jesus takes precedence over all others as the Christ, so the gospels about Jesus are first. The primitive post-Easter church in Jerusalem inherited the Spirit of Christ to become the generative matrix from which the later church received its life, so Acts follows Gospels. Paul was the major agent in carrying the gospel to the Gentile world, so his letters come third. Finally, the various churches had to find their place in the world of ideas and struggles, so those writings come last on the list.

One can sense already a *chronology* entering into the canonical ordering: Jesus was first, the post-Easter church second, Paul's mission third, etc. However, this can be confusing for the average reader. The chronology stated thus is what one might call 'narrative chronology'. That is, events and people *narrated* in the documents are presented chronologically in the literature. But the various books were not *written* according to that chronology.

The very earliest writings of the New Testament come from the one who penned the third part of the canon, the letters of Paul. His writings about Jesus as the Christ of God pre-date by many years the writing of the Gospels that present the figure of Jesus.

What is the point of distinguishing between canonical chronology and compositional chronology? Just this: the writings that narrate accounts of events and people prior to Paul's mission and theology, came under the influence of these developments. Much had happened to various branches of the developing church: controversies with the Jewish community, Rome's suspicion of the emerging movement, the delay of the return of Christ and end of the age, etc. Moreover, the thinking that is an integral part of the later time is bound to enter the narration of the circumstances of the earlier time. By analogy, a Jewish resident of Germany who survived the Nazi ideology and the gas chambers of that regime may choose to write about Jewish life in a community in pre-Nazi Germany of the early 1920s. In such a narrative one would expect to find traces of the experiences of losing family members to the death camps in a discussion of the earlier time.

The same holds for many of the writings of the New Testament. Jesus lived during the heyday of the Temple period. But many of the writings, including the Gospels, were written after the bloody four-year war in Palestine that brought down the magnificent Temple to a heap of rubble. Knowledge of that onslaught was bound to colour the narration of the events that occurred during the Temple period in which Jesus lived. Consider the way the parable of the Wedding Banquet is told in Matthew 22.2-10. Some of the invited guests who declined the invitation killed the messengers who delivered the invitation. In turn, the king had his troops burn their city! All of this in a story about an invitation to a wedding banquet for a king's son? (Cf. Lk. 14.16-24). Sounds more like an allegorical re-'telling' of the parable by a Jewish believer in Jesus after the destruction of the city of Jerusalem in 70 CE.

2. Genre

If it is important to acknowledge the interworking of canon and chronology in reading the literature of the New Testament, it is equally important to recognize the various texts according to *genre*.

The word 'genre' comes from the French meaning 'kind' or 'sort'. One might ask, 'What sort of book are you reading?' 'What kind of art is that?' The term 'genre' is a rather loose way of talking about works of literature. It is a way of categorizing a work of literature or other art forms as belonging to works with similar characteristics. By so categorizing a work of literature the reader approaches the work with certain expectations and assumptions. One would not approach an epic poem in the same way one would approach Tolstoy's *War and Peace*. The one is an epic poem, while the other is a novel. The approach and the expectation of the reader to each of these would be commensurate with the genre, the kind of literary writing that each of them represents.

The canon of the New Testament consists of several literary genres, the identity of which should be recognized as the point of entry into the substance of the particular work. The intent of the rest of this chapter is to identify and describe briefly the various genres within the collection of documents that make up the New Testament canon. Later chapters will explore each of these in more detail.

a. Gospel

As a genre, 'gospel' applies to a significant number of documents that tell the story of the ministry, death and resurrection of Jesus, four of which are in the New Testament (Matthew, Mark, Luke and John). The genre is called 'gospel' because it represents *good news* of God's gift of life and wholeness to humankind through the ministry of Jesus. Moreover, a 'gospel' is not a biography in the sense of describing Jesus going through every stage of his 30-year life. Rather, a gospel brings out the saving character of Jesus for the purpose of bringing comfort and grace to the lives of those who would put their trust in him. In this respect, gospels are missionary documents designed to persuade readers to follow Jesus in their lives. For example, the Gospel of John concludes with the following summary statement of purpose:

> Jesus did many other signs in the presence of his disciples, which are not written in this book. But these are written *so that you may come to believe* that Jesus is the Messiah, the Son of God, and that through believing you may have life in his name. (Jn 20.30-31)

Within the genre 'gospel' in the New Testament a further division can be observed. Three of the four (Matthew, Mark and Luke) are called 'synoptic'.

As the term implies, the three tell the story from the same perspective. They 'see together' (*syn* + *optic*). But the three are not identical. If they were, the presence of two of them in the canon would be redundant, if not ridiculous. While much of the material is the same, each gospel bears its own stamp. A more detailed analysis of each of the Synoptic Gospels in the next chapter will confirm as much.

The Fourth Gospel, John, has very little in common with the other three beyond the fact that it is a 'gospel'. The few places where there is overlap with the Synoptics the episode is rendered differently. The vocabulary is different. The literary structure is unique. The theological themes are distinctive. Only in the Fourth Gospel do we find Jesus attending four Passovers in Jerusalem. Hence the traditional view of a 3-year ministry of Jesus. The other three gospels have Jesus attend only one Passover, making his ministry last about 18 months.

The Gospel of John has three companions in another genre, namely Epistles. They are companions in that they share much the same vocabulary, and some of the same tensions and theological viewpoints, making them Johannine. The Johannine literature will be discussed in more detail in Chapter 7.

b. Acts

Only one book in the New Testament falls under the name Acts of the Apostles. It is nonetheless a genre in that Acts of the canon has many partners outside the New Testament. The genre is so named because these writings are about the acts of the earliest believers in Jesus after his resurrection and the receiving of his Spirit. The other non-canonical Acts include the Acts of Paul, the Acts of Peter, the Acts of John, the Acts of Andrew, and the Acts of Thomas. The canonical Acts is the most comprehensive. It makes connection between the missionary acts of Paul in the Gentile world and the earlier acts of Peter and others in the environs of Jerusalem. Many other such links are made in the canonical Acts, such as the implicit connection between Jesus in the city of Jerusalem and Paul in the city of Rome. Moreover, Acts accounts for the movement of the gospel out of its first humble environs in rural Galilee into the most powerful centre of the world, by virtue of the call and conviction of Paul. The Acts of the Apostles comes up for further analysis in Chapter 8.

c. Letter

Unlike the Acts genre, with only one such represented in the canon, the 'letter' genre has 13, all of them under the name of Paul. The 'letter' was common throughout the Graeco-Roman world, and Paul used it as a way of keeping faith with churches he established throughout the north Mediterranean provinces, including Rome in Italy.

A Graeco-Roman letter was personal and directed to particular matters of the moment. It could be official, as in a letter from the army general to a centurion, but it would still be personal and specific. Because of the shared context between sender and receiver, the letter could assume certain social, cultural and personal details in the course of the correspondence without spelling out the knowledge common between sender and receiver.

Paul's letters, like those common in the world of the time, followed an established pattern:

(1) *The opening salutation*, which consisted of three elements: (a) the name of the sender(s). With the name may be some qualifying character-istics, 'apostle of Jesus Christ', for example; (b) the designation of the receiver(s). If the letter was to a group of readers then the designation could include their locale and their character, as in 'to all God's beloved in Rome, who are called to be saints;' (c) A greeting, which is usually aimed directly at the readers: 'grace to you and peace from God our Father and the Lord Jesus Christ'.

(2) *The Thanksgiving*, which hints at the purpose and content of the main part of the letter. The hint lies within the lofty language of prayer and thanksgiving for the good life and good will of the recipients of the letter. The 'thanksgiving' in Paul's letter to the congregation at Thessalonica is a case in point: 'We always *give thanks to God* for all of you and mention you in *our prayers*, constantly *remembering* before our God and Father your work of faith and labor of love and steadfastness of hope in our Lord Jesus Christ. For we know, brothers and sisters beloved by God, that he has chosen you, because our message of the gospel came to you not in word only, but also in power and in the Holy Spirit and with full conviction; just as you know what kind of persons we proved to be among you for your sake' (1 Thess. 1.2-5). The telltale phrases are 'give thanks', 'our prayer' and 'remembering'. The faith and labour of love are commended in the thanksgiving, and these in turn become part of the discussion in the subsequent parts of the letter.

(3) *The Body*, in which the various issues that gave rise to the letter come into full view. The body of the letter deals with issues that pertain to both sender and receiver. Often the matters are weighty. An argument ensues. Argument has to do with proving a point. A thesis statement is set out, and then proofs are developed to establish the validity of the thesis. The proofs are not simply lined up. They are textured into persuasive discourse. There may be rhetorical questions, as illustrated in 1 Corinthians 9 of Chapter 2 above. Appeals may be made to authoritative sources, such as Scripture. Analogies may be made. The literary possibilities are many for making an argument. And Paul's letters overflow with the various forms of argument. The argument usually leads to practical application. How then should the readers behave given the conclusion(s) to the argument? This kind of practical, ethical advice is called *paranesis*, of which there is plenty in Paul's letters.

(4) *The Closing*, in which final greetings are extended and a benediction pronounced. In this closing part of the letter the writer may give travel plans, especially if he plans to visit the community to which this letter is going.

Perhaps the best example of the letter form that includes all of these elements in compressed form is the little letter to Philemon 'and to the church in [his] house' (Phlm. v. 2). It would be worthwhile to locate that letter at the end of the collection of Pauline letters and scan it for the elements outlined above.

i. Authenticity

As noted earlier, there are 13 letters under the name of Paul. But not all scholars agree on the ones that came directly from the hand of the historical Paul. The question is one of *authenticity*. It is not enough to rely on the opening salutation in which the writer identifies him/herself. The practice of writing under the name of an important figure from the past was not uncommon in the Graeco-Roman period. A number of letters outside the canon bear the names of the early church leaders long since dead, among them Paul. The question that troubles some modern Christians has to do with the lack of authenticity in the ones under Paul's name *within* the canon. A modern Christian might expect a letter that bears the name of the writer to be the true identification of that person. But it is also true that we have to take into account the accepted practice of writing under an assumed name for purposes of bringing the authority of the assumed writer to bear on the new situation at hand. That practice was also 'true' at the time.

Scholars have found that the substance and texture and details of some of the 13 letters are not consistent with the content, texture and details of other letters in the collection. Based on careful literary and historical analysis scholars have been able to identify 7 letters *unquestionably from the historic Paul* of the fifties CE: Romans, First Corinthians, Second Corinthians, First Thessalonians, Galatians, Philippians, and Philemon. All of these reflect the mission and mind and activity of Paul during his preaching expeditions from 49/50 to 57/58 CE. The other 6 letters written under the authority of Paul's name reflect a later development in the life and thought of the emerging churches. The conflicts and tensions are different. Hence the thought and vocabulary are of a different vintage from that of Paul a generation or two earlier.

Two stages of development seem to be reflected in the 6 disputed letters. Colossians and Ephesians appear to be earlier than First and Second Timothy and Titus, and are labelled deutero-Pauline. They are so named because they appear to speak to a second (*deutero*) stage in the development of Paul's thought. Colossians and Ephesians are more general in nature; more 'catholic' in their appeal. They call for *the churches* of Paul's mission to become *the Church*: one Church, not many. The other three, called the Pastorals – because they contain instructions to two pastors of congregations – grapple with different matters: church order, Gnostic myths that threaten orthodoxy, false doctrine, ordination of qualified individuals to lead the congregations, etc. These Pastoral letters are sometimes referred to as trito-Pauline, representing a third phase in the thought and life of the Pauline churches.

ii. Integrity

There is another matter with which interpreters of the Pauline letters grapple: *integrity*. Questions about integrity focus not on the authorship of a letter, but on the literary coherence of the letter. Did all of the parts of this document originate at the same time in response to the same situation? There seems to be some disparity from one part to the next? It was a practice of the time to put more than one document onto one papyrus scroll in the process of copying. When additional copies of documents were required some people had the job of copying the text onto a new papyrus by quill and ink. For example, when some of the post-Pauline leaders engaged in collecting Paul's letters for distribution, they probably found fragments of letters, which they then incorporated into one scroll along with another letter (or part thereof). A good example of this product can be observed in 2 Corinthians. The first 9 chapters of that document are generally conciliatory and patient with the Corinthian readers. But the last 4 chapters are defensive, sarcastic and judgmental. There is no question about the authenticity of the two parts, but there is serious doubt about the integrity of the letter. That is, the two literary parts are so incongruent as to throw into question the occasion of writing each part. Something gave rise to the writing of chapters 1–9 that led Paul to write those chapters in a mode of forgiveness and reconciliation. But something quite different gave rise to his way of writing in chapters 10–13. In those chapters he is 'ready to punish every disobedience' (10.6).

This brief overview of the complex 'letter' genre in the New Testament paves the way for expanded discussion of the character and content of the Pauline and post-Pauline letters to follow in Chapters 10 and 11.

d. Epistle

A distinction is being made between 'letter' and 'epistle' for the purpose of identifying the difference between the two forms. The 'letter', as we have seen, follows a pattern already in place in the Graeco-Roman world. The architects of the 'epistle', on the other hand, adapted the letter-function for a wider audience. The 'epistle' should therefore be treated as a subgenre. The post-Pauline church leaders cashed in on the idea behind Paul's personal, specific letters, which was to give guidance to his various congregations. Paul's genuine letters were directed to particular congregations located in very particular places in the territories of his mission. The needs were specific, and Paul's word was targeted to the situation at hand. The 'epistle', on the other hand, is more general. It has a whole group of churches in view in its address. Its instructions apply to a broad spectrum of issues that were common to many congregations.

The epistle-form came into its own during the move towards *catholicity*. Bishops in charge of churches scattered over large areas used the 'epistle' as a way of keeping all of the churches of a large area in line with the doctrine and practice deemed appropriate by the bishop(s). Eventually all areas were welded together into one, to form One Church, the Catholic Church. In that later stage the epistle was still a vehicle for keeping all of the churches in tune with the doctrine and practice hammered out by bishops in council. Recall the 39th Festal Epistle of Athanasius in 367 CE.

The documents of the New Testament that fall under the subgenre 'epistle' are Hebrews, James, First and Second Peter, First, Second and Third John, and Jude. All of these are general in nature, some more than others. Hebrews opens with a thematic preface, not a personal salutation. It reads more like a sermon than a letter. It retains some of the letter form at the end, including a lofty benediction at 13.20-21. Hebrews is anonymous. Later tradition attributed it to the historical Paul, but the whole tenor and texture of Hebrews is un-Pauline.

The three Johannine epistles are also anonymous. But later tradition attributed them, along with the Fourth Gospel, to John the disciple of Jesus. Even though the Johannine epistles exhibit the same vocabulary and themes as the Fourth Gospel, they probably come from a later situation in that circle of churches in the Mediterranean basin.

All of the other 'general epistles' are under the names of well known leaders of the early primitive church: James and Jude, presumed to be brothers of Jesus, and the Apostle Peter. Their general character and purpose will come to light under closer scrutiny in due course.

e. Apocalypse

Finally, the genre called 'apocalypse', or 'apocalyptic'. 'Apocalypse' is derived directly from the Greek term *apocalupsis*. It is usually translated 'revelation'. Even though there is only one document in the New Testament that qualifies for this genre, there are others outside the New Testament that have the same literary imprint. Daniel of the Hebrew Bible is a case in point; so also *1 Enoch* among others. And there are parts of documents in the New Testament that contain some of the marks of apocalyptic, Matthew 24–25 being a good example.

Scholars have debated the definition of the genre called 'apocalyptic' for some time. How much of apocalyptic is prophecy, eschatology, letter, drama, wisdom? J. J. Collins crafted a definition of the apocalyptic genre after his research into numerous such literatures in Judaism and Hellenism, one that fits Revelation in the New Testament. Apocalyptic is a genre of 'revelatory literature with a narrative framework in which a revelation is mediated by an otherworldly being to a human recipient, disclosing a transcendent reality which is both temporal, insofar as it is envisages eschatological salvation, and spatial insofar as it involves another, supernatural world' (1998, p. 5). Such a genre of literature is 'intended for a group in crisis with the purpose of exhortation and/or consolation by means of divine authority' (1998 p. 41).

The apocalyptic vision of history sees God in ultimate control of the affairs of human beings. Those who suffer in the present under the oppressive structures of the ruling hierarchy will be vindicated, and their suffering for righteousness rewarded. Those who oppress and oppose justice will be judged accordingly, and their regime destroyed.

Christian apocalyptic literature seems to have arisen out of a socio-political situation that threatened the life of the communities, especially the leaders of the communities. If communities and their leaders were seen to be subversive of the ruling powers, they suffered, even to the death. The last book of the New Testament most likely came to expression in such a time of persecution of the Christian churches in Asia Minor towards the end of the first century or the beginning of the second century. The mythic symbolism of apocalyptic concealed the real identity of the oppressors and their schemes under code words and images recognized, presumably, by the insiders to whom the literature was directed. Babylon, the power that destroyed Jerusalem and took the Judaeans captive many years before, became an apocalyptic cryptogram for Rome, the contemporary oppressor of the churches. The masking of the real oppressor of the time served to protect the writer and his community from recrimination.

One of the purposes of apocalyptic literature was to hold out hope to suffering communities. The seer in the book of Revelation envisions a new heaven and a new earth after the judgment of the evil doers, and with these new realms also a New Jerusalem coming down from God out of heaven. The new city will be just and merciful. The former things will have passed away. He sees a time and place and situation in which all tears will be wiped away. Beyond this purpose, apocalyptic also serves to indict the oppressor using transcendent, cosmic categories, authorized by the heavenly mediator of the vision. A more detailed inquiry into the book of Revelation is reserved for the last chapter of the book.

3. Conclusion

The purpose of this chapter was to identify the pluralistic literature of the New Testament canon by genre. The 27 documents on the list, with all their diversity from one to the other, together constitute a reference point for the faith and life of the members of the Christian communities worldwide. The idea of a 'canon' serves that function in the ongoing life of the Church in the world.

However, the use of the canon as a singular reference point tends to run the risk of glossing over the literary variation from one document to the next. Some readers in faith communities feel at liberty to pick and choose texts from one document and another in support of some system of thought or practice without regard to the integrity and particularity of documents. Responsible interpretation takes into account the kind of literature under consideration. That much is at least an important starting point for work within the variegated canon. A text from apocalyptic cannot be combined uncritically with a proverb of Jesus or an argument of Paul without violating the type and texture of each of the texts.

It is hoped that in laying out the literature of the New Testament by genre a reading of the New Testament will be enhanced. The point to the exercise was not to denigrate the canon of the New Testament, but to draw attention to what it really is: a collection of *diverse literary compositions* on which the Orthodox Church has put its stamp of approval.

Further related reading

A new book by Kyle Keefer (2007) investigates the writings of the New Testament using the lens of literary criticism – plot, character, genre, etc. – to explain its influence not only among Christians, but in the larger world. *The New Testament As Literature: A Very Short Introduction*, Oxford, is accessible, clear, insightful, and resourceful for interpretation of texts.

Stephen Cox (2005) in *The New Testament and Literature: A Guide to Literary Patterns*, Open Court, identifies the literary genres and devices operating in the New Testament as its DNA. Beyond identifying the literary DNA, Cox's book demonstrates the influence of the literary character of the New Testament on other great literature, including hymns, especially in English.

One in Three:
The Synoptic Gospels

Even though the first three gospels in the New Testament are the primary sources for any study of the historical Jesus, they are not historical writings in the modern sense of the term 'historical'. Each one of them purports to be a gospel, not a history. That is, they claim to be 'the good news of Jesus Christ, the Son of God' (Mk 1.1). This opening statement in the Gospel according to Mark is a confession of faith. The author of Mark is up front with the reader. He declares Jesus 'Son of God' immediately and without apology.

At the same time, Mark proceeds with a *narrative* that underwrites the confession. Each of the other two gospels does likewise in its own way.

The confessional elements are essentially the same in all three. And the figure of Jesus is essentially the same in all three. Yet there are three complementary Gospels about one person. In the case of Luke the 'compliment' is rather large – almost 9 chapters! Clearly, the author of Luke had access to material that the other two did not. Or if they had access to it, they chose not to include it in their presentation of Jesus of Galilee.

Good tools help in the study of the Synoptic Gospels. One of the most helpful is a 'gospel parallels'. This tool enables the reader to view at a glance the rendering of each pericopè (bounded text), and thus compare the similarity and difference between the three, or the two as the case may be. The *Gospel Parallels* edited by Burton Throckmorton Jr. has been a standard work for many years. It is now available in the NRSV English translation. Any English version is not the best way to compare the wording from one gospel to the next. The Gospels were written in Greek, and should be compared in Greek. But for those without facility in Greek, the NRSV edition of Throckmorton's work is useful. More recently Robert Funk edited a *New Gospel Parallels* in two volumes in which he pays close attention to the Greek text of the Gospels, and includes parallels in John and non-canonical gospels such as the Gospel of Thomas. It would be advantageous to have one of these tools at hand during the reading of the next sections of this chapter.

1. The Synoptic question

Scholars have identified what they have called the 'Synoptic problem', or 'question'. The question about Synoptic Gospels presents itself because of the *synoptic fact*.

There are several parts to the synoptic fact. (1) All three Gospels were written in Greek, not the Aramaic dialect of Jesus. Some scholars have tried to argue that Matthew was first written in Hebrew/Aramaic and later translated into Greek. But there is no hard evidence to support that theory. Aramaic echoes do exist in all three gospels, as might be expected, given the original setting of the Jesus tradition in Jewish Galilee. Jesus almost certainly taught in Aramaic. But the common language of the extant gospels is Greek. That fact conjoins with the second. (2) There is remarkably close agreement in language patterns between the three Greek gospels. Vocabulary is the same at many points, as also syntax. Compare the underlined words and word order between two texts from Mark and Luke, and two from Mark and Matthew in Table 6.1.

Table 6.1 Comparison between Texts

Mark 5.5-7	Luke 8.28
When he saw Jesus from a distance, he ran and bowed <u>down before him; and he shouted at the top of his voice, 'What have you to do with me, Jesus, Son of the Most High God?</u> I adjure <u>you</u> by God, <u>do not torment me'.</u>	When he saw Jesus, he fell <u>down before him and shouted at the top of his voice, 'What have you to do with me, Jesus, Son of the Most High God?</u> I beg <u>you, do not torment me'.</u>

Mark 9.2-3	Matthew 17.1-2
<u>Six days later, Jesus took with him</u> Peter and <u>James and John, and led them up a high mountain</u> apart, <u>by themselves. And he was transfigured before them, and his clothes became dazzling white.</u>	<u>Six days later, Jesus took with him Peter and James and</u> his brother <u>John and led them up a high mountain, by themselves. And he was transfigured before them,</u> and his face shone like the sun, <u>and his clothes became dazzling white.</u>

(3) The sequence and setting in a number of the narratives is the same between Matthew, Mark and Luke. But (4) when Matthew and Luke carry similar material that is not found in Mark they do not follow the same sequence of events or the same setting for the events. For example, many of the sayings of Jesus in Matthew appear in Luke. But the setting and sequence of their utterance is not the same in Luke as in Matthew. Jesus' famous Sermon on the Mount of Matthew 5 to 7 is also in Luke 6, but in Luke the 'sermon' is given after he came down from a mountain to a level place. And the Lukan version of the sayings in the 'sermon' is not in the same sequence as they are in Matthew. In addition to the shared sayings material between Matthew and Luke, (5) each of these two has text material, both narratives and sayings, unique to the respective gospel. Finally, (6) where there is remarkable similarity between two or three of the Synoptic Gospels, there is also some difference. Consider the illustrated texts in Table 6.1 above. With the underlined words that the gospels share, there are words in the same pericopè that are distinctive to each gospel.

These are the basic facts about the Synoptic Gospels, from which comes the Synoptic problem: How do we account for the similarity between the three on the one hand, and the two on the other? How do we account for the unique material in Matthew and Luke? And how do we account for the differences between them?

2. Jesus-tradition

The culture of ancient agrarian society was largely *oral*. Only an educated class could write anything remotely approaching a gospel. Their writings, including the Synoptic Gospels, have come down to us as proof that there were indeed writers in Christian communities towards the end of the first century. But the majority of the population did not write, and certainly not to the extent to which we are accustomed today. The interest of most people of that time lay in keeping body and soul together.

Jesus served the peasant class above all, it seems. As noted earlier, he spent his time in ministry in rural village communities, not urban centres. His preaching was not first written out in polished text and then delivered. He spoke out of an interior reservoir of insight and experience. And the people who listened to his words were not taking notes. They learned from their master how to speak out of the heart without notes. The sayings of Jesus were remembered. The events were talked about, and passed down in story form to those who had not observed them first hand. It was an oral culture in which the shaping and transmitting of sayings and events in oral form became the sustaining '*tradition*' for the believing communities.

Much has been made of eyewitness accounts, as well it should. Eyewitnesses to the actions and sayings of Jesus vouchsafed the initial transmission of the experiences they had had with Jesus. The stories were then picked up by non-eyewitnesses and repeated over and over in an ever widening circle of audiences. It is quite conceivable that the *writers* of the Gospels had received the traditions about Jesus and used that material in their composition of the gospels. If the tradition was completely stable from one locale to another that would account for the similarity between the several gospels. The problem with that scenario is that all three gospels were written in Greek, not Aramaic. The Aramaic traditions – there were probably several – went through translation at an early stage, and were then transmitted in the Greek language to the time of the writing of the Synoptic Gospels. Translated traditions were probably present in the communities at large after the successful mission to Gentiles in the Greek-speaking world. These traditions in Greek could possibly be the reason for the identical wording and syntax between all three Gospels. The 'sameness', however, speaks more to *literary dependence* than to availability of identically translated material orally transmitted to the different locations where the compositions were carried out.

The other factor that speaks against the theory of the Evangelists' drawing on the same tradition is that Matthew and Luke do not agree on the wording and setting of the sayings of Jesus they share. Why would these two agree with each other when they use the same material as Mark but not when they use material not found in Mark? Witness the rendering of the parable of the Great Supper/Wedding Banquet in Matthew and Luke, noted above (Mt. 22.1-14/Lk. 14.16-24). The core parable is the same, but the narrative details are quite different from one to the other, as also the wording and the setting. The same is true for numerous other sayings in both Matthew and Luke. If that part of the tradition that Matthew and Luke share was not completely stable why would the tradition these two share with Mark be stable? Doubtless, Jesus-tradition underlies the Synoptic Gospels, and is traceable therein. But it does not address adequately the question arising out of the synoptic fact.

3. Sources option

For some time now scholars have argued that sources account for the Synoptic fact and the problem it presents. 'Sources' refers to literary material. This train of thought is not recent. As early as Irenaeus of the second century Matthew was considered the first gospel to have been written. Mark and Luke knew Matthew and used it for their own compositions. Some scholars, particularly William Farmer, upheld that notion with well reasoned arguments. In that case the shorter Gospel of Mark would be a summary of Matthew, drawing directly on selected parts from the first Gospel. Luke then followed both Matthew and Mark and added tradition and sources not in the other two.

Still, the majority opinion today is that Mark is the most primitive of the three gospels. The other two drew on Mark independently of each other, and added to Mark's account material they had gleaned from elsewhere. The argument for the priority of Mark is convincing. Where Matthew and Luke carry the same narrative material as Mark, the order of the events is the same as Mark's. Where Matthew and Luke depart from Mark's narrative, the order and context of events and sayings they share are not the same. This latter observation points to a source with minimal narrative structure. More on that point in a moment.

Meanwhile, an illustration of the way Matthew used Mark should help in understanding the situation. Matthew 15.1–16.12 follows the same events in the same order as they appear in Mark 7.1–8.21. Suddenly Matthew leaves out a healing miracle in Mark 8.22-26. Then Matthew picks up Mark's events and sequence immediately after the miracle story. Why skip the miracle story? The miracle is one where Jesus heals a blind man from Bethsaida, but in two stages. Jesus had put saliva on the man's eyes and touched him and then asked the man if he could see. The man replied: 'I can see people, but they look like trees, walking.' Then Jesus put his hands on his eyes a second time and the man could see clearly. It seems as though Matthew preferred not to have Jesus appear as an imperfect healer, so he skipped over the story.

Matthew sometimes modifies an internal inconsistency in Mark's account, rather than leaving out the whole story altogether. The story of the cursing of the fig tree is a case in point. Mark's account reads: 'Seeing in the distance a fig tree in leaf, he went to see whether perhaps he would find anything on it. When he came to it, he found nothing but leaves, **for it was not the season for figs**. He said to it, "May no one ever eat fruit from you again"' (Mk 11.13-14). Matthew (21.19-20) has the story, but without the purpose clause at the end of Mark's verse 13. If it was not the season for figs, why would Jesus expect to find figs on the tree? And why would he curse such a tree for not bearing figs out of season? By omitting Mark's trouble-some clause Matthew resolved the problem and kept the story. It would appear, therefore, that Matthew followed the Mark source, rather than the other way round. If Mark were following Matthew why would Mark muddy the Matthaean waters where Jesus is concerned?

About 90 per cent of Mark is in Matthew. Much less in Luke. But another part of the Synoptic puzzle remains unresolved. How do we account for the abundant material in both Matthew and Luke that is not in Mark? And why does that material appear at different points in the narrative time-frame and in different contexts in Matthew and Luke? Again, the answer is sought in a source-theory. Most of the material that Matthew and Luke share apart from Mark is in the form of sayings of Jesus. Scholars have posited a *sayings source* for this material, which the authors of Matthew and Luke used independently of each other. Since that source, unlike Mark, is not extant, it has been named simply Q (from the German *Quelle*, 'source'). It is often referred to as the Q Gospel. But that source hardly qualifies as a 'gospel' in the sense described in this chapter. The sayings seem to have been strung together loosely, much like the Proverbs in the book by that name in the Hebrew Bible. Without a narrative context, the sayings could be picked up from Q and placed where the writers of Matthew and Luke chose. The Q source probably pre-dates the composition of Mark, making it the earliest source to have come from the Jesus-tradition.

There remains one factor in the Synoptic problem that needs some discussion. Each of Matthew and Luke has material *unique* to their respective gospels. Both have birth and infancy narratives, but the content is very different from one to the other. Even the genealogies in Matthew and Luke exhibit marked differences. This factor has led to the conclusion that Matthew and Luke had access to sources beyond Mark and Q, sources that were independently shaped and transmitted.

The preface to Luke is unequivocal about the writer's use of sources already in existence: 'many have undertaken to set down an orderly account' (1.1). The writer then admits that 'after investigating everything carefully' he too decided to write an 'orderly account'. That account (canonical Luke) includes a large amount of material about Jesus that occurs nowhere else in early Christian literature. The source of the exclusively Lukan material is unknown, so it is given the simple designation 'L'. Again, it is possible that some of the Lukan sayings and narratives came from an oral tradition

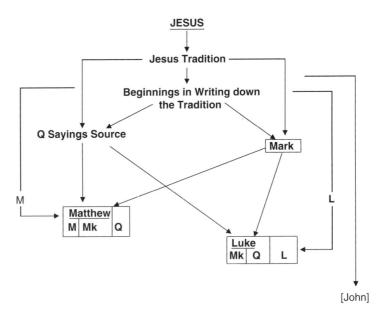

Figure 6.1 Source Solution to the Synoptic Puzzle.

carried in a community to which the author had access. Or it is possible, although less so, that the author composed much of the unique material in his gospel in line with his vision of what Jesus was saying and doing. The 'L' source theory is still the most likely option.

Matthew too has material about Jesus uniquely Matthaean. As mentioned, Matthew's birth and infancy narrative has very little in common with Luke's. Origin and genealogy were important in establishing the character and authority of heroic figures in the ancient world. The miraculous birth of Jesus corresponds with his unusual life and ministry and resurrection. Beyond the infancy narrative, Matthew has other material unique to that gospel, although not to the extent that Luke has. The source of the uniquely Matthaean material is labelled 'M'.

Figure 6.1 illustrates the source theory said to resolve the Synoptic question. In it I have tried to show the proportion of Mark, Q and M and L in the respective boxes for the Gospels of Matthew and Luke.

4. Form analysis

The handing down of tradition involves couching the oral material in memorable, transmittable forms. Martin Debelius and Rudolf Bultmann, two noted scholars in the early part of the twentieth century, carried out an analysis of various forms embedded within the Synoptic Gospels. Analysis of forms takes into account several conditions that go into the making of forms of speech, which then become forms within literature. One important condition is the *situation in life* (German, *Sitz im Leben*) textured into the form in the process of transmission. When the transmitted form ends up in literary compositions, such as the Synoptic Gospels, several layers of the transmitted tradition can be detected and peeled away to find the earliest tradition. The recent quest for the historical Jesus has used form criticism, as it is called, to come as closely as possible to the very words and actions of Jesus.

Already we have found in the illustration of the parable of the Wedding Banquet in Matthew how a situation in life shaped the final form of the parable (Mt. 22.2-10). Either the writer of Matthew, or his source, had knowledge of the destruction of Jerusalem. The event was shattering for people of Jewish heritage. The Jewish *Christian* writer of Matthew worked the burning destruction of the city into his telling of the parable of the Wedding Banquet. In the process the parable was layered with *allegory*. The king was God; the invited guests were the Jewish leaders who rejected Jesus; God (the king) punished them by burning their city. This layer on the parable form was not part of the original parable Jesus told in Galilee. Form criticism strips the later part away to discover the original word of Jesus. It is noteworthy that Luke carries the same parable, but with very different layering. Luke is less allegorical, but much more socially conscious (Lk. 14.16-22). The invited guests were the rich people who could afford to refuse the invitation. They were not hungry. Their refusal opened the door to the 'the poor, the crippled, the blind, and the lame'. In Luke also there is a layer of material having come out of a situation in life. It too has to be detected and removed to find the primitive parable in the form that Jesus used originally.

Part of the analysis of forms in literature consists in naming the forms. A number of different forms appear in the Synoptic Gospels. *Parable* we have seen already. A parable is metaphoric. It can be a short metaphor, or a longer narrative metaphor. An example of a short parable is the new wine in old wine skins: 'No one puts new wine into old wineskins; otherwise, the wine will burst the skins, and the wine is lost, and so are the skins; but one puts new wine into fresh wineskins' (Mk 2.22). The parable of the Wedding Banquet/Great Dinner is an example of a narrative parable. The genius of the parable is in its shock value. It takes elements from everyday life and gives them an unexpected turn that challenges the accepted social order. The alternative order falls under 'the kingdom of God'.

Many short pithy sayings of Jesus have come down into the Synoptic Gospels. They are wisdom sayings in keeping with the overall action and teaching of Jesus. This form is called *logia*. Numerous examples can be found in the Sermon on the Mount (Mt. 5-7) and in the Sermon on the Plain (Lk. 6): 'Blessed are the meek, for they will inherit the earth' (Mt. 5.5); 'Blessed are you who are hungry now, for you will be filled' (Lk. 6.21).

Another form is the *miracle story*. The actual happening of a miracle cannot be transmitted without language. Language recreates the situation and event by the use of words woven into story. The resulting miracle story becomes effective in its telling and retelling: Jesus is powerful; Jesus makes people well; people should love and follow Jesus. The restoration of the widow's only son at the village of Nain is a case in point (Lk. 7.11-16). The people who observed the miracle 'glorified God'. Some miracle stories have a negative effect. The miracle power of Jesus puts conventional values on notice. The miracle story of the healing of the Gerasene demoniac is such a miracle (Mk 5.1-17). The demons left the man and entered a herd of pigs. The pigs in turn ran into the sea and were drowned. The owners, among others, begged Jesus to leave their territory. They had lost their livelihood. The owners may not have been Jewish. If they were, then their business of pig farming violated their own kosher regulation (Deut. 14.6-8). In the end, the issue is not about the pigs but about the demon possessed man. His quality of life is of more value than pigs, the miracle story seems to suggest.

Some of the forms of speech have been called *pronouncement stories*. An event is narrated for the purpose of making a pronouncement related to the narrated situation. A good example of this form is the story of the disciples plucking heads of grain as they walked through the grain fields on the Sabbath (Mk 2.23-28). The setting is one of controversy between the Jewish leaders who observe Sabbath Law rigorously, and Jesus who is more relaxed about keeping the Sabbath. The situation in the life of the later churches was one of controversy with Jewish leaders, following the destruction of Jerusalem, about which day to observe as the Sabbath and how to observe it. The Christian answer to the matter of proper Sabbath observance comes at the end of the story in the voice of Jesus in the form of two pronouncements: 'The sabbath was made for humankind, and not humankind for the sabbath; so the Son of Man is lord even of the sabbath' (Mk 2.27-28).

One form of speech Bultmann called *myth*. The name does not sit well with people who believe the Bible to be the Word of God. 'Myth' is commonly thought to be fictitious story told as true. But in Bultmann's analysis, 'myth' is a technical way of identifying that which is undeniably above and beyond history but told in the context of history in support of faith. A myth-form of speech arises out of a faith experience. In the case of Christian faith in Jesus, the later believers saw in him the power of God and the Spirit of God. After his baptism in Jordan at the hands of John the Baptizer, 'just as [Jesus] came up from the water, suddenly the heavens were opened to him and he saw the Spirit of God descending like a dove and alighting on him. And a voice from heaven said, "This is my Son, the Beloved, with whom I am well pleased" ' (Mt. 3.16-17). The baptism is a fact of history. In this pericopè it is linked with a supra-historical confessional affirmation. The God of heaven puts the divine seal on this figure, with a heavenly 'voice' that declares him 'my Son, the Beloved'. How do the heavens open? What kind of 'voice' speaks without larynx? Scientific history, which deals with human intentionality, is not the domain from which these questions find an answer. This voice and the action in the Gospel are divine, not subject to the scrutiny of historical criticism. What is historical, however, is the faith community that holds and fosters this confessional form of speech. (Cf. Mk 1.10-11; Lk. 3.21-22; Mk 9.2-7; Mt. 17.1-5; Lk. 9.28-35).

5. Redaction

When all is said and done, what we have before our eyes is the final product of collecting and arranging tradition and sources into three respective gospels, each one with its own recognizable character. The process of collecting and piecing together the sources in a particular way is called *redaction.*

Redaction does not mean a random combining of sources, but *intentional and artful* activity. The end product is a new document. To be sure, the sources are present, but in a particular way that serves the purpose of the respective Evangelist. In this sense, therefore, the gospel writers were authors. Their particular selection of the sources they employed together with the way they embedded and combined them into their respective gospels was a creative act. In a sense, the redactor imprinted his name on the gospel he wrote. His words bind the selected sources and traditions together in a purposeful way. Vocabulary is identifiable as belonging to one gospel and not another. Themes and imagery are highlighted in one gospel in a way that they are not in another. The redactor makes his particular gospel serve the needs and interests of his community, from where he sits. In that light, we approach each gospel *according to* the stamp that the redactor put upon it: according to Matthew; according to Mark; according to Luke.

6. Redaction and literary criticism

Since the 1970s literary criticism has been applied to the study of Synoptic Gospels increasingly. Redaction, as described above, bears the mark of literary creation upon it already. Yet redaction criticism is not quite the same as literary criticism. Where redaction criticism questions how the selected sources were combined to create a gospel with a particular purpose, literary criticism looks for such qualities as characterization, plot, location, time, symbolism, opposition, choice of words and their repetition, narrator, implied readers and implied author. This kind of analysis of a gospel takes seriously the idea that the ones who wrote the gospels were authors, not merely collectors and arrangers of sources.

Literary analysis treats a gospel as an artful creation that *affects* the reader(s) in a particular way. The gospel artist used sources, of course, but in a literary way. The arranging and shaping of the sources towards the literary end-product was nothing less than a work of art. A gospel has focus and force that generates a response in the reader/audience. Response to the reading of a gospel is not random. It is guided by two factors at least: (1) the texture and tone of the literary character of the gospel, and (2) the situation in the life of the reader. These two work together dynamically in forming a response to reading the gospel according to Mark, Matthew or Luke.

7. According to Mark

Mark is *the shortest* of the Synoptic Gospels. It does not have a birth and infancy narrative. The focus rather is on the ministry of Jesus in Galilee and Jerusalem. The 'gospel' (good news) consists in the saving word and work of Jesus conducted in the last year or two of his earthly life. Most important to this Gospel is the redeeming word and work of Jesus in Jerusalem in the last week of his life, which culminated in his death by crucifixion. More than one-third of the Gospel of Mark is given over to the last week in Jerusalem.

The *pivotal point* of Mark occurs at 8.27-30. This pericopè is generally called the confession near Caesarea Philippi. The confession of the disciples, represented by Peter, is that this Jesus who preaches and heals and feeds the hungry is none other than the promised Messiah. 'You are the Messiah,' Peter declares. Whatever others are saying, the disciples see in this man the character of Deliverer of the people of Israel. He is the anointed of God, as King David of Israel was, for the purpose of bringing victory and peace to the people of God.

But Mark was written after the crucifixion of Jesus. How does crucifixion tie in with Messiah? Where is the victory of God in the crucifixion of the anointed One, Messiah? Mark wrestles with those questions. The Messiah (Christ) is supposed to be able to overcome the enemy who kills people, not to become one of the victims himself. This tough issue is addressed in Mark in terms of *discipleship*.

The Markan Jesus radically redefines the Messianic confession near Caesarea Philippi. The Messiah of the Gospel goes beyond traditional Jewish expectation of Messiah as deliverer of the oppressed nation and people. But the new conception and conviction do not come easily. They require insight that comes from following Jesus. Discipleship is a process of learning from someone wiser by following in their footsteps literally and figuratively. It means eating with the Master when he eats. Sleeping when he sleeps. Walking when and where he walks. It means going with the Master to the end of the line, even if the end means death by crucifixion. The Gospel according to Mark accents the *process and progression* of discipleship. One can become a disciple of Jesus, but not without some painful lessons in life and thought.

If the pivotal point of Mark comes at the confession near Caesarea Philippi, then there is a leading up to that point, and a leading away from that point.

First the leading up to that point. The *introduction* to Mark (1.1-15) presents John the Baptizer announcing the coming of 'the Lord'. John is merely the one preparing the way, 'the voice of one crying in the wilderness' (1.3). He calls the people to repentance (*metanoia*, 'change of mind') by baptizing them in the Jordan as a sign of renewal. Jesus enters the introduction towards the end as One affirmed by the heavenly voice of God directly. He receives the very Spirit of God immediately after his baptism by John. He is tested in the wilderness, and passes the test. At that point he is ready for ministry. All of this happens quickly in the short introduction. It is part of the character of Mark to present scenes concisely and with dispatch. One of the repeated connectives between scenes and episodes in this Gospel is 'immediately'.

Once Jesus has been introduced, baptized and affirmed by God from heaven, he *proclaims* immediately: 'The time is fulfilled, and the kingdom of God has come near; repent, and believe in the good news.' This is the key theme of Mark, which carries over variously into Matthew and Luke. The '*kingdom of God*' was a loaded term at the time, related to the title 'Messiah'. Messiah in Mark is the agent through whom God brings about true justice and mercy for the people. The 'kingdom of God' on the lips of Jesus in Mark is a political term. There was a kingdom already operating in Palestine at the time. Caesar was the king of that vast empire that included Palestine. The announcement from Jesus that the kingdom of God has come near begins already to threaten the kingdom of Caesar. Far from being compatible partners, the two oppose each other: the Roman king oppresses people, while God's king seeks to relieve the oppressed.

As soon as the announcement of the nearness of the kingdom of God is made, Mark then pushes forward with narratives and sayings that point to Jesus as that king who will rule in God's stead in the world. He calls disciples, twelve men in particular. They are to be his emissaries after they have learned *who he is* and what he expects of them (10.5-16). This is the renewed Israel coming on the scene: Israel in the process of being restored. Even the biological Jewish family of Jesus is reconstituted in the new group of faithful followers, depicted in Mark 3.31-35. People from the crowd sent word to Jesus that his mother and brothers and sisters were asking for him. His reply in Mark is striking: ' "Who are my mother and my brothers?" And looking at those who sat around him, he said, "Here are my mother and my brothers! Whoever does the will of God is my brother and sister and mother." ' In other words, Jesus has formed a new fictive family around him: disciples who do the will of God.

But the will of God is not easy to understand, and even less easy to obey. *Understanding* the Messiah of God will be a challenge even for the most promising of disciples in Mark. *Seeing* is a prominent symbol for understanding in this Gospel, which comes through in subtle ways, and sometimes not so subtle. If the followers stay with the process of discipleship (learning) they will discover the secret having to do with Messiah. This motif of *secrecy* in Mark is worth following through the Gospel. The disciples are given 'the secret of the kingdom of God' (4.11), which they do not grasp immediately. What appears in secret at one moment will come to light eventually, 'for there is nothing hidden, except to be disclosed; nor is anything secret, except to come to light' (4.22). Often Jesus tells his disciples not to tell anyone about him. The secrecy has to do with the nature of Messiahship, which, in Mark, breaks the bounds of the conventional wisdom of Judaism of the time. The Jewish disciples – and all of them are Jewish – will have to learn patiently and progressively the meaning of the Messiahship of Jesus.

This progressive discipleship in Mark comes through in cleverly construed dress. Leading up to the confession in 8.27-30, Jesus had miraculously fed a crowd of five thousand (6.30-44), and then did the same for four thousand a while later (8.1-10). Shortly after that the disciples and Jesus went off on a trip, but the disciples forgot to bring bread. They realize they have made a mistake and mumble among themselves. Jesus, sensing their dilemma, says: 'Why are you talking about having no bread? Do you still not perceive or understand? Are your hearts hardened? Do you have eyes, and fail to see? Do you have ears, and fail to hear? And do you not remember? When I broke the five loaves for the five thousand, how many baskets full of broken pieces did you collect? They said to him, "Twelve." "And the seven for the four thousand, how many baskets full of broken pieces did you collect?" And they said to him, "Seven". Then he said to them, "Do you not yet understand?" ' (8.17-21). Discipleship has to do with 'seeing' with the mind in a way that the disciples do not see apart from following Jesus progressively.

Not surprisingly, this 'seeing' is accented in Mark through the healing of the blind man of Bethsaida. Recall the earlier discussion. Some people brought a blind man to Jesus to be healed. Jesus touched his eyes, and then asked him if he could see. The man reported that he could see people walking as trees. Jesus had to touch him a second time. Then he could see clearly. The miracle in Mark serves a purpose in showing discipleship as an ongoing affair with Jesus until the understanding becomes clearer. Immediately following the progressive healing of the blind man, Jesus asks his disciples who they think he is. Peter replies, 'You are the Messiah' (8.29). But does he see clearly when he declares his understanding of Jesus? Mark will answer that question in the succeeding interaction between the character of Peter and that of Jesus. The teaching towards greater understanding will continue to the end of the Gospel.

During that extended teaching on the way to Jerusalem, Jesus repeatedly speaks about the Messiah in the third person, as though not talking about himself. He calls the Messiah 'the Son of Man'. The teaching of the disciples comes in *three progressive stages*, each stage launched by a variation on the theme of the suffering death and vindication of the Son of Man: 'the Son of Man must undergo great suffering, and be rejected by the elders, the chief priests, and the scribes, and be killed, and after three days rise again' (8.31); 'The Son of Man is to be betrayed into human hands, and they will kill him, and three days after being killed, he will rise again' (9.31); 'See, we are going up to Jerusalem, and the Son of Man will be handed over to the chief priests and the scribes, and they will condemn him to death; then they will hand him over to the Gentiles; they will mock him, and spit upon him, and flog him, and kill him; and after three days he will rise again' (10.33-34). Just as each of the statements expands the theme of the suffering and death and vindication of the Son of Man, so the understanding of the disciples expands.

But the full understanding of the death of Jesus Messiah will not come until the vindication of Jesus happens with the resurrection. That will be the defining moment for the followers, when Jesus' true Messiahship will be revealed, fearfully and radically (16.8).

Jesus' teaching about the *Son of Man*, and the kingdom of God that he represents, is not pleasant to the ears of the disciples. Consider Peter's response to the first mention of the *suffering and death* of Jesus at 8.31. Remember, the suffering-theme statement comes immediately after Peter's confession of Jesus as the Messiah. When he hears about the suffering of Messiah, 'Peter took [Jesus] aside and began to rebuke him' (8.32), because of his incomplete understanding. Peter spoke out of his conventional under-standing of the meaning of Messiah, but Jesus will teach him otherwise. The kingdom of God is not conventional, not of human origin. In turn, Jesus rebukes Peter in the sternest possible way. 'Get behind me, Satan! For you are setting your mind not on divine things but on human things' (8.33). Peter's thinking is not merely conventional and human, but *adversarial*. 'Satan' means adversary. Peter, with his partner-disciples, will have a long way to go before they understand the secret of Jesus' Messiahship.

Even after the third and last theme-statement about the suffering Messiah, the disciples still had not learned the inner meaning of Jesus as Messiah. This time the characters in the story are James and John, two brothers. They ask a favour of Jesus: 'Grant us to sit, one at your right hand and one at your left, in your glory' (10.37). They want power positions in the coming kingdom of God. But they too fail to understand Jesus, as Peter had done earlier. Jesus responds by asking them, 'Are you able to drink the cup that I drink, or be baptized with the baptism that I am baptized with?' (10.38).Of course, they say they are able. They fail to understand that the cup is that of suffering, and the baptism is that of death that he will die. Are they able for that?

Placed at the end of the third teaching about the suffering Messiah is another miracle story of the healing of a blind beggar, Bartimaeus of Jericho (10.47-52). When asked what he wants from Jesus, Bartimaeus says, 'My teacher, *let me see again*.' This time Jesus the teacher simply speaks a word to the man, and 'immediately he regained his sight and followed [Jesus] on the way' (10.52). By becoming a willing and obedient disciple of Jesus, Bartimaeus could see, viz. understand.

By chapter 11 Jesus and his disciples enter the city of Jerusalem. The entry is often described as 'triumphal', but the narrative does not fit the conventional sense. Jesus rides on the back of an unbroken colt, a *humble and peaceful* ride into trial, suffering and death. In Jerusalem he clears the Temple court and curses the barren fig tree (chapter 11). In that setting he tells parables, denounces the scribes, and points out a widow who put all the money she had to live on into the Temple treasury (chapter 12). There in Jerusalem he delivers his apocalyptic vision of things to come, including the destruction of the Temple, the coming of the Son of Man, and the need for watchfulness (chapter 13). There in Jerusalem a woman anoints him; he celebrates the Passover with his disciples and institutes a new way to thinking about that meal; he prays in Gethsemane. There in Jerusalem Jesus is betrayed and denied by his own disciples. They do not understand (chapter 14). Finally, Jesus is seized in Jerusalem, tried in both Jewish and Roman courts, and found guilty of insurrection. The Roman authorities lead him outside the holy precincts to execute him by crucifixion. A man named Joseph buries him in a new tomb cut out of a rock (chapter 15).

But Mark knows of the resurrection. The account is short, a mere eight verses in chapter 16. The longer endings are later additions to original Mark (see Appendix IV). For Mark, however, the secret of Jesus' *redemptive Messiahship* is not in his resurrection, but in his suffering and death. The resurrected Jesus will bring that secret to light in the surviving community of disciples who will carry forward the work of Jesus. The resurrection-revelation of such a Messiah is 'amazing', 'terrifying', 'frightening' (16.8).

This concludes the examination of the literary aspect of the Gospel of Mark. Interlaced with the literary character is a theological lining. Those on the inside of the Christian community should understand the meaning of the death of Jesus as Messiah. Those on the outside will not get it. Disciples need to stay with Jesus, have him live with them as the resurrected One, and they will learn thereby what the Kingdom of God is like in the brave new world of the kingdom of God.

A final word about the *compositional history* of Mark. The best guess is that it was written close to the time of the destruction of the Temple of Jerusalem in 70 CE. Perhaps a few years before that event. Tradition places its origin in Rome, and there is no good reason to dispute that claim. Neither is there solid scientific or literary evidence to affirm it. Similarly, the Gospel of Mark does not disclose the name of the author. Tradition attributes it to John Mark of Acts (12.12, 25; 15.37), said to be the young man who fled when Jesus was arrested (Mk. 14.51-52). When the arresting officers tried to catch him, they pulled from him the linen garment he was wearing. He escaped and ran away naked. That this young man was John Mark of Acts is conjecture. That the same young man must have written this embarrassing story and the whole Gospel in which it sits is also conjecture. The Gospel of Mark is anonymous. The title at the top of the Gospel (*kata markon*, 'according to Mark') was added later to identify the scroll from among others.

8. According to Matthew

Nearly all of Mark is contained in Matthew, but with a Matthaean stamp upon it. Consider the example of the temptation pericopè in Table 6.2 below. Mark's brief version is elaborated substantially. For Matthew, the event of *testing Jesus* for the ministry carries great weight. Readers can trust themselves to this tested teacher-healer. The material added to Mark would have come from Q, since it appears in more or less the same form in Luke 4.1-13, except for the sequence of the tests.

This way of wrapping other source material around Mark shows the redactional hand of the author. But the Gospel of Matthew is also a literary composition. Vocabulary is Matthaean, and the structure distinctive. It sets its own literary stage to make its own theological points in a purposeful and persuasive way.

The aim in this section is to demonstrate the distinctive literary and theological character of the Gospel of Matthew. That will mean highlighting those parts of the Gospel that are uniquely found in this Synoptic Gospel. Not surprisingly, Mark's themes, such as the secrecy motif, come through, but not accented in Matthew to the extent they are in Mark. Matthew has other concerns to set before his readers/audience for their response.

We begin with Matthew's *birth and infancy* narrative. Each of Matthew and Luke has a rather lengthy narrative detailing the beginning of Jesus' life, but the two are not at all the same. Some elements are the same, such as the miraculous conception of Jesus in the womb of Mary. In virtually all other areas Matthew and Luke present different narrative images. Later Church pageantry to the present time selects from both, and makes a composite presentation despite the incongruity: kingly magi and lowly shepherds both visit the baby Jesus in an animal shelter. (In Matthew Jesus was born in a house, 2.11).This combining of elements from the two gospels does not advance the inquiry into the unique character of the Gospel of Matthew. It tends, rather, to hinder the inquiry.

Table 6.2 Temptation Pericopè

Mark 1.12-13	Matthew 4.1-11	Luke 4.1-13
And the Spirit immediately drove him out into the wilderness. He was in the wilderness forty days, tempted by Satan; and he was with the wild beasts; and the angels waited on him.	Then Jesus was led up by the Spirit into the wilderness to be tempted by the devil. He fasted forty days and forty nights, and afterwards he was famished. The tempter came and said to him, 'If you are the Son of God, command these stones to become loaves of bread.' But he answered, 'It is written, "One does not live by bread alone, but by every word that comes from the mouth of God."' Then the devil took him to the holy city and placed him on the pinnacle of the temple, saying to him, 'If you are the Son of God, throw yourself down; for it is written, "He will command his angels concerning you," and "On their hands they will bear you up, so that you will not dash your foot against a stone."' Jesus said to him, 'Again it is written, Do not put the Lord your God to the test.' Again, the devil took him to a very high mountain and showed him all the kingdoms of the world and their splendor; and he said to him, 'All these I will give you, if you will fall down and worship me.' Jesus said to him, 'Away with you, Satan! for it is written, Worship the Lord your God, and serve only him.' Then the devil left him, and suddenly angels came and waited on him.	Jesus, full of the Holy Spirit, returned from the Jordan and was led by the Spirit in the wilderness, where for forty days he was tempted by the devil. He ate nothing at all during those days, and when they were over, he was famished. The devil said to him, 'If you are the Son of God, command this stone to become a loaf of bread.' Jesus answered him, 'It is written, One does not live by bread alone.' Then the devil led him up and showed him in an instant all the kingdoms of the world. And the devil said to him, 'To you I will give their glory and all this authority; for it has been given over to me, and I give it to anyone I please If you, then, will worship me, it will all be yours.' Jesus answered him, 'It is written, Worship the Lord your God, and serve only him.' Then the devil took him to Jerusalem, and placed him on the pinnacle of the temple, saying to him, 'If you are the Son of God, throw yourself down from here, for it is written, He will command his angels concerning you, to protect you, and On their hands they will bear you up, so that you will not dash your foot against a stone.' Jesus answered him, 'It is said, Do not put the Lord your God to the test.' When the devil had finished every test, he departed from him until an opportune time.

The uniqueness of Matthew's narrative can be found even in the *genealogy* of Jesus from Abraham to Joseph, husband of Mary. Abraham was the father of the faithful Israel in Jewish thought. To show a genetic link between Jesus and Abraham through the generations of Israel bespeaks a theology of Israel being restored in this new-born child. Matthew's generational symmetry in the genealogy further underwrites the veracity of the *divinely ordained origin* of Jesus: 'So all the generations from Abraham to David are fourteen generations; and from David to the deportation to Babylon, fourteen generations; and from the deportation to Babylon to the Messiah, fourteen generations' (1.17).

Another poignant characteristic of Matthew is the pervasive appeal to selected texts from Jewish Scripture to authenticate the narrative event and the claims that it makes. The tag phrase is 'fulfill'. Jesus *fulfils* the recorded hopes and dreams of Israel. For example, the miraculous conception of Jesus in the womb of a virgin calls up Isaiah 7.14: 'Look, the virgin shall conceive and bear a son, and they shall name him *Emmanuel*,' which means, 'God is with us' (Mt. 1.23). The Greek version of the Jewish Scriptures that Matthew quotes has 'virgin' (*parthenos*), not the less specific designation, 'young woman', of the Hebrew text. This opening idea of God's presence with his people embodied in this newborn baby is echoed in the closing promise of the resurrected Jesus given to encourage the disciples: '*I am with you* always, to the end of the age' (28.20).

Other striking features in the infancy narrative bear the mark of Matthaean ideology. The magi ('wise men') from the east point to Jesus as the Teacher of Wisdom in the tradition of Hebrew religion and culture. Later in Matthew, Jesus as sage becomes the hallmark. The wise men identify with him, bringing him gifts of honour. Wise as they are, they bow to the child Jesus (2.1-11).

Dreams are also important to this Gospel. As in the dreams of the patriarch Joseph who ended up in Egypt, so dreams in Matthew are the medium through which God directs the steps of another Joseph. In his dreams, this Joseph discovers the *revelation* of God concerning the safety of the child Jesus. In one dream Joseph is warned about Herod's plan to eliminate Jesus, along with other children 2 years and under (2.13-16). In another dream Joseph was told to go to Egypt. Joseph obeyed, because he was a '*righteous*' man (1.19). When Herod died Joseph dreamed again in Egypt, and was told to leave that place and return to Israel with the child. 'This was to fulfill what had been spoken by the Lord through the prophet, "Out of Egypt

I have called my son" ' (2.15). The prophecy from Hosea 11.1 pictures the 'son' as Israel, whereas in Matthew Jesus as 'son' is restorer of Israel. One can hear a loud echo of the Exodus of the ancient Hebrews in this new exodus in Matthew.

The little family set up house in Nazareth in Galilee, 'so that what had been spoken through the prophets might be fulfilled, He will be called a Nazorean' (2.23). There is no corresponding prophecy in this instance. The reference may be to the messianic 'branch' (Heb. *netzer)* of David in Isaiah 11.1. Or 'Nazorean' may be a Matthaean way of referring to a Nazarite, a holy person who vowed to abstain from wine and from cutting his hair. The latter seems least likely. The appeal to 'the prophets' as a whole in this last fulfilment formula in the infancy narrative may well be Matthew's way of saying the exact prophetic text is not available, but there is a prophetic sense that Nazareth is the visionary place for Jesus to live and from which to launch his ministry.

Dreaming in the opening of Matthew appears also at the closing trial narrative, but nowhere else in the Gospel. At *the trial*, Pilate's wife warns her husband not to have anything to do with this 'righteous' man, because she had been dreaming about him. But Pilate is not a 'righteous' man like Joseph and Jesus, so he sentences Jesus to death by crucifixion.

We come now to the central section of the Gospel. The accent falls on Jesus the sagacious teacher. To be sure, Jesus heals as he does in Mark. But in Matthew Jesus is above all the Master teacher, the great Rabbi of Jewish tradition. He has been compared to the Teacher of Righteousness epitomized in the Dead Sea Scrolls of Jewish Qumran. Five blocks of instruction are set out in Matthew, each one closing with a similar *concluding formula* having to do with the teaching ministry of Jesus. It may be going beyond the literary bounds of Matthew to hear an echo of the five scrolls of the Law in the five divisions of teaching material in Matthew, but the insight is tantalizing nonetheless.

The first occurrence of the concluding formula is at 7.28: 'Now when Jesus had *finished* saying these things, the crowds were astounded at his teaching'. This concludes the well-known Sermon on the Mount to which we shall return shortly. The second occurrence of the formula comes at 11.1: 'Now when Jesus had *finished* instructing his twelve disciples, he went on from there to teach and proclaim his message in their cities'. Numerous proverbial sayings make up this section, in the manner of the Proverbs of the Hebrew Bible. The third section ends at 13.53: 'When Jesus had *finished* these parables, he left that place'. Many of the shorter parables of the kingdom are grouped together in this section. For example, 'the kingdom of heaven is like a merchant in search of fine pearls; on finding one pearl of great value, he went and sold all that he had and bought it' (13.45-46). The fourth section closes at 19.1: 'When Jesus had *finished* saying these things, he left Galilee and went to the region of Judaea beyond the Jordan.' Among other matters, this section highlights the need for forgiveness in the community. Matthew is the only Gospel to have the term 'church' (*ekklèsia*). It occurs in this section at 18.17: 'If the [offending] member refuses to listen to [witnesses], tell it to *the church*; and if the offender refuses to listen even to the church, let such a one be to you as a Gentile and a tax collector.' The fifth and final section ends at 26.1: 'When Jesus had *finished* saying all these things, he said to his disciples, "You know that after two days the Passover is coming, and the Son of Man will be handed over to be crucified."' At this point Jesus is in Jerusalem. He will be arrested, tried and executed there. Matthew follows the basic structure of the Passion Narrative of Mark.

We return now to the Sermon on the Mount (5.1–7.29). First of all, *the setting* seems to be that of post-Temple Judaism in the process of reconstituting itself at Jamnia in Gaza. The Pharisees who survived the destruction set up a school in Jamnia in an effort to revitalize the tradition in the absence of their central symbol, the Temple. The Matthaean community seems to be aware of this movement within Judaism, which has not accepted Jesus as Messiah.

W. D. Davies has made a cogent case for this setting, among other possibilities. The *six antitheses* especially in the Sermon point in the direction of an opposing group rebuilding itself around a strict adherence to the Law. All six antitheses are couched in the same formula. Here is one example. 'You have heard that it was said to those of ancient times, "You shall not murder"; and "whoever murders shall be liable to judgment". **But** I say to you that if you are angry with a brother or sister, you will be liable to judgment; and if you insult a brother or sister, you will be liable to the council; and if you say, "You fool," you will be liable to the hell of fire' (5.21-22; cf. 27-44). The point of the contrast between the ancient word and the new word of Jesus is to highlight the *greater righteousness*. Righteousness, or justice, is a major theme in Matthew, related very much to the keeping of the Law of God. The righteousness characteristic of the Matthaean community must outweigh the righteousness of the scribes, for 'unless your righteousness exceeds that of the scribes and Pharisees, you will never enter the kingdom of heaven' (5.20).

Even in the list of beatitudes (blessings) from Q that open the Sermon, the hunger and thirst are not for physical food and drink, but for righteousness (*dikaiosunè*). 'Blessed are those who hunger and thirst for righteousness, for they will be filled' (5.6). Compare the same beatitude in Luke: 'Blessed are you who are hungry now, for you will be filled' (Lk. 6.21). We have already seen Joseph as a 'righteous' man. Jesus of the same lineage should be righteous too. Moreover, his baptism in Matthew is not for repentance, but 'to fulfill all righteousness' (3.15).

In keeping with the new way of doing the will of God found in Jesus and his teaching, the disciples are called upon to do likewise. Their commission at the end is to 'make disciples . . . , baptizing them in the name of the Father and of the Son and of the Holy Spirit, and teaching them to obey everything that I have commanded you' (28.19-20). Their job will be to bring *new life* to the keeping of the law of God as embodied in Jesus and his teaching. The Sermon says they are to be revitalizing 'salt of the earth' (5.13).

This little salt-metaphor has been misread repeatedly in the history of interpretation. Commentaries and translations both consider the salt to be table salt, sodium chloride. The compound is said to lose its 'taste', which sodium chloride does not do under any condition. Moreover, the disciples as salt preservative, according to most commentators, are supposed to preserve the good in society, or at least to add flavour to an otherwise good situation. But the chemical in this little parable is not sodium chloride for the preservation, or flavouring, of meat, but fertilizer for *the land*. The Greek word is *halas*, a general term like the English word 'chemical'. It is called, after all, salt of the 'earth' (*gè*), not salt of the table. The chemical in question infuses the barren soil so that new life may come out of it. That is what the disciples are supposed to be and to do. They are followers of the new Messiah, the new Teacher of righteousness who sets forth a renewed set of laws on a new mountain in Israel.

The rest of the Sermon on the Mount counsels on matters of marriage, adultery and divorce, prayer, (including the model prayer now called 'the Lord's prayer'), non-retaliation, loving enemies, giving to the poor, wealth and poverty, and finally warnings about disobeying the directives of the Sermon, and thus not entering the kingdom of God. 'Not everyone who says to me, "Lord, Lord," will enter the kingdom of heaven, but only the one who does the will of my Father in heaven' (7.21).

Another element peculiar to Matthew is the occurrence of *supernatural events* at the moment of Jesus' death on the cross. 'At that moment the curtain of the temple was torn in two, from top to bottom. The earth shook, and the rocks were split. The tombs also were opened, and many bodies of the saints who had fallen asleep were raised. After [Jesus'] resurrection they came out of the tombs and entered the holy city and appeared to many' (27.51-53). One of the remarkable pieces of this pericopè is the mention of the resurrection of Jesus prior to the narration of the event. Here is one of the clear signs that the author of the Gospel narratives intended backwards, from a post-Easter perspective and experience.

The construction of this narrative of the death scene is puzzling. At the moment of Jesus' death, extraordinary events happened. Tombs were opened, and bodies of deceased saints were raised (27.52). But according to the next sentence in the structure, these bodies did not come out of their tombs until Jesus had come out of his. At one level the resurrection of the saints is a precursor to the resurrection of Jesus. At another, it prefigures the general resurrection. Either way, the structure presents a problem. The resurrection of Jesus was viewed in earlier tradition, reflected in 1 Corinthians 15.20, as 'the *first fruits* of those who have died'. Knowledge of this belief may have led to a narrative restraint concerning the raised saints in their tombs until **after** the resurrection of Jesus. The structure is awkward in the extreme, and curious to this reader.

The *compositional history* of the Gospel of Matthew is not certain, as with other gospels. A person called Matthew appears in the gospel records as a tax collector who became a disciple of Jesus (Mt. 9.9). The same man, apparently, is called Levi in Mark 2.14 (cf. Lk. 5.27). According to early church tradition – beginning in the second century CE – this man Matthew is said to be the author of the first gospel in the canon. If that were so, it would be strange indeed to have the author rely on sources and traditions to write his gospel. One thing we can say with assurance, this Gospel was written by a well-educated Jewish person, one who had access to funding for papyrus and time enough to carry out the task. But as with all the gospels, Matthew itself is silent about its real author. What matters more than naming the author is the character of the implied author. That is, the *kind of author* who would write the literary, religious, social and theological texture of the gospel as it is in the canon.

The time of composition is again an educated guess. It reads as though written some time after the destruction of the Temple of Jerusalem. As we have seen already, echoes of the event reverberate in a number of narratives.

Moreover, it was probably written sometime between 75 and 90 CE. Its place of origin may have been Antioch of Syria, at the edge of Palestinian Judaism under reconstruction.

9. According to Luke

As with Matthew so also with Luke, only those aspects that make this Gospel unique among the Synoptics will be examined. Luke has much less of Mark than Matthew has. Abundant material not found anywhere else makes this Gospel truly Lukan. The literary configuration of the material serves to accommodate Lukan theology.

We begin the survey with the *distinctive preface* to this Gospel, Luke 1.1-4. This is in line with classical introductions to treatises in Hellenistic literary practice. It contains the purpose and method used in the composition, together with a dedication to a patron:

> Since many have undertaken to set down an orderly account of the events that have been fulfilled among us, just as they were handed on to us by those who from the beginning were eyewitnesses and servants of the word, I too decided, after investigating everything carefully from the very first, to write an orderly account for you, most excellent Theophilus, so that you may know the truth concerning the things about which you have been instructed.

The Gospel of Luke is one among 'many' such accounts already in circulation at the time of writing. The 'orderly account' (*diègèsis*) refers to narrative writing of events, as compared to other kinds of literature: poetry, philosophical treatises, proverbs, etc. The resources used to create the narrative are not given directly, but are alluded to as 'handed on' through two media: 'eyewitnesses and servants of the word'. Of course these two designations could be referring to the same group, but not likely. The author seems to view himself in a third category of transmitters of the events. The dedication to a person named Theophilus bespeaks a *patron–client* relationship. The practice was quite common, and quite necessary, in that world. The cost of papyrus and the expense of finding the sources and then writing the account required money beyond everyday living expenses. The figure of Theophilus qualifies as a worthy patron. He is called 'most excellent', perhaps denoting a term of nobility. And according to the last purpose clause he had already accepted the Christian way of life and thought. The notion that the name Theophilus ('god-lover') is merely symbolic of anyone who loves God is not convincing. More will be said about the author at the close of this section.

We come now to the Lukan *birth and infancy narratives*. If the author of Luke knew Matthew, he has distanced himself dramatically from Matthew's infancy narrative. The central feature remains: the miraculous conception of Jesus in the womb of the Virgin Mary by the power of the Holy Spirit. Surrounding the birth are stories depicting the lowliness of the Messiah. Mary's song of acceptance of the miracle accents her lowly estate (1.46-55). The same is true for the other speakers of poetry in the narrative: Elizabeth, Mary's cousin who was barren (1.25); Zechariah, a priest who could not have offspring (1.67-71); Simeon, who is old and about to die (2.28-32); and Anna, a prophetess in the Temple and a widow aged eighty-four; she does not speak in her own voice but is described as speaking praise of the child out of her humble life (2.36-38).

While we are in the context of the *Temple*, consider the prominent role it plays in Luke, and with the Temple the *Law*. Jesus was circumcised after eight days, and then presented to the Lord in the Temple. The name 'Jesus' ('the Lord saves'), previously given by the angel, became official at the time of circumcision. Jesus' parents then offered sacrifice in accordance with the Law. Luke makes bold effort to connect the coming of Jesus with the symbols of Israelite faith and life. For Luke there is only one history of salvation, and that came through Israel into Judaism and thence into Jesus and the new community that bears his name. This concern in Luke can be traced through the Gospel and also throughout Acts (written by the same author). The bond Luke seeks to make between the new Jesus-movement and historic Judaism and Israel is further seen in the presence of the twelve-year-old Jesus in the Temple talking to the leaders there. He and they are at one with each other (2.41-47).

Outstanding in the infancy narrative are *the shepherds* and the animal shelter, probably a cave. The shepherds are the ones to hear the *angelic announcement* about the birth of this unusual child. Shepherds were about as lowly as one could get in that society. An angel of the Lord declared to them: 'I am bringing you good news of great joy for all the people: to you is born this day in the city of David a Savior, who is the Messiah, the Lord. This will be a sign for you: you will find a child wrapped in bands of cloth and lying in a manger.' Then the heavenly host joins in the glad refrain that has been the classic theme of Christmas to the present time: 'Glory to God in the highest heaven, and on earth peace among those whom he favors!' (2.8-14). The fact that the lowly shepherds hear the announcement and obey the heavenly call to go and find the child in the animal shelter, that fact in this early part of Luke sets up one of the major themes for the whole gospel: the poor receive the kingdom of God (6.20); the rich have to be on guard lest they lose the kingdom for the sake of their wealth.

Whereas Matthew opens his infancy narrative with *a genealogy* of Jesus, Luke closes his with a genealogy. Or perhaps it would be better to say the genealogy opens onto Jesus' public ministry when 'Jesus himself began to be about thirty years of age' (3.23). The genealogy functions thus to ground the word and work of Jesus in the history of salvation. Internally also Luke's genealogy is rather different from Matthew's at several points. Matthew's starts with Abraham and moves forward to Jesus. Luke's genealogy begins with Jesus and moves backward through Abraham all the way to Adam, 'son of God' (3.38). In effect Luke's genealogy embraces all of humanity without prejudice.

At the same time, the genealogy locates Jesus at once squarely within humanity, and through humanity constitutes him 'son of God'. In short, the genealogy of Jesus is such that all of humanity can trust his good character and lineage: Abraham is his forefather, but so also Adam, and ultimately God. The *universal appeal* of the genealogy is stunning. A number of names in the lineage are different from those on Matthew's list. Surprisingly, Ruth and Rahab, two unusual females from the sacred past of Judaism, are missing in Luke. With Luke's concern for women in communion with Jesus one would expect him to delight in citing these two as forebears of Jesus. It appears that the author of Luke drew on a different source for his genealogy.

Time now to consider the text in which Jesus launches his ministry (4.14-30). There again, key Lukan emphases come to the fore. The setting is Nazareth, the hometown of Jesus. In the synagogue he reads from Isaiah (Isa. 61.1-2; 58.6): 'The Spirit of the Lord is upon me, because he has anointed me to bring good news to the poor. He has sent me to proclaim release to the captives and recovery of sight to the blind, to let the oppressed go free, to proclaim the year of the Lord's favor' (4.18-19). After the reading he sat down, as was the custom, and said, 'Today this scripture has been fulfilled in your hearing'. Everyone was pleased with what they had seen and heard, until Jesus began to tell them that God favoured a non-Israelite widow in Elijah's time, and a Syrian leper in Elisha's time. When the congregation heard this they were 'filled with rage'. They drove him out of town to the brow of a hill as an attempt on his life, but he escaped. The scene is a literary foreshadowing of the trial and death of Jesus. What then are the themes here that parade through the rest of the Gospel? They are wrapped up in the text of Isaiah in the mouth of Jesus thus: Jesus is the Spirit-anointed One to bring good news to the poor; release to the captives; recovery of sight to the blind; to let the oppressed go free; and to call for a Jubilee year, when debts are forgiven and lands restored to the original owners.

Another strikingly Lukan part of the Gospel is in the *commissioning of the seventy-two* (10.1-11; some ancient manuscripts have 'seventy'). This commissioning is in addition to the sending of the Twelve (9.1-6), taken from Mark. The sending of the seventy-two is symbolic. Whereas the Twelve represents Hebraic Israel centred in Palestine, the seventy-two point to Hellenistic Israel in the larger world. In the legendary tale in the *Letter of Aristaeas*, seventy-two scribes are said to have translated the Hebrew Scriptures into Greek in seventy-two days. That translation was used by Jewish people in the Greek-speaking world from about 200 BCE to 100 CE. The same translation by the 'seventy-two' was the Bible used in spreading the gospel during the Gentile world mission, and in the churches formed thereby. Paul quotes from it in all his missionary letters. Moreover, the two commissions in Luke – those of the Twelve and of the Seventy-two – correspond rather well to the two-phase mission in Acts. Peter's missionary preaching represents the Aramaic-speaking Twelve of Judaea (Acts 1–13), while Paul's missionary preaching represents the Seventy-two in the larger Hellenistic world (Acts 14–28).

Paramount in Luke is the large block of material in the middle of the Gospel found only there in all of early Christian literature (9.51-19.27), with a few pieces from Mark included for good measure. The selection of material from the 'L' source forms the literary context for the *journey motif* characteristic of the section. Repeatedly the reminder is given throughout the section that Jesus and his disciples are on their way to Jerusalem. The journey in Luke is the way of the Christ moving towards suffering and death. Throughout the travel narrative virtually all of the major Lukan themes spring to expression. In this space we can discuss only a small part of that material.

We discover first of all that the Gospel of Luke has a special place for *Samaritans*. From the Jewish perspective Samaritans were the off scouring of the earth. They descended from the Northern Tribes, intermarried, and had a version of the Torah (law) that did not correspond with the Torah of Jerusalem. Yet the Jewish Jesus in Luke has a special place in his mission for Samaritans. He enters a Samaritan town with his disciples (9.52-55). The townspeople do not receive them well, knowing them to be Jewish. The disciples want to call down fire from heaven to consume them, as Elijah had done to the priests of Ba'al centuries earlier. But Jesus rebuked his disciples: the Samaritans must not be destroyed.

On another occasion when Jesus healed *ten lepers*, only one of them returned to thank him, and he was a Samaritan (17.11-19). The other nine presumably were Jewish. But the most striking appearance of a Samaritan in the Lukan block of material comes in a parable (10.25-37). The context of the parable is important. A Jewish lawyer had asked Jesus how he could attain eternal life. In response Jesus tells the now-well-known parable called the Good Samaritan. What is noteworthy in the story is that the victim in the ditch could not count on the Temple clerics to take pity on him. They passed him by. But the character of the Samaritan stops and pours out overflowing compassion on the man. Remarkably, salvation comes to the victim, presumably Jewish, in the person of a hated Samaritan. And Jesus stands behind the Samaritan as God's healer, saviour, and eternal life-giver. (Cf. Lk. 18.9-14 for another example of an outcast who receives mercy, but not from the Temple elite).

Other outcasts figure prominently in Luke. The parable of the son who takes his inheritance and squanders it among Gentiles is an example. How will he re-enter his village home? How can he rid himself of his *shame and impurity* within his Jewish village community? Under everyday conditions of that time and place he could not re-enter without some serious repentance and cleansing. But in the story Jesus tells in Luke, the disgraceful son is welcomed back by his father. Like the victim in the Samaritan parable, the prodigal is showered with compassion, and given a banquet in his honour. Not a sign of disgrace, except in the mind of his stay-at-home brother. The brother represents the conventional wisdom of the society that would likely exclude the prodigal from table-fellowship.

One of the repeated themes relates to *accumulated wealth*. A very telling parable in the Lukan block of material tackles that issue (12.15-21). The land of a rich man yielded a great surplus of crops. The man decided to build bigger barns to store the produce for himself. He would eat, drink and be merry as an elite person of wealth. But the end of the parable has God speak to the man: 'this night they will require your life from you.' There is no way of knowing who 'they' are that will require his life. But it could be the very ones from whom he took land, and to whom he gave nothing back from his surplus. In any case, Luke cites a problem with the hoarding of wealth while others go hungry. The hoarder could lose his life!

Luke's concern for *the place of women* in the community also comes through in this major section of the Gospel. We have already met several women in the infancy narrative. They occupy places of religious importance. Who else in Luke composes such as song as that of the young Mary? Later in the ministry some women provide for Jesus and his disciples out of their resources (8.2-3). But outstanding among them all is Mary the Magdalene. From her Jesus cast out seven demons, and she became an ardent disciple. It was this Mary who travelled from Galilee with Jesus, and witnessed his death. She and other women also experienced the appearance of the resurrected Jesus. Mary and the others were the first to bring the news of the appearance of the risen Jesus to the apostles (24.8-10).

There is yet another Mary with her sister Martha in this gospel. These two women offer *hospitality* to Jesus in Martha's home. While Martha busies herself making the dinner for Jesus, Mary simply wants to be near Jesus. She sits at his feet drinking in his every word while Martha attends to the meal. Mary should be helping her, Martha tells Jesus. 'Martha, Martha', Jesus replies, 'you are worried and distracted by many things; there is need of only one thing. Mary has chosen the better part, which will not be taken away from her' (10.38-42). The better part that Mary chose was *discipleship*. Her position at the feet of Jesus was that of a learner. It was a position held usually by men who wanted to gain wisdom from a master. But the woman in the story, Mary, chose that position, and Jesus accepted her in that posture. She 'listened to what he was saying' (10.39).

Other themes and concerns that find a place in Luke include the prominent role of the *Holy Spirit* in the life of Jesus (and later in the life of the post-Easter communities pictured in Acts); prayer as communion with the God who directs Jesus' life and ministry; and the *innocence of Jesus*. On this last one, attention should be drawn to the saying on the lips of a Roman centurion at the foot of the cross. Whereas Mark has the centurion confess, 'Truly this man was God's Son' (Mk 15.39), Luke has him say, 'Certainly this man was innocent' (23.47). The innocence of Jesus was important to the author of Luke. Both Luke and Acts exhibit a pro-Roman slant, and at the same time Christian. The implied author's concern seems to be that the Christian community and its founder are innocent of insurrection or any other crime. To have a Roman centurion confess the same of Jesus is an effective way of staving off recrimination from Rome.

Finally, Luke has a unique narrative about *an appearance* of the resurrected Jesus to two disciples who witnessed the cruel crucifixion (24.13-32). They were walking to a village called Emmaus. They were doleful after the horrendous events of trial and bloody execution of their Master, who, they thought, would deliver Israel. A third unknown traveller joined them on the road. He explained the events in light of Scripture. The two did not recognize the third. When the two came to their lodging place, they urged the unknown traveller to stay there with them. He did. And as they broke bread together during a meal the two disciples recognized the third traveller as Jesus. They were elated and returned to tell the others that he was alive in resurrected form.

Here the breaking of bread together seems like an act of hospitality and friendship. Throughout Luke there is much made of eating and drinking together (e.g. 7.36-47; 14.7-24). But Christian readers of Luke would doubtless view *the breaking of bread* in the presence of the resurrected Jesus in more theological categories. Something had happened at the last Passover meal that Jesus observed with his disciples. Jesus had instituted a new way of thinking about the significance of Passover. The usual body of sacrifice for Passover was changed. The traditional body was that of a lamb whose blood was shed. But now in the world of Jesus it was the everyday bread and wine, the staff of life for everybody, even for those who could not afford a lamb. 'This [bread] is my body, which is given for you. Do this in remembrance of me; this cup [of wine] that is poured out for you is the new covenant in my blood' (22.19-20). It was a most unusual thing to say in the ritual meal. It was unforgettable in their Jewish minds. Forever after, the meal in Christian community would be observed with those words during the breaking of bread and the drinking of wine. This later Christian ritual, based on Jesus' last Passover meal with the disciples, was read back into the meal that the two disciples shared with the stranger. He came to them on the road as one unknown, but became known to them in the breaking of the bread (24.35).

It goes without saying that there was a *real author* of this gospel. But whoever the author was he/she kept personal identity out of the picture. As the Christian tradition developed in the later church, it became important to the bishops to put a credible name to every document the communities were reading in worship. This was especially so in the move towards a Christian canon. For the third Gospel, a friend of Paul was put forward, a man named Luke (*Lukas*), 'the beloved physician' of Colossians 4.14

(see also 2 Tim. 4.11). It was said that this Luke's education and special interest in healing made him a likely candidate for author. But this *Lukas* was Gentile, whereas the third Gospel reads as the composition of a learned Jewish person, well versed in the Greek Scriptures of Diaspora Judaism. The fact remains, the Gospel of Luke is anonymous. The author that matters for interpretation is the one *implied* in the composition. That one is Jewish, but well disposed to Rome; he had accepted Jesus and the new community as a way of life and thought; he had concerns as a Christian about social issues such as poverty and riches in the community; about male and female relationship/discipleship; about the problem of discontinuity with the Jewish-Israelite heritage, etc.

The *time of writing* the Gospel must post-date the 'many' (1.1) other such writings of the Christian communities in the post-Pauline world. He used Mark and Q, and possibly Matthew. If the 'many' were already in circulation, then the time of writing was probably after that of Matthew, probably between 85 and 95 CE.

The *place of writing* the Third Gospel is uncertain. There is some evidence in Acts that the implied author is familiar with Macedonia. He knows the local names for government officials in cities of the area. It is possible that he belonged to a Greek-speaking synagogue in Thessalonica or Philippi, and then joined the new community of Christians that had formed in one or another of the Macedonian centres.

For the *occasion and purpose* for writing the Gospel we may look no further than the preface (1.1-4): 'so that you may know the truth concerning the things about which you have been instructed'. Conflicting voices may have come into the communities regarding the person and work of Jesus. Luke purports to set such matters straight for Theophilus, and for the extended Lukan community.

10. Conclusion

The Synoptic Gospels are three highly important documents of the New Testament, in that they focus directly on the central figure of the New Testament, and founder of a movement that was to become a world religion known as Christianity. But more than that, in their presentation of the central figure these three Gospels also pose some problems for interpretation. Why are the three the same yet different? Where did they find the information for their respective narratives? How does each of them treat the material they use? And what are the literary and theological characteristics of each of them? These have been the questions for discussion throughout. It is hoped that this introduction to the Synoptic Gospels will mark a beginning for further in-depth study of this celebrated literature and theology.

Further related reading

In a 'revised and expanded' edition of his 1980 work on the Synoptic Gospels, Keith F. Nickle's (2001) book is a very useful guide to understanding: *The Synoptic Gospels: An Introduction.* Westminster/John Knox.

Craig A. Evans and Stanley E. Porter, eds. (1995) edited a collection of valuable essays that investigate a variety of issues and themes in relation to the Synoptics, *The Synoptic Gospels: A Sheffield Reader.* Sheffield Academic.

First published in 1958, Joachim Jeremias' (1982) *Jesus Promise to the Nations*, translated by S. H. Hooke, Fortress, is still a valuable contribution to the question about Jesus' attitude towards Gentiles.

Jewish scholar, Ellis Rivkin (1984), addresses astutely a critical question growing out of the Synoptic presentation of Jesus in Judaea: *What Crucified Jesus?* SCM.

More recently, Amy-Jill Levine (2006) provocatively sets forth the Jewishness of Jesus, against some questionable Christian caricatures in *The Misunderstood Jew: The Church and the Scandal of the Jewish Jesus.* HarperSanFrancisco.

Consult also the relevant commentaries under 'Gospels' in the Bibliography.

Jesus Reconfigured Theologically: The Johannine Writings

Chief among the Johannine writings of the New Testament is the beloved Fourth Gospel (alternately 'John'), which will therefore occupy most of the discussion of this chapter. Because John shares distinctive literary and theological elements with three Epistles, these will come up for discussion as well.

Links between John and the Synoptic Gospels could be explored with profit in a venue beyond the scope of this chapter. A brief comment must suffice. The author of John may have had access to one or another of the Synoptics, and may at points have contravened the Synoptic narrative. Or the Johannine author may have had access to some strands of Synoptic tradition together with other material from which to construct the extant Gospel according to John. Theories of underlying sources and stages of composition have occupied Johannine scholars for many years. To enter into meaningful dialogue with the various points of view on these theories would take us far afield. The intent of the chapter, in the main, is to focus on the Fourth Gospel as we have it in the New Testament, to appreciate the sweep of its literary and theological pattern, pausing periodically to compare narrative points in John with similar ones in the Synoptic Gospels.

We begin with some broad strokes about the character of this Gospel, followed by an analysis of the shape and substance of both Gospel and Epistles.

1. Time to reflect

A post-Easter understanding of the character and work of the Galilaean Jesus developed relatively quickly in the new communities that believed in him. Reflection on his life and death in the experience of the Spirit of Jesus led the communities to state their new faith in transcendent categories. The very name 'Jesus' itself became meaningful without saying much more about the acts and words of the historical figure by that name. The name became symbolic, especially so when linked with other transcendent terms of dignity and divinity: Lord, Christ, Saviour, Son of God. The earliest confession seems to have been 'Jesus is Lord.' Hymns were composed in honour of Jesus as Lord and Christ. For example, Paul's letter to the Philippians, written in the mid-fifties, contains a hymn (2.6-11) that probably pre-dates Philippians, making the hymn very early indeed. The Philippians hymn celebrates the 'form' of the divine Christ embodied in the human Jesus, who humbled himself to the point of death on a cross. Then God 'highly exalted him' and called on everyone in the universe to bow in worship at the name of 'Jesus', calling him Lord, 'to the glory of God the Father'.

The earliest creedal formulations that celebrated the saving work of Jesus as the Christ were short and memorable. Candidates for baptism could repeat them as they entered the baptismal waters. One of the most carefully sculpted of these is found in 1 Corinthians 15.3-5. This faith formulation was not composed by Paul. He received it from a tradition already operating before his time, possibly first formed at Antioch. It has four lines as follows:

> that Christ died for our sins in accordance with the scriptures
> and that he was buried,
> and that he was raised on the third day in accordance with the scriptures,
> and that he appeared to Cephas, then to the twelve.

The two principal lines affirm *two propositions* for understanding Jesus in the communities of faith that prevailed after Jesus was crucified. (1) The death of Jesus was an expiation for sins in accordance with the sacrificial system required in the Scriptures of Judaism; (2) the reality of the risen Jesus in the life and thought of the community connects the members with the character of Jesus who died for their sins.

The hymns and faith formulations of the early Christ-communities seem to have developed in Greek-speaking, Jewish-Christian settings outside Palestinian Judaism. Antioch appears to have been such a contemplative Christian community, according to Acts. The development of Christological thinking of this vintage requires some time to take shape. Remarkably, by the time of Paul's letter writing, about *twenty years* after the Easter event, these well-crafted Christological affirmations were in place in the church.

The Christology of John outweighs all of the others in sophistication. The sweep of thought in the Prologue to John (1.1-18, discussed below) is wider than the universe, stretching right into Eternity with God. The thought is about the *Logos* (reason, mind, word), its creative power and grace and truth. Then the same overarching *Logos* becomes 'flesh' in time and space in the historical figure of the Jewish Jesus, Messiah of God (1.20-41). There can be no doubt that the author of this Prologue was keenly aware of the higher Hellenistic thinking of the world of the day. Philo of Alexandria, a Hellenistic Jewish philosopher, had already worked out a synthesis between Greek philosophy and the Jewish Scriptures. The Word (*Logos*) of God in the Scriptures was the same Word of the Eternal God of philosophers like Plato. Philo had written widely about the divine *Logos* 40 or 50 years before the publication of the Gospel of John. But Philo's *Logos* could never have become 'flesh'. Flesh corrupts. Flesh is mortal and dies. Philo's *Logos* is incorruptible. Flesh is tied to time and change. God and God's *Logos* are unchangeable. Philo wrote a whole treatise titled 'The Unchangeableness of God'. Against this powerful and pervasive philosophy, the Fourth Evangelist boldly states: 'the *Logos* became flesh and lived among us, and we have seen his glory, the glory as of a father's only son, full of grace and truth' (1.14). From this proposition in particular, Christian theologians construed the *doctrine of incarnation.*

The rest of the Fourth Gospel then works out the implications of that paradoxical connection between the eternal *Logos* and the historical Jesus located within Palestinian Judaism. The narrative about the historical figure of Jesus following the Prologue, so unlike the sophisticated texture of the Prologue, is not thereby detached from the Prologue. With every new scene in the narrative drama of Jesus' earthly ministry an intrinsic connection is made between his word-and-act and the divine *Logos* of God. Jesus works in history as God works in creation and recreation. Here are some examples of the Johannine framing of this inextricable connection between the will and work of Jesus (called 'Son') in history and the will and work of God (called 'Father') over history:

> the Son can do nothing on his own, but only what he sees the Father doing; for whatever the Father does, the Son does likewise. (5.19)
>
> My Father is still working, and I also am working. (5.17)
>
> Just as the Father raises the dead and gives them life, so also the Son gives life to whomever he wishes. (5.21)
>
> I have told you that no one can come to me unless it is granted by the Father. (6.65)
>
> I do nothing on my own, but I speak these things as the Father instructed me. (8.28)
>
> What my Father has given me is greater than all else, and no one can snatch it out of the Father's hand. The Father and I are one. (10.29-30)
>
> If I am not doing the works of my Father, then do not believe me. (10.37)
>
> What I speak, therefore, I speak just as the Father has told me. (12.50)
>
> I am the way, and the truth, and the life. No one comes to the Father except through me. If you know me, you will know my Father also. (14.6-7)

One of the prominent marks of the Christology of John is the generative metaphor to describe Jesus as issuing uniquely from the Uncreated God, as a son issues from the loins of his father. The function of the metaphor is to forestall any notion that the character inhabiting the 'flesh' of Jesus was created. In this light, therefore, the *Logos* did not come into being as a mortal, nor did the *Logos* die when the earthly Jesus died. The *Logos* of God cannot die, any more than the Eternal God can die as mortals do. This way of thinking is ingrained in the literary and theological workings of the Gospel of John. Jesus of history enshrines the mind of God, but is not the mind of God in total. Jesus, after all, repeatedly refers to the Father God as being responsible for his earthly existence, his words and his work.

Here are some other indications in John of the divine mind in the person of Jesus. He knows what people are thinking before they speak or act (e.g. 1.47-51). He 'needed no one to testify about anyone; for he himself knew what was in everyone' (2.25). The woman of Samaria who met him at a well in her neighbourhood could not keep her life hidden from him. She tells her friends, 'Come and see a man who told me everything I have ever done!' (4.29).

In John there is no holding back the understanding that Jesus is the promised Messiah of God. He confesses as much himself from very early in the Gospel to the end of it. This is so unlike the Synoptics where the *Christological identity* of Jesus is held in reserve. The Synoptic authors had almost as much time to contemplate the significance of Jesus for their life and thought, but their writings are restrained on the matter of Christology in comparison to John. It may be, of course, that the Synoptic writers occupied a different world of thought. Compared to them, the implied author of John is immersed in Hellenistic patterns of thinking, and deftly works his thinking into the network of Christian faith traditions.

There are several ways in which the Fourth Gospel is '*fourth*'. Obviously it is fourth in the canonical order, which could mean fourth in importance as compared to the Synoptics. Or it could be that John was put on the list after the Synoptics, and thus fourth. But John is also fourth chronologically, being composed most likely after the other three gospels. John is also fourth in terms of its developed theology and Christology. If such a pattern of thought was known to the other Evangelists they did not express it in their Gospels, at least not to the same degree that the Fourth Evangelist did. Given this scenario, the Gospel of John almost certainly post-dates the other three, written shortly after 90 CE.

Around this time the Pharisees of Jamnia were reconstituting Judaism post-70 CE, as noted earlier. According to some Johannine scholars, particularly J. Louis Martyn (2003, pp. 46–51), there seems to be in John awareness of a decision made at Jamnia to exclude Johannine Christians from the synagogue. Where 'the Jews' (*Ioudaioi*) are portrayed negatively in John, the term may point to the rabbinic leaders of the restored Judaism at Jamnia. But the evidence for *the exclusion* of Johannine Christians from the synagogue because of their belief in Jesus-Messiah is not spelled out specifically in the revised Benedictions of Jamnia. A note about an exclusion of Christ-followers from worship/fellowship in the synagogue is sounded three times in John. The first occurs when the parents of the man born blind appear before the Jewish council: 'they were afraid of the Jews; for the Jews had already agreed that anyone who confessed Jesus to be the Messiah would be put out of the synagogue' (9.22). The second occurs at the end of the Book of Signs. Some Jewish leaders are said to have believed in Jesus secretly, 'but because of the Pharisees they did not confess it, for fear that they would be put out of the synagogue' (12.42). And the third comes up in the farewell discourses in the mouth of Jesus: 'They will put you out of the synagogues' (16.2). The narrative-time situation (the ministry of the historical Jesus) may be a throw-back from the later composition time. The only evidence of official exclusion of Jewish believers in Jesus as Messiah is in the prayer of 'curse' on heretical Jewish sects. Daniel Boyarin affirms that the curse (*Birkat Ha-minim*) inserted into the Eighteen Benedictions under the rule of Gamaliel at about 90 CE was indeed against Christians, but makes no direct connection between that action and the exclusionary statements in John. (Boyarin 2006, p. 262).

If that prayer should prove to be the implied reference in the 'exclusion' texts of John, then the Gospel would post-date the prayer, putting the composition of John into the last decade of the first century. But the three references to the expulsion of Jewish believers in Jesus from the synagogue may have more to do with a local synagogue setting rather than the official decision coming out of Jamnia. Whether the exclusion came from Jamnia or from a local synagogue setting, the move towards separating reconstituted Judaism from the emerging Jewish Christ-communities outside Palestine was not likely to have occurred until about 15 to 25 years after 70 CE. Thus, 90 CE remains a fairly reasonable date of composition of the Fourth Gospel. (See further on the three 'exclusionary' texts in Reinhartz (2001), pp. 38–53).

2. Real author and implied author

Who was the 'real author' of John and the Johannine Epistles? By *real author* is meant the historical person who decided to write for some reason. His identity, including his name, is said to be recoverable, even though the Gospel itself makes no mention of such a 'real author'. Tradition from the late second century attributed the Gospel to John the son of Zebedee, disciple of Jesus. That tradition about the 'real author' has remained in the church to the present time. For some the case is air tight. Who else could the Beloved Disciple be if not John, son of Zebedee? At the crucifixion scene the 'author' is said to have identified himself as the one who witnessed the event: 'He who saw this has testified so that you also may believe. His testimony is true, and he knows that he tells the truth' (19.35). But this comment does not address authorship, much less the identity of the one who 'saw' and 'testified'. But the clincher, so it is said, comes in chapter 21: 'This is the disciple who is testifying to these things and has written them, and we know that his testimony is true' (21.24). Here, so it is claimed, we have the identity of the writer of the Fourth Gospel. Actually, none of these statements speaks directly to the identity of the real author of John. And they certainly do not put a name to the 'other disciple'! In short, this Gospel, together with the other three, is anonymous.

The most compelling evidence against the proposal of John the son of Zebedee as the historical author is the character witness of the Fourth Gospel itself. The language and style are that of a well versed Greek-speaking writer. As stated above, the patterns of thought show native familiarity with Hellenistic culture. The literary quality of the work tells of a writer who had grown up with the culture of Greece, and had become rather well acquainted with both Jewish and Hellenistic literature. He was one of the elite of the church, educated and well disposed to writing a long account about Jesus as the Messiah, Son of God and Word of God. It is difficult to believe that the Aramaic-speaking fisherman of Galilee would have become so fluent in the Greek language and so baptized in Greek philosophical ideas following the death of Jesus. Furthermore, he would have been a very old man at 90 CE, a rarity in those days. What we have is an *implied author* and a *literary narrator*.

Discovery of the implied author is much more rewarding than naming a so-called 'real author'. The implied author needs not a name tag, any more than the disciple whom Jesus loved needs one. This much can be said of the implied author: (1) he was Jewish, respectful of Jewish Scripture and sufficiently acquainted therein to quote and echo it at will; (2) he was Hellenistic, in that he was thoroughly conversant with the Greek language and philosophical thought of the Greek world; (3) he was a committed follower of Jesus as the Christ, who probably paid a price for his confession of that faith; (4) he was an evangelist serving the interests of his congregation(s) through the writing of a Gospel.

The *place of writing* is also unknown. Traditionally Ephesus has been named as the place to which John the son of Zebedee went to live, and from which he wrote his gospel. Interestingly, the fragments of manuscripts of the Fourth Gospel have not been found in that excavated city. Plenty have come to light in Egypt. The earliest fragmentary papyrus manuscript of the New Testament is a tiny portion of John 18 (31-33; 37-38), measuring 2 ½ by 3 ½ inches. It is dated in the first half of the second century, very early indeed.

With this evidence before us, it seems not unreasonable to suggest that the first home of the Gospel of John was somewhere in Egypt, not far from the great centre of learning in Alexandria where Philo lived and taught and wrote his treatises. In the end, though, a definitive place of origin cannot be stated with confidence, except to say that John was written somewhere outside Palestine in close proximity to Jewish synagogues.

The *purpose for writing* such a Gospel may have been several-fold. Stated in the words of the Gospel itself: 'these [signs of Jesus] are written so that you may come to believe that Jesus is the Messiah, the Son of God, and that through believing you may have life in his name' (20.31). Moreover, the purpose at one level is missional. 'Sending' is thematic in John: the Father sent the Son; the Son in Jesus sends the ones God called to be with him; the resurrected Jesus sends his Spirit-endowed disciples. 'Peace is with you. As the Father has sent me, so I send you' (20.21). Equally, the implied purpose was to sustain the flock already baptized into community: that they may keep on believing in the Messiahship of Jesus in the face of controversy and even persecution.

3. The beloved disciple and his community

The Gospel of John knows the tradition about 'the twelve' Palestinian Jewish disciples that Jesus designated as a symbolic group. The group number, 'twelve', occurs at the end of the miracle story of the feeding of the multitude (6.67-71). In that story also twelve baskets of food were left over. Beyond that scene, the group number 'twelve' is used to identify Thomas the twin in chapter 20.24: he is 'one of the twelve'. But *the twelve disciples of Jesus*, known to us by name from the Synoptic Gospels, are not listed in this Gospel. Only six of the Synoptic twelve are mentioned: Andrew, his brother Simon Peter (1.40), Philip (1.43), Thomas the Twin (11.16), Judas Iscariot (6.71) and Judas not Iscariot (14.22).

One might have expected the name of Matthew the tax collector to have entered the drama, or brothers James and John. But they do not appear. Strangely, another man is named as one who joined the early disciples of Jesus: Nathanael, meaning 'gift of God'. Philip found him and brought him to Jesus. Thereupon Nathanael confessed Jesus as Son of God and King of Israel. Nathanael does not appear on the list of twelve disciples in the Synoptic Gospels, or anywhere else in the New Testament for that matter. His absence from the Synoptic lists has led to the notion that Nathanael is another name for Bartholomew, one of the twelve in the Synoptics. Bartholomew (Heb. *bar-tolmai*, 'son of Tolmai') is said to be a family name. Nathanael was his given name. The argument is rather forced, driven, it seems, by the need to harmonize John with the Synoptics on this point. It is best to approach John on its own merits. Bartholomew is not significant in the Synoptic Gospels, whereas the story of Nathanael is significant in John. Jesus looks very favourably on him and says: 'Here is truly an Israelite in whom there is no deceit!' (1.47). And Nathanael in return makes a *two-fold confession* that unites a familiar Graeco-Roman formula with a distinctively Hebraic one: 'You are the Son of God!' (Graeco-Roman), 'You are the King of Israel!' (Hebraic).

This Nathanael has the character of a disciple that the Johannine Jesus could love! He reappears by name in the Appendix (chapter 21) to the Gospel as one of the disciples to whom the risen Jesus made himself known. Nathanael would be a better candidate for the role of the Beloved Disciple than John the son of Zebedee. In the end, though, the Fourth Evangelist has kept the personal name of 'the disciple whom Jesus loved' out of the picture. He is a character in the literary unfolding of the story, an ideal character with whom any interested reader would be inclined to identify. That is his literary and theological role in this Gospel. To name him would be to rob him of his role, and thus to minimize the effect of his characterization and corresponding action.

What is interesting about this disciple-character is that he does not enter the stage until the second main part of the Gospel (chapters 13–20). The second part is all about the death and resurrection of Jesus: departure and return. The pervasive theme of the section is *love*. In this second part the disciples receive instructions from Jesus about their life together after his death. It will be life in the Spirit of Jesus, who laid down his life for them. They are to love one another as he had loved them. At the heart of the whole Passion discourse and the subsequent Passion narrative, stands this enigmatic figure of a disciple whom Jesus loved. He is singled out during the dramatic meeting of the disciples around a table for a meal with the Master. 'One of his disciples – the one whom Jesus loved – was reclining next to him' (13.23). The position is one of learning, and also one of intimacy.

To be close to Jesus is to know him well. Hence, Peter – the figurehead of the disciples in the Synoptics – has to go through the Beloved Disciple to ask Jesus a question.

Peter in John is second to the Beloved Disciple at every turn, which is remarkable given the other tradition that has set him on a rather high ecclesiastical pedestal. In John, Peter outspeaks himself in the supper scene and has to be corrected (13.6-9). He promises to 'lay down his life' for Jesus rather than deny him. But Peter does deny Jesus when the time comes to confess him. The Beloved Disciple, without saying much, remains faithful to the end. When Peter wanted to get inside the courtyard where Jesus was tried, the other disciple had to vouch for him (18.15-16). After the news of the resurrection of Jesus had reached the disciples, Peter and the Beloved Disciple ran to the tomb, 'but the other disciple outran Peter and reached the tomb first' (20.4). Clearly, the hero among the disciples in this Gospel is the one unnamed, the one whom Jesus loved. He is a disciple who knows the virtue of *receiving the divine love* before attempting to love others.

Even in the last scene in chapter 21, where Peter and the Beloved Disciple are with Jesus, Peter's response to Jesus is less than flattering. The dialogue reads thus:

> [Jesus]: Simon son of John, do you love [*agapaò*] me more than these?
> [Peter]: Yes, Lord; you know that I love [*phileò*] you.
> [Jesus]: Feed my lambs.
> [Jesus]: Simon son of John, do you love [*agapaò*] me?
> [Peter]: Yes, Lord; you know that I love [*phileò*] you.
> [Jesus]: Tend my sheep.
> [Jesus]: Simon son of John, do you love [*phileò*] me?
> [Peter]: Lord, you know everything; you know that I love [*phileò*] you.
> [Jesus]: Feed my sheep

A few observations should be made here to clarify how this dialogue relates to the character and action of the Beloved Disciple. First, notice *the interchange* between the two Greek words for 'love' in the dialogue. The word Jesus uses in the first two questions (*agapaò*) is the word used throughout the Gospel for the love of God for the world (3.16), and the self-sacrificial love of Jesus, which he passes on to the disciples (15.9-13). Peter responds in the dialogue with another word for love, *phileò*. This is a friendship kind of love, but not as demanding as *agapaò* in the context of the Gospel. Second, Jesus switches words in the third question, using Peter's word *phileò*.

At that point Peter is hurt, says the narrator, not because Jesus asked the question a third time, but because Jesus changed words in the third question to the weaker one of the two. Peter still answers with the weaker one. Third, the unnamed disciple, meanwhile, is standing silently in the wings. Peter, having heard from Jesus about the kind of death he would die, sees the Beloved Disciple standing there and asks Jesus about the fate that will befall that one: 'Lord, what about him?' In so many words Peter is told to mind his own business. His business is to follow Jesus wherever that may lead.

Peter is not the ideal disciple in John. He comes across in John 21 as one who wants to be able to claim for himself that he loves Jesus, even if it is only a friendship kind of love. At least he can say, 'I love Jesus.' The other disciple implicitly resigns himself to *being loved by Jesus*, which becomes the model for community life.

Receiving the love of Jesus becomes the *enabling grace* for community life. How else could the 'new commandment' of Jesus be obeyed, 'that you love one another. Just as I have loved you, you also should love one another'? (13.34).The First Epistle echoes the same theme: 'not that we loved God but that he loved us and sent his Son to be the atoning sacrifice for our sins' (1 Jn 4.10). The character of the Beloved Disciple is not only the ideal towards which the individual disciple should aspire, but also the symbol of the community associated with the Fourth Gospel and the Johannine Epistles.

4. The shape and substance of the Fourth Gospel

New Testament scholars have analyzed John this way and that, and not surprisingly. One of the characteristics of this Gospel is its *simplicity* on the one hand and its *depth* on the other. C. H. Dodd's (1953) analysis of John still makes good sense, and will be used as a base from which to develop the discussion that follows.

The Fourth Gospel consists of two large blocks of material about the ministry of Jesus, the first may be called The Book of Signs comprising 11 chapters, and the second part called The Book of the Passion, comprising 8 chapters. Bracketing these two large sections is an introduction, chapter 1,

Table 7.1 A Structural–Thematic Analysis of the Gospel of John

Introduction

1. *Prologue* (1.1–18): sets forth in lyrical form all elements of the theme, and sets the stage for the unfolding of this gospel story.
2. *Testimony* (1.19–51): a series of different witnesses (as in a court trial) testify to the virtuous character and beneficial mission of Jesus in the world.

I The Book of Signs: narrative > discourse (Chapters 2–12)	II The Book of the Passion: discourse > narrative (Chapters 13–20)
The 'signs' (*semeia*) are episodic. That is, the narration of the 'sign' is followed with discourse about the significance of the narrated event, beyond the response of wonder. The numbers to the left represent the sign-discourse unit. The suggested titles seek to capture the prevailing theme that moves to and fro throughout the text. Reference to the text of the 'episode' appears in brackets.	The Passion discourses read as though the death and resurrection had already taken place. They serve to strengthen the community of the Beloved Disciple in the absence of the historical figure of Jesus. The Spirit as Helper (*paraklētos*) continues the work of Jesus, extending it beyond the bounds of Palestine.
1. New creation out of the old (2.1–4.42)	**A. Passion Discourses**
2. A new quality of life by the Word (4.46–5.47)	1. The making of true disciples (13.1–30)
3. Life Sustained by the Word (6.1–71)	2. Going Away and Coming Again: A Dialogue (13.31–14.31)
4. Life Revealed by The Light: Received and Rejected (7.1–8.59)	3. Union of Christ with His Community (15.1–16.33)
5. Sin Judged by the Light (9.1–10.21) (Complement: 10.22–39)	4. The Manifold Prayer of Christ (17.1–26)
6. Mortality Reversed by the Power of the Word (11.1–53)	**B. Passion Narrative**
7. Life through Death (12.1–36)	• Arrest (18.1–11)
Summary of the seven episodes (12.37–50)	• Trial (18.12–19.16)
	• Crucifixion/burial (19.17–42)
	• Resurrection (20.1–29)

SUPPLEMENT

Jesus continues in the church (21.1–25)

and an appendix, or supplement, chapter 21. A skeletal analysis of the thematic structure of the Gospel appears in Table 7.1 (p. 110) for reference: (i) *The Introduction* consists of a Prologue (1.1-18) and a Testimony reminiscent of the word of witnesses in a court trial (1.19-51). The Prologue is lyrical, except for a few narrative pieces concerning the character and role of John the Baptizer (hereafter JB). The poetic parts are all about the *Logos* of God as creator of the universe and revealer of the grace and truth of God to the world. The relationship of the *Logos* to the Eternal God is that of transcendent oneness. *Logos* was in the beginning with God, and in that relationship was thus divine. Through the *Logos* God created the world and every thing and person in the world. The *Logos* is creative light that dispels darkness and governs 'all things'. The *Logos*-light came into its own created realm, but the created people in the world did not receive the *Logos*-light. But there were some who did. To that remnant God gave the right to be called children of God, because they were born of God. Then the *Logos* took on human form, and in that form revealed the glory of the One God. The *Logos* was the only revealer of the God of the universe, and Jesus was *Logos* incarnate. That in brief is the essence of the Prologue. As mentioned earlier, the *Logos* doctrine has roots in the Hebrew Scriptures, especially in Genesis and the Wisdom tradition, but those roots were nourished in Hellenistic soil, such as that of Philo of Alexandria. A *theme statement* of the Prologue, and, by extension, of the whole Gospel, might read as follows:

> The God (*ho theos*) of the universe (*ta panta/kosmos*) has revealed the mystery of life (*zôê*) to human minds by loving the world uniquely through the word-and-act (*Logos/sêmeion*) of the divine Son (*theos-huios*) in the historical figure (*sarx*) of Jesus, to be received by believing (*pisteuô*) and thereby knowing (*ginôskô*) this same Jesus as saviour of the world (*anthropos/kosmos*).

The second part of the introduction may aptly be called 'testimony', a prominent term of reference in John. Credible witnesses testify to the virtuous character and power of the One to bring salvation to the world. He is Messiah of Jewish expectation and Son of God for the Greeks. JB is the principal witness. When the authorities from Jerusalem send priests and Levites (P&L) to inquire into the identity of JB, he repeatedly denies any messianic aspirations. The texture of the dialogue has the effect of diminishing JB (1.19-23):

P&L: Who are you?
JB: I am not the Messiah.

P&L: What then? Are you Elijah?

JB: I am not.

P&L: Are you the prophet?

JB: No.

The visual-literary effect is that of reducing JB to a mere voice that speaks about the other person coming after him. JB is not the light (1.6-8), and he is definitely not the Messiah (1.19-20). A visual representation of JB's answers underscores the diminishing effect:

I am not the Messiah

I am not

No

Instead, JB bears witness to the person of Jesus as 'the lamb of God who takes away the sin of the world' (1.29). That one, says JB, 'must increase, but I must decrease' (3.30).

There are other witnesses, including disciples of JB, who become followers of Jesus. Nathanael, as mentioned earlier, is one of the most important of these. His character is (1) truly Israelite, and (2) guileless (1.47). His witness avers two salient qualities in Jesus. He is *Son of God* and *King of Israel*. That implies he is universal saviour of all peoples of the world.

(ii) *The Book of Signs* (narrative > discourse) is long and somewhat complex. This short excursion into its landscape hardly does justice to its rich texture. The discussion should at least mark a beginning to what could become a life-long journey with the Beloved Disciple and his Gospel.

A word about the term 'sign' (*sèmeion*) in John. It is used as a descriptor for a miracle story in the ministry of Jesus. As such, the miracle points to a reality beyond itself, although not divorced from itself. The sign is not Reality in the final and ultimate sense, but reality as prefiguring the Reality yet to come. Reality is otherwise called 'truth' (*alètheia*) in John.

Sign can also be found in narrated acts of Jesus other than 'miracles'. The overturning of the tables in the Temple is sign. A new kind of temple is underway, one not built with human hands, but raised up by God. The narrator then slips in the insightful comment: 'but he was speaking of the temple of his body. After he was raised from the dead, his disciples remembered that he had said this' (2.21-22).

The narrated sign is followed by a corresponding discourse. The two together, sign and discourse, Dodd calls an *episode*. The author of John does not allow the narrated sign to speak for itself, nor the reader to settle on a meaning apart from the one assigned in the discourse. Consider the first two signs in chapter 2, for example. The changing of the water to wine celebrates a new 'beginning' (*archè*) in the context of a wedding feast. It was the 'beginning' of Jesus' signs, says the narrator (2.1-11). The other 'beginning' was at the creation of the universe as cited in the Prologue (1.1-2). Now there is a new beginning in the work of Jesus in the world. The new wine is better vintage than the old. The new living Temple is better than a stone structure. The change-over depicted graphically and symbolically in these two signs in the first episode is enhanced by subtle details. The changing of water to wine happens 'on the third day'. Any Christian reading the story would not try to look for the first and second day chronologically in the text, but think immediately of the confessional line: God raised Jesus 'on the third day, in accordance with the Scriptures'. The search for a chronological first and second day would be in vain in any case; they are not in the text.

There may be an echo in John 2.1-11 of the Greek myth of Dionysius – also called Bacchus – who was believed to be the god of wine and intoxication. If an echo exists in the narrative it is faint, and scarcely relevant to the thrust of the Johannine narrative. The comparison internal to the narrative is not between Jesus and Dionysius, but between Jesus and Judaism. The sign depicts the drawing out of the water from Jewish water pots, the primary source of the new wine which the Jewish Jesus creates. A Johannine Jewish believer in Jesus could make connection with the wine of the Communion ritual, which seems to have been widely observed in the post-Easter Christian communities. (Cf. 1 Cor. 11.23-26; Mk 14.22-25; Mt. 26.26-29; Lk. 22.19-20).

Exchange and transformation – as in water to wine, stone temple to resurrected Jesus – are very much part of the Gospel of John. The good news in Jesus was heard and received first in Palestinian Judaism, but then transferred and transformed into 'good news' for the whole world. Even small details such as *the translation of terms*, so characteristic of John, should not be dismissed lightly. 'Messiah' is translated into *Christos*, 'Cephas' into *Petros*, 'Siloam' into *Apestalmenos*, etc. In every instance the translation is out of Aramaic into Greek, out of the limits of the Palestinian environs into the larger Hellenistic world. (Shillington 2004, pp. 54–70. Cf. also 7.35; 12.19-23).

Following the two narrated signs are two complementary discourses in the form of dialogue. The first is a dialogue between Jesus and a leading Jewish Rabbi named Nicodemus (3.1-21). The second is between Jesus and a woman of questionable morality from Samaria (4.4-26). The contrasts between the two are stark and the irony brimming. Symbolism in and around each of these dialogues is pungent.

Nicodemus comes to Jesus 'by night' (3.2). He is not a person of the light, as Jesus and his followers are (3.10-11). He does not *know* as they do. It is expected then that he will stumble through the dialogue with Jesus without enlightened understanding. When he is told he and his fellow Jewish leaders will have to be 'born again' (*anòthen*, lit. 'from above'), he misses the point and wonders how an adult man could be born a 'second time' (*deuteros*), Nicodemus' term. Then he is told he will have to be born of *water and Spirit*. This is almost certainly a Johannine allusion to Christian baptism with which the giving of the Spirit was closely associated in the primitive church (Acts 1.5; 2.38; 1 Cor. 12.13). The new birth by water-and-Spirit will mean for Nicodemus – and others like him – that he will have to cross over openly into the new community through the waters of baptism in the name of Jesus. The move would have social implications. If he should join with the Jesus-Messiah community he could be ostracized by his own community. Implicitly, Christian discipleship comes at a cost socially and politically. Nicodemus could lose his status in the Jewish academy if he were to join the Jesus-group.

Ironically, the woman of Samaria meets up with Jesus at 'about noon', the brightest hour of the day (4.6). She exhibits greater insight than Nicodemus in her dialogue with Jesus, but her understanding is still faulty. She has had five husbands, which, to her surprise, Jesus knows about. The number 'five' may hint at the five scrolls of the Samaritan Pentateuch, which the Jewish hierarchy viewed as a perversion of the Mosaic Law. The male disciples, meanwhile, are befuddled by the whole scene, especially that Jesus was talking with a woman, and a Samaritan woman at that (4.27). At any rate, the woman submits to the word of Jesus in her own way. She asks for the living water that Jesus can give, and then goes off to her village to tell her story to her friends. In the end, the Samaritans invite Jesus *to stay* with them, and he did stay for two days (4.40). 'Staying', or 'abiding', (*menò*) is a key word in John. It comes up prominently again in the farewell discourses, where it has to do with a dynamic interrelationship between the living Jesus and those who receive him by believing. In this present text, the believing Samaritans have received the witness of Jesus-Messiah. Implicitly, believing Samaritans belong to a community faithful to Jesus. The crowning irony comes when the Samaritan villagers make their confession: 'this is truly the Savior of the world' (4.42). They were able to see the light in Jesus to a far greater degree than the Jewish Nicodemus had demonstrated earlier.

The rest of the signs and their corresponding discourses in the Book of Signs appear in an ascending order of gravity. The *first sign*, as we saw, was set in a joyful wedding feast. The wine had run out. Jesus made new wine for the occasion. The new wine enhanced the celebration. The *last sign* occurs in a setting of mourning the death of a loved one named Lazarus. In that setting Jesus raises Lazarus having been dead four days (chapter 11). Between these two are other signs and discourses that increase in intensity and significance: Jesus heals a sick child of a royal official (4.46-54); then he heals a lame man in Jerusalem by the pool with five porches, having been lame for thirty-eight years (5.1-9); then he feeds 5,000 people, with twelve baskets of bread left over (6.1-15); then a speech-sign about the water-Spirit at the end of the great festival of booths (7.1-39); then the healing of a man blind from birth (9.1-12); and finally the raising of Lazarus from the dead (11.1-44). Following that last sign that Jesus performed, Mary of Bethany, sister to Lazarus, performed a sign on Jesus: she anointed him with costly ointment for his burial (12.1-8).

Accompanying each of these sign-narratives is a discourse about its significance. Within both narrative and discourse, *controversy* is plentiful. It could be about breaking Sabbath law, or about the extravagant claims Jesus makes for himself and his work as Son of God. Whatever the controversy, it involves the religious hierarchy. Jesus breaks the bounds of orthodoxy, and the keepers thereof have to find some way to remove his maverick work and word from their traditional environment. Ironically again, when he gives new life to the dead Lazarus, the system is disturbed and the religious authorities are at a loss as to what to do about Jesus.

So the chief priests and the Pharisees called a meeting of the council, and said, 'What are we to do? This man is performing many signs. If we let him go on like this, everyone will believe in him, and the Romans will come and destroy both our holy place and our nation'. But one of them, Caiaphas, who was high priest that year, said to them, 'You know nothing at all! You do not understand that it is better for you to have one man die for the people than to have the whole nation destroyed'. He did not say this on his own, but being high priest that year he prophesied that Jesus was about to die for the nation, and not for the nation only, but to gather into one the dispersed children of God. So from that day on they planned to put him to death. (11.47-53)

The role of *the narrator* throughout the Book of Signs is striking, as in this last passage. The narrator is the informant throughout. His explanatory comments are the literary gel that makes this gospel such a fascinating read. His knowledge of Jesus – his origin, motives, purpose and destiny – is boundless. Among his many functions, the narrator translates Aramaic into Greek, describes characters, sets the time and place of a scene, and explains some cryptic sayings of Jesus. For example, when Jesus announces his manifesto on the last great day of the festival of booths, the narrator has to explain it for the novice reader.

> **[Jesus]:** Let anyone who is thirsty come to me, and let the one who believes in me drink. As the scripture has said, Out of the believer's heart shall flow rivers of living water.
>
> **[Narrator]:** Now he said this about the Spirit, which believers in him were to receive; for as yet there was no Spirit, because Jesus was not yet glorified. (7.37-39)

So much more could be said about the Book of Signs, but that would take the discussion well beyond the bounds of this chapter. Attention should be drawn, at least, to the two principal symbols operating variously throughout: *water* and *light*. Water in the ancient near eastern world was a symbol of life. If the rainy season failed to give enough water for the crops, famine could result, and death ensue. Even the watery tears on the cheeks of Jesus at the graveside of Lazarus are not incidental in the text (11.35). The tears are a 'sign' of life flowing from the innermost being of Jesus, who brings life out of death in the raising of Lazarus.

The water of life in relation to Jesus runs through this Gospel from beginning to end. The last sign of water issues forth from the pierced side of Jesus on the cross. When the soldiers pierced his side 'at once blood and water came out'. He had already given up his Spirit in death, with his final word to the world on his lips: 'It is finished' (19.30-37). This is the sign of life through death. This sign gathers all the others into itself, the sign of the cross on which Jesus was 'lifted up' (3.14) in life-giving death in order to draw all kinds of people to himself (12.32). 'Lifted up' is an ambiguous term in John. Its common meaning would be that of being lifted up in glory, not in death. But in John, Jesus' being lifted up in crucifixion is the badge of honour and glory Jesus wears, because he willingly gave himself up to that death for the sake of others (10.11).

The other dominant symbol in the Book of Signs is light. Its function is two-fold: (1) to reveal the truth, especially the truth about the person and work of Jesus, and (2) to judge right from wrong in the world of humankind. The symbol of light moves off stage at the end of the Book of Signs, giving way to the all-embracing theme that was held in reserve until that point, *the theme of love* (*agapè*). With the turning of the first page of the Book of the Passion, self-giving love shines forth like the rising of the sun, and remains visible to the end. Over against that radiant love-light, the dull glimmer of the world's light tries in vain to shine in the darkness, as in the soldiers' flickering lanterns and torches at the time of Jesus' arrest.

The scene is striking in its subtle irony. 'So Judas brought a detachment of soldiers together with police from the chief priests and the Pharisees, and they came there with lanterns and torches and weapons' (18.3). Jesus then asked them for whom they were searching. They said, 'Jesus of Nazareth'. He replied, 'I am[he]' (*egò eimi*). At that point 'they stepped back and fell to the ground' (18.6). A strange reaction indeed! But from the standpoint of this Gospel, and the community it represents, the reaction would be understandable. Jesus uses the shorthand, but loaded phrase, 'I am'. The phrase had come up in the Book of Signs and in the Passion discourses a number of times – '*I am* the door', '*I am* the good Shepherd', '*I am* the way', '*I am* the true vine.' The same two words on the lips of Jesus at the arrest-scene bring the soldiers to the ground, either in astonished obeisance or in paralysis. The narrator does not tell. The point is, the 'I Am' had spoken; eternal majesty was present; divine light broke through the gloom of betrayal.

One final point needs to be made before turning the page from the Book of Signs to the Book of the Passion. In speaking pointedly about his approaching death, Jesus prays out of his troubled soul (12.27). The wording is reminiscent of the Synoptic prayer in the Garden of Gethsemane. Yet it is quite different from the Synoptic prayer. In the Synoptic prayer Jesus asks that the cup of suffering be removed, and then adds, 'not what I want, but what you want' (Mk 14.36, par). The prayer in John reads quite differently: 'Now my soul is troubled. And what should I say—"Father, save me from this hour?" No, it is for this reason that I have come to this hour' (12.27). The tone and texture have a corrective note, especially in the rhetorical question. The Johannine Jesus goes to his sacrificial death willingly, without flinching. He will **not** ask for the cup of suffering and death to be removed, because 'it is for this reason that I have come to this hour.'

(iii) *The Book of the Passion* (discourse > narrative) is structured in the reverse of the Book of Signs: the discourse comes before the narrative. But the several discourses echo the death and resurrection as though they had already taken place. From the standpoint of the time and situation of the Gospel, of course, the death and resurrection of Jesus are indeed in the past.

The discursive parts of the Book of the Passion may be called 'farewell discourses' (13.1–17.26). In them Jesus speaks of his departure from his disciples. They will be able to cope well, because Jesus will send another One to be alongside them to help and counsel them. In that sense, the departed Jesus will return to them to carry them through their tough times, enabling them to speak boldly in his name. The other One is called the Spirit, not different in character from Jesus, but in form. A closer inspection of the Passion discourses should bring these themes to light.

In chapter 13 the setting is a meal Jesus shares with his disciples *before Passover* (13.1). Some churchly interpreters construe this meal to be the same as the Passover meal represented in the Synoptics in which Jesus utters the words of institution. But the text of John forbids such a construal. It was a 'supper' (13.4) 'before the festival of Passover' (13.1). The Gospel of John makes very clear that Jesus was crucified on the day of Preparation for Passover (19.14, 31, 42). Therefore, the supper he shared with his disciples in chapter 13 could not have been the Passover meal. Noteworthy also is the absence of the words of institution from the meal of chapter 13. The closest John comes to the Synoptic words of institution occurs in chapter 6.51-56:

> Very truly, I tell you, unless you eat the flesh of the Son of Man and drink his blood, you have no life in you. Those who eat my flesh and drink my blood have eternal life, and I will raise them up on the last day; for my flesh is true food and my blood is true drink. Those who eat my flesh and drink my blood abide in me, and I in them.

The day of Preparation for Passover was the day when the lambs were slaughtered, a point John apparently wants to make with reference to the death of Jesus (cf. 1.29). What is odd in the words of institution, whether the Johannine version in chapter 6 or the Synoptic version, is the symbolic drinking of the blood. Jewish kosher regulation forbade the *consumption of the blood* of the sacrificial animal. The blood of the passive lamb was sprinkled on the doorposts and the lintel of the house, but not consumed. 'Only be sure that you do not eat the blood; for the blood is the life, and you shall not eat the life with the meat' (Deut. 12.23). Perhaps John is revising that law with respect to the Passover sacrifice of Jesus. Believers are to receive the life-blood of Jesus figuratively.

Central to the dramatic scene of chapter 13 of John is the washing of the disciples' feet. Jesus acts as a slave would in that society. Peter refuses to have Jesus wash his feet. The act of Jesus deconstructs Peter's world. Servants wash feet. Masters do not. Here Jesus the Master takes on the posture of a slave and invites the disciples to do the same to each other. No one ranks higher than the other in the new kingdom of Jesus. Anyone who hopes to lead will have to do so from within the circle, not from the top of a pyramid structure.

The washing with water may relate to the practice of *baptism* within the Johannine community. When Simon Peter eventually asks for a washing of his hands and head as well as his feet, he is told that someone who has bathed needs only to wash the feet. One can hear the echo of the once-for-all baptism of inclusion in the faithful community, and then an ongoing confession within the community. The teaching-scene culminates with the giving of the new commandment, with a word about its effect as witness to Jesus: 'that you love one another. Just as I have loved you, you also should love one another. By this everyone will know that you are my disciples, if you have love for one another' (13.34-35).

The discourses that follow expand the implications of the *new commandment* with reference to the community of the Spirit of Jesus. The 'I am' in Jesus becomes the way, the truth and the life in relation to God and to each other. The two are never separated. Relationship with God comes to expression in the context of relationship in community-life. Jesus will not leave the disciples orphaned by his death. He will come to them through the Spirit and give them *shalom* (peace). 'Peace I leave with you; my peace I give to you. I do not give to you as the world gives. Do not let your hearts be troubled, and do not let them be afraid' (14.27).

Throughout the discourses in chapters 14 through 16 the One replacing the earthly Jesus has a special title of *paraklètos*, translated variously as Comforter (KJV), Counsellor (RSV/NIV), Advocate (NRSV), Helper (NASB). No other writer in the New Testament uses this title for the Spirit. Etymologically the sense is that of one who is 'called alongside'. The disciples will not be alone with their own thoughts, unable to answer when they bear witness in the courts. The one alongside them 'will guide [them] into all the truth; for He will not speak on His own initiative, but whatever He hears,

He will speak' (16.13). In this sense the Spirit is Advocate, one who speaks on behalf of a client. 'When the Advocate comes, whom I will send to you from the Father, the Spirit of truth who comes from the Father, he will testify on my behalf. You also are to testify because you have been with me from the beginning' (15.26).

One of the most poignant images of Christian community in John is that of the vine and the branches (15.1-17). Jesus in the Spirit is the vine supplying the branches with the nourishment for fruit-bearing. God is the vine dresser. Pervasive throughout the vine discourse is the idea of *mutual indwelling*. 'Just as the branch cannot bear fruit by itself unless it abides in the vine, neither can you unless you abide in me. I am the vine, you are the branches. Those who abide in me and I in them bear much fruit, because apart from me you can do nothing' (15.4-5). Mutual indwelling – Christ in the members of the community and the members in Christ – produces fruit. Any branch that does not produce fruit should not be drawing from the fruit-producing vine. Such branches are suckers, and as such are pruned away. Applied to members of the community of Christ, this can only mean that a non-fruit-bearing member is removed from membership in the community of the Messiah. Insofar as this is the sense of the 'pruning', expulsion from the Johannine community is on par with expulsion of heretics from the synagogue.

There cannot be much doubt about the nature of the fruit. 'My Father is glorified by this, that you bear much fruit and become my disciples. As the Father has loved me, so I have loved you; abide in my love . . .. This is my commandment, that you love one another as I have loved you. No one has greater love than this, to lay down one's life for one's friends' (15.7-13).

The farewell discourses close with a *mediatorial prayer* in chapter 17. In it Jesus acts as a high priest would in the Temple worship. The prayer of Jesus unites the true worshippers with the 'I am' God, the eternal One, and with each other, 'so that they may be one, as we are one' (17.11). The form of the prayer may be viewed as having a number of concentric circles. At the centre is the 'glory' of the Son who, by his nature as *Logos*-Son, glorifies the Father-God. The Son prays for the first disciples God gave through the Son's choosing them from the world (see 15.16-19). Jesus also prays for those who believe through the word of the disciples, that all may be one, as the Son is one with the Father. The outside circle is the world that God loves through the Son (3.16). The world (*cosmos*) enters the prayer as the place of God's saving action, the context from which the new community is drawn

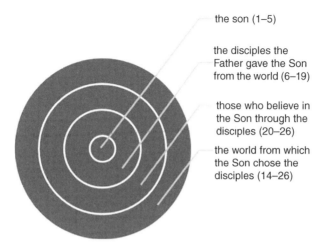

the son (1–5)

the disciples the
Father gave the Son
from the world (6–19)

those who believe in
the Son through the
disciples (20–26)

the world from which
the Son chose the
disciples (14–26)

Figure 7.1 Literary Contours of the Prayer of Jesus.

to the Father-God through the Son. The form of the prayer may be viewed as having a number of concentric circles, illustrated in Figure 7.1.

The Passion narrative, beginning at 18.1 and closing at 19.42, has a sequel in the Resurrection narrative, 20.1-31. Both of these have been mentioned already in the discussion. A few points on each will bring this brief exploration of the Gospel of John to a close.

As with the Synoptic Gospels, so also in John, the events leading up to the end of Jesus' earthly life are seen as fulfilling *the divine plan* as recorded in the Jewish Scriptures. For example, the custom was to break the legs of the crucified criminals so that they could no longer hold themselves up. They would then suffocate. In keeping with the Johannine theme of his willing self-sacrifice, Jesus did not hold himself up so as to live as long as possible. 'When [the Roman soldiers] came to Jesus and saw that he was already dead, they did not break his legs. Instead, one of the soldiers pierced his side with a spear, and at once blood and water came out' (19.33-34). The narrator then calls in the Scripture texts that these events are said to fulfil: 'These things occurred so that the scripture might be fulfilled, "None of his bones shall be broken". And again another passage of scripture says, "They will look on the one whom they have pierced" '. Several texts may underwrite the first quotation about none of the bones being broken: Psalm 34.20, Exodus 12.46, Numbers 9.12. It seems likely that the regulation in the

Law (Exod. 12, Num. 9) about not breaking the bones of the Passover lamb is in view. The second quotation about the piercing of Jesus' side fulfils Zechariah 12.10.

An important point coming out of the Passion narrative concerns *the role of the Roman authorities* in the death of Jesus, in particular the character and behaviour of Pilate. The argument by David Rensberger on this issue is telling. Pilate in John is not a weakling, swayed by the Jewish leaders in Jerusalem to act against his better judgment. Pilate is a calloused, calculating and manipulative Roman official who uses the accusations against Jesus to put the Jewish hierarchy in its subservient place under Roman rule. The Jewish people have no earthly king of their own, apart from the Emperor. Pilate questions Jesus about his claim to kingship. And in John Jesus is not silent on the matter. He is a king, but his kingdom is not of this world (18.36). It is a kingdom nonetheless, and Pilate will have none of it. He manoeuvres the proceedings to the point where the Jewish leaders make an affirmation contrary to the Passover refrain that celebrates God as king and deliverer. After flogging Jesus, and allowing the soldiers to ridicule his kingship (19.1-7), Pilate brings out this thorn-crowned, beaten figure to the Jewish leaders saying, 'Here is your king' (19.14). The Jewish leaders are offended, understandably, and call for the crucifixion of Jesus. 'Shall I crucify your king?' Pilate asked. By asking thus, he managed to elicit a kind of confession: 'We have no king but the emperor.' (19.15).

The Romans led Jesus outside the religious precincts to be crucified. He went out 'carrying the cross by himself' (19.17). From the syntax of the sentence, John seems to be aware of the Synoptic tradition that has another man carry the cross for Jesus (Mk 15.20). In John Jesus bears the full weight of the punishment in his own person. Pilate had an inscription made, written in the three principal languages of the world (Hebrew, Greek and Latin), and put the inscription on the cross over the bleeding head of Jesus. It read, 'Jesus of Nazareth, the king of the Jews' (19.19). The Jewish leaders who saw it asked Pilate to change the wording to read, 'This man said, I am the king of the Jews.' But Pilate refused. The wording stands. This is what happens to anyone in Jerusalem who would be king: they will be mocked and crucified.

In the burial narrative, Nicodemus returns. He is still a person of the night (19.39). He, along with a man named Joseph, wrapped the body of Jesus and placed it in a tomb 'according to the burial custom of the Jews' (19.40). Nicodemus disappears from the narrative after the burial.

The resurrection of Jesus marks his *return* to his chosen ones, not to the unbelieving Romans, and not to the unbelieving Jewish leaders either. Only his faithful followers witness his resurrected body. In that body Jesus 'appears' to the believers, both women and men (20.11-23). The question is, how does 'appearance' relate to reality? Thomas, one of the disciples, is not convinced by appearances (20.24-29). He requires *physical reality* before he will believe. 'Unless I see the mark of the nails in his hands, and put my finger in the mark of the nails and my hand in his side, I will not believe' (20.25). The resurrected Jesus accommodates even Thomas, tied as he is to the notion that the physical is more real than the spiritual. 'Put your finger here and see my hands. Reach out your hand and put it in my side. Do not doubt but believe' (20.27). What the incident affirms is that the person of Jesus resurrected is the same Jesus that lived and died. The same self-sacrificial character of Jesus continues in the resurrected state. The believing community is expected to take its cue from the 'signs' on the resurrected body of Jesus and embody the same character in their communal life.

While Thomas is accommodated, his focus on the physical is not affirmed. Yes, he believes when his physical senses affirm the reality of the risen Jesus. But the last word of the resurrected Jesus is this: 'Blessed are those who have not seen and yet have come to believe' (20.29).

5. The shape and substance of the Johannine Epistles

In all likelihood the three Johannine Epistles were written after the Gospel, 1 John being the most substantive of the three, and the focus of this section. The theology and vocabulary of the Gospel carry over into 1 John, but with some differences. If there were opponents behind the Gospel, as seems likely, then opponents are out in the open in the language of 1 John. They may not be the same people, but they appear to be openly opposed to the community from which this Epistle comes. What makes them difficult for the implied author to handle is that they were at one time members of the Johannine community. 'They went out from us, but they did not belong to us; for if they had belonged to us, they would have remained with us. But by going out they made it plain that none of them belongs to us' (2.19). The situation reflected in 1 John is, in several respects, beyond that of the Gospel.

The Epistle is trying to stay the traditional course against some kind of spiritualized gospel. No one knows exactly what the opponents believed. But the rhetoric implies that they no longer confess that the Christ of God had come in the flesh of Jesus of Nazareth. 'By this you know the Spirit of God: every spirit that confesses that Jesus Christ has come in the flesh is from God, and every spirit that does not confess Jesus is not from God' (4.2-3). Such people are labelled 'antichrists', and as such signal the eschatological wind-up of history: now that many antichrists have come 'we know that it is the last hour' (2.18).

Some scholars find in the *implied opponents* of the Epistle the beginning of Docetism in the early church. This doctrine held that the Christ of God could not have become flesh, as the Gospel affirms. Christ could not be subject to suffering and death; therefore, Jesus who suffered and died was not the divine Christ.

1 John urges the *ones remaining* to continue in the message they heard from the beginning 'concerning the word of life' (1.1). There is no mistaking what that 'word of life' is in this Epistle. It is the word of love, the major theme carried over from the Fourth Gospel. The act of God in Christ was a loving act, 'for God is love' (4.8). But the human response to the love of God in Christ is not individualistic or selfish in 1 John. It is communal and self-giving. A person born of God is, by that nature, loving. 'Beloved, let us love one another, because love is from God; everyone who loves is born of God and knows God. Whoever does not love does not know God, for God is love' (4.7-8). Accordingly, the opponents who went out from the community were considered unloving, and therefore 'antichrist' in thought and action. If members of the true community are to *abide in Christ* and in God they do so by loving one another. Loving one another makes the word real in life. 'Let us love, not in word or speech, but in truth and action. And by this we will know that we are from the truth' (3.18-19).

The 'world' is still very much in view in the Epistle, as it was in the Gospel. Jesus performed an atoning sacrifice 'for the sins of the whole world' (2.2). The 'world' is the realm of sin, darkness and death. People caught in that sphere hate the members of the community of Christ (3.13-14). Yet 'God sent his only Son into the world so that we might live through him' (4.9).

The name of the writer of the three Johannine Epistles is not given in the text. But 2 John and 3 John designate the writer 'the Elder'. Tradition named this Elder, John, referring to the disciple of Jesus by that name. But an elder is not an Apostle, and much less one of the first disciples of Jesus.

He is simply the Elder, as in 'leader', by virtue of age and wisdom, of the communities to which these two short letters were sent. Given the similarity of vocabulary and thought pattern throughout the three documents it seems likely that the same hand penned all three Johannine Epistles. The most that we can say about the identity of the real author is that he belonged to a community that had a distinctive way of thinking and writing about the grace of God in the person of Jesus the Christ. Hence the designation Johannine. The writer could be the same one who wrote the Gospel, but just as likely the Gospel and the Epistles were written by different people from the same community setting, the community of the Beloved Disciple.

If the Epistles post-date the Gospel by 8 to 10 years, then they were written at the turn of the century, perhaps in the early years of the second century.

6. Conclusion: Jesus, John and Judaism

The Fourth Gospel is more complex than it appears on the surface. Its narrative texture is woven together with intricate symbolism and irony that culminates with the self-sacrificial death of Jesus on a Roman cross. The resurrection sequel serves to carry forward into the community of the Beloved Disciple the kind of life Jesus lived and the kind of death he died. That disciple-figure in John becomes the model of how the community should put the *Logos*-love into practice: they are to love one another as the Christ in Jesus loved them, and by so doing to testify to the world that they belong to the Word made flesh in Jesus. The Johannine Epistles sustain the same themes as the Gospel, rehearsing them in and for a new setting in life.

Even though one is able to identify a purposeful literary structure in the extant Gospel, the text is not without 'seams'. For example, in John 3.2 Nicodemus speaks of the 'these signs' that Jesus performs, while the narrator speaks of the healing of the royal official's son as the 'second sign' (4.54). Similarly, Jesus ends a discourse in chapter 14 with a directive to the disciples, 'Rise let us be on our way', and then launches immediately into the discourse on the vine and branches without any spatial movement apparent. The disconnection between the two sentences is difficult to reconcile. Redaction analysis may account for such 'seams' in John, but should not detract from the literary and theological shape of the Gospel as it stands in the canon.

One matter not sufficiently developed in the discussion of the Gospel was that of the anti-Jewish sentiment in a number of texts. The designation, 'the Jews' (*hoi Ioudaioi*) is often used pejoratively in the Fourth Gospel. Scholars have debated variously the uses of the term in John. Sometimes the plural implies the historic people who identify themselves thus, as in the dialogue between Jesus and the Samaritan woman in John 4. Jesus tells the woman, 'Salvation is from the Jews' (4.18). While the theme lies undeveloped in the text, 'the Jews' appears in a rather positive light. In the context of the dialogue, a reasonable inference is that the historic people called 'the Jews', rather than Samaritans, constituted God's agent through whom salvation comes.

Other apparently positive or neutral uses of the designation, 'the Jews', comes through in John. One such is in 8.31-33. In that immediate context the narrator has Jesus instructing 'the Jews who had believed in him'. If they continue in his word they will know the truth and the truth will make them free. A more neutral use of the 'the Jews' is found in the narrative about the death of Lazarus, where 'many of the Jews had come to Martha and Mary to console them about their brother' (11.19). Jesus was there too, and there he wept in mourning along with 'the Jews' and Martha and Mary.

At other points in John, however, 'the Jews' seems to refer to the leaders of the Jewish community opposed to Jesus, and by extension to the community of the beloved disciple. In the episode of the healing of the man born blind (9.1-41), for example, 'the Jews' are identified specifically with the Pharisees in the court scene where the man and his parents are called to bear witness against Jesus (9.16-22). Clearly, 'the Jews' in that context are cast in a negative light. But the most damning evidence of an anti-Jewish bias in John comes at 8.44 where Jesus says to 'the Jews' in dialogue with him about ancestral descent: 'You are from your father the devil.' What is puzzling about Jesus' statement is that the dialogue partners seem not to have changed from 8.31 to 8.44. At 8.31 'the Jews' are said to be those who had believed in Jesus. At 8.44 they are said to be descended from the devil (*diabolos*), because they 'look for an opportunity to kill [Jesus]' (8.37). Of course, the narrator wants to show the name-calling moving in both directions: at 8.48 'the Jews' accuse Jesus of being a Samaritan and having a demon.

There is no easy explanation for the anti-Jewish tone and texture at a number of points in John. If the antagonism between Jesus and the Pharisees in the narrative context is taken at face value, then Jesus being Jewish is engaged with fellow Jewish leaders in heated theological debate. Similar name-calling can be found in texts of the sectarian Jewish community at Qumran against the priests of Jerusalem. In both the Qumran texts and in John the antagonism resulted from opposing positions from within the same religion and ethnic identity.

But the narrative antagonism can be read at the level of the Johannine community in tension with post-70 Judaism. In that reading, the Johannine community may have consisted of mixed membership of Jewish and non-Jewish believers in Jesus. In that scenario, the border lines between the two communities would have been more clearly recognizable, and the polemic more discernibly anti-Jewish. But if the author(s) of the Fourth Gospel were of Jewish heritage, then what appears as anti-Jewish rhetoric may be construed as intra-Jewish, rather than non-Jewish Christian diatribe. The question of the separation of the Christ-community from its parent Judaism is critical in dealing with the issue. Had the Johannine community declared itself non-Jewish Christian by the time of writing? Was the author(s) writing as a non-Jewish Christian? My own tentative answer is that the author was a Hellenistic Jewish person who still had ties with the synagogue, and was in dialogue with the synagogue leaders about belief in Jesus as the Messiah viewed through the paradoxical lens of crucifixion-resurrection.

The 2,000-year history of Judaism and Christianity has been a chequered one at best. With the ascendency of Christianity following the accession of Constantine, Christian supersessionism flourished, and with it anti-Jewish rhetoric of racist calibre, contrary to the more inclusive teaching of the Jewish Jesus of history who gave birth to the primitive Christian community. 'The Jews' (*Ioudaios-oi*), as used in the first-century context by both Jewish and non-Jewish people, would probably not have carried the same connotation as it does in the Anglo-European world of the twenty-first century. Moreover, from this point forward in the ensuing discussions, another translation of *Ioudaios-oi* will be proposed to designate people of the first century of Israelite heritage and religion. A case for the alternate translation will be made in the next chapter on Acts, where the term occurs numerous times, usually with negative overtones.

Further related reading

An illuminating study of the Jewish *Logos* doctrine, traced from the Hebrew Scriptures through John and into early Christianity and Judaism, is that of Daniel Boyarin (2006), *Border Lines: The Partition of Judaeo-Christianity*. University of Pennsylvania.

In her clear and careful analysis of John, Adele Reinhartz (2001), probes the Fourth Gospel from various angles to come to terms with anti-Jewish elements, among other striking features of the Gospel: *Befriending the Beloved Disciple: A Jewish Reading of the Gospel of John*. Continuum International.

David Rensberger (1996) explores John through a reconstruction of the social history, with some novel results, *Johannine Faith and Liberating Community*. Westminster/John Knox.

Paul Duke (1985) points out helpfully the presence of ironic elements in John, *Irony in the Fourth Gospel*. John Knox.

Raymond E. Brown (1979) masterfully reconstructs the history of the community connected with the production and reception of the Gospel and Epistles in *The Community of the Beloved Disciple*. Paulist

Consult also relevant commentaries under 'Gospels' in the Bibliography.

Second Volume of a Two-part Work: The Acts of the Apostles

Chapter Outline

The book of Acts, by its own testimony, is not an independent work, but a continuation of the Gospel of Luke. The two documents share the same world view and redactional hand. By these alone one can see the relationship between the two volumes. But the author/redactor of Acts does not leave the reader guessing and deducing. He opens Acts with a backward glance at Luke: 'In the first book, Theophilus, I wrote about all that Jesus did and taught from the beginning' (1.1). There can be no mistaking the allusion to the Gospel of Luke, since Luke alone has the name Theophilus. Granted, the preface to Acts is not as handsomely crafted as the preface to Luke, but the former serves both volumes by the simple allusion to 'the first book'.

Because of the tightly knit relationship between Luke and Acts the two are often referred to as Luke-Acts. From the standpoint of the implied author, the second book is a necessary sequel to the first. The work of the historical Jesus did not end with his cruel death, nor yet with his resurrection.

That which Jesus initiated within the bounds of historical Israel continued in the community inspired by the outpoured Spirit of Jesus. Continuity from Jesus to the primitive church is important to the implied author, and just as important to Luke-Acts is the continuity between the community of Jesus and the Israel of God to whom the promise of salvation was made. In Jesus and the church the promise finds fulfilment, but not apart from historic Israel.

1. Narrative time and place

Narrative time and place are very much part of the *heuristic context*, within which to understand the Acts schema of the story. As indicated in the introduction above, continuity matters greatly to the implied author of Luke-Acts, so the Acts narrative begins by connecting with the risen Jesus, who ascended before the eyes of his Apostles. The events happened in the environs of the city of Jerusalem. While Acts nuances Luke's narrative about the resurrected appearance of Jesus, together with his ascension, connection between the Gospel and Acts is still evident.

At the ending of Acts, the city is no longer Jerusalem, but Rome. And the key figure is no longer Jesus, but Paul. In a way, Jesus is present in Rome, but only in the word of Paul and in the Spirit that fills his heart and mind. Some 28 years elapsed from the beginning of Acts to the end. Between those two temporal and local points, the missionary impact was significant. The news of the saving word and work of Jesus spread from Jerusalem into the rest of Judaea, Samaria and further north to Antioch of Syria. From Antioch the word spread to the Gentile world, ending in Rome.

But the spread of the news from the Jerusalem centre was not without opposition. One group of Greek-speaking Judaeans ran into trouble with the Aramaic-speaking authorities. The persecution scattered the Greek-speakers throughout the region as far north as Antioch (8.1). Questions crossing the minds of the scattered disciples of the risen Jesus would probably have run along these lines: How far can this news go? Into what social, ethnic groups can it penetrate? Can non-Jewish people come into the new community of Jesus the Christ? And if so, by what means are they to be incorporated?

The one to extend the news into regions where it had not gone was a man named Paul, a Jewish man who had an epiphany of Jesus the Christ

(Acts 9), which transformed his vision and widened his horizon. His call – by his own testimony – was to go to the Gentiles with the news of Jesus (Gal. 1.16; 2.8). In following his call, Paul travelled from one city to another to gather in believing Gentiles into the new community of Jesus Christ. Finally, Paul ended up in Rome, the centre of the world of the day. And Acts is happy to leave the story there, with Paul preaching in the capital of the Empire unhindered. The notion that the author of Acts had a third volume in view is pure conjecture. By all other accounts, Paul died a violent death in Rome (c.63–67) under the tyranny of Emperor Nero (EH 2.15).

2. Composition time, place and person

Important as the narrative time and place of Acts are, they do not stand alone. A subtext runs through Acts like an aquifer, present but not immediately visible. The *subtext informs the narrative* out of the consciousness of a later situation in life. The new community, with its beginning in Palestinian Judaism, had penetrated successfully into the minds of non-Jewish people of the Roman world. The new Christian movement had become a force to be reckoned with by the time of writing. The Jerusalem Temple had fallen in 70 CE, and Judaism through its leaders was actively reconstituting itself as a viable religion in the world without its central symbol. Meanwhile, the gap between the new Jesus movement and the new Judaism was widening. The new movement of Jesus Christ could think of itself as the inheritor of the salvation of God through Israel, but the new Judaism claimed the same without including the Jesus movement. All the while Rome was keeping a close eye on both groups. If one or the other should become seditious they could suffer loss. Acts seems very aware of the need to keep within the good graces of Rome, while casting a negative light on the Jewish community.

Besides this situation, Acts (and Luke) sees a need to keep the growing community in line with its roots in the teaching of Jesus about the poor, the widows, the sick, and the marginalized. By implication, Acts urges members of the Christian communities to remember the Spirit of Jesus poured out on the community after his ascension (Acts 2). To lose the Spirit would be to forfeit the distinctive character that makes the Christian community the eschatological fulfilment of the promise to Israel.

Moreover, while the narrative time of Acts is between 30 and 60 CE, the composition time is after Luke, which places it in the last decade of the first century. As in the case of Luke, the place of writing Acts would have been outside Palestine, probably in a city of Macedonia well known to Acts (see Acts 16 especially). The historical person who wrote this book is the same one who wrote Luke, unknown to us by name but present in his writings. To call him 'Dr. Luke', as some do, is to assume far more than the text of Luke-Acts supports.

A number of scholars have argued that the author must have been a companion of Paul, if not Luke the physician of Colossians 4.14, then another travelling companion. Proponents of this view appeal to what is usually called *the 'we' sections* of Acts. Most narratives in Acts have a third person narrator. But several narratives dealing with Paul's missionary travels have a first person plural narrator. One of these 'we' sections is in chapter 16, the narrative about a trip from Troas to Philippi and the activity in that city. But the only two missionaries in view in that narrative are Paul and Silas. These two alone, according to the narrative, went to the place of prayer in Philippi on a Sabbath day and found women there. The same two got into trouble with the Roman authorities, were beaten and thrown in prison. Was there a third companion besides these two? If so, the third party kept a safe narrative distance from Paul and Silas. He is not mentioned as being with Paul and Silas in Lydia's house, nor was he thrown into prison with them. Too much has been made of the first person plural narrator in Acts. It could simply be an alternate way of narrating, using something like a 'collective we'. Or the 'we/us' narrator could have been integral to a travel diary source that the author used without changing the first person plural narrator. (See other 'we' narratives in 20.6-15; 21.1-17; 27.1–28.16).

In short, the 'we' narratives do not prove authorship of Acts by a travelling companion of Paul, and they certainly do not prove that Luke the physician wrote Acts. The author of Acts appears to have been unaware of Paul's letters. No appeal is made to any part of them, much less to a collection of letters. Paul's letters were probably not collected at the time of writing. Even so, after reading the preface to Luke, one might have expected such a writer who claims to have investigated 'everything carefully from the very first' (Lk. 1.3) to have investigated congregations at such locations as Corinth or Philippi or Thessalonica where one or another of Paul's letters would have been lodged. That seems not to have been the case.

3. The structure and quality of the work

The book of Acts falls essentially into two principal parts: (1) narrated activities of the Apostles up to the crucial Jerusalem conference of chapter 15; and (2) narrated activities of Paul and companions from chapter 15 to Paul's preaching under house arrest in Rome. Chapter 15 marks *the turning point* in the development of the story of the church. Historically, the decision coming out of the Jerusalem conference (*c.*49 CE) was pivotal for the success – or failure – of the mission to bring non-Jewish people to faith in Jesus Christ.

Peter, representing the original twelve Apostles, dominates the first part of Acts set in Jerusalem, and oversees the work of others. As such, Peter announces Israel restored in the person of Jesus resurrected. Paul, as a post-Easter apostle, dominates the second part of Acts, and announces the new call of God in Jesus resurrected for the inclusion of Gentiles in the promise of salvation. As soon as Paul occupies his place in the narrative drama of Acts, the figure of Peter moves of the narrative stage for the remainder of the story.

But the activity of these two, and those with them, is not simply their activity, but that of the Spirit of the resurrected Jesus. After the introduction in which the missionary commission (1.8) is reformulated from Luke (Acts 1.8), the most important event is the outpouring of the Spirit on the Jewish Day of Pentecost (2.1-4). The gathered disciples, including the women from Galilee, especially Mary the mother of Jesus (1.14), experience the rush of a mighty wind. The recipients of the wind of the Spirit exhibit its effects, especially in their ability to speak in languages other than their own native tongue.

The Jewish festival of Pentecost (50 days after Passover) attracted Jewish pilgrims from 'every nation under heaven', each with its own language (2.6-13). The list of 'nations' may have come from ancient histories or geographies known to the author. At any rate, upon hearing the Apostles speak in the *languages of the 'nations'*, the diverse visitors were amazed. Language can be a barrier between peoples. In Acts 2, the demonstration of the Spirit in the gift of languages is a sign of the promise of salvation for all the 'nations' of the world. As professor Lamin Sanneh has argued cogently, part of the genius of the Christian message is its *translatability*, not only from the original language into others, but more broadly from one culture to another, from one social group to another, without either the gospel or the culture being eroded (1989, pp. 1ff.).

Still in Acts 2, the outpouring of the Spirit is the occasion of Peter's sermon, speaking on behalf of the Twelve. He grounds his explanation of the event on the fulfilment of the prophecy of Joel:

> In the last days it will be, God declares, that I will pour out my Spirit upon all flesh, and your sons and your daughters shall prophesy, and your young men shall see visions, and your old men shall dream dreams. Even upon my slaves, both men and women, in those days I will pour out my Spirit; and they shall prophesy. And I will show portents in the heaven above and signs on the earth below, blood, and fire, and smoky mist. The sun shall be turned to darkness and the moon to blood, before the coming of the Lord's great and glorious day. Then everyone who calls on the name of the Lord shall be saved. (2.17-21; cf. Joel 2.28-32)

There is very little change from the wording in Joel 2 to that of Peter's speech. The function of the Joel text in Acts 2, however, proves the demolition of boundaries that separate: the boundary of language, boundary of gender, social boundary between slave and free, young and old, and the boundary that separates the human mind from the mind of God.

In the early chapters of Acts, the Jerusalem community in continuity with Jesus is of one mind and one heart. The members live out of a common fund, so that 'there was not a needy person among them, for as many as owned lands or houses sold them and brought the proceeds of what was sold . . . and laid it at the Apostles feet' (4.34-37). When this spirit of *common life* was threatened, judgment fell. Chapter 5 depicts such judgment on a husband and wife team who sold their possessions, but held part back while declaring they had surrendered the entire proceeds. The judgment of death was because they lied to the Holy Spirit of God, so says the text (5.3-5). The ideal of a common fund did not hold for long, once the gospel moved into the Hellenistic cities of the Roman world. In that environment, Paul asked merely for a collection proportional to the church members' income to go to the poor saints of Jerusalem (1 Cor. 8 and 9). There is nothing in Paul's appeal to the Corinthians remotely like the description of the common fund in Acts 4.

An important figure rises to prominence in chapters 6 and 7 of Acts, namely Stephen. Even though he appears in Jerusalem, he is not a native Judaean. He speaks a different language and manifests a different Jewish world view. His testimony to Jesus as God's 'Righteous One' (7.52) serves as a *transitional bridge* between what Peter represents and what Paul represents. An account of Stephen's character and testimony comes up for discussion shortly. Meanwhile, it is worth noting Paul's connection with Stephen in Acts: Paul consents to his violent death (8.1). By so doing, Paul doubtless believed he was protecting Jewish orthodoxy against the radical openness represented in Stephen's speech. Later, when Paul received his call to follow Jesus the Christ and engage in mission to the Gentiles (9.1-20), he identified with people like Stephen, whom he had persecuted earlier.

One of the distinctive aspects of Acts is the *speech-form*. Different characters make speeches representing different perspectives in the developing community of Jesus. As already noted, Peter's speech in Acts 2 represents the early stage of the Aramaic community of Jerusalem. Stephen's speech (Acts 7.2-53), in contrast to Peter's, gets him into trouble with the Jewish authorities in Jerusalem: he was killed, and a 'severe persecution' broke out against the Stephen-group (8.1-2).

Paul also has many speeches in Acts. His speeches represent the third stage in the development of the growth of the community of Jesus. For example, one of his speeches in Acts is delivered in Athens, heartland of Greek philosophy (17.22-31). Not surprisingly, in that speech Paul cites Greek poets in support of his doctrine of the resurrection of Jesus. In short, the speeches in Acts in the mouths of particular apostolic characters are designed to reflect the mind-set of the speaker and his enterprise. But in many respects all the speeches, regardless of the speakers, reflect the purpose and program of the redactor of Acts.

The speeches in Acts have been the subject of much scholarly discussion. What sources did the author/redactor use in the production of the speeches? Were there actual documents containing the speeches? Or were the speeches the free creations of the author? It seems unlikely that the speakers in each case would have written out the speech before delivering it in the given context. Most probably the historical speakers would have spoken out of their heart-experiences. The parables of Jesus belong to the same practice, characteristic of a predominantly oral culture: the sayings were constructed and spoken out of experiences in the environment of Galilee and Judaea. One of the assumptions ancient writers of history made about the historic figures was that they spoke out of their understanding of the situation in an effort to explain and correct misgivings that might occur. Moreover, it was a common practice in ancient historical writing to put appropriate speeches into the mouths of key figures in given historical contexts.

Acts follows that practice. Judging from the tradition about Peter, and what he represents, the author of Acts gives the Peter-character a fitting speech. The same holds for Stephen and Paul, and for other figures in the historic drama of Acts. But it bears repeating, that the author in so giving the respective figures their speeches also speaks through them. Themes and concerns embedded in the overall work of Acts will appear in the speeches of the characters. For example, the resurrection of Jesus and the outpouring of the Spirit are vital theological underpinnings of the book of Acts. In one way or another, these factors come into the speeches of the various characters.

Rather than go further into a detailed analysis of selected texts of Acts, it seems prudent to examine a number of *interfaces* that come through at several points in the texture of Acts.

4. Interface

By using the interface-metaphor in the context of Acts, I mean the lines that connect people-groups made up of similar and dissimilar features. Groups are important in Acts: what unites and divides them, what creates tensions between them, etc. In the next several sub-sections of this part, the designation 'Judaeans' will come up repeatedly. 'Judaeans' is one way of translating the Greek word *Ioudaioi*. The plural term occurs sixty-two times in Acts, six times in the singular, and is usually translated 'the Jews', 'Jews' and 'Jew'. In an attempt to deconstruct the modern, post-Holocaust use of 'the Jews' in favour of a first-century one, 'Judaeans' could serve the purpose, however imperfectly.

One of the problems with 'Judaeans' as a way of designating people who observed the Law of Israel's God is that it comes across as more geographical than religious-ethnic. On the other hand, geography in the tradition of Israel was laden with religious and ethnic connotations: Judaea got its name from one of the sons of Jacob/Israel. Furthermore, the Land, like the Law, was a gift from God. The Temple of the Lord stood within the geography of Judaea, and the Judaeans who returned from Exile in Babylonia to their Holy Place were the architects of Second Temple religion. Their descendents, expatriated to Jamnia after the destruction of the Second Temple in 70 CE, kept the tradition of Judaea, and ensured that the scattered people who avowed the religion of Israel did the same. Hence, the name 'Judaean'/'Judaeans' may serve as a fitting translation of *Ioudaios-oi* in the time and circumstances reflected in the New Testament.

a. Between Judaeans in Judaea and Judaeans elsewhere

When the faithful remnant of post-exilic Israelites was given the opportunity to return to what was their Holy Land, they set up their religious house in Jerusalem of Judaea. A tradition had already cemented the people together around the idea of Jerusalem of Judaea as the special place of God's presence. It was Zion, 'city of the Great King' (Ps. 48.2). When the Judaeans were deported to Babylonia, or when others escaped to Egypt and other parts of the world, they remembered Zion of Judaea as the home where their hearts belonged. Here is a classic example of the longing for the land of Judaea in which the central shrine of the Lord their God once stood.

> By the rivers of Babylon – there we sat down and there we wept when we remembered Zion. On the willows there we hung up our harps. For there our captors asked us for songs, and our tormentors asked for mirth, saying, 'Sing us one of the songs of Zion!' How could we sing the LORD's song in a foreign land? If I forget you, O Jerusalem, let my right hand wither! Let my tongue cling to the roof of my mouth, if I do not remember you, if I do not set Jerusalem above my highest joy. (Ps. 137.1-6)

That sentiment continued after the returnees had rebuilt the Temple. The Ones who did not return continued to support the Temple system. They thought and wrote as though present themselves in the sacred place. The Babylonian Talmud bears testimony to the devotion of the Babylonian Diaspora to the Jerusalem symbolism and authority.

But there were tensions between the Palestinian Judaeans and some of the *scattered communities*. The community in Alexandria will serve as an example. The Judaeans who continued to live there became so embedded in the culture of Egypt that they lost their innate facility in the language of Judaea, Aramaic/Hebrew. Their request to the Jerusalem authorities for a translation of the Law out of Hebrew into Greek was granted at about 200 BCE. The Greek translation of the ancient Law became Scripture for the Judaean residents in Alexandria, and then also for other Jewish and Jewish-Christian communities in the Greco-Roman world. Mention was made already about Philo, the Jewish writer of Alexandria. He was Judaean in background and faith. But he had openly espoused aspects of Greek philosophy, a factor that would not have sat well with the leadership in Judaea. As a Hellenized Judaean living in Alexandria, Philo epitomized the difference between a thoroughly Hellenized Judaean and his fellow Judaeans living in Palestine. The Palestinian Judaeans had faced hard times in Judaea under the ruthless rule of the Hellenistic overlords such as Antiochus IV in the second century BCE. Judaean resistance against the Hellenization of the Land of Judaea was hard fought and won some 160 years before Philo. Loyal residents of Judaea thereafter honoured the victory on their behalf. Expatriated Judaeans like Philo had not fought in that battle. Moreover, the Hellenization of the dispersed Judaeans like Philo was bound to incur some criticism from the orthodox hierarchy of Jerusalem. Acts is well aware of the difference between a native Judaean and a Judaean native to another place, and even mentions Alexandria as the home of a Hellenized Judaean to become a missionary of Jesus. Apollos, said to have been a 'Judaean' (*Ioudaios*) and 'a native of Alexandria', was 'an eloquent man, well-versed in the scriptures' (18.24). This could just as well be a description of Philo of Alexandria.

b. Between Judaeans and Gentiles

Understandably, the cultural differences between the faithful Judaeans living in the Land of Judaea and their Gentile neighbours generated some ideological distance and name-calling. Palestinian Judaeans might label Gentiles 'dogs' (Mk 7.27; cf. Mt. 7.6; cf. Phil. 3.2; Rev. 22.15), indiscriminate in their eating habits, debased in sexual practices and preferences, and idolatrous in their worship. They were devoid of the high and holy Law of the Lord, and therefore 'far off' (*makran*, Eph. 2.13, 17). They did not bear the covenantal mark of circumcision on their body. Observant Judaeans outside Palestine were of much the same mind. But because of their Greek language, common commercial interests and practices, Greek-speaking Judaeans outside Palestine by the sheer force of cultural, social, geographical and economic circumstances may have compromised aspects of their Judaean religion. Their world view as Judaeans in the larger Hellenistic environment would have broadened. These interfaces enter the fabric of Acts. As we shall see shortly, Paul's mission to the Gentile world was a monumental *breakthrough*. Law-observant Judaeans and non-observant Gentiles had little in common culturally, religiously, and socially. If the Christian mission could be called a breakthrough (and not a break-away from Judaism), then the credit in large measure should go to the more liberal group of Hellenistic Judaeans, such as Stephen, who had accepted the resurrected Jesus as their Lord.

c. Between Aramaic-Judaean Christians and Hellenistic-Judaean Christians

If *Ioudaioi* in Acts requires a new English translation for the group belonging to formative Judaism, then perhaps 'Christians' needs another term as well to distinguish the primitive groups of Jewish believers in the resurrected Jesus from the later worldwide institution of Gentile Christianity. The plural, 'Christians', appears only once in the New Testament at Acts 11.26: 'it was in Antioch that the disciples were first called Christians.' The singular occurs twice, once at Acts 26.28 and also in 1 Peter 4.16. The English word comes directly from the Greek original, *christianos-oi*. When it was first applied to the believers in Jesus resurrected, it may have been a term of derision. It signifies one who adopted the teaching about Christ. Followers of Jesus confessed him as the Messiah of the Judaeans. Translated into Greek, Messiah becomes *Christos*. It was quite natural to call the group who thus confessed Jesus as *Christos* by the diminutive *Christianoi*. Moreover, the use of the term 'Christian/Christians' in this section should not be identified directly with its use when Christianity had become a major world religion.

Acts 6 recognizes two distinct groups of Jewish Christians present in Jerusalem. Tension grew between the two groups over the daily distribution of food for widows of one group. Acts *labels* the two groups: *Hebraioi* and *Hellenistai* (6.1). Both are Jewish and both are Christian. The full weight of the labels is not immediately obvious. Language is doubtless one important factor. The *Hebraioi* probably spoke Aramaic, while the *Hellenistai* spoke Greek. Nor should the language factor be taken lightly. Language difference has a way of separating groups. In the case of the *Hebraioi* their language was that of Jesus, and also that of the native Judaeans who maintained the Mosaic Law and worship in the Temple. The *Hebraioi* may have succumbed to the notion that their language entitled them to a more important place in the Christian community having originated with the Aramaic-speaking Jesus. Noteworthy also, the Twelve Apostles of Jesus would have belonged to the Aramaic-speaking *Hebraioi*. The widows neglected in the daily distribution of food of Acts 6.1 belonged to the *Hellenistai*.

If language is a significant factor in the two designations, then culture and world view may also be inferred. The *Hellenistai* probably espoused a more liberal interpretation of the Law of Moses than the *Hebraioi* did. Members of the group of *Hellenistai* had probably lived elsewhere, but came to Jerusalem in honour of the sacred tradition associated with Judaea, Jerusalem and the Temple. One can see how a controversy could have erupted between the two Jewish-Christian groups.

Acts 6 records the resolution to the controversy. The Apostles, not about to give up their ministry of the Word to serve tables, instructed the *Hellenistai* to appoint seven trustworthy men from among them to look after the matter. The names of the seven are given in 6.5, all of them of Greek origin. Two of the named *Hellenistai* come to prominence in the subsequent narrative of Acts.

Stephen is one of the seven. Immediately after the narrative about his appointment to an administrative duty, he begins to preach the gospel. His preaching in Acts 7, not completely unlike Peter's, exhibits something of a Hellenistic outlook: a more free interpretation of the Law and the Temple. To preach such a message in Jerusalem ran the risk of recrimination from the more conservative Judaeans. The speech – too long to discuss in detail here – recites a brief history of the Jewish people, but with a rather *liberal slant* and not a little criticism of some of their leaders. They are 'stiff-necked people, uncircumcised in heart and ears' (7.51).

Two matters in particular about Stephen's preaching come to the attention of the Aramaic-speaking Judaeans, who call him to account. First, he is said to have spoken against 'this holy place', and second, against 'the law' (6.13). These two put him in serious danger. The Aramaic-speaking Judaeans see it as their duty to protect the holy place and its environs and to observe the Law of Moses. To speak against these two in any way is to threaten the foundation of the Judaeans. Stephen, being Judaean himself, should know that. But he is also Hellenistic and Christian. And that stance seems to have made a significant difference. The upshot of Stephen's preaching in the environs of Jerusalem was death by stoning for violating the sacred traditions of Judaism.

According to Acts 8.1-2, widespread persecution broke out after the discovery of Stephen's offence that led to his death. Others of the same mind were scattered throughout the whole region of Judaea and beyond. Some went to Samaria, at least one to Gaza, and others as far north as

Antioch in Syria. A telling phrase enters the narrative about the scattering of the *Hellenistai*: 'That day a severe persecution began against the church in Jerusalem, and all *except the apostles* were scattered throughout the countryside of Judaea and Samaria' (8.1). Why not the apostles? One would think they above all the people preaching Jesus as the Christ should have been persecuted and scattered. But they were not, presumably because they did not belong to the Stephen-group. Their view of the holy place and the Law was not as radical as that of Stephen and his group of *Hellenistai*.

The second member of the seven *Hellenistai* that comes to prominence in Acts is Philip. He goes to Samaria and preaches the gospel there. The Samaritans receive Philip's message. Word of the conversion of the Samaritans came to the ears of the Aramaic-speaking Jerusalem group. The group sent Peter and John to check out the evangelistic work of Philip. According to Acts 8, the two from Jerusalem approved, but qualified the work of Philip by laying their hands on the new Samaritan converts so that they too would have in them the same Spirit as that already present in the Jerusalem group (8.4-17). *Deviance* from the teaching of the original Apostolic *Hebraioi* could not be permitted. How long the Jerusalem *Hebraioi* would be able to keep the burgeoning movement of Christian communities in step with the thought and practice of Jerusalem remained to be seen. The one bold step that would test the ability of the Jerusalem *Hebraioi* to maintain control was the launching of the Gentile world mission under the leadership of Paul, discussed below.

After their approval and qualification of Philip's evangelistic work in Samaria, Peter and John went back to Jerusalem (8.25). Philip did not go with them to Jerusalem. Instead, an angel of the Lord – not Peter and John – told Philip to go down the wilderness road away from Jerusalem to Gaza. En route he met up with *an Ethiopian* on his way home from Jerusalem. As he rode in his chariot the Ethiopian was reading from the scroll of the prophet Isaiah. Philip joined him and asked, 'Do you understand what you are reading?' The man replied, 'How can I, unless someone guides me?' Thereupon he invited Philip to join him in the chariot (8.30-31). Here Philip acts on his own as guide to the Ethiopian traveller, pointing him to Jesus as the Christ resurrected. Philip then baptizes the new convert into the faith. All of this Philip did on his own, without the oversight of the Jerusalem Apostolic *Hebraioi*. Philip, the one-time administrator of food for widows in his group of *Hellenistai*, had become an apostle of Christ in his own right.

The scattered *Hellenistai* became *the bridge* between the Aramaic-speaking Christians of Jerusalem and the new converts to Jesus Christ from the Gentile world. By launching the Gentile world mission, the proponents could hardly have known at the time the full extent of the massive historic project they had undertaken.

d. Between sacred history and world history

Both Luke and Acts keep two kinds of history before the reader: salvation history and world history. The former is worked out within and for the benefit of the latter. In Luke the saving events associated with the birth and death of Jesus happened in the reign of certain emperors, governors and procurators (Lk. 2.1-3; 3.1-2). Similarly in Acts, the development of the new community of the resurrected Jesus happens in relation to the governing powers of Rome. Roman political rule in Acts is benign for the most part, and at times beneficial to the Christian cause. Sometimes the powers are hostile to the Christian witness, as in Acts 16 when Paul and Silas were beaten and thrown into a Roman prison (16.22-24). But even there, the city magistrates had made an understandable mistake: they did not know Paul and Silas were Roman citizens. The magistrates apologized to the two missionaries and sent them on their way (16.35-39).

Meanwhile, in the throes of the ordeal for Paul and Silas, a miracle happened. While the two prayed and sang, an earthquake caused the prison gates to open. Thinking the prisoners had escaped, the jailer was about to kill himself rather than face the shameful consequences of his dereliction of duty. Paul stopped him. The jailer thereupon asked the missionaries, 'Sirs, what must I do to be saved?' (16.30). From the jailer's perspective it was a pragmatic question, which Paul turned into a religious one. 'Believe on the Lord Jesus, and you will be saved, you and your household' (16.31). That night the jailer and his household were *baptized*, and a new Christian community was born in that important Roman colony (16.12). Moreover, the Roman imprisonment (world history) of the missionaries aided their Christian project (salvation history).

Acts is keenly aware of the need to recognize the power of Roman rule, and seems to affirm that rule. At the same time, the rule of God in Jesus Christ transcends the rule of Rome, even in Acts where every effort is made to show Rome in a fairly positive light. At Thessalonica, for example, Paul and Silas ran into problems with the city authorities. Some people of the city brought charges against the missionaries, saying, 'they are all acting contrary to the decrees of the emperor, saying that there is *another king* named Jesus' (17.7). Of course, in Acts the real offenders and accusers are the unbelieving Judaeans. They incited the city people against the missionaries. In short, Acts presents the new Christian movement as an active agent in the larger world history, not cloistered outside world history. The interface between salvation history and world history, however tense and tenuous it may be, is a necessary element in the spread of the message of Jesus and the Spirit in Acts.

We come now to the interface between the two principal spokespersons in the development of primitive Christianity according to Acts.

e. Between Peter and Paul

Little more needs to be said about Peter's role as spokesperson for the Twelve. His relation to Paul in Acts does merit some comment before exploring the critical event in the Acts narrative: the launching of the Gentile world mission.

Peter is constantly tied in with Jerusalem, and all that Jerusalem symbolizes. Even when he visits Caesarea he is still oriented towards Jerusalem. A centurion in Caesarea named Cornelius, 'a God-fearing man', sent for Peter. Meanwhile, Peter had a vision of a sheet filled with all kinds of unclean animals coming down from heaven. A voice tells him to kill and eat. He declines: 'By no means, Lord; for I have never eaten anything that is profane or unclean' (10.14). The voice corrects Peter: 'What God has made clean, you must not call profane' (10.15). Later when Peter enters the centurion's house he still has to make his Jerusalem-oriented speech to the Gentiles gathered under Cornelius' roof: 'You yourselves know that it is unlawful for a [Judaean] to associate with or to visit a Gentile.' He then proceeds to tell them, 'God has shown me that I should not call anyone profane or unclean' (10.28). When Peter returned to Jerusalem his compatriots criticized him: 'Why did you go to uncircumcised men and eat with them?' they ask him (11.3). Eating with uncircumcised Gentiles was seen as a contaminating association. How then can the message of Jesus resurrected reach into Gentile homes and hearts? That is a burning question in Acts, and in Paul's letters. Acts is concerned to show that Peter had a kind of conversion that opened the door for him to enter into Gentile lives, in the same way that Paul would do later on.

However, when Paul in his letter to the Galatians (2.11-14) relates a story about Peter at Antioch, the image is rather different. Here is what Paul recalls from that experience, which post-dates the narrative time of Acts 10:

> But when Cephas (Peter) came to Antioch, I opposed him to his face, because he stood self-condemned; for until certain people came from James [of Jerusalem], he used to eat with the Gentiles. But after they came, he drew back and kept himself separate for fear of the circumcision faction. And the other [Judaeans] joined him in this hypocrisy, so that even Barnabas was led astray by their hypocrisy. But when I saw that they were not acting consistently with the truth of the gospel, I said to Cephas before them all, 'If you, though a Judaean, live like a Gentile and not like a Judaean, how can you compel the Gentiles to live like Judaeans?'

Several points are worth noting from this text from Galatians in relation to Acts 10. First, Paul gives Peter his Aramaic name Cephas, a hint that his orientation is still towards the Jerusalem conservative mentality. Second, James the brother of Jesus (Gal. 1.19; cf. Acts 12.2) had become a major voice in the post-Easter community of disciples of Jesus. His orientation is even more tightly tied into the Jerusalem Aramaic mentality concerning the Law of the Judaeans. Two elements in that Law had to do with the signs of covenantal election, namely circumcision and the regulation regarding clean and unclean foods. In Paul's recollection Peter had not come around completely to the idea that the gospel of Jesus had now opened the door to both Gentiles and Judaeans in a way that required the observance of neither circumcision nor food regulation. Peter/Cephas was afraid of the ones who had come from James of Jerusalem. Third, Paul opposed Peter for causing Gentiles to *live like Judaeans*, which could mean they submitted to circumcision or they practised kosher food laws, or both.

Acts 10 and 11 shows Peter more in line with Paul's attitude, but not completely removed from the Jerusalem mind-set. Still, Acts softens the disparity between Peter and Paul that exists in Paul's recollection of the episode at Antioch recorded in Galatians 2. It is part of the Acts schema to present the emerging community of the Spirit of Jesus Christ resurrected as one community bound together in one mind. Yet Acts cannot but allow some of the early tensions to enter the narrative. Tensions associated with the launching of the Gentile world mission from an avowed Judaean base were bound to happen.

5. The Gentile world mission

A number of the scattered *Hellenistai* settled at Antioch in Syria, one of the three largest and most influential cities in the Empire (*War.* 3.2.4) – the other two being Rome and Alexandria. According to the description in Acts, the members of the group spread the word about Jesus whom God raised from the dead. Their open-mindedness, like that of Stephen, opened the door of their meetings to Hellenized Judaeans and Gentiles who believed their message. News of this missionary activity reached the Aramaic-speaking Apostles at Jerusalem. They in turn sent a man named Barnabas to oversee the activity, and to ensure that the group kept faith with the original community of the risen Jesus at Jerusalem.

Barnabas was a native of Cyprus, probably fluent in Greek, but loyal to the tradition associated with Jerusalem (4.36-37). Even though oriented toward Jerusalem, Barnabas could relate to the *Hellenistai* scattered throughout the region. The group at Antioch seemed to have been especially zealous in spreading the news about Jesus. The assignment for Barnabas, apparently, was to ensure that the enthusiastic group at Antioch remained faithful to the Lord as preached by the Apostles of Jerusalem (11.22-24).

Barnabas, finding the growing community at Antioch in need of leadership, sought out Paul (sometimes called Saul in Acts) in his home city of Tarsus. Paul had encountered the risen Jesus some time earlier. The chronology in Acts is not explicit. Paul in his letter to the Galatians provides an account of his movement following his epiphany and call. His own recollection of the sequence of events may help in understanding the timeframe in which he and Barnabas exercised leadership in Antioch.

> But when God . . . was pleased to reveal his Son to me . . . I went away at once into Arabia, and afterwards I returned to Damascus. Then after *three years* I did go up to Jerusalem to visit Cephas and stayed with him *fifteen days*. Then I went into the regions of Syria and Cilicia, and I was still unknown by sight to the churches of Judaea that are in Christ; they only heard it said, "The one who formerly was persecuting us is now proclaiming the faith he once tried to destroy". . . .. Then after *fourteen years* I went up again to Jerusalem with Barnabas (Gal. 1.15–2.1).

According to these time references, Paul had spent three years in Arabia (the Transjordan) before moving into the regions of Syria and Cilicia. He makes no mention of Barnabas seeking him out at Tarsus. He seems to have been active in preaching among Gentiles, but with no evidence of communities resulting from his ministry. By bringing Paul's account to bear on Acts, we could say that Barnabas enlisted Paul's help for Antioch some time after Paul's foray into Arabia, and perhaps sometime within the 'fourteen years' before going up to Jerusalem with Barnabas.

Why Barnabas wanted Paul in particular to help him in the work at Antioch is not stated in Acts or in Paul's letters. Was it because Paul had already proven himself an effective missionary teacher? There is no clear evidence of that from Acts or from Paul's letters. *Paul's effectiveness* came after he entered into fellowship with the Antioch community. Barnabas may have thought of Paul, rather, to be one he could trust not to let the Antioch community become too liberal in relation to the Jerusalem *Hebraioi*. After all, Paul's reputation had preceded him. He had previously persecuted the *Hellenistai*, Stephen in particular, for their open interpretation of the Law and the Temple. Perhaps Barnabas thought Paul's call to Christ would be more in line with the Jerusalem group, and would therefore keep the Antioch group in play with the Jerusalem group. These are merely educated guesses. One thing is clear: Paul's involvement with the Antioch community of Christian *Hellenistai* impelled him into an effective ministry to Gentiles, including their incorporation into the community of Christ as full members on their way to final salvation.

But how was he incorporating them exactly? The answer is not hard to find. Prompted by the conciliatory thinking of the Antioch community, Paul was incorporating believing Gentiles into full membership *without the mark of circumcision for males*. Acts recounts a critical moment when word reached the ears of the Jerusalem *Hebraioi* that this was in fact happening. Representatives from Jerusalem had come to Antioch and found Gentiles worshipping alongside Hellenistic Judaeans as equals. The representatives from Jerusalem found the situation entirely unacceptable. 'Unless you are circumcised according to the custom of Moses, you cannot be saved', they said (15.1). The propagators of this liberal practice at Antioch were summoned to a meeting in Jerusalem to give an account of the matter. Paul and Barnabas were appointed to bring the issue before the 'apostles and elders' in Jerusalem. The proceedings of this crucial meeting are recorded in Acts 15.

The more orthodox members of the assembly at Jerusalem insisted that 'it is necessary for them to be circumcised and ordered to keep the Law of Moses' (15.5). The issue was not only circumcision, but the proper observance of the Law of Moses. Circumcision was the critical issue, of course.

But Gentiles probably found the practice repulsive, considering circumcision a mutilation of the human body. Thus, circumcision was a serious hindrance to the incorporation of Gentiles into membership in the community. But the orthodox leaders of Jerusalem were calling for the observance of the Law, not just circumcision. That meant also the kosher food regulations. This too was difficult for Gentiles to accept.

The chief speakers at the meeting, according to Acts 15, were Paul and Barnabas for the liberal Antioch side of the issue, and Peter and James accommodating the more orthodox Jerusalem side. James, being the principal leader of the Jerusalem group, struck down the final decision as follows: 'we should write to [the Gentile converts] to abstain only (1) from things polluted by idols and (2) from fornication and (3) from whatever has been strangled and (4) from blood' (15.20). From the Judaean perspective, one of the horrors of Gentile religion was idolatry. Not surprisingly, abstinence from idolatry would be a requirement. But the ruling has to do with 'things polluted by idols', referring to offerings of food in the temple of idols. Abstinence from such food is also required in the decision of James. Sexual immorality was also perceived as rampant among Gentiles. Again, no surprise that abstinence from sexual immorality would be required of Gentile converts to Christ. The last requirement relates to the kosher regulation. Abstinence from eating the flesh of animals killed by strangulation was prohibited in Jewish law. The blood did not drain properly. The eating of the blood of the slaughtered animal was also ruled out by law (Lev. 17.12-14). These then were the requirements placed upon the new converts to Christ and his community according to Acts. Circumcision, by its absence from the decision statement of James, seems not to have been imposed on the new converts.

What is odd about this resolution regarding the inclusion of Gentiles into membership in the new community of Christ is that it does not correspond with Paul's view and practice alluded to in his letters. In 1 Corinthians 8 and 10, Paul has no problem with his Gentile believers at Corinth eating food that had been sacrificed to idols. Nor does he raise the issue of how an animal had been slaughtered. He encourages the Corinthians to 'eat whatever is sold in the meat market without raising any question on the ground of conscience' (1 Cor. 10.25). Paul's concern relates to the *worship of idols*. On that point he will not compromise. If a Gentile convert to Christ were to eat meat sacrificed to an idol as an act of worship, then that practice would be in violation of the exclusiveness of Christ and his body, the church.

Acts seems unaware of this Pauline tradition. Could it be that the author/ redactor of Acts observes the kosher food laws in his Christian community and so reads his experience into the earlier resolution? No clear answer is forthcoming. This much can be said, the Gentile world mission was launched successfully by setting aside those parts of Jewish Law that traditionally kept Gentiles from entering the covenant community: circumcision and food rules. The successful mission among Gentiles could be viewed as a breakthrough, the end of the clashing between two different cultures (cf. Eph. 2.15). Or it could be seen as the beginning of an unintentional break-away from the parent Judaism. Perhaps the success of the first, of necessity leads to the realization of the second.

6. Conclusion

While the Acts of the Apostles is a favourite with church people, it presents several challenges to the scholar. What sources did the author/redactor use in creating his narratives? Why is Acts so favourably disposed to Rome, and so antithetical towards unbelieving Judaeans? It is clear that Paul is the unchallenged hero of Acts. Yet the redactor's gathering of Pauline material for the composition of his Acts seems not to have included the letters of Paul. Paul's rendering of incidents, such as the one between him and Peter at Antioch, scarcely squares with Acts. In Acts, Paul continues to defend himself as a Pharisee, observant of the Law of the Judaeans (23.6; 26.5). But in his letter to the Philippians, Paul considers his *former life* as a Pharisee so much 'rubbish' in comparison to knowing Christ and the power of his resurrection (Phil. 3.4-11). Even more puzzling, Paul's recognition of the death of Jesus 'for our sins', which he says he received from those before him (1 Cor. 15.3-5), is altogether absent from Acts. The reason for its absence is difficult to understand.

Acts does highlight the success of the Gentile world mission in the midst of hostilities from the powers of the world, especially from unbelieving Jewish authorities. Remarkably, Acts signs off when Paul is under house arrest in Rome. Paul had appealed his case to the Emperor (Nero) during his Jewish court trial in Jerusalem. He then lived for two years in Rome, welcoming people to his home and preaching the gospel freely to any who would listen. But then Acts becomes silent concerning the years following the two spent under house arrest. From other sources we are led to believe that Paul was killed in Rome during Nero's tirades (EH, 2.15; *Annals*, 15.44).

The redactor of Acts surely knew this fact, but chose to omit Paul's death from his account. His motive cannot be recovered. One can only imagine that his purpose in writing Acts was to promote the Christian faith and the representative communities to the Roman world. It would hardly serve that purpose to depict Rome as the instrument of death for the innocent apostle Paul. The real disturbers of the peace in Acts are the Judaeans who reject Jesus and continue to persecute the communities that live by the Jesus 'Way' (9.2; 18.25-26; 19.9, 23; 22.4; 24.14).

Further related reading

A valuable, and very accessible resource for the period represented in Acts is that of Raymond E. Brown and John P. Meier (1983), *Antioch and Rome: New Testament Cradles of Catholic Christianity.* Paulist.

An insightful and well documented analysis of the Judaean and Greek cultures, and the ostensible resolution of the clash between them, is in Gregory Dix (1953), *Jew and Greek: A Study in the Primitive Church.* Dacre.

Ecclesiology, an important characteristic of Acts, is explicated well by Philip Esler (1987), *Community and Gospel in Luke-Acts. The Social and Political Motivations of Lukan Theology.* Cambridge University.

Still unsurpassed is the study by Martin Hengel (1979), *Acts and the History of Earliest Christianity.* Translated from the German by John Bowden. SCM.

My own work (2007), *An Introduction to the Study of Luke Acts,* Continuum International, tests various approaches to reading multiple textures in the two-volume composition.

9 Urban Centres of Paul's Missionary Letters

An urban dweller from birth, Paul focused his missionary endeavours on cities. On his travels he may have spoken to rural village folks about Jesus, but the records in Acts and in Paul's own letters testify to his interest in bringing the gospel of Christ into areas of concentrated population. The letter addressed 'to the churches of Galatia' is a special case dealt with below (Gal. 1.2; cf. 1 Cor. 16.1). Galatia was a region, not a city.

1. Which cities?

Our interest here is with the cities to which Paul wrote letters that have survived. Each of the city centres had its own urban characteristics and its own demographics. Paul's letters should be read in relation to the target group in the particular city. The life-experience and mind-set of congregations of Corinth, for example, would not have been the same as those of 'the churches of Galatia' (Gal. 1.2). Citizens living in Rome, by comparison, were doubtless well aware of the political and cultural power resident in their city, so Paul in writing to the Romans weaves something of the particularity of living in Rome into his letter to the groups of believers meeting in that locale (e.g. Rom. 13.1-7).

In short, the cities discussed in this chapter are those of the addressees in Paul's genuine letters. A glimpse into the character of each of the cities (or groups of cities) should help in understanding the character of Paul's rhetoric in the respective letters. The cities are Corinth in Greece, Thessalonica and Philippi in Macedonia, Ankyra, Pessinus and Tavium in Galatia, Colossae in Phrygia of Asia Minor and Rome in Italy.

2. How urban?

When we think today of major urban centres we have in mind such places as Toronto, London, New York, Manila, or Sydney, each of them teaming with millions of people spread out over a large metropolitan area. Cities in the Graeco-Roman world were much smaller geographically and in population size. A number of them were city states, in the sense that the city proper controlled not only its inner population but also the region immediately surrounding the boundary of the city. Evidence of the actual population size is scant in the literature, but judging from the area of the cultural remains of cities such as ancient Jerusalem, Jericho, Corinth, Ephesus, Colossae and Rome, the population could hardly have exceeded 100,000 for the largest of these, unless the residents lived in high-rise apartments, which is highly doubtful. Still, these were the urban centres of the time and place. Cities such as Athens and Corinth among others could boast of theatres, libraries, schools and religious shrines. The excavated architecture in many of the cities of the time remains as a monument to the vision and skill of the urban artisans. Witness, for example, the remains of the Parthenon of Athens or the library of Ephesus or the coliseum of Rome.

City people of the New Testament times had educational opportunities, along with economic possibilities. Skills were honed in cities; trade and commerce flourished there. And, of course, city elite invariably came to the top as the driving force. There were rulers and ruled, masters and slaves, powerful and powerless, privileged and oppressed. The cities of Paul's mission really were urban in the sense that we understand the term today. Each of the cities under review in this chapter would have exhibited all of these qualities to one degree or another.

3. Location, character and demographics

It would be well to consult the map of the north Mediterranean (p. 37) in conjunction with this sketch of the cities of Paul's letters.

a. Corinth, Greece

The city of Corinth in which Paul first set foot was a relatively new city, or at least renewed. Founded in the tenth century BCE, the old Corinth gained a reputation over time of being one of the wealthiest cities of the world of the day. Located as it was on the isthmus between the Peloponnesus and mainland Greece, Corinth became the largest city of Greece and the richest. It was a port city, located between two ports of call to the east and the west with only a few miles between them: Lechaeum to the west, trading with Italy and Sicily, and Cenchreae to the east, trading with countries of the eastern Mediterranean. Cargo was transferred between ships in the eastern harbour and ships in the western harbour (*Geog.* 8.6.20, 378). It was not until the nineteenth century that a canal was cut through the rock, thus connecting the waters of the Adriatic and the Aegean Seas. The canal saved about 320 kilometres of sea voyage.

The region in which the old city of Corinth was located was called Achaia, Corinth being the major city of the region. An arrangement was made between the cities and towns of the region, initiated by the elite of Corinth, to form a kind of coalition with Corinth as the lead city. Rome eventually called for dissolution of the coalition in Achaia. Corinth resisted. The Roman consul, Lucius Mummius, did not take kindly to the Corinthian resistance, so he destroyed 'wealthy Corinth', as it was called (*Geog.* 8.6.20), in 146 BCE. He killed the leading men of Corinth and sold their women and children into slavery. Some of the wealthy men escaped to the island of Delos. Corinth was desolate for the next 100 years, except for a few squatters.

Julius Caesar took up the challenge of rebuilding Corinth in 44 BCE. He populated the new Corinth with people from different parts of the Empire, including Italians, Egyptians, Syrians, Greeks and Judaeans. The reconstructed Corinth became a cosmopolitan centre, serving the aspirations of various cultures and religions. Its wealth returned as it serviced the ports to the east and the west. Corinthian residents considered themselves gifted by the gods. Even the virgin spring at one end of the city was revered as coming to the residents from one of the deities. (Cf. 1 Cor. 12–14).

Part of the service provided by some Corinthians was prostitution. As in any port city, sailors sought out women to satisfy their sexual desires. So notable was Corinth for its promiscuity that a Greek verb for certain sensual acts was coined using the name of the city as its root: *korinthiazomai* (cf. 1 Cor. 5–7).

There is no solid evidence that points to sacred prostitution in the Greek or Roman temples of the new Corinth. But polytheistic religion was well represented in Paul's Corinth, including an Emperor cult and also a mono-theistic Jewish synagogue. Acts 18 describes Paul's efforts to persuade the Judaeans of the synagogue of the grace of the Jewish Jesus, the Messiah resurrected. His preaching in the synagogue apparently failed to persuade the Jewish worshippers. He then turned to the non-Jewish population, gained a hearing from them, and founded Judeo-Christian communities alongside the Jewish synagogue. The new communities met in the homes that could accommodate the group. The groups may have ranged from 20 to 30 persons per home. None of the homes in excavated Corinth would have accommodated a larger number with any comfort.

As with all ancient cities, Corinth had its sacred mountain to the south. According to Strabo, Acrocorinth was the elevated site of the temple to the goddess Aphrodite, whose temple 'was so rich that it owned more than a 1,000 temple slaves, courtesans, dedicated to the goddess' (*Geog.* 8.6.20). But the Athenian Strabo was almost certainly referring disparagingly to the old Corinth. Sacred prostitution was not a Greek custom, and was probably not in vogue in Corinth when Paul was preaching in the city.

The city of Corinth of Paul's mission was eventually destroyed, most likely by earthquakes to which the area was subject. But the city has since been excavated, revealing such notable structures as the *bema* (place of judgement, Acts 18.16), the forum, shops, temples and more. A museum has been set up on the site where many interesting artefacts from sculptures to objects used for healing to a portrait of the young Nero are on display. The first Christians in that thriving centre of trade, religion, education, architecture, entertainment and artisanship were without doubt urban in orientation. Into this mixture of urban life at Corinth, Paul managed to plant the seed of the gospel of Jesus Christ, originating as it did with rural Galilee.

b. Thessalonica, Macedonia

The ancient city of Thessalonica in Macedonia had several claims to fame, not least of which was the honour of being the home city of Alexander the Great. Alexander's father, King Philip II, was buried in the area in full armour, which provided archaeologists with a meaningful clue to the identification of the one who wore the armour: one leg piece was shorter than the other, corresponding to the physical condition of Philip II who had one leg shorter than the other. The armour is on display in the museum in modern Thessaloniki. Alexander's grave was not discovered at the site where he might have been expected to be buried, had he died at home. Alexander died in Babylonia, probably from a disease he contracted there, a long way from home. His grave has not yet been discovered.

Another claim to fame is that Thessalonica was the home of the great philosopher–teacher Aristotle. Aristotle taught both Philip II and his son Alexander. In addition, the well known orator, Cicero, also lived in the city for a time, and delivered orations there periodically to captive audiences.

The Thessalonica that Paul entered in the early 50s CE was founded in 315 BCE by the army general, Kassander, successor to General Alexander the Great. Formerly a cluster of villages dotted the area. Then in celebration of his victorious campaigns against the Persians, Kassander drew the villages together into an urban centre, and gave the city the name of his wife, Thessalonike, daughter of Philip II, and half-sister of Alexander. Having amassed huge resources from his campaigns, Kassander was able to build a thick and high wall around the city to fortify it against invaders.

A strategic seaport city, Thessalonica became the largest and richest urban centre in all of Greece/Macedonia. Its population (estimated at 65,000) at the time of Paul was surpassed only by such cities as Rome and Alexandria. But Thessalonica was subject to attacks from outsiders, most of which the inhabitants were able to withstand successfully. The Celts attacked the city and destroyed some of the defensive walls, but were eventually sent packing. The Romans also were repelled for a time. Eventually, though, the city surrendered to the Romans after the defeat of King Perseus of Macedonia in 168 BCE.

Under Roman rule Thessalonica's fortunes increased. It was declared the capital city of Macedonia. During the Roman Civil War of 49–31 BCE, Thessalonica sided with Octavian and Mark Anthony, both of whom stayed in the city at the height of the battles. After his victory in the Battle of

Philippi in 42 BCE, Octavian gave Thessalonica freedom to appoint its own magistrates (*politarchai*; see Acts 17.6-7).

Situated as it was (and is) on a natural harbour in the north Aegean Sea, Thessalonica was one of the star cities of the Roman Empire from the second century BCE onward. As such the city was served by the Via Egnatia, which the Romans constructed in the second century BCE. The road connected the Roman provinces of Illyria, Macedonia and Thrace. It ran through terrain that is today part of Albania, Macedonia, Greece and European Turkey. Running for some 1,120 kilometres in total, part of this famous Roman road lies today at the base of modern Thessaloniki. Part of the road that ran through the ancient city has been uncovered, and is integrated into the modern city. Paul would have entered through the city gate of Thessalonica on the same Via Egnatia.

Religion was popular in Thessalonica, perhaps to an even greater extent than in Corinth. The whole Greek pantheon was represented in Thessalonica, including also an Emperor cult, a cult of Isis, Serapis, Osiris and Mithra. The presence of such an array of religions is testimony to the mixed population in the city. And according to Acts 17, Paul visited a Jewish synagogue in the city. Some worshippers in the synagogue believed, according to Acts, but others resisted Paul and his message. They claimed Paul and his friends were 'acting contrary to the decrees of the emperor, saying that there is another king named Jesus' (Acts 17.7). Sure enough, Paul's message about the rule of Jesus Christ had strong political overtones. In any case, Paul's target audience was non-Judaeans as his call demanded (Gal. 1.16). In his letter to the church at Thessalonica, Paul makes no mention of a synagogue, or of a Jewish resistance to his gospel in that city. But he does address his non-Jewish converts to Christ, complimenting them on their stalwart faith and labour of love in the face of persecution from their own compatriots (1 Thess. 1.3). They had 'turned to God from idols, to serve a living and true God' (1 Thess. 1.9). It was probably their turning away from the idolatrous cults of Thessalonica, including the cult of the Emperor, which led to the persecution (1 Thess. 1.9). The abandoning of idols may have been construed as a form of insurrection, especially so if the cults of Thessalonica enjoyed the approval of the imperialist magistrates of the city.

As an aside, Thessalonica appears to have had a Jewish community present from the time of Paul up to the Second World War. Some sources say the Jewish residents fled the city to safety, fearing the incursion of the Nazi army. It is more likely, however, that during the war the Nazi regime deported every Jewish resident to one or another of the concentration camps.

Thessalonica of Paul's mission was clearly an impressive urban centre, with all the attending characteristics of an imperialist *polis* (city). The non-Jewish believers, having turned from their idols, gathered together in new communities of faith in Jesus Christ. The first members were likely not from the ruling class of the city, judging from Paul's directive to work for a living. They appear to have been labourers, perhaps even slaves, who looked forward to a better life to come. Their interest, implicit in Paul's letter, in the coming age of peace and joy that Messiah brings, without the hard labour of their hands, prompted Paul to write a corrective, yet encouraging word in his letter known to us as 1 Thessalonians.

c. Philippi, Macedonia

Founded around 700 BCE, the site that was to become the city of Philippi soon came to prominence as a leading city of the region. Its name for some 400 years was Crenides, meaning 'springs' or 'fountains'. It appears that the presence of these springs in a group may have led to the building of the city edifices around them. The city was located 15 kilometres northwest of the harbour of Neapolis, the city from which Paul is said to have travelled to Philippi (Acts 16.11-12), and 185 kilometres northeast of Thessalonica.

As with all ancient cities of importance, Crenides had its sacred mountain called Pangeo, the mountain of the god Dionysus. The son of the highest god of the Olympians, Dionysus was worshipped as the god of wine and drunkenness, or madness, and also the god of vegetation. He was also associated with the theatre. But the mountain was not merely the sacred high place of the god; it contained rich resources, especially gold and silver. When king Philip of Macedon took over the city he used the gold and silver from mount Pangeo to fund his army. Alexander did likewise.

King Philip took control of the city at about 358 BCE. To show that he had control he gave each of the 'springs' (Crenides) his name. Hence the name of the city thereafter, the *plural of Philip*: Philippi. The name was retained after the Roman occupation of the territory.

When Perseus, the last king of Macedonia, was defeated by the Romans, Macedonia was recognized as a province within the Empire in 148 BCE. Philippi became an important outpost for the Roman military. The famous Via Egnatia ran through the city, connecting Byzantium to the east with

Thessalonica to the west. As mentioned earlier, the Via Egnatia was built mainly for the military on their missions throughout the Empire. But the road also served Paul and his companions for their mission in bringing the gospel of Jesus Christ to cities such as Philippi.

The Roman city of Philippi was the scene of one of the most notable battles of the time. After Cassius and Brutus had assassinated Julius Caesar, Octavian and Mark Anthony determined not to let the assassins gain power in Rome. The armies of Octavian and Anthony fought against the forces of Brutus and Cassius in the autumn of 42 BCE and defeated them. Thereafter, Octavian granted Philippi the status of a Roman colony with all the privileges pertaining thereto. One of the most important of those privileges was exemption from paying taxes to Rome. Another was the right to own and sell property, and the right to civil action. The colony controlled an area of some 1,200 square kilometres, making Philippi a very powerful city, not unlike the mother city of Rome.

Rome populated Philippi with Italians mostly, and others who, like Paul, had been granted the rights of Roman citizenship. The gods of Rome, as one would expect in such a city, occupied a privileged position, although other religious cults were present as well, including the worship of Aphrodite. Few, if any, Judaeans lived in Philippi. There is no archaeological evidence of a synagogue from the period. The story in Acts 16 about Lydia and other women worshipping beside the nearby river – doubtless the river Gangitis – suggests that there was no synagogue building in the city. It should not be assumed that Lydia and her household were Judaean in character and religion before they met up with Paul and Silas. They were Greek/Macedonian women sympathetic towards the religion of Judaism, to the point of adopting the monotheistic form of worship. Acts 16.14 calls Lydia 'a worshiper of God' (*sebominè ton theon*).

Modern excavation of Philippi started in France in the early nineteenth century under the sponsorship of Napoleon Bonaparte. Archaeological work on the site is ongoing, sponsored by the Archaeological Society of Athens and the University of Thessaloniki. Excavations have revealed a forum and a theatre, a jail and a latrine among other structures. The jail is likely not the one that Paul and Silas occupied on the night the earthquake shook open the gates of the prison (Acts 16.24-31). With the baptism of Lydia and her household, and also the baptism of the jailor and his household, a church was born in Philippi. Christian churches in that city continued to grow. Excavations have confirmed the presence of a number of Byzantine church buildings, making them the earliest evidence of buildings dedicated to the worship of God in the name Christ. When Paul wrote his letter to this city, however, the believers would still have been meeting in homes.

The public latrine is one of many in the city with which Paul would have been familiar. The waste of the latrine may be what he has in mind in his comparison between his former life as a observant Pharisee and his new life in Christ, alluded to in Philippians 3.8: 'I have suffered the loss of all things, and I regard them as *rubbish* (*skubalon*, 'excrement') in order that I may gain Christ' (Phil. 3.8).

Citizens of Philippi had every reason to be proud of their privileges and their place in such a celebrated *polis* of Rome. But Paul urges them to take on the mind of Christ who humbled himself, and regarded the welfare of others above his own (Phil. 2.1-11).

d. Colossae, Phrygia in Asia Minor

Of the cities Paul visited during his mission, Colossae is the only one not mentioned in Acts, which does not mean he did not visit the city. The Pauline letter addressed to the church in Colossae – even if it did not come directly from the hand of the historical Paul – together with the letter to Philemon, attests to the likelihood of Paul's having been there. Questions surrounding the authenticity of the letter to the Colossians will be addressed in Chapter 11.

In the meantime, the epistle to the Colossians sheds some light on *the membership of the church* in that city, and on the development of philo-sophical ideas that threatened to undermine the original gospel that Paul had preached in the region years earlier. More than that, the epistle to the Colossians names people of the church in the city that correspond with people named in the unquestioned letter to Philemon. It is mainly on account of this little letter about a slave and his master who live in Colossae that a discussion about this urban centre finds a place in this chapter. Three names in Colossians, said to be residents of that city, appear also as such in Philemon: Onesimus (4.9), Epaphras (1.7; 4.10) and Archippus (4.17).

Colossae is a largely unexcavated site in modern Turkey (At least it was so when I visited the site in 1995). An Australian team has made application to dig on the site, and may indeed have started at the time of this writing. Enough evidence exists in the writings of geographer Strabo and Roman historian Tacitus, among others, to be able to get a picture of the city and its environs. Surveys of *the tell* (mound of cultural remains) have revealed a city wall, a pit lined with stones, possibly a silo of some sort, a necropolis (cemetery), and a theatre.

Colossae was one of three cities in close proximity to each other in the beautiful Lycus River Valley in what was Phrygia. The other two cities were Laodicea and Hierapolis, each one 20 kilometres from Colossae, and both of them mentioned in Colossians 4.13. Colossae lay 200 kilometres east of the great city of Ephesus, where Paul of Acts is said to have lived and worked for two years (Acts 19.10). During his time there he doubtless moved from place to place, and may have visited the three cities of the Lycus Valley region. It is possible also that one of his missionary companions, Epaphras maybe (Col. 1.7; 4.12), brought the word of Jesus to the city initially. Colossae was the home city of Epaphras. From Paul's letter to Philemon we know of Paul's plan to visit the city some time after his release from prison (Phlm. 22).

Colossae lay on the road running from Ephesus all the way east to the Tigris–Euphrates region. Greek historian Herodotus describes it as a centre for a thriving *woollen industry*. Apparently the wool of the region was a dark red, and earned the special name of *colossinium*. Such a thriving industry meant wealth for the city, which in turn drew people of various backgrounds to its centre. Jewish, Phrygian and Greek traders gathered in the city to ply their wares and set up house. They doubtless brought their philosophical thought patterns with them. Hence the warning to the church in the epistle to the Colossians not to allow their Christian thought to be corrupted by 'philosophy and empty deceit, according to human tradition' (Col. 2.8).

The city of Colossae suffered *a great earthquake* in 60 CE, according to Tacitus. If Paul had in fact written the epistle to the Colossians from a Roman prison after 60, as the traditional view holds, it is strange to find him not making any reference to the destruction in the wake of the earthquake. Of course, if the letter were written some years after the quake, and after Paul's death, when the city had regained some of its past glory, then silence about the earthquake might be expected.

Two of the important members of the church in Colossae, namely *Epaphras and Onesimus*, may have been responsible for the collection of Paul's letters some years after his death. Onesimus especially had good reason to preserve the letters of his 'father' in the faith, and liberator from slavery, and include his own short letter with the rest. One may well conjecture that the city of Colossae was as likely a centre as any for the earliest collection of Paul's letters to have come into being.

e. Cities of Galatia

Two features of Paul's letter known to us as 'Galatians' make it unique: the absence of a 'thanksgiving' and the broad designation of the recipients, 'the churches of Galatia' (1.2). The latter of these is the concern of this section.

Galatia is *the name of a territory*, sandwiched between Cappadocia to the east and Bithynia and Asia Minor to the west. 'Galatia' is derived from 'Gallo', otherwise known as *Cleat* (*Geog.* 4.1.14). At least three Celtic tribes moved across the regions of Thrace, Macedonia and Thessaly, battling with inhabitants en route. These Celts settled eventually in the region of Ancyra in Anatolia in the late third century BCE. Their settlement in that central plateau around Ancyra was not without serious difficulty. Battle followed battle as the Celtic outsiders dared to claim the territory for themselves.

The Galatians thus were neither Greek nor Roman, and certainly not Judaean. As Celts they were, in Paul's term, *'barbarian'* (Rom. 1.14). They had their own gods and their own language. The Celtic dialect was still spoken in the region as late as the writing of St. Jerome's commentary on Paul's letter to the region. Overlords not of Celtic origin used the newcomers as mercenaries, an activity these Celtic warriors used to bolster their holdings. These Galatians, as they came to be known, managed to gain territory for themselves as a result of their battles.

At about 189 BCE the Romans invaded the territory of the Galatians and defeated them on their own ground. Subdued, the *Galatians became pro-Roman* in an effort to maintain their place in the region. Their ability in battles came in handy when the Romans moved forward into other areas of Anatolia. The Galatians aided the Romans in their expansionist efforts. For their loyalty and hard work on behalf of Rome, Pompey granted to the territory of Galatia the status of a client kingdom, with the Galatians choosing their own rulers.

When Caesar Augustus came on the scene (27 BCE–14 CE), he transformed the region of Galatia into a *Roman province*, adding to the old territory the regions known as Pisidia, Isauria, Pamphylia, Lycanonia and Paphlagonia. The ruling elite class of the Roman province of Galatia took on elements of Greek culture (Hellenization) coupled with a Roman way of life and thought. The less powerful in the Galatian cities would have retained their Celtic dialect and religious cultic rituals. Paul's readers most likely were city dwellers, not the rural poor class. The question is not one of urban versus rural, but of which cities. Were the 'churches of Galatia' (1.2) to which

Paul wrote located in the Galatian region of the original settlement, or in the more southerly cities annexed by Augustus?

Even though Acts makes no mention of Paul's travelling to the three cities of the central region of the Roman province of Galatia, it is quite likely that Paul would have visited the three principal cities of the Celtic Gentiles on his travels west to Macedonia and Greece. Paul's letter addressed to the 'churches of Galatia' gives no further designation of the recipients, at least not in plain speech. His emphasis on *freedom in Christ* may well speak to the heart of the Celtic Galatians who knew so little freedom during their many years of battles against overlords. In his famous egalitarian Magna Carta of Christian community, Paul may be appealing to their ethnic background: 'no longer Jew or Greek, . . . no longer slave or free, . . . no longer male and female; for all of you are one in Christ Jesus' (3.28). The Galatians who earlier occupied the territory in central Anatolia were *neither Judaean nor Greek*. They were 'barbarian'. Paul's preaching aimed at liberating them from 'the elemental spirits' to which they were 'enslaved' (4.3, 9).

The *three principal cities* of Galatia in the region of the first Celtic settlement were Ankyra, Pessinus and Tavium. By the time of Paul's mission the cities had taken on all the characteristics of urban political, social and religious life. Paul's monotheistic religion probably appealed to the working class. His preaching of Christ as liberator from oppression (sin) would doubtless have struck a chord in the hearts of the Galatians. Paul's strong polemic against those who would enslave the Galatians again under the yoke of the Law may be understood against the experience of the Galatians, released as they were from 'the elemental spirits' of their Galatian religious and cultural life by the power of the Spirit. 'How can you turn back again to the weak and beggarly elemental spirits? How can you want to be enslaved to them again?' (4.9). He is here comparing 'the works of the law' (viz. Jewish circumcision) with the traditional religions of the Galatians of Celtic background. Remarkable!

One of the unique aspects of Paul's rhetoric in Galatians is his *labelling* of the readers as 'foolish Galatians' (3.1, 3). Its rhetorical economy is shocking and insulting on the surface. Twice he calls the readers 'foolish' (*anoètoi*). Who would not feel insulted? Such labelling can hardly be dismissed as rhetorical flourish. It seems that the Galatians may have understood themselves as the 'foolish' folks among the more sophisticated Graeco-Roman types in the surrounding cities. Paul may be reminding them of their earlier self-understanding before he brought the freedom and grace of Christ to their hearts and minds. By this outlandish label he seems to be wrestling them back to the freedom they experienced in the Spirit of Christ (3.2).

Paul had established a relationship with the members of 'the churches of Galatia'. In his earlier travels in the region he became ill, which meant a longer stay in one of their cities while he regained his strength. He praises them in his letter for their kindness, because they had welcomed him 'as an angel of God, as Christ Jesus' (4.14). So kind were they to him, he says, 'had it been possible, you would have torn out your eyes and given them to me' (4.15). This may be an allusion to the nature of his infirmity, an eye infection perhaps.

Whatever their ethnic and cultural background, the Galatians receive high praise from Paul, as long as they do not take on 'the works of the Law' (2.16; 3.5, 10, 12). The evidence from clues in Paul's letter favours the identity of the recipients as *Galatians of Celtic origin.*

f. Rome, Italy

When Paul composed his large letter to believers in Rome, the city had become the *dominant capital* of a powerful empire. But Rome was not always so. It was once a shepherds' village, among others of the same kind. Over time it gained supremacy over neighbouring tribal villages by virtue of its location in the centre of Italy, not far from the sea, and sitting strategically on the Tiber River. By the eighth century BCE a number of shepherd tribes banded together to form a larger settlement. At first the expanded town was ruled by kings, but by the early sixth century it had become a republic. As such it governed itself by elected magistrates. By the end of the third century BCE Rome controlled all of Italy. With Italy under its control in the second century BCE, Rome exerted its influence over territories to the east and the west. Provinces were organized successively. By the middle of the first century the city of Rome had become the centre of a powerful empire, with the occupied provinces paying taxes to the central government.

Three generals governed Rome: Pompey, Crassus and Julius Caesar. Pompey won much of the eastern Mediterranean including Judaea in 63 BCE. After the assassination of Julius Caesar *Octavian* became the sole ruler in Rome. He ruled for 41 years (27 BCE until 14 CE). To him the senate in Rome gave the title '*Augustus*', meaning 'venerable'. From there it was an easy step to the notion of divinity for the Emperor. Augustus devoted himself to creating a peaceful world, and to some extent he succeeded. He developed the city of Rome in the area of performing arts among other things.

He named the Roman forum after himself. The city had become a complex network of elaborate buildings, which Augustus did his best to protect from fire. A later ruler of his dynasty in some sort of mad rage set the city alight, and blamed the arson on Christians (*Annals* 15.44). That was Nero in the latter part of his reign. He ruled from 54 until 68. In the first five years of his rule the Roman populous enjoyed all the benefits of the good urban life that Rome afforded. Those early years were the best since Augustus. It was during those first five years of Nero's rule that Paul wrote his letter to the Roman Christians. The *peaceful bounty of Rome* at the time may account, to some extent, for Paul's generous attitude towards Roman authority in Romans 13.1-7. Had he written at the height of Nero's tyrannical behaviour he might not have been so generous in his instruction to the Christian communities in the city.

Rome attracted many people from the conquered provinces. Among those moving to Rome were some believers in Jesus. They may have originated in Judaea where the gospel of Jesus was first proclaimed by Peter, James and others. There is evidence of a Jewish attitude present in the church in Paul's corrective instruction about 'strong' and 'weak' members on the subject of acceptable foods to eat (Rom. 14.1-23). Having conceded that much concerning the ethnic-religious origin of the earliest Christian community in Rome, it should not be assumed further that the Apostle Peter went from Jerusalem to Rome as an evangelist. There is no evidence in the record of any active missionary effort in Rome like that of Paul elsewhere. *People of different backgrounds converged in Rome*, some of them Christian Judaeans and some Gentile believers from different parts of the empire. We know from Paul's letter to the church in the city, and from Acts, that Aquila and Priscilla had made their home in Rome. By the time Paul wrote his letter in 57/58 CE, the Gentile constituency seems to have grown in numbers and in power. His various statements about the believing Gentiles in the community, especially at 11.13-21, points to a significant number of Gentiles – perhaps greater than Judaeans – in the church at Rome. A more detailed exploration of the composition of the church of Paul's letter appears in Chapter 10.

Because of its importance as the capital of the empire, Rome had among its *inhabitants* slaves from conquered territories, merchants who found a ready market for their goods, artisans who could find an open door for their craftsmanship and artists for the performance of their art forms. In short, the church in Rome was almost certainly the most cosmopolitan church in the world of the day.

A further word is in order concerning *the expulsion* of Jewish Christians – and perhaps also some nonbelieving Judaeans – from the city of Rome. The event and its cause were recorded briefly by Roman historian, Suetonius, of the early second century. 'The Jews he [Claudius] expelled from Rome, since they were constantly in rebellion, at the instigation of Chrestus' (*Claud.* 25). There can be little doubt that *Chrestus* is a Suetonian rendering of the Greek *Christos*, which the Jewish Christians would have been using in their debates. Most likely the disturbance referred to in Suetonius had to do with heated debates between Judaeans believing in Jesus as the Christ (Messiah) and nonbelieving Judaeans. Disturbances of this sort in Rome were not taken lightly. Rome had come to pride itself – since Augustus – in being the city of peace. Disturbers of the peace were expelled. Aquila and Priscilla are two of those said to be among the expelled Judaeans of Rome (Acts 18.2), *c.*49 CE.

4. Conclusion

Paul's missionary forays into urban centres of population in the Roman Empire seem to have been deliberate. The reason is not immediately obvious. It could be that he was himself a city person from birth and was innately drawn to urban centres. More likely Paul's call to reach the Gentile world with the Gospel of Jesus Christ led him to *places with the highest concentration of people* of different backgrounds. Village groups may have emerged out of the city centres. For example, in the salutation of 2 Corinthians Paul addresses 'the church of God that is in Corinth, including all the saints throughout Achaia' (2 Cor. 1.1b). The first place name is a city, while the second is an area. The message probably fanned out from the city either as a result of rural people frequenting the city and returning to their village homes, or as a direct result of the city converts spreading the word. The same could be said of the 'the churches of Galatia' (Gal. 1.1). Galatia was a region. The cities of the region would have been the first target for Paul. But by the time of Paul's writing his letter, small communities of Christians in the surrounding areas of the cities had probably sprung up.

By and large, though, the first Gentile Christians were urban in orientation, with all of the patterns of thought and behaviour attending a city context. With urban believers in view, Paul could use the best rhetoric at his disposal, ply analogies and illustrations drawn from city life, and assume his readers would be familiar with institutions and policies ingrained in urban society.

But each city setting had its own history and its own distinctive character. Paul was well aware of the particularity of each of the city centres, and wrote his letters accordingly. Any reading of Paul's letters without due diligence paid to the city in which the letter was first read short-changes the interpretation of the text.

One wonders what direction Christianity would have taken had Paul followed the geographic–demographic model of Jesus' ministry that avoided the chief cities of Galilee, Tiberias and Sepphorus.

Further related reading

I heartily recommend the classic work of Wayne Meeks (2003), *The First Urban Christians: The Social World of the Apostle Paul*, Yale University, with an updated 'Introduction' from the 1983 edition. In this book Meeks analyzes the character of Paul's arguments in relation to the urban social texture of the congregations, especially the Corinthians and the Galatians.

Jerome Murphy-O'Connor's (1983), *St. Paul's Corinth: Texts and Archaeology*, Michael Glazier, on Corinth serves two purposes: it provides an excellent introduction to the context of the two long letters of Paul to that city, and it points to key sources of information from the period of the New Testament for further investigation into other aspects of city life in the Graeco-Roman world.

Consult also the 'Introductions' in the respective 'Commentaries' section of the Bibliography.

10 Paul's Textured Thought: Seven Undisputed Letters

Chapter Outline

One of the great literary treasures of the New Testament canon is the collection of letters from the hand of a man called Paul, the great Apostle to the Gentiles. They are the earliest surviving literature of the Christian heritage, written in the decade of the fifties CE. Paul's letters are the primary points of entry into his thought and life during the rigorous years of his missionary endeavours. That which persons have to say about themselves and their work should surely take precedence over what others, friends or foes, have to say about them. Having said that, though, secondary accounts should not be discounted out of hand. They can provide valuable insights into how the subject person is perceived, which may not tally exactly with self-perception. In Paul's case, Acts is one such secondary source. Too often, however, Acts has been made the starting point for understanding Paul's thought and mission. Similarly, the post-Pauline writings have traditionally been conflated with the genuine letters, resulting in a mixed – if not conflicting – account of Paul's thought and practice. Moreover, accounting for the man and his mission is best accomplished by examining what he wrote to his congregations about his life and thought in relation to them.

And so it is that we turn now to the seven letters that have the Pauline stamp of authenticity on them. The Graeco-Roman letter-form, explained in Chapter 5, needs no further comment here. Likewise, the importance of the historical figure of Paul in the development of the new movement following the death and resurrection of Jesus, discussed in Chapter 4, serves as a backdrop to the present discussion of the texture of the letters. Additional insights will, of course, come to the fore.

1. Features in general

A few points about the letters should be set out in preparation for the interpretation of the distinctive character of each of them.

a. Situation-specific

An important mark of Paul's letters is their situation-specific texture. *Situations differ* from one community to another. The letters were first directed to particular issues having arisen in the given community. In the churches in the region of Galatia, for example, itinerant missionaries had entered Paul's churches to encourage the Gentile members in that area to submit to circumcision in order to be recognized as full members. He found out about it and wrote in response to the churches in the region. In Corinth the situations were quite different. Paul had received reports about the church's thinking and practice, and the church had also written to him about issues with which they were grappling. The situations were specific to that congregation. The result was letters now called 1 Corinthians and 2 Corinthians.

The same is true for all of the genuine letters: they were prompted by some matter that had arisen in the community, or within the Apostle himself. The letter to the church at Rome, which he had not founded, was prompted by Paul's plan to visit that church en route to Spain. Romans was also an occasion for him to review his stance on the major tenets of his missionary thought before going to Jerusalem with the collection of money from the Gentile churches.

The reason for paying attention to the specificity of the letters is because Paul's arguments are tailored to meet *the demands of the situation* of the moment in which the persons involved find themselves. As such, the arguments in the letters should not be read as universal philosophy or theology, but as rhetorically charged directives to particular congregations.

b. Argument and conclusion

Paul's convictions in relation to his Jewish heritage on the one hand, and to his call in relation to Jesus as the resurrected Christ on the other, guide his arguments in response to the situations in his churches. Arguments are meant to persuade an audience or a reader. They make a case. Sometimes an argument may be heated, depending on the nature of the situation being addressed. The texture of the rhetoric will be commensurate with the 'heat'. The letter to the Galatians is ironic and polemical, aimed at cutting down the position of opponents. The letter to Philemon is conciliatory, aimed at reconciling a runaway slave become Christian with his Christian master.

Arguments have conclusions that arise out of the convictions of the person making the argument. An important principle to keep in mind for reading Paul's letters is to distinguish between the *form of argument* and the *conclusion* to which the argument is supposed to lead. Simply put, the reason for making an argument should not be confused with statements inside the argument. Sometimes Paul makes statements within an argument that are not identical with the convictions he holds on the issue. For example, he believes in the universality of the plight of Sin that affects every human being in Adam, whether Judaean or Greek. He believes also that Christ reverses the plight for all who believe in him. In Romans 5, Paul makes the comparison between the two figureheads, Adam and Christ. Inside the argument he states, 'Just as one man's trespass led to condemnation for all, so one man's act of righteousness leads to justification and life for all' (Rom. 5.18). Does he believe that *all* human beings caught in the Sin of Adam of Genesis will be made right with God by the righteous act of Jesus? I think not. He believes all *in Christ* will be made alive (1 Cor. 15.22). The typological comparison internal to the argument leads Paul to make a statement that does not square exactly with his conviction. Those who say Paul believed in the universal salvation of all humanity, based on his statement in Romans 5.18 (and 1 Cor. 15.22), are confusing the formal texture of the argument with the reason for the argument.

Sometimes Paul will quote from a source inside an argument as though the source were his own words. For example, in 1 Corinthians 7.1 he most likely quotes from a letter he received from the Corinthians without making clear to non-Corinthian readers that he is doing so. As a result some interpreters conclude that he was opposed to Christians having sexual intercourse. 'It is well for a man not to touch a woman' is a line from the Corinthians' letter, which Paul then qualifies as he moves through the argument. Again, sorting out the elements within an argument from the thought that drives the argument helps in the interpretation of his letters.

c. Intertexture: Paul's use of Scripture

In Chapter 2 I drew attention to the way intertexture works in the New Testament. Observing its dynamics facilitates an understanding of what is going on in Paul's argumentation.

One of the principal sources on which he draws in the course of his arguments is the Greek version (LXX) of his Jewish Scriptures. He sometimes *appeals to that authority* explicitly to make a case: 'Isaiah says, "Lord, who has believed our message?"' (Rom. 10.16). Even when he is arguing in Galatians against the circumcision of Gentile believers in Jesus he appeals to the very Scripture that requires circumcision of all members of the covenant community (Gen. 17.9-14). Of course, Paul does not quote the text of the covenant with Abraham in which circumcision is demanded. Instead, he cites a text from the same source that affirms *the faith of Abraham* as the saving factor: '[Abraham] believed God; and it was reckoned to him as righteousness' (Gen. 15.6 in Gal. 3.6 and Rom. 4.3). At one point he even appeals to the Law to prove that the Law has been rendered inoperative in the presence of the Spirit of the Christ crucified and raised (2 Cor. 3.7-18). These Scripture texts that Paul incorporates into his argument are nuanced by him in keeping with his new experience of Christ and his call to incorporate Gentiles into covenant community.

At times he will allude to the texts of Scripture without citing them explicitly. In that case he puts a particular spin on the incorporated text in keeping with the direction of his thought on the issue under consideration. Sometimes Scripture is echoed in an argument, so nuanced is it in his discussion. In this pattern of intertexture the source text is virtually rewritten. Some examples are as follows. The story of the Exodus of the Hebrews from Egypt and the subsequent idolatry and punishment of some of them in the wilderness is echoed in 1 Corinthians 10, where Paul warns the Corinthians to 'flee from the worship of idols' (10.14). The account of Moses shining face when he turned to the Lord (Exod. 34) is echoed in 2 Corinthians 3, where Paul contrasts the 'fading glory' of Moses with the permanent glory of Christ present in Paul's mission. The priestly regulations about atonement for sins in the commonwealth of Israel (Lev. 16–18) is echoed in

1 Corinthians 5, where he instructs the community in Corinth 'to hand over' an immoral man to Satan to rid the community of its complicity in his sin. Hearing echoes such as these in Paul's letters helps in unravelling some of the complex texture in many of his arguments. He interprets his Scripture in the freedom of the Spirit, from his knowledge of Christ, and in connection with his call to gather believing Gentiles into a new community of faith in Christ.

d. The relevance of dating the letters

Efforts have been made to date each of the letters precisely, even to a time of year in some cases (e.g. Thiessen 1947, p. 194). What is appropriate for interpretation, however, is the knowledge that Paul's letters were all written *during his missionary activity* in the decade of the fifties CE, following the critical meeting in Jerusalem. The earliest letter could have been written in 49/50, and the latest in 57/58. This knowledge affects how we read the letters. If he had lived to see his churches well established – with ordained bishops, pastors, deacons, appointed to oversee the work – he would doubtless have written differently. As it happened, he was actively engaged in putting his call into practice when he wrote his thoughts to the new congregations living in the Spirit of Christ. His sense of mission meant leaving his churches to fend for themselves. Issues arose in his absence, which in turn led to the writing of letters in an attempt to help the churches sort out the issues.

Personal *presence* and *spoken word* were believed to be more powerful and persuasive than any text. In several of his letters, Paul draws attention to the present–absent syndrome. He tries in his letters to lead the readers to imagine his personal spirit present while they read the letter: 'For though *absent* in body I am *present* in spirit, and as if *present*, I have already pronounced judgment' (1 Cor. 5.3). Or he will point out that the statement by letter in his absence will be the same in speech when present: 'Let such people understand that what we say by letter when *absent*, we do when *present*' (2 Cor. 10.11; 13.2). Again he may affirm a congregation to live as though he were always present to them: 'Only let your manner of life be worthy of the gospel of Christ, so that whether I *come and see you* or am *absent*, I may hear of you that you stand firm in one spirit' (Phil. 1.27).

The presence–absence continuum was part of Paul's missionary experience in relation to his churches. He could not stay long with the newly formed congregations in one location, and seemingly did not organize the leadership before he left for another city. Instead, he expected the 'spiritual gifts' within a congregation to come to life and be exercised, and he also wrote letters to be read aloud. Evidently some members in the congregations could read, otherwise the letters would have been to no avail. Reading ability was highly valued in the world of Paul's time. Relatively few people were educated to the point where they could read and understand complex thought encoded in text. Some urban people of the time were more likely to acquire an education than were their rural counterparts who made up about 95 per cent of the population in that agrarian society. Readers in the congregations would not only have read the letter aloud in the congregation, but would also have explained difficult parts of the argumentation, however long it took. It is likely that a letter would have been read in its entirety on one occasion.

Moreover, precise dating of each of the letters is not nearly as important as the recognition that the letters were written during a 10-year period of vibrant missionary activity, 20 to 30 years after the Easter experience. Formative birth pains in the churches' experience are evident in Paul's letters. The issues addressed differ from one church to another, from one area to another, and from one time to another. Yet the central convictions remain remarkably coherent throughout his 8-year letter-writing mission.

The order in which each of the letters is discussed below is an attempt at a sequence of composition from earliest to latest. A guiding principle seems to underwrite them all: *freedom and peace* through the grace of the Lord Jesus Christ: 'Now the Lord is the Spirit, and where the Spirit of the Lord is, there is freedom' (2 Cor. 3.17). 'It is to peace that God has called you' (1 Cor. 7.15). Any interpretation of Paul's genuine letters that undermines these two characteristics of salvation in Christ dishonours the Apostle and the 'truth of the gospel' he preached (Gal. 2.5, 14).

2. Surveying the texture of the letters

a. 1 Thessalonians

One of the major urban centres of the territory of Macedonia was Thessalonica, described in chapter 9. Paul's letter to the congregation(s) in that city, far from being critical of the members, congratulates them for their good *example* of faith and love. A report of their good life of faith in Jesus Christ had reached well beyond their own borders. One point in particular in that report is singled out: the Thessalonian believers had 'turned to God from idols, to serve a living and true God'. As such they are 'to wait for [God's] Son from heaven, whom he raised from the dead – Jesus, who rescues us from the wrath that is coming'. All of this appears in the thanksgiving (1.2-10). The last point is eschatological, waiting for God's Son. Eschatology is the principal issue in 1 Thessalonians. The telltale phrase gives the signal: 'we do not want you to be uninformed, brothers and sisters' (4.13). That which follows deals with the specific issue that came to Paul's attention, and prompted this letter.

Timothy, one of the three named as sending the letter (1.1), had just recently returned from a visit with the congregation. Paul had sent him all the way north from Athens to inquire about the spiritual and practical well-being of the congregation, and to encourage them in their faith (3.1-5). Timothy's report from and about the congregation was overall positive (3.6). Why then would Paul write this letter? If all is well he should have no reason to follow up on Timothy's good news. Something in Timothy's report led Paul to find a substantial piece of papyrus, a pen and ink, and stop what he was doing to write this letter. He wrote letters, not because he had nothing else to do, or merely to keep in touch. His letter-writing was deliberate and purposeful, arising out of some situation in life.

The implied purpose in 1 Thessalonians is at least three-fold: (1) to encourage the members to continue in the faith in the face of opposition (3.2-3); (2) to urge them to continue to work with their hands while they wait for the coming (*parousia*) of the Lord (4.11-13); and (3) to instruct them about their concern for those who had died before the *parousia* (4.13-18). In connection with this third purpose, 1 Thessalonians 5 deals with a related concern about the signs of the end of the age. It may be that the Thessalonians went so far as to put the 'signs of the times' question in a letter to Paul, delivered by Timothy. Why is that probable? The little phrase 'now concerning' (*peri de* 4.9; 5.1) is likely a way of addressing a question that had come to Paul in written form. We know explicitly from 1 Corinthians 7.1 that each time he tackles one of the questions from their letter to him he introduces his reply by this same phrase, 'now concerning'. In 1 Thessalonians, however, it is possible that Timothy brought their questions personally to Paul.

How does Paul enunciate the three purposes in his letter?

First, the opposition the believers faced was from their own compatriots (2.14). Not only were these people from the city of Thessalonica, they were also Gentile in religion and culture. The exact situation that would have led to the *opposition/persecution* is debatable. The most likely could have been that they 'turned to God from idols' (1.9), which meant they no longer supported the local temple cult with their offerings. From their 'turning from idols' we know that the congregation was mostly, if not completely, Gentile. Their new religion would have looked strange to their fellow residents of Thessalonica. Talk of the resurrection of a crucified criminal – by Roman jurisprudence – may have been offensive to the state officials. What is interesting is that Paul compares their persecution with the persecution of the Judaean believers, including himself, by their nonbelieving Judaeans. His judgement language in this text against his own people (2.14-16) is unique in the letters. It reads like *hyperbole* for effect. Nevertheless, it is strange to have Paul say, even for rhetorical force, that the Judaeans 'displease God and oppose everyone by hindering us from speaking to the Gentiles so that they may be saved' (2.15-16).

The Judaeans did not hinder him from *speaking* to Gentiles; they objected to *what* he was speaking to Gentiles concerning their incorporation into covenant community on the basis of faith apart from observance of the Law, which included circumcision among other matters of Jewish identity. He himself once persecuted believers like Stephen on similar grounds. The rhetoric in Romans about unbelieving Judaeans, by contrast, is respectfully compassionate: the Judaeans are 'Israelites, and to them belong the adoption, the glory, the covenants, the giving of the law, the worship, and the promises; to them belong the patriarchs, and from them, according to the flesh, comes the Messiah, who is over all, God blessed forever. Amen' (Rom. 9.4-5).

Second, the ethical advice to the Thessalonians about 'working with their hands' is expanded beyond a mere injunction in general. Paul points to his own work to support himself as example (2.9). On this point he tells them 'to work with your hands, as we directed you, so that you may behave properly toward outsiders and be dependent on no one' (4.11). It could be that their 'waiting for [God's] Son from Heaven' led them to suspend their *regular work* from which they earned their daily bread. Immediately following this injunction to continue working for a living he instructs them about the eschatology, which they seem to have misappropriated after he had left them.

Third, what happens to believers who had died before the coming of the Lord? On this matter Paul does not want them to be uninformed. He answers out of his experience of the resurrected Christ, in light of which he envisions resurrection for all those who are 'in Christ'. Their relationship to Christ guarantees them life like that of the resurrected Jesus. That appears to be his conviction in his answer to the inquiry from the Thessalonians: 'Through Jesus, God will bring with him those who have died. For this we declare to you by the word of the Lord, that we who are alive, who are left until the coming of the Lord, will by no means precede those who have died' (4.14-15). At that point Paul launches into an *apocalyptic scenario* in elaborating his hopeful vision for the believers at Thessalonica. 'For the Lord himself, with a cry of command, with the archangel's call and with the sound of God's trumpet, will descend from heaven, and the dead in Christ will rise first. Then we who are alive, who are left, will be caught up in the clouds together with them to meet the Lord in the air; and so we will be with the Lord forever' (4.16-17). Only here in all of the New Testament does this image of rapture into the air at the coming of the Lord occur. Elsewhere Paul deals with the resurrection of the dead and the eternal life that ensues. But not once again does he mention a metaphysical ascent into the clouds to meet the Lord. Apocalyptic visions by their very nature vary, depending on the situation that gave them birth in the first place. His point in presenting this vision to the believers is *to encourage them*, to give them hope in the midst of persecution (4.18)

Finally, in connection with the third purpose, the times and the seasons of the coming end are not given. Instead, the coming is said to be like a 'thief in the night' (5.2). That is, there will be no warning. According to Paul's statement here and elsewhere, he believed the coming of the Lord to be *imminent*, 'any time soon'. And indeed he seemed to believe that he would likely live to see the Day of the Lord (see 4.17 and 1 Cor. 15.51-51). But imminent can also mean without warning or signs of any kind, which appears to be the sense in this letter. And that hope-filled eschatology is supposed to motivate a corresponding ethics within the membership: 'So then let us not fall asleep as others do, but let us keep awake and be sober; for those who sleep sleep at night, and those who are drunk get drunk at night. But since we belong to the day, let us be sober, and put on the breastplate of faith and love, and for a helmet the hope of salvation' (5.6-8).

Paul's benediction in concluding his letter includes the word '*blameless*' (5.23; see also 2.10; 3.13). Apparently he expects converts 'in Christ' to live unimpeachable lives in the presence and power of the Spirit before the world until the coming of the Lord. There is no notion here or elsewhere in the letters that a member of Christ remains 'under the power of Sin', transgressing God's Law inevitably (Rom. 3.9; cf. 8.1-4).

b. 1 Corinthians

The urban centre of Corinth, as we learned in Chapter 9, was one of rich commerce and diverse religion. The population was mainly Gentile. According to Acts, however, there was a Jewish synagogue in Corinth where Paul tried unsuccessfully to convince the participants of the virtue of knowing Jesus crucified and resurrected (Acts 18.1-16). By his own account, Paul concentrated on Gentiles in Corinth, of whom his congregation of believers was composed.

He was not the first Christian to enter Corinth. A Jewish-Christian couple named Aquila and Prisca ('Priscilla' in Acts) had reached the city before Paul. Their presence in the city prior to his coming, however, was not purposefully missional. Among those expelled from Rome by an edict of Emperor Claudius, they ended up in Corinth of Greece. When Paul met up with them, they became friends, probably also sharing the same trade of tentmaking (Acts 18.3). At the time of Paul's writing 1 Corinthians, possibly from Ephesus, Aquila and Prisca were with him, and sent greetings to the church at Corinth (1 Cor. 11.19).

From two factors implied in 1 Corinthians we can infer the occasion for writing the letter: an *oral report about* the church (1.11), and *a letter from* the church (7.1). The report came from 'Chloe's people', a phrase that implies Chloe was a woman of means, with a household of slaves or hired free people able to move around in the Empire. The report identified two matters in particular: divisions in the community (11.1) and sexual immorality permitted in the community (5.1)

The letter from the Corinthians involved issues about marital ethics, spiritual gifts in the community, eating food that had been offered to idols, the resurrection of the dead, and concern about a man named Apollos. While the letter is said to have come from the Corinthians themselves, clearly the whole group did not actually write it. One of their number would have had the skill to hear what the members were saying, and then to write their inquiries to Paul. In the process, though, the writer was also an interpreter. His/her own thoughts doubtless entered the texture of the letter, so the letter to Paul may not have represented entirely the thoughts and intentions of every member of the congregation. Nevertheless, we can reasonably assume that the letter from Corinth was a fair reflection of interests and concerns of the church in that area of Achaia. From his reply in the second part of his letter it is possible to recapture at least some parts of the Corinthians' letter to him.

These two, then, the report and the letter from Corinth, left Paul little option but to rise to the occasion and write a reply. In addition to dealing with the divisions and the sexual immorality from the report, his letter covers marriage, celibacy, divorce, eating food offered to idols, the proper conduct in worship, spiritual gifts, and resurrection. Chapter 15 on the resurrection of the dead is the longest sustained argument in all of the letters. It appears that resurrection of dead bodies had little appeal for the Corinthians. Their interest theologically may have been in the direction of gaining a spiritual experience of the world to come in the present.

1 Corinthians has *integrity*, in that it reads as though written at one time out of one occasion. What is called for now is at least a brief foray into the texture of the arguments in response to the report and the letter from the Corinthians.

i. The report

Quarrels that lead to division in the ranks of the community of Christ do not fit with Paul's ecclesiology, his understanding of the community of Christ. The symbolism of the Lord's Supper itself rules out division. 'Because there is one bread, we who are many are one body, for we all partake of the one bread' (10.17). Even though the spiritual gifts in the community are diverse, the body politic is one, not many. 'For just as the body is one and has many members, and all the members of the body, though many, are one body, so it is with Christ' (12.12). This is the conviction from which Paul's response to the divisions springs.

According to his response, the factions have to do with leaders in the new Christian community. Some members are drawn to one or another of the leading teachers of the Christian mission. Some identify with Paul, some with Cephas (Peter), some with Apollos, and some with Christ (1.12). One would think the last group, identifying with Christ, would be applauded. But even they fall under Paul's critique. A group within the 'body of Christ' cannot set themselves up under any name, even the name of Christ, as better than the others. That is so because Christ in the person of Jesus gave himself away for the sake of others. And that latter point becomes critical in the argument against any kind of division in the community of Christ.

Paul focuses on *the efficacy of the cross of Christ* in the first chapter of 1 Corinthians in a way unparalleled in any other part of the New Testament. The rhetorical force of the argument in 1.18-31 renders any divisive member defenceless. 'For the message about the cross is foolishness to those who are perishing, but to us who are being saved it is the power of God' (1.18). Apparently wisdom and folly played a vital part in the language and thought of the members at Corinth. Their place near Athens on the one hand and near a busy port on the other gave them access to the philosophies and the sophists of the day. Wisdom (*sophia*) was believed to be a great gift, one that led to the divine mind. Well aware of the Corinthians' desire for wisdom, Paul acknowledges his preaching of the cross sounds foolish, 'a stumbling block to [Judaeans] and foolishness to Gentiles' (1.23), so he has to argue otherwise. 'God chose what is foolish in the world to shame the wise; God chose what is weak in the world to shame the strong; God chose what is low and despised in the world, things that are not, to reduce to nothing things that are, *so that no one might boast* in the presence of God' (1.27-29).

Paul eventually gets to one particular line of division in the congregation: devotees of Apollos on one side, and devotees of himself on the other (3.4-8). *Apollos* had become a believer in Jesus and a missionary. He was not exactly a partner with Paul, as Silas and Timothy and Titus were, but visited the church at Corinth after Paul had left (Acts 19.1), and spoke to the congregation in his absence. He and Paul had met up at some point, of course, but they seemed not to have been in Corinth together as apostolic partners. The argument against partisanship with regard to the two men may have been more far-reaching than its immediate context in 1 Corinthians envisions. It is possible that Apollos eventually spoke disparagingly of Paul's apostleship in Corinth. (See e.g. 2 Cor. 10.10).

Here in 1 Corinthians 3, however, Paul is simply aware that Apollos has a following in Corinth. He seeks a fair balance in his rhetorical response, but will not give up his place as the pioneer agent of God who brought the congregation into being.

> What then is Apollos? What is Paul? Servants through whom you came to believe, as the Lord assigned to each. I planted, Apollos watered, but God gave the growth. So neither the one who plants nor the one who waters is anything, but only God who gives the growth. The one who plants and the

> one who waters have a common purpose, and each will receive wages according to the labor of each. (3.5-8)

While the texture of the figurative language is ameliorating in tone, it does not assign identical status to each of Paul and Apollos. Paul plants; Apollos does not. Apollos comes along afterward and waters merely what Paul had planted. But still God is the one who gives growth. Neither of the men can boast of his own work. Remember, the cross rules out boasting of any kind.

Another part of the report cites a case of a sexually immoral person in the congregation, with full membership status (5.1-13). It is a case of incest, in which 'a man is living with his father's wife' (5.1). The woman is most likely his step-mother. The man's father may have died or divorced his wife. In either case, the Law of Leviticus rules out such a marital relationship. And according to Paul, even the law of the Gentiles does not condone this kind of union. He calls it 'sexual immorality' (*porneia*, 5.1), and will have none of it in the community of the Christ. The man may call himself a brother (5.11), but as far as Paul is concerned his moral behaviour contradicts his claim.

But the problem is not merely that the individual man is immoral, but that the Christian community condones fellowship with such a man. The members of the community are called upon to rid the community of the contaminating member. The ritual of riddance reflects the atonement ritual in Judaism in which the sins of the community are taken away in the flesh of a goat dedicated to the task. The goat is led to the wilderness and then 'handed over' to the desert-dwelling demon, Azazel, for the destruction of the flesh of the goat (Lev. 16.8-26). When the ritual was completed the community could consider itself purged of its sin. This *ritual of atonement* is echoed in 1 Corinthians 5.5: 'you are to hand this man over to Satan for the destruction of the flesh, so that [the] spirit may be saved in the day of the Lord.' The implication is that the man thus led out of the community and handed over for 'the destruction of the flesh' is expected to die physically as a result. (Käsemann 1969, p. 71.)

The result for the community would be that 'the spirit will be saved in the Day of the Lord'. Most modern translations render the article – '*the* spirit' – with the pronoun '*his* spirit', which means the spirit of the expelled man will be saved in the day of the Lord. It is characteristic of modern thinking to highlight the ultimate importance of the individual. But first-century agrarian mentality was communal. The one individual would be sacrificed to save the many (cf. Jn 11.50). Paul is concerned, in the texture of 1 Corinthians 5, for the salvation of the contaminated community, the body of Christ indwelt by the Spirit. In practical terms, the 'handing over to Satan' likely involved banning the man from fellowship in the Christian community, without which he would probably not survive.

ii. The letter from Corinth

Discussion of sexual matters continues through chapters 6 and 7. Beginning at chapter 7, however, Paul is answering concerns coming out of the letter from the Corinthians (7.1). All of chapter 7 deals with conjugal rights (1-5), marriage and celibacy (6-9), marriage and divorce, marriage to a nonbe-liever (10-16), and instructions to virgins and others (17-40).

Chapters 8 and 10 deal particularly with *food offered in an idol's temple*. If a Christian chooses to eat such meat Paul has no scruples. But eating such food as an act of worshipping an idol would be a problem. He will not tolerate that practice, because 'you cannot drink the cup of the Lord and the cup of demons. You cannot partake of the table of the Lord and the table of demons' (10.21). If the eating of the meat leads a 'weak' member of the community to worship an idol, then it would be better for the 'strong' member not to eat such food (8.10-13). The section ends with instructions about behaviour in a worship setting.

Both women and men are assumed to be participating in leading worship. But they should do so as women and as men: a woman should not try to take on the persona of a man in leading worship. Follow the accepted cus-tom of dress and general decorum for men and women, the Apostle seems to say, and so lead in prayer and prophecy. Paul is often accused of setting men above women in chapter 11. What needs to be remembered is that he is replying to a letter from the Corinthians, which doubtless assumes the conventional ideology of hierarchy (cf. Col. 3.18–4.1; Eph. 5.21–6.6). Sometimes he cites, or echoes the letter without letting subsequent readers like ourselves know it. Very likely the Corinthians had an idea of hierarchy related to men and women, and Paul affirms a certain hierarchy (11.3-5) in order to instruct men and women on fitting decorum for the two genders in worship. In the end, though, he abandons any rigid hierarchy *in favour of equality*: 'Nevertheless, in the Lord woman is not independent of man or man independent of woman. For just as woman came from man, so man comes through woman; but all things come from God' (11.11-12).

An addendum is called for at this point. Clearly, chapter 11 assumes both women and men pray and prophesy in the worship service. Paul affirms the gender-inclusive practice. But later in chapter 14 of the same letter we find a text prohibiting women from speaking in church. Here is how the ruling reads:

> As in all the churches of the saints, women should be silent in the churches. For they are not permitted to speak, but should be subordinate, as the law also says. If there is anything they desire to know, let them ask their husbands at home. For it is shameful for a woman to speak in church. Or did the word of God originate with you? Or are you the only ones it has reached? (14.33b-36)

This is such an outright contradiction to the argument in chapter 11 that the only responsible decision to make about the prohibition against women speaking in church is that this out-of-place text is *an interpolation* by a later copyist. Concrete manuscript evidence is not available in support of this position, but the restriction fits better with a later time and situation in the church when some of Paul's interpreters restricted unlearned women from speaking in the church service (see 1 Tim. 2.11-15).

Returning to chapter 11, the tradition about the Lord's Supper was handed down to Paul, and he quotes it as the basis for his instruction to the congregation on how to partake of the sacral meal:

> For I received from the Lord what I also handed on to you, that the Lord Jesus on the night when he was betrayed took a loaf of bread, and when he had given thanks, he broke it and said, 'This is my body that is for you. Do this in remembrance of me.' In the same way he took the cup also, after supper, saying, 'This cup is the new covenant in my blood. Do this, as often as you drink it, in remembrance of me.' (11.23-25)

The *Eucharistic words* here are consonant with the Synoptic tradition. Paul knew the tradition and respected it, although he did not slavishly rely on it to guide his congregations. This in one of the very few places where he cites the tradition (see also 7.10; 9.14; cf. 1 Thess. 4.15)

Chapters 12–14 take up the matter of *spiritual gifts*. Paul acknowledges the gifts in which the Corinthians seem to delight, but the way the gifts function in the community of the Spirit should not become a cause for division. 'For just as the body is one and has many members, and all the members of the body, though many, are one body, so it is with Christ. For in the one Spirit we were all baptized into one body – Jews or Greeks, slaves or free – and we were all made to drink of one Spirit' (12.12-13). Sandwiched between chapters 12 and 14 is the great love poem of chapter 13. In the final analysis, *love (agapè)* is the all-encompassing gift and thus 'a still more excellent way' than all other gifts (12.31).

As mentioned earlier, chapter 15 on the resurrection of the dead is the longest argument. Apparently the Corinthians had a problem with the resurrection of the physical body. They knew – as all of us do – that the physical body decomposes. The Corinthians wished for a kind of life in relation to God that would no longer be subject to corruption. In response, Paul explains the nature of the resurrected body, based on a traditional faith formulation already resident in the churches:

> that Christ died for our sins in accordance with the scriptures,
> and that he was buried,
> and that he was raised on the third day in accordance with the scriptures,
> and that he appeared to Cephas, then to the twelve. (15.3-5)

Resurrection of the body belongs to the new creation in Christ. The old creation in Adam has been created anew in the second Adam, Christ resurrected. Those in Christ will be resurrected as he was, not with a physical body that will die again, but with a *spiritual body* like that of the resurrected Christ. Paul uses several analogies to prove his thesis. One is that of the seed sown in the ground. What comes up is not exactly the same as the seed that was sown. So also the resurrected body: 'it is sown a physical body, it is raised a spiritual body. If there is a physical body, there is also a spiritual body' (15.44).

The clinching point of the whole argument comes at verse 50: 'What I am saying, brothers and sisters, is this: flesh and blood cannot inherit the kingdom of God, nor does the perishable inherit the imperishable.' In the end, however, Paul admits he is dealing with *a mystery*. Somehow a change must take place for human experience to become free from the sting of death (15.55-56). How that transformation happens is God's business, hence a mystery to human minds.

Two final matters from the letter from the Corinthians bring a response from Paul. We know the questions come from the letter because of the introductory phrase, 'now concerning' (16.1, 12; cf. 7.1). First, the question of *the collection* of money for the saints in Jerusalem. The members are to set aside 'whatever extra they earn' in preparation for the time when the money is collected for the trip to Jerusalem. Second, they enquired about Apollos. Paul says he urged Apollos to visit Corinth, but he was not willing to go at this time. He will come when he has the opportunity (16.12).

The comment, while not derogatory, is not overly complimentary to Apollos either.

This long and complex letter ends – as all of the seven letters do – with final instructions, final greetings and benediction (16.13-24).

c. 2 Corinthians

While the integrity of 1 Corinthians is beyond dispute, the integrity of 2 Corinthians is not. The canonical shape of 2 Corinthians consists of *two distinct parts*. The first nine chapters, in the main, are patient and conciliatory in tone. The rhetoric is generally pastoral and caring. The last four chapters, however, are anything but patient. The rhetorical texture is biting, sarcastic, ironic, and punitive. In those chapters, Paul is 'ready to punish every disobedience when your obedience is complete' (10.6). The occasion for writing the first nine chapters appears to have been different from the occasion related to the last four chapters. One is led to conclude, therefore, that we have in the canonical 2 Corinthians a composite of at least two letters from Paul to the Corinthians written on two different occasions. The two may have come together on one papyrus at the time of the collection of the letters towards the end of the first century.

Even within the first nine chapters several *seams appear*, which has led some scholars to detect several fragments that are not integral to the nine chapters: 2.12-13 does not fit well with what precedes and follows; 6.14–7.1 is completely out of sync with what precedes and follows the section; 8.1-24 argues for the collection to be completed; 9.1-15 advances a similar argument. The two appeals may be from two separate letters.

All but one of these parts of 2 Corinthians doubtless originated with Paul at one time or another, and all of them directed to the Corinthians. One part, 6.14–7.1, about *the unequal yoke* is characteristically un-Pauline: numerous words in the section do not appear elsewhere in genuine letters; his word for Satan (viz. Beliar) is unique to this text; Pauline Christology is all but missing. The tenor of the text reads like an edict from the Dead Sea covenanters. Still, a case could be made in support of Paul's composition. The occasion may have been so different as to call forth this kind of language not found elsewhere in the genuine letters. Either way, this text is not integrated with the surrounding texture.

Aside from these observations that challenge the integrity of 2 Corinthians, what can be said for the canonical letter? A title for the whole could be 'Variations on the Theme of Ministry'.

i. Conciliation (2 Cor. 1–7)

In chapters 1 through 7 Paul reflects on his *pastoral relationship* with the Corinthians, and longs for their spiritual wellbeing. He had visited them recently and was offended by a member. The congregation did nothing to discipline the offender, so Paul wrote a 'tearful', 'painful' letter to the congregation about the matter. That letter is lost. The congregation then did exercise discipline on the offender. Paul, upon hearing of their action, wrote to encourage the members and to advise them to lift the disciplinary measure they had imposed on the man before he becomes overwhelmed with 'excessive sorrow' (2.7). Paul forgave him and so should they. (2.1-10; 7.8-13). We have that letter in 2 Corinthians 1–9.

Some at Corinth – whether members or interlopers is not certain – have called for *letters of recommendation* from Paul. He declines to give such letters. 'You yourselves are our letter', he tells the Corinthians, 'written on our hearts, to be known and read by all' (3.2). Mention of 'letter' leads him to discuss the difference between *letter and Spirit*. The written letter of the Law has been superseded by the Spirit, 'for the letter kills, but the Spirit gives life' (3.6). Paul's ministry in the name of Christ is conducted 'with unveiled face' in the freedom and power of the Spirit (3.7-18). But his ministry is not without hardship. At times, especially in 2 Corinthians, he will *list hardships* for effect, and with figurative flare. One of the best of these is found in chapter 4 as follows:

> But we have this treasure in clay jars, so that it may be made clear that this extraordinary power belongs to God and does not come from us. We are afflicted in every way, but not crushed; perplexed, but not driven to despair; persecuted, but not forsaken; struck down, but not destroyed; always carrying in the body the death of Jesus, so that the life of Jesus may also be made visible in our bodies. (4.7-10)

One of the captivating themes of 2 Corinthians is *new creation*, which includes a new kind of life for those who are in Christ Jesus. His vivid description of exchanging the mortal body for the heavenly is both puzzling and promising (5.1-10). When he comes to the notion of new creation he couches the idea in the language of reconciliation. The creation has been estranged from God, especially the human family in that old creation. Renewal is already under way since the resurrection of Jesus. 'So if anyone is in Christ, there is a new creation: everything old has passed away; see, everything has become new!' (5.17). He speaks as one already involved in the new creation, even though he holds the final outcome in reserve. 'All this is from God,' he says, 'who reconciled us to himself through Christ, and has given us the ministry of reconciliation'(5.18). But Paul's ministry is not simply that of 'saving souls' individualistically. The reconciliation is large scale. 'That is, in Christ God was *reconciling the world* to himself, not counting their trespasses against them, and entrusting the message of reconciliation to us' (5.19).

ii. The collection (2 Cor. 8–9)

As mentioned earlier, the collection of money for Jerusalem was important to Paul. The rhetoric of chapters 8 and 9 implies that the Corinthians had not been setting aside monies for the final collection to go to Jerusalem. He had instructed them in 1 Corinthians to gather the money piece-meal until the day of his departure to Jerusalem. Now here in 2 Corinthians 8 and 9 he makes a case for the collection. 'For you know the generous act of our Lord Jesus Christ, that though he was rich, yet for your sakes he became poor, so that by his poverty you might become rich' (8.9). He also uses the generosity of the Macedonian churches to the north to urge the Corinthians in the south to give. Though much poorer than the Corinthians, the Macedonians gave abundantly. In chapter 9 he reverses that example. He says he sang the praises of the Corinthians to the Macedonians, telling of their eagerness to give (9.2). He concludes his second argument with a paean of praise to the giver of all gifts: 'Thanks be to God for his indescribable gift!' (9.15).

Why the urgency of the gift of money for the saints at Jerusalem? It was not merely a gift to help poor people. There were poor people in many of the centres of the mission, but he urges a collection for those in *Jerusalem specifically*. Paul saw his mission as the fulfilment of the divine plan for the salvation of the world. That plan had been focused in Jerusalem through many generations, going back to the time of King David (1 Chron. 11.5). In short, Jerusalem was the chosen city of God's revelation and salvation, where prophets had preached and priests had sacrificed and kings had ruled. Third Isaiah especially had announced the good news about the ingathering of the nations with their offerings to Jerusalem in the coming day of salvation (see Isa. 60.3-5; 66.18-20). The collection for Jerusalem was symbolic of the ingathering of the Gentiles to the historic city of God's salvation. When Paul later wrote Romans, he was ready to go there with the collection from the Gentiles, which he considered 'the priestly service of the gospel of God' (Rom. 15.16-31).

iii. In defence of apostleship (2 Cor. 10–13)

We come now to the second main part of the canonical 2 Corinthians, chapters 10–13. If the first nine chapters could be called a letter of reconciliation, then these last four chapters should be labelled a '*letter of defence*'. In it Paul has to defend his apostolic status. Some missionary interlopers, whose identity is embedded in his super-charged rhetoric, had preached in the Corinthian congregations and had called his apostolic ministry into question. News of that opposition was the occasion of this 'letter of defence'. He quotes his opponents thus: 'For they say, "His letters are weighty and strong, but his bodily presence is weak, and his speech contemptible"' (10.10).

These *opposing missionaries* call themselves ministers of Christ, with full credentials (11.22-23). Paul casts them as ministers of Satan (11.14-15). They claim to be first-class apostles of Christ. He calls them ironically 'super-apostles', and also plainly 'false apostles' (11.13). What makes them false is their boastful self-praise, and that over against the very apostle who brought the congregation into being in the first place.

To counter his opponents, and their influence among the Corinthians, Paul engages in a powerful reverse rhetoric called the Fool's Speech (11.1–12.11). The super-apostles claim to be wise and wonderful as ministers of Christ. They can speak boldly and persuasively. Their bodily presence is compelling in public oratory. Paul, by contrast, claims to be a fool in two senses: (1) he boasts as only a fool would boast to show up the folly of the opponents; (2) He speaks as a fool *to show his weakness* as a minister of Christ. In doing so he lines himself up with the cross of Christ (1 Cor. 1.18ff). But out of his physical, human weakness he qualifies as God's true minister. He alludes to his 'thorn in the flesh' as a sign of his weakness, having prayed for deliverance from his debilitating physical malady. But God did not heal him (12.7-8). Instead, he received from God *an oracle of divine grace* that carried him through his mission. The oracle is one of the most telling paradoxes in literature: 'My grace is sufficient for you, for power is made perfect in weakness' (12.9a). Then he expounds that paradox personally: 'So, I will boast all the more gladly of my weaknesses, so that the power of Christ may dwell in me. Therefore I am content with weaknesses, insults, hardships, persecutions and calamities for the sake of Christ; for whenever I am weak, then I am strong' (12.9b-10).

To end his letter of defence Paul tells his audience at Corinth about his plan to visit the community for a third time. This time he will not be lenient.

They want proof he speaks for Christ? He will give them proof (13.1-3). The letter closes with one of the most used benedictions in church liturgy to this day: 'The grace of the Lord Jesus Christ, the love of God, and the communion of the Holy Spirit be with all of you' (13.13).

d. Galatians

The letter to the Galatians is in some respects the harshest of all the letters. Only in this letter does Paul call his converts 'foolish' (3.1-3), and only here does he belittle ironically those who 'compel' circumcision for membership: 'I wish those who unsettle you would castrate themselves!' (5.12; cf. 2.3, 14; 6.12).

This is our cue to deal with the *occasion* for the letter. Some people had come to the region after Paul had left, and unsettled the Galatian believers in Jesus. Where they came from no one really knows. Their *orientation*, judging from the rhetoric in this letter, was toward Jerusalem where a conservative group of Jewish believers had expressed the need for circumcision (Acts 15.1, 5; Gal. 2.4). They were probably not Peter and friends, although Peter's behaviour at Antioch was not altogether unlike that of the interlopers at Galatia (2.11-14). Although the next alternative is unlikely, it is possible that the visitors in Galatia came from James of Jerusalem, who seemed to take a more conservative stance on matters Jewish (Gal. 2.12). Whoever they were, Paul judged their gospel to be 'another gospel', other than the gospel he had preached in Galatia earlier (1.6-7). Working out of the rhetorical language of Galatians, we can imagine the message the intruders preached in the congregations of Galatia. Here is a possible reproduction:

> You did well to accept Jesus as the Messiah of God. The God of Israel promised a Messiah to his people. Jesus was and is that Messiah. But even though you have come a long way to being accepted into the new people of God through your believing in Jesus as the Messiah, you need to go all the way to be fully included in the covenant that God gave to Abraham. That covenant required the mark of circumcision on the body. At this point you do not have that mark. Paul did not insist on it. But he should have. You should know that all of God's people to the present time have had that mark on their bodies. Jesus himself was circumcised. By submitting to circumcision you will then be identified not as Gentiles, but as the new people of God. God's Law has always required circumcision for full membership, and the Law of God endures forever.

Against a backdrop like this, Paul wrote this letter 'to the churches of Galatia' (1.2). His implied purpose was to forestall the Galatians from submitting to circumcision. He seems to know about some in the communities of Galatia who 'want to be justified by the law' (5.4). For him, that would be unacceptable, having ruled out the requirement of circumcision as a mark of membership in the community of Christ. If some Gentile believers were to submit to circumcision it would set a precedent for others, or create division in the community. The problem is that Paul appears to be in violation of the Law when he rules against circumcision as a covenantal mark of incorporation. He will argue that Christ has set people free from the *Mosaic Law* to live in relationship to Christ and so 'fulfill *the law of Christ*' (6.2).

The letter to the Galatians is the only one lacking a 'thanksgiving'. Perhaps the matter before Paul was so upsetting that he could not bring himself to praise God for the Galatians willing to listen to 'another gospel'. Here they are, paying heed to some interlopers who would persuade them to take on the marks of Judaism, particularly circumcision, in order to be saved. Whatever his motivation, it is strange to have a letter missing one of the formal parts, especially the 'thanksgiving'.

i. The call (Gal. 1.15–16)

Paul begins the letter by citing his call. It was like that of Jeremiah, prenatal and specific (cf. Jer. 1.5). Like Jeremiah, he was appointed to bring the good news to the 'nations' (*ethnè*, 'Gentiles'). He needed no endorsement from Jerusalem to sanction his mission, nor did he need to be instructed about the content of the gospel of Jesus the Christ. He respected the Jerusalem group of Christians, but he found no reason to submit to their authority with respect to his call and his gospel. Thus, his word should be accepted by the Galatians as a word from the Lord.

ii. Analogy from Antioch (Gal. 2.11-14)

Paul uses an incident at *Antioch as analogous* to the situation in Galatia. At Antioch Peter's action caused some Gentiles to take on the marks of Judaism (2.11-14). And he opposed Peter 'to his face, because he stood self-condemned'. In like manner, those who unsettle the Galatians stand condemned for their urging the Galatians to submit to circumcision.

iii. Thesis (Gal. 2.16)

Paul's thesis is stated in 2.16:

> We know that a person is justified not by the works of the law but through faith in Jesus Christ. And we have come to believe in Christ Jesus, so that we

> might be justified by faith in Christ, and not by doing the works of the law, because no one will be justified by the works of the law.

The thesis is essentially negative: *not by works of law*. And Paul will argue that case throughout the rest of the letter. His term translated '*justified*' (*dikaioō*) could convey a forensic notion of acquittal, as in being declared righteous in the name of Christ. As Paul uses the term in the passive form, however, it connotes 'being changed', i.e. 'being put right'. Thus, E. P. Sanders coined the word 'righteoused' to account for the sense of being transferred out of a state of Sin into a state of righteousness before God. Paul believed that a person 'in Christ' could not at the same time be under the power of Sin (Rom 3.9; 8.2).

iv. Making a case (Gal. 3.1–4.31)

To argue his case, Paul makes several appeals. First, he appeals to the *experience* of the Galatians in becoming Christian. They did not become believers in Jesus crucified and raised by doing the works of the Law (3.1-2). Second, he appeals to *the Spirit* versus the Law. Through the Spirit the Galatians were incorporated into Christ, not by doing the Law (3.3-5). Third, he appeals to *Abraham in Scripture* (3.6-10; cf. Gen. 15.6). Abraham 'believed God, and it was reckoned to him as righteousness'. On the basis of his faith Abraham was given the promise that in him 'all the Gentiles shall be blessed' (cf. Gen. 12.3). Based on these appeals, Paul argues that those who rely on the works of the Law are 'under a curse' (3.10).

No one is really sure what Paul has in mind for the 'curse'. Is it by doing the works of the Law, including circumcision? Is it by not being able to do the works of the Law perfectly? Is it by observing the demands of the Law and becoming proud and thus condemned? The line of argument is not clear on the matter. The point he will eventually make is that God's salvation does not come by keeping the law. 'For if a law had been given that could make alive, then righteousness would indeed come through the law' (3.21). This is what is called a contrary to fact conditional sentence. No such law had been given; therefore, righteousness and life do not come through the works of the Law. In Galatians 3, Paul comes dangerously close to declaring the Law itself a curse, but stops short of doing so (3.10-14).

Given his polemic against doing the works of the Law in order to be saved, Paul is pushed by his own rhetoric to ask and answer the question: 'Why then the law?' (3.19). His answers would scarcely be compelling to educated Jewish readers of the day. There are two points in particular:

1. The law was '*added because of transgressions*, until the offspring would come to whom the promise had been made; and it was ordained through angels by a mediator' (3.19-20). The offspring is Jesus whom God raised from the dead. There was a tradition in Judaism that angels attended the mediating of the Law to Moses. Paul uses the tradition against the supremacy of the Law, and in favour of the offspring. The Law was not bad; it was simply not intended to give life (3.21).

2. 'The Law was our disciplinarian (*paidagògos*) until Christ came, so that we might be justified by faith. But now that faith has come, we are no longer subject to a *disciplinarian*, for in Christ Jesus you are all children of God through faith' (3.24-25). The allusion here is to an educational practice related to school children. One person, perhaps a slave, would be designated to keep the pupil under control *until the real teacher came.* When the teacher arrived with the students the work of the disciplinarian was finished. If one were to take the analogy to its limit, it would imply that Paul believed the Mosaic Law had run its course and was no longer necessary for life in Christ. The faithfulness of Christ in giving life, and the faith of people in receiving this life matter most.

If Paul were to allow circumcision for some, it could divide the community. One group could think of themselves as superior to another, an intolerable state of affairs. We have seen a version of such division already in 1 Corinthians. The unity of the community of Christ matters much to Paul. There is no difference in Christ between a circumcised Judaean and an uncircumcised Gentile. One of the strongest affirmations of oneness in Christ comes at 3.28 of Galatians. 'There is no longer [Judaean] or Greek, there is no longer slave or free, there is no longer male and female; for all of you are one in Christ Jesus.' True enough, this is a soteriological disposition, a way of viewing the status of those who are being saved through Christ. But the sociological and communal implications of the equalizing thought in this language are inescapable. In the community and ministry of Christ, role assignments, like the status of righteousness and life in Christ, should exist on a level playing field.

Perhaps the weakest of the arguments against doing the works of the Law in order to be saved comes at 4.21-31. There Paul uses an *allegorical interpretation* of the story of Sarah and Hagar. The strange reversals in the allegory are hardly persuasive – ironic maybe, but not persuasive. The two women represent two covenants. Hagar was the slave wife of Abraham who bore a child of slavery. Hagar and her son were of the flesh. And she is from

Mount Sinai in Arabia, which corresponds to Jerusalem. Sarah is the free woman. She corresponds to the Jerusalem above. 'She is free, and she is our mother' (4.26). Paul is not given to this kind of allegorical interpretation in his letters. But here it stands as a closing argument in Galatians. The method was acceptable in the ancient world of Judaism, especially in Alexandria of Egypt. The Galatians may also have found it palatable.

v. Ethical advice (Gal. 5.1–6.18)

The arguments lead, as in all of the letters, to final ethical instructions about living in community and in the world in relation to the Christ and the Spirit. Part of ethical instruction of the time included a *catalogue of vices and virtues*. Paul follows that practice in his instruction to the Galatians:

> *Vice list*: Now the works of the flesh are obvious: fornication, impurity, licentiousness, idolatry, sorcery, enmities, strife, jealousy, anger, quarrels, dissensions, factions, envy, drunkenness, carousing, and things like these. (5.19-21)

> *Virtue list*: By contrast, the fruit of the Spirit is love, joy, peace, patience, kindness, generosity, faithfulness, gentleness, and self-control. There is no law against such things. (5.22-23)

The final word, before the benediction, sums up his argument intended to persuade the Galatians not to submit to circumcision. 'For neither circumcision nor uncircumcision is anything; but a new creation is everything!' (6.15). The marks on the body that matter are the marks of Jesus that Paul has branded on his person in mission (6.17).

EXCURSUS: Meetings in Jerusalem and Antioch (Gal. 1.18–2.14; Acts 15.1-35)

Among all of the letters, only Galatians offers anything like a sustained historical narrative of Paul's career as an apostle to the Gentiles. One of the most important turning points was the meeting in Jerusalem to determine whether, and with what conditions, believing Gentiles could be recognized as full members in 'the Israel of God' (Gal. 6.16). We saw the Acts 15 rendering of the proceedings of the meeting. Paul's own memory of the meeting recalls the details differently, coloured perhaps by the rhetoric characteristic of Galatians. His recitation of the events in Jerusalem has the effect of rendering the current incursion in the Galatian congregations detrimental to 'the truth of the gospel' (2.5).

From Paul's perspective about the meeting at Jerusalem, the ones called in secretly were there 'to spy on our freedom' (2.4). He labels them 'false brothers' (*pseudadelphoi*). Both the metaphor of spying and the label 'false brothers' are the rhetorical means of making the point that those who require the Galatians to adopt the marks of Judaism are of the same mind as the Judaeans of Jerusalem that Paul derides. They were out of step with 'the truth of the gospel'. But the parties thus characterized by Paul would hardly have seen themselves in the same light. They were Judaeans of Jerusalem, convinced in their minds that the covenant of Israel required the marks of inclusion set out in Israel's Law.

Peter, James and John seem to have represented a middle ground between the so-called 'false brothers' and Paul. Paul's recollection of the outcome of the meeting was that the word of the three 'pillars' in Jerusalem won the day for him. They asked only that he remember the poor in Jerusalem in his mission among Gentiles. The division of missionary labour that grew out of the meeting – Peter to the 'circumcised' and Paul to the 'uncircumcised' – could be seen as the thin edge of the wedge that ultimately separated the new Christian movement from its parent religion, Judaism. From a Jewish perspective other than Paul's, the Jewish brothers that participated in the meeting in Jerusalem to help chart the course for the inclusion of Gentile believers in Jesus could be viewed as true brothers within the Israel of God. They sought to preserve the Law and tradition that had guided their steps and guarded their faith from Exodus through Exile and Return.

The other meeting recounted in this part of the letter to the Galatians took place at Antioch in Syria. Peter, representing the middle ground, visited the community with Paul present (2.11-14). Paul remembers Peter eating with Gentiles until some people came from James of Jerusalem, at which point he withdrew strategically from the table 'for fear of the circumcision faction'. Did James belong to the circumcision faction? Were the 'false brothers' members of the circumcision faction? However one might answer these questions, one thing seems clear: James held a rather more conservative Jewish view than Paul did about membership in the community of Christ, the 'Israel of God'. And Peter was caught between the vision of James and that of Paul's more liberal 'truth of the Gospel' that declared believing Gentiles full members of the community of Christ without the traditional Jewish marks of inclusion. Peter's action, according to Paul, led even Barnabas, along with other Judaeans, to behave inconsistently concerning 'the truth of the gospel'. Paul opposed Peter for his vacillating behaviour at Antioch.

One thing is reasonably clear from the narration of the events in the two centres of missionary activity: Paul's Law-free mission to the Gentiles would be hard-pressed to keep theological ties with the Jerusalem Jewish group from which the gospel of Jesus emerged after Easter. History has proven the challenge too great to succeed in the long run, as Paul would doubtless have wished.

e. Philippians

The letter to the congregation at Philippi is both uplifting and disturbing at the same time. The *theme of joy* and rejoicing, giving thanks for the generosity and good will of the Philippians, runs through the letter from beginning to end (1.4, 25; 2.2, 17, 18, 28-29; 4.15-17). But at the same time, Paul is in prison, *suffering* for the sake of the gospel of Christ, and faced with rival missionaries who 'proclaim Christ out of selfish ambition, not sincerely but intending to increase my suffering in my imprisonment' (1.7, 13-17).

As with all of Paul's letters, Philippians was not written in a vacuum. The occasion for writing was the coming of a man named Epaphroditus with gifts from the Philippians. Paul was grateful for their love and financial support, and so writes back with thankfulness and joy. Of course, Epaphroditus brought a news report as well from the congregation at Philippi, most of it seemingly positive. After writing Philippians, Paul then dispatched Epaphroditus back to Philippi with the letter.

i. In a prison (Phil. 1.7-14; 4.22)

One of the debated issues arising out of Philippians has to do with *the place of the imprisonment* when Paul wrote this letter to the Philippians in Macedonia. The traditional position is that he was in prison in Rome when he wrote. Two clues are given in support of that view. First, Acts speaks of a 2-year imprisonment in Rome at the end of the north Mediterranean mission in which he was able to welcome people and tell them of Christ (Acts 28.30). Second, Philippians refers to the 'imperial guard' (1.13) and 'Caesar's household' (4.22).

However, several factors speak against this traditional view. Paul was imprisoned in a Roman-run jail more than once, and the imperial guard (viz. 'Caesar's household') was in all major centres of the empire. When Paul wrote Romans at the end of his mission in the north Mediterranean regions, before he went to Rome, he cites an imprisonment he already had (Rom. 16.7). Elsewhere he claims to have had 'far more imprisonments' than his opponents (2 Cor. 11.23). These latter also happened before he went to Rome.

But the compelling factor against Rome as the place of his prison-letter to Philippi is the ease with which he and his friends are said to travel back and forth from his place of writing to the city of Philippi. Rome in Italia was a long way from Philippi in Macedonia. Yet Epaphroditus came to Paul from Philippi, then Paul sent him back directly with the letter in response, and he hopes to send Timothy shortly thereafter. Furthermore, if Paul is released from prison, which he believes will happen soon (1.26; 2.24), he too will travel to Philippi to visit the congregation. If his place of imprisonment were in Rome when writing, then his plan would be to push forward to Spain, not to return to Macedonia (so Rom. 15.24, 28). Moreover, his place of writing Philippians was not Rome, but some city in the provinces north of the Mediterranean. Ephesus is a likely candidate, where Paul figuratively 'fought with wild animals' (1 Cor. 15.32; cf. Acts 19.24-41).

ii. Suffering with Christ (Phil. 1.29; 3.10)

Paul saw his imprisonment for preaching Christ as a way of participating in the sufferings of Christ. Christ had become his life in the present world, and his hope for life in the world to come. One of his most telling statements about this conviction comes through in Philippians. 'For to me, living is Christ and dying is gain' (1.21). It was not simply a matter of believing in Jesus as the Christ of God. That truly was important to his. But he argues in Philippians that believing with commitment will result in suffering for the cause. 'For [God] has graciously granted you the privilege not only of believing in Christ, but of suffering for him as well' (1.29). The suffering is not merely a matter of the lot that befalls all of humanity. It is a suffering related to giving oneself away for the higher good, the greater cause. The cause to which Paul was called and to which he committed the remainder of his life on earth was his relationship to Christ and the mission to bring the good news of Christ to the Gentiles.

Suffering went with the mission. In this respect Paul saw suffering as redemptive and life-giving in relation to Christ. *Knowing Christ* was uppermost. It was not merely intellectual, but relational and personal, ongoing and growing. Here is his own poignant statement to this effect: 'I want to know Christ and the power of his resurrection and the sharing of his sufferings by becoming like him in his death, if somehow I may attain the resurrection from the dead' (3.10). Knowing Christ relationally appears to be the source of Paul's joy in Philippians, not just a momentary joy at having received money from the Philippians. The relationship was also mind-changing. In 2 Corinthians he speaks of knowing Christ once 'according to the flesh', but now knowing him thus no longer (2 Cor. 5.16). His new way of knowing comes from the indwelling Spirit of the crucified Christ of God, the suffering servant who brings life and hope and new creation to the world of humankind.

iii. The mind of Christ (Phil. 2.1-11; 4.8)

If a major theme in Philippians is joy in Christ, then a second theme has to do with *the way a person in Christ thinks*. Paul will urge his audience at Philippi to 'let the same mind be in you as it is in Christ Jesus' (2.5). This injunction comes on the heels of instructing his readers not to regard their own interests merely, but the interests of others. They should not be vying for position in the community, but should act out of one mind. Conceit has to be ruled out to let love reign supreme. How one thinks, Paul implies, determines how they will act in relation to others. The mind of Christ is the mind that puts others above one's own self-interest. Hence the later advice *to think* on virtuous matters, and so *to live* that way. 'Whatever is true, whatever is honorable, whatever is just, whatever is pure, whatever is pleasing, whatever is commendable, if there is any excellence and if there is anything worthy of praise, think about these things' (4.8).

That which is honourable, just, pure, pleasing, and commendable goes beyond contemplative thinking to that which works itself out in the issues of life and death for good. 'Work out your own salvation with fear and trembling,' he tells his friends at Philippi, 'for it is God who is at work in you, enabling you both to will and to work for his good pleasure' (2.12-13). For Paul, the work is missional. To receive the message and the Spirit of Christ will bring newness of life (cf. Rom. 6.4), deliverance from sin, peace of mind, love in community, service without counting the cost.

But one cannot leave a discussion of this letter to the Philippians without focusing on the unique hymn in which the mind of Christ is poetically set forth (2.6-11). Ernst Lohmeyer (c.1930) detected the formal hymn-quality in the text, and scholars have since expanded on his thesis. One of the conclusions reached is that Paul drew the hymn from a source other than his own creative mind. He may have heard it in Antioch, that dynamic centre of Christian thought and life (cf. Acts 11.26). The vocabulary is unique, and

Table 10.1 Philippians Hymn Celebrating the Christ

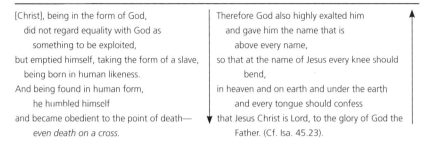

[Christ], being in the form of God, did not regard equality with God as something to be exploited, but emptied himself, taking the form of a slave, being born in human likeness. And being found in human form, he humbled himself and became obedient to the point of death— *even death on a cross.*	Therefore God also highly exalted him and gave him the name that is above every name, so that at the name of Jesus every knee should bend, in heaven and on earth and under the earth and every tongue should confess that Jesus Christ is Lord, to the glory of God the Father. (Cf. Isa. 45.23).

the *self-emptying* of the divine Christ is not stated elsewhere in the letters. Be that as it may, Paul was doubtless capable of writing poetry using words and ideas he had not written before. Either way, the hymn is rich in texture and design.

As Table 10.1 illustrates, the hymn has two parts. The first may be called the descent of the Christ of God, and the second the ascent. The claim implied in the hymn is that the Christ is pre-temporal, divine, and eternal, 'being in the form of God' (*en morphè theou huparchòn*). The self-emptying could be construed as self-limiting for purposes of revealing the salvific character of God. The last line, 'even death on the cross', on the descent side, may be Paul's addition to the hymn. The kind of death Jesus died was important to Paul's proclamation. It showed the utter humiliation of the Christ of God on behalf of humanity (see 1 Cor. 1.18ff.).

The place of the hymn in Philippians is not merely for the appreciation of its poetic quality. Paul inserted it poignantly where he urges his readers to 'regard *others* as better than yourselves' (2.3). It appears that the Philippians were not altogether free from human self-interest. Epaphroditus probably reported something of this. Two women of the community, Euodia and Syntyche, are cited in particular as disagreeing with each other. Paul urges them 'to be of the same mind in the Lord' (4.2). He grounds his ethical demand in theology, more particularly in Christology. The mind of Christ in the hymn was not a matter of systematic speculation, but for embodiment in human life and thought.

f. Philemon

The shortest of Paul's letters, Philemon has but one case to argue: the status of a runaway slave become Christian and his relationship to Paul and to his owner, Philemon. A careful reading of this short letter of 25 verses reveals Paul the rhetor at his best.

Slavery was a fact of life in the world of that time. People could end up as slaves through debt or as a result of a hostile takeover of native territory. After the destruction of the Temple of Jerusalem, for example, a number of Palestinian Judaeans ended up in slavery. In a number of Paul's letters slavery is a metaphor with both positive and negative connotations. People outside of Christ are said to be 'slaves of sin' (Rom. 6.20); in Christ they become 'slaves to righteousness for sanctification' (Rom. 6.19). Paul calls himself a 'slave of Jesus Christ' (Rom 1.1), insofar as the Spirit and love of Christ have taken over his life.

In the matter of the letter to Philemon and to the church that meets in his house, the issue of slavery is a socio-cultural one. With respect to that reality we discover *the occasion* for writing this short letter to the slave's owner. Paul met up with this runaway slave named Onesimus while in prison. Having listened to Paul speak of the grace of Jesus Christ, Onesimus believed in Jesus and began serving Paul. Following proper protocol, however, Paul sent the slave back to his Christian owner, Philemon, with this short letter.

One would think the purpose would be straightforward: Paul wants to do the right thing by sending Onesimus back to his owner with a plea not to punish this slave now become Christian. And that has been the traditional interpretation. But the *special pleading* in the argument seems to call for an alternate interpretation beyond compassion for Onesimus. In 1959 Professor John Knox developed another way of reading this little letter, partially reflected in what follows.

Slavery was a particular kind of *relationship* in Graeco-Roman society. Slaves were part of a household. Children of parents also belonged to the household, in that they were the offspring of their parents. But children become adults and, if they are free citizens, they can leave the household and forge other relationships. Slaves cannot do the same unless their householder grants their freedom. Relationship is the issue in the letter to Philemon: Paul's relationship to Philemon as a brother in Christ; Philemon's relationship to Onesimus as his legal owner; Paul's relationship to Onesimus as the one to bring him to faith in Jesus; Onesimus' relationship to Paul as disciple and free helper; Philemon's and Paul's relationship to the church that meets in Philemon's house. The question is, what is Paul aiming to achieve by playing out these relationships? I submit he is politely and persuasively asking Philemon to free his slave to be a helper to Paul, especially during his time in prison for the sake of the gospel.

The case is made in several ways. First, as a runaway slave, Onesimus (meaning 'useful') was useless to Philemon, but now as a believer he is useful (v. 11). Paul plays with the meaning of the slave's name. Second, he compares the two well-known household relationships, parent–child and master–slave. He then highlights his relationship with Onesimus as one of a father to his child (v. 10), and implicitly invites Philemon to compare his relationship to Onesimus with Paul's relationship to him. Third, while sending Onesimus back out of respect for Philemon's relationship to his slave, Paul says, 'I am sending . . . my own heart' (v. 12). Fourth, he accents his good relationship with Philemon as ground for keeping Onesimus as his helper in Philemon's place (v. 13). Yet he feels obligated to respect the law that says the slave belongs to Philemon and should be returned. Fifth, he compares the relationship of master to slave with brother to brother in Christ. Philemon and Paul are brothers in Christ; Onesimus and Paul are brothers; now Philemon and Onesimus are brothers (vv. 16-17). That relationship ranks higher in the household than master–slave. Thus, Philemon is asked to welcome Onesimus back as a brother, as he would welcome Paul.

One more relationship is at play in the rhetoric, that of debtor and creditor. Paul wonders if Onesimus had stolen anything from his master, and offers to have Philemon charge it to his account (vv. 18-19). But then he adds that Philemon owes him his new life in Christ, his 'own self' (v. 19).

In short, Paul asks Philemon for *the benefit* of Onesimus in his ministry, especially now when he is in prison. What else could 'this benefit' of verse 19 mean? The last persuasive point Paul makes is a promise to come to Philemon's household as soon as he is released from prison. 'Prepare a guest room for me,' he asks Philemon (v. 22). Imagine Paul arriving at Philemon's house and church and Philemon not having granted the benefit requested!

As an aside, the prison from which Paul hopes to be released was most likely not in Rome, and the letter therefore not written in the early sixties CE. Philemon apparently lived in the city of Colossae, according to the epistle to the Colossians. (See the names of Onesimus, Epaphras, and Archippus in 1.2, 24 and also in Col. 1.7, 4.9-12, 17. See also the discussion in chapter 9). In addition to the great distance from Rome to Colossae, Paul's intention to visit Philemon in the Lycus River Valley in Phrygia would contravene his plan to go to Spain from Rome. The prison was almost certainly somewhere closer to Colossae, and the time probably between 55 and 58 CE.

Slavery, which included slave trading, as a socio-political and socio-economic fact of the modern western world of the nineteenth century was a blight not easily wiped out. To their shame, proponents of the slave industry in the United States grounded their practice in Scripture texts such as Philemon. Like other socially acknowledged practices of New Testament times that ran their course in the history of civilization – from child sacrifice to crucifixion – slavery is one that should have vanished with the rest. Does Paul argue for the abolition of slavery in his letter to Philemon? Not quite. But I contend that he does plead for the freedom of one slave on the basis of good will, compassion, and the new household of faith in Jesus Christ. In Pauline thought, the only slavery that is in any way good is that of belonging to Christ, which paradoxically is true freedom (cf. 1 Cor. 7.21-22). On the strength of his conviction that Christ is God's agent for setting people free from bondage, Paul could hardly be a supporter of slavery in principle. Slavery may be according to the law of Rome, but it could not be according to the law of Christ (Gal. 6.2).

A tantalizing question has to do with the inclusion of this small letter, so personal and specific, in the collection of Paul's letters in the first place. Why was it important? To whom was it important? Above all, it would be encouraging to anyone valuing personal freedom. It would be especially meaningful to young Onesimus, the bearer of the letter. A likely scenario is that Onesimus treasured the letter and preserved it. Devoted to the great Apostle as he was, and freed to become a recognized leader among the churches, Onesimus may have been the collector of the other letters to which he added this short letter that earned for him the gift of freedom.

g. Romans

Paul's masterful letter to the church at Rome was prompted by his two-pronged plan at the end of his mission in the north Mediterranean: (1) to go to Jerusalem with the collection of money from the Gentile churches (15.19, 25-26, 31), and (2) to visit the church in Rome en route to Spain (15.24, 28).

The purpose of Romans is related to both of these plans, not just the second one. True enough, Paul wanted to make himself and his ministry known to the church at Rome, because he had had no part in founding the community in that city. No one knows exactly how the church in Rome came into being. Quite likely it formed as a result of the convergence of Christians from other parts of the world into the capital. Socio-political magnet that Rome was, people were drawn to it. If the members of the church were not known to Paul, or he to them, then this weighty letter surely would inform them of his thought and ministry. And if he hoped to receive financial support from them for his trip to Spain, then he should indeed make himself known to them (15.24).

But Paul's purpose in writing Romans doubtless arose as much out of his other plan to go to Jerusalem before proceeding to Spain via Rome. Going to Jerusalem was dangerous for Paul at that point. He had been busy for at least seven years incorporating believing Gentiles into the community of the Jewish Messiah without requiring the marks of Judaism for them. Ironically, he used the Jewish Scriptures in support of his action. From a traditional Jewish perspective, his action violated the norms of Judaism based on the Law. Hence the danger that would have awaited him in Jerusalem (see 15.31; cf. Acts 20.22-23; 21.4). He would have to give an account of himself and his mission before the highest court of the Judaeans in Jerusalem.

Paul surely would have known the charges being brought against him upon his arrival in Jerusalem. In response, he will have to present a case concerning his use of the Jewish Scripture in support of the incorporation of Gentile believers into covenant community, giving them the assurance of salvation that accrues from that. The interrelated subjects of Romans constitute the substance of his case. One could say, then, that the letter to the Romans is Paul's way of preparing his defence for the Jerusalem court. The implied question for him would almost certainly have been: Will this argument persuade the religious hierarchy in Jerusalem to recognize the validity of the mission to the Gentiles? The precarious connection between Paul's Gentile churches and traditional Judaism will hang in the balance for the future during his court appearance in Jerusalem. The offering of money from the Gentiles for the poor saints of Jerusalem may bolster his case, but will it be enough to win the day for him and his mission? With the benefit of history on our side, we can give an answer: Judaism and Christianity parted company not many years after Paul's death.

Before approaching the literary structure of the letter, a word about the composition of the congregation(s) in Rome would be useful. Paul seems to know that the membership is made up largely of Gentile believers. He addresses them as such in the salutation (1.5) and thanksgiving (1.13). In addition, he cautions the members of the church at Rome not to think of themselves as independent of the Jewish people through whom God's

Messiah came. Figuratively, he calls the members wild olive shoots grafted into a cultured root. He cautions them not to boast over the other branches broken off the olive tree because of unbelief (11.17-20). There can be little doubt that a significant number were Gentiles.

The structure of Romans is fairly straightforward. In the first seven chapters Paul argues mainly for the universality of the Sin-plight of humanity, with a strong hint of the solution woven into the texture of his arguments. Chapter 8 then focuses on the solution, the state of having been delivered from the tyranny of Sin by the grace of God in the Son, Jesus Christ, whom God raised from the dead. Chapters 9 to 11 take up one pressing issue: What will become of the Jewish people who do not believe in Jesus as God's Messiah for the salvation of the world? In those three chapters Paul identifies completely with his Jewish compatriots, longing for their participation in what he believes to be the fulfilment of the plan of God for the ages. The remaining chapters (12–16) deal with practical matters pertaining to community life in relation to Christ, with chapter 16 devoted entirely to personal greetings and benediction.

i. Theme statement (Rom. 1.16-17)

Within the constraints of this chapter the investigation has to be limited to highlighting salient points in each of the parts of the letter outlined in the previous paragraph. Following the lengthy and complex opening to his letter (1.1-15), Paul states his thesis in a nutshell:

> For I am not ashamed of the gospel; it is the power of God for salvation to everyone who has faith, to the [Judaean] first and also to the Greek. For in it the righteousness of God is revealed through faith for faith; as it is written, 'The one who is righteous by faith will live.' (1.16-17)

The quotation at the end of verse 17 is from Habakkuk 2.4 – the NRSV translation at v. 17 being modified slightly in keeping with Paul's thought in his argument. In the LXX from which he quotes the text reads, 'the righteous one will live by my faith/faithfulness' (*ho de dikaios ek pisteòs mou zèseta*). In Habakkuk the Lord is the speaker. The point there is the faithfulness of God toward the righteous person. In Paul's rendering, however, the 'my' is omitted. For his thesis, he highlights how a person becomes righteous before God. His answer in his argument will be as it was in Galatians, by *faith apart from works of Law*. But he does not at the same time abandon the Habakkuk angle of the faithfulness of God, acted out in Jesus Christ who brings people of faith into a right relationship with God. The two operate together: the faithfulness of Christ in doing the will of God on behalf of humankind, and the faith principle in the heart of the human person whom God transfers into Christ by the power of the Spirit.

One of the main planks in the thesis statement applies the gospel to 'everyone who has faith'. If the plight is universal, then the principle by which everyone is delivered is universal as well, taking in the two main cultural groups: Judaeans and Greeks. After the two cultural groups had been clashing for centuries, Paul, in so many words, announced a breakthrough that will bring an end to the hostility between them. As far as the end-time salvation of humanity is concerned, the Judaean has priority over the Greek. Paul believed that God elected Israel in the first place to bring the good news to the other nations of the world (2.19; 10.15; cf. Isa. 52.7). So also in Paul's time. The Messiah in Jesus came first to the Judaeans, and thence to the rest of the world. Yet the priority inflection in his phrase – Judaean first – is more theological than chronological, more vertical than horizontal. The plan of God for the world comes through Israel represented in the Judaeans.

One wonders why Paul would mention the possibility of being ashamed of the gospel. Perhaps because at the heart of his gospel is a crucified Messiah. Proclaiming a crucified Messiah in Rome could sound rather absurd. The only ones the Roman jurisprudence system crucified were criminals. Rome used that barbaric method of execution as the ultimate punishment for criminals tried in their courts. He could be ashamed of a gospel that proclaims a crucified person as saviour of the world. But he is not ashamed, because the God who saves humanity uses the most abhorrent thing in humanity to bring about a new creation in which such abhorrent practices are brought to an end. Thus he can say, in the gospel he preaches the righteousness/justice of God is revealed, as compared to the justice of Rome that imposes the despicable penalty of crucifixion on sentenced criminals, some of whom, like Jesus, could be innocent.

One phrase in the thesis statement is somewhat puzzling. The righteousness of God is revealed 'through faith for faith'. Literally, 'out of faith into faith' (*ek pisteòs eis pistin*). Perhaps Paul has in mind the principle of faith that leads to salvation and then the life of faithfulness that results. The Greek word for faith (*pistis*) can mean trustworthiness or faithfulness. The person transferred into Christ by faith should thereafter be faithful to the new life in Christ.

ii. Indictment (Rom. 1–2)

The section in 1.18 to 2.29 indicts the whole human family as *transgressors* of God's Law. As mentioned above, Paul views humanity as consisting of two main cultural groups, Judaeans and Gentiles. Chapter 1.18-31 catalogues the sins of Gentiles, the most abhorrent of which being idolatry: Gentiles have 'worshiped and served the creature rather than the Creator' (1.25). A Jewish person would recognize the Gentile sins immediately, and would applaud Paul for citing them and indicting those who commit them. But then chapter 2 proceeds to indict the Jewish people for their sins. 'While you preach against stealing, do you steal? You that forbid adultery, do you commit adultery? You that abhor idols, do you rob temples? You that boast in the law, do you dishonor God by breaking the law? For, as it is written, The name of God is blasphemed among the Gentiles because of you' (2.21-22).

As part of the indictment of Judaeans in chapter 2, Paul makes statements about the Law he would scarcely make in another context. Considering his thesis for the letter, his statement at 2.13 is out of character: 'For it is not the hearers of the law who are righteous in God's sight, but the doers of the law who will be justified.' Is it possible that Paul is drawing on a sermon he heard in a synagogue? Or maybe one he preached himself in his earlier pre-Christian life? Why on earth would he say that 'the doers of the law will be justified?' In the next chapter he reveals his deeply held conviction which is so unlike his statement at 2.13: 'For we hold that a person is justified by faith apart from works prescribed by the law' (3.28). Context may be the better way through this conundrum. In chapter 2 Paul addresses fellow Judaeans about the problem of transgressing the law while judging Gentiles for their sins. In doing so, he is led to say what he would say as a Judaean preacher to a Jewish congregation.

Particular statements, such as the one at 2.13, should not be taken out of the larger context of 1.18–2.29 in which Paul simply wants to demonstrate that both groups of the human family have their own way of breaking God's law. Both groups stand condemned, and in need of God's grace in Christ. The plight is one of *Sin-power*, and all are caught in the same universal web. That point comes through loudly and clearly in chapter 3: 'What then? Are we [Judaeans] any better off? No, not at all; for we have already charged that all, both [Judaeans] and Greeks, are under the power of sin' (3.9). Sin as 'power' in the universe means human beings cannot struggle free by any means. They may repent, but repentance alone does not deliver them. Repentance, prominent in Judaism, is rare in Paul (Rom. 2.4; 2 Cor. 7.9-10).

People 'are now justified by [God's] grace as a gift, through the redemption that is in Christ Jesus' (3.24).

iii. Abraham (Rom. 4)

Enter Abraham as proof that God makes the ungodly righteous through the principle of faith apart from works of the law. As in Galatians so here, Paul uses one text from the Abraham story as proof: 'Abraham believed God, and it was reckoned to him as righteousness' (4.3). But unlike his use of Abraham in Galatians, in Romans he admits that Abraham was indeed circumcised. Paul is, after all, preparing his case for Jerusalem. His Jewish judges are bound to cite Abraham's circumcision. But he appeals to the time when Abraham was reckoned righteous: 'Was it before or after he had been circumcised? It was not after, but before he was circumcised' (4.10). Paul's argument from chronology is appealing, but may not persuade a higher court in Jerusalem.

iv. Adam (Rom. 5)

Enter Adam of Genesis. Adam serves as the progenitor of the whole human family, Judaean and Gentle alike. Again, Adam's function in the overall argument is to declare both Judaean and Gentile under the power of Sin. But the argument in 5.12-21 is in the form of *typological reversal*. The trespass of the one man Adam at the head of the human family led to condemnation for all. But there was another man, Jesus Christ, who stands at the head of the new human family. His act of righteousness has led to justification and life for all. He reversed the Sin/death state of Adam's family. While the two 'alls' may appear to refer to the same people, Paul probably does not have that in mind. Rather, just as the character of all the humans in the one man Adam is that of Sin, so the character of all the humans in the one man Christ is that of righteousness.

The question Paul wants to press is this: How does one become a member of the righteous family that belongs to Christ? The next two chapters, 6 and 7, demonstrate mainly how they do NOT become members of Christ: it is not by keeping the Law. Paul has already charged that all people in Adam are under the power of Sin. Such people do not simply decide to keep the Law, as though they were not under the tyranny of Sin and death. He uses the *imagery of slavery* repeatedly in chapter 6 to make this point. Human beings are 'slaves of sin' (6.20). The only solution as far as Paul is concerned is the operation of another power for good that frees the person from slavery to Sin to become a slave of righteousness before God (see 6.16-20). God provides the person and the power, namely Christ and the Spirit.

v. The Law vindicated (Rom. 7)

Chapter 7 of Romans is still about *the plight*, not the solution. Christians, especially those of Protestant persuasion, have taken chapter 7 to be Paul's description of normative Christian experience. They point to his personal frustration, so-called: 'I do not understand my own actions. For I do not do what I want, but I do the very thing I hate' (7.15). Rather, Paul's 'I' (*ego*) – repeated some 21 times – is a rhetorical 'I' that stands in for all human egos in Adam. The whole text of Romans 7.7-25 accomplishes two goals: (1) it illustrates further the charge made earlier that 'all are under the power of sin' and as such are not capable of becoming righteous on their own; (2) it exonerates the Law, which almost ended up on the side of Sin that enslaves (7.6). Paul does not want to say that the Law is part of the problem for humanity. 'If it had not been for the law, I would not have known sin . . . So the law is holy, and the commandment is holy and just and good' (7.7, 12). The Law reveals Sin for what it is, but the Law does not deliver the transgressor from Sin, nor can the transgressor free her/himself. That in brief is the struggle depicted in Romans 7.7-25. It is the struggle of those related to the first Adam caught in the plight of Sin. The anguished *human Paul* cries out: 'Wretched man (*anthrōpos*) that I am! Who will rescue me from this body of death?' (7.24). The *rescued Christian Paul* answers: 'Thanks be to God through Jesus Christ our Lord!' (7.25).

vi. Solution (Rom. 8)

Enter Christ and the Spirit. Condemnation and death can be overcome, not by the Law of Moses, but by 'the law of the Spirit of life in Christ Jesus' (8.2). The solution in Christ has two sides to it, both of them described in chapter 8. First (1-17), the *present life* of persons in relation to Christ should not be lived 'according to the flesh but according to the Spirit' (8.4), because, he says, 'you are not in the flesh; you are in the Spirit, since the Spirit of God dwells in you' (8.9). The change happened by the grace of God through the principle of faith 'apart from works prescribed by law' (3.28b). Second, the present experience of the Spirit of Christ is the 'first fruits' of the new creation about to be revealed (8.18-39). New creation will be altogether good, and all things now at work in the world are working out towards that greater good 'for those who love God, who are called according to his purpose' (8.28). In short, Paul's eschatology is captured in chapter 8 as nowhere else.

The new creation has begun already in the action of Jesus as the redeeming Christ of God. The Spirit bears witness to that reality in the present experience (8.16). Then the new creation will come into full flower in *the future*. Meanwhile, those in Christ through the power of the Spirit can rest assured that nothing in all the world will separate them from the love of Christ (8.33-39).

vii. Israel and the Gentiles (Rom. 9–11)

Chapters 9 to 11 take up the case of the success of the Gentile mission in contrast to the resistance of the majority of Jewish people to the message of Jesus as the Christ of God who rescues both Judaeans and Gentiles from the power of Sin. Paul grieves over *the resistance* of his fellow Judaeans. In his words, 'I could wish that I myself were accursed and cut off from Christ for the sake of my own people, my kindred according to the flesh' (9.3). With all their advantages, their rejection of the gospel of Jesus is a mystery to the Jewish Paul. The whole texture of the three chapters deserves much more discussion than this space allows. (See further in Nanos 1996, pp. 16–26; 239–288). One part of chapter 11 should come into focus, however. Paul describes *the mystery* for his audience (and for himself!): 'a hardening has come upon part of Israel, until the full number of the Gentiles has come in. And so all Israel will be saved' (11.25b-26a).

'The full number of the Gentiles' remains a mysterious turn of phrase for the most part. At any rate, the success of the mission to the Gentiles, according to the structure of the text, will result in the gathering of 'all Israel' into relationship to Messiah, Jesus. Paul has only one plan of salvation for all, not a separate plan for 'all Israel'. That term, 'all Israel', is just as puzzling as 'the full number of the Gentiles'. 'All Israel' probably does not mean every Jewish person in the world, any more than the 'full number of the Gentiles' means every non-Jewish person. Something of *remnant theology* seems to be at work here. A representative number of Jewish people have already accepted the gospel of Jesus as the Messiah, with more to follow. Eventually a believing remnant from both cultural groups, Judaeans and Gentiles, will constitute the Israel that God had planned all along. Perhaps 'all Israel' is Paul's inclusive term used theologically rather than ethnically or historically. This much is clear from the text: he will not set aside historic Israel represented in Judaism from his mission to the Gentiles. Addressing Gentile believers specifically, he says of Judaeans, 'As regards the gospel they are enemies of God for your sake; but as regards election they are beloved, for the sake of their ancestors; for the gifts and the calling of God are irrevocable' (11.28-29). From this we may conclude that Paul does not envision an eschatological Israel apart from the incorporation of historic Israel *along with Gentiles* into the new community of Christ. The two together will make up Israel as a whole, the 'Israel of God' (Gal. 6.16).

viii. *Ethical and communal implications (Rom. 12–15)*

Chapters 12 to 15 hammer out the implications of Paul's thesis and conclusions for the community of faith in Jesus Christ on its way to salvation. Every member of the community of Christ should consider themselves already transferred into Christ, and in that state continue to be transformed by the renewing of [their] minds. This ongoing renewal of mind is spiritual worship; this is 'the good and acceptable and perfect' will of God (12.1-2). But the instruction is communal, not individualistic. The rest of chapter 12 assumes *community*, and describes how the particular community of Christ should be. The words echo those of 1 Corinthians 12: 'For as in one body we have many members, and not all the members have the same function, so we, who are many, are one body in Christ, and individually we are members one of another' (12.4-5).

Beyond Paul's high regard for community life in relation to the Christ, he is not unaware of the *world politics* in which he with others are forced to live in the present time. How are the new communities supposed to live out their faith responsibly in an imperialist situation? Romans 13 points the way to an appropriate response to the Roman powers that ran the world of the day. In some respects Paul seems a bit naive with regard to the governing authorities of his time. He seems to think that good conduct will win the approval of the rulers. In principle one would expect that to be so, of course. 'For rulers are not a terror to good conduct, but to bad. Do you wish to have no fear of the authority? Then do what is good, and you will receive its approval' (13.3).

But surely he recalls the Roman punishment and imprisonment he received for his 'good' preaching of Jesus as Messiah! (2 Cor. 11.25; Acts 16.22-23). Surely he knows that it was Roman authority that crucified Jesus! And it will be that power under the rule of Emperor Nero that will bring about his own death. How can he say, then, 'do what is good, and you will receive its approval?' It is, of course, possible that Paul is writing tongue in cheek: saying implicitly to those living in the immediate environs of the greatest political authority in the world, '*God's* good political/judicial authority will not judge you harshly when you do right.' Conversely, he may be implying: 'If you, while doing your good Christian duty in society, are called before judges and punished for doing wrong when you are not, then that power is in violation of its God-ordained responsibility to society.' Divinely ordained rule in society is for good and not evil. If a particular configuration of political power punishes people for doing the good, then that power has become corrupt and as such is not from God, for God is good.

It should be noted further that Paul almost certainly wrote Romans in the early years of Nero's reign. In those years Nero had not yet become the tyrant emperor with which his name later became synonymous.

Paul knew he was writing to people living in Rome. He could put their lives in jeopardy by making a political statement. His *political rhetoric* in chapter 13 guards against inciting his readers to insurrection, while he paves the way for his own proposed visit to the city. If word got out that he criticized the Roman government, it would not sit well for him when he arrived on the scene. In this regard Paul advises his Christian readers to pay their taxes as part of their duty within Roman occupied society (13.6-8). Otherwise they will incur the punishment of the state. Christians are to owe no one anything, 'except to love one another; for the one who loves another has fulfilled the law. The commandments . . . are summed up in this word, "Love your neighbor as yourself." ' (13.8-9). In the context of Romans 13, the neighbour is as much the Roman ruler who will sentence him to death, as the Roman Pilate who sentenced Jesus to death. The politics of Paul, like those of his Lord, is a politics of unfettered love.

Paul's *ethical instructions* continue in chapter 14. The subject matter of the whole chapter (1–23) is two-fold: which *foods* to eat and not to eat, and which *days* to observe as holy. The first of these occupies the most space on the page. The problem arises when one member passes judgment on another over an issue such as food. Which is more important, the kind of food a fellow member eats or the life and faith of the member? A *judging attitude* over such things injures the other, and threatens the very foundation of the community of Christ, whose law is to 'love your neighbour as yourself' (13.9b).

> Let us then pursue what makes for peace and for mutual upbuilding. Do not, for the sake of food, destroy the work of God. Everything is indeed clean, but it is wrong for you to make others fall by what you eat; it is good not to eat meat or drink wine or do anything that makes your brother or sister stumble. (14.19-21)

Recall Paul's liberal application of the so-called 'apostolic decree' of Acts 15.20. As in Galatians 2 and 1 Corinthians 8 and 10, so here he either disregards the decision of James, or he remembers the particulars of the decree differently from the rendering in Acts 15.

ix. All those acquaintances (Rom. 16)

The *final greetings* in Romans 16 raise a number of interesting questions. Observe, first, the commendation of the bearer of the letter, a woman named Phoebe (16.1-2). She had become a minister (*diakonos*) of the church in the port city of Cenchreae, near Corinth, and now she is about to leave for Rome. She seems to have been a woman of means, 'a benefactor of many and of [Paul] as well' (v. 2). As for the greetings, there are some 26 persons named by my count, a significant number of them women. How could Paul have known personally so many people in Rome? Some scholars believe chapter 16 to be a fragment from a different letter to somewhere else, perhaps Ephesus. A scribe later added these greetings to Romans, which may not have had any greetings originally. In support of this theory also is the appearance of a benediction at the end of chapter 15 (v. 33), as though the original letter ended there.

What are *Prisca and Aquila* doing in Rome? They are said to be hosting a church in their house there. The last time we met them was in 1 Corinthians 16.19. There too they are said to be hosting a congregation in their house. But their house was probably in Ephesus where Paul wrote 1 Corinthians (cf. Acts 18.2-26). It is possible, of course, that between the time of writing 1 Corinthians, and later Romans, Aquila and Prisca had returned to Rome and had set up a house church there (16.5).

Another husband and wife couple, *Andronicus and Junia*, are greeted at verse 7 as 'prominent among the apostles'. In almost all English translations prior to the NRSV the second name was spelled 'Junias', which makes the person a male. The translators were relying on manuscripts that had the masculine ending. However, with the discovery of the much earlier Chester Beatty texts of Paul's letters the feminine spelling came to the fore. The question is, Why would the later copyists be inclined to change the feminine ending to masculine? Motives are never easy to determine. A few educated guesses might be: (1) that the church by the time of the later copying had become more *male-dominant* in its leadership, (2) that *the idea* of 'apostles' was associated with the twelve men Jesus commissioned, and/or (3) that by the time of copying, *the term* 'apostles' was believed to mean men exclusively.

Used as it is in Romans 16.7, however, 'apostles' were missionaries, persons sent out with a message for others. On the strength of the evidence from the earliest available manuscripts, Andronicus and Junia were a man and woman team in the same sense that Aquila and Prisca were.

In the final greetings of chapter 16, the writer of the letter, Tertius, sends his greeting as well. As such Tertius was an *amanuensis*, someone trained to take dictation. It was not that Paul could not write, but the custom of using an amanuensis freed up the author to think and speak constructively. It is possible also that Paul's vision was impaired, thus affecting his legibility (cf. Gal. 4.15).

3. Conclusion: Paul's thought extrapolated

Paul's thought in his letters appears to be complex because of his arguments. Elements within arguments should not be taken by themselves as belonging to Paul's prevailing thought. For example, did Paul believe and practice baptism on behalf of the dead who were not baptized? Probably not. Yet the practice among some at Corinth becomes a point in his argument about the resurrection of the dead (1 Cor. 15.29). He may or may not have approved of the belief and practice of baptism for the dead. In 1 Corinthians 15 he seems to allow it at Corinth without criticism. His use of the practice in his argument does not mean he holds the belief that the living baptized believers should be baptized on behalf of the unbaptized dead. Readers of his letters should distinguish between his thought that undergirds his arguments, and the rhetorical texture of the arguments. Having said that, it is time to lay out what may be construed as principal lines of Paul's prevailing thought woven into the texture of his arguments.

1. Paul believed he was living at the turn of the ages. 'The fullness of time had come' at which point 'God sent his Son, born of a woman, born under the law, in order to redeem those who were under the law, so that we might receive adoption as children' (Gal. 4.4-5). The *old age* had run its course, and the new had already begun to dawn with the resurrection of Jesus by the power of God. He believed that he and his converts were living at the end of the old and the beginning of the *new age*. They were the people 'on whom the ends of the ages have come' (1 Cor. 10.11), with the final wind-up just around the corner: 'The appointed time has grown short' (1 Cor. 7.29).

2. Along the same line, Paul believed that the age to come had *already* begun to break through to those who had put their faith in Jesus Christ. Their knowledge of the revelation of God in the person of Jesus Christ opened the door to the future. But Paul holds some matters *in reserve* until the final outcome, 'for the Lord himself, with a cry of command, with the archangel's call and with the sound of God's trumpet, will descend from heaven, and the dead in Christ will rise first,' and the ones still alive at the time 'will all be changed, in a moment, in the twinkling of an eye, at the last trumpet' (1 Thess. 4.16; 1 Cor. 15.51-52).

3. What brought about the turn of ages was the *Christ-event*. Central to that event was the death of Jesus by crucifixion, which God then used to bring about a new creation out of the old (2 Cor. 5.17; Gal. 5.16). This same Jesus, humiliated to the uttermost by human hands, God raised from the dead. Resurrection language is end-time language. The resurrection of Jesus became the 'first fruits' of the final harvest when all who had died in Christ would be raised with a new spiritual body like that of the resurrected Jesus (1 Cor. 15.20, 23).

4. In the meantime, the congregations in waiting have the Spirit of the resurrected Jesus Christ, which is the Spirit of the age to come. For believers living in the present, the Spirit is the '*first instalment*' of resurrection life to come, the '*guarantee*' that they will participate in the new creation with Christ at its head (2 Cor. 1.22; 5.5). Again, the image of 'first fruits' of the harvest applies to the experience of the Spirit in the life of the community of believers in Christ: they have 'the first fruits of the Spirit' while they 'wait for adoption, the redemption of [their] bodies' (Rom. 8.23).

5. As noted repeatedly, Paul thought in *communal categories*. The individual believer mattered, of course, but there was no such thing as a solitary believer in Christ. Christ has a body in the world, and that body is not that of an individual merely, but of a cohesive group. It is the body of members one of another, each of them bearing the same testimony to the grace of God in the faithfulness of Jesus Christ, and each having gifts suited to the member. But the members together are the body of Christ (Rom. 12.4-5; 1 Cor. 12.12-27). When one member behaves out of character with the will of God in Christ, that member is expelled from the community, as in the case of the immoral man at Corinth (1 Cor. 5.1-13). In keeping with his strong belief in the community of Christ, Paul deplores factions in the church (1 Cor. 1.11–3.23). Above all, the community of Christ is made up of

Judaean and Gentile, slave and free, male and female, all of them serving with *equal honour* according to their gifts and abilities (Gal. 3.28; cf. Phlm. 4-25; Rom. 16.1-23).

6. How one becomes a member of the new community of Christ was an issue that brought Paul into serious tension with his Jewish counterparts. The question was for him, *How does one become righteous before God* and thus qualify for membership in the community of those on their way to final salvation? His answer came in connection with his epiphany of Christ and his call to gather in Gentiles. Within Jewish thought, the acceptance of Gentiles into full membership in the synagogue meant repentance of transgressions of the Law, a promise to obey the Law, including the external signs of election: circumcision, Sabbath observance and kosher observance. Paul probably soon noticed a resistance of adult Gentiles to taking on these marks, especially the circumcision of adult males. His new experience of Christ as God's unique revelation enabled him to come to the conclusion that righteousness before God came not through the external marks of Judaism, but through faith in the saving grace of Jesus Christ, *apart from works of the Law.*

7. Out of his experience of Christ crucified and resurrected and his corresponding call to gather in the Gentiles came his *revised view of the Law*, revised from his earlier view prior to his encounter with the Christ. He says so many things about the Law in his letters that it is difficult to find the measure of his coherent thought on the matter. He continued to regard the Law as 'holy, and the commandment . . . holy and just and good' (Rom. 7.12), but not the means by which one becomes righteous in the presence of Christ crucified and resurrected. Only the faithfulness of Christ can give life to those caught in the plight of Sin and death. The Law of Moses 'came in alongside' the transgressions already being committed 'with the result that the trespass multiplied; but where sin increased, grace abounded all the more' (Rom. 5.20). In short, the Law does not give life. The life-giving grace of Jesus Christ makes one righteous before God. 'For if a law had been given that could make alive, then righteousness would indeed come through the law' (Gal. 3.21). But no such law exists, for Paul. In some sense, he believed the Law had run its course, like the guardian of school children awaiting the teacher. When the teacher comes the guardian is no longer required. Paul will even go so far as to say '*Christ is the end of the law* so that there may be righteousness for everyone who believes' (Rom. 10.4). 'End' could mean temporal end or purposeful end. Either way, Christ has taken over the role

of the Law while giving life and love and hope to all who put their faith in him. 'For God has done what the law, weakened by the flesh, could not do: by sending his own Son in the likeness of sinful flesh, and to deal with sin, he condemned sin in the flesh, *so that the just requirement of the law might be fulfilled in us,* who walk not according to the flesh but according to the Spirit' (Rom. 8.3-4).

8. Paul did not believe that God had abandoned historic Israel represented in *the Jewish people* of his day (Rom. 11.1). Somewhere in the mystery of the single plan of God for the ages, Israel would be included in the *final salvation* along with believing Gentiles. 'For the gifts and the calling of God' with respect to historic Israel 'are irrevocable' (Rom. 11.29). God had promised Abraham to make him 'the ancestor of a multitude of nations' (Gen. 17.2-5). He believed the covenantal promise to Abraham was being fulfilled in his Gentile world mission. Without the inclusion of the Jewish people along with believing Gentiles in the new community of Christ, however, God's promise to Abraham would become empty. 'And so all Israel will be saved; as it is written, "Out of Zion will come the Deliverer; he will banish ungodliness from Jacob"' (Rom. 11.26).

These eight points are far from final. Paul's thought within the texture of his letters will continue to generate debate, insight, and multiple publications. These eight points are offered as prompters towards further investigation and clarification.

Further related reading

I wholeheartedly recommend a serious reading of Stephen Westerholm's (2004) updated (1988) work on Paul, in which he traces a history of interpretation from Augustine through Luther, Calvin and Wesley to the present time. This is one of the most lucid and incisive books on Pauline thought, vis-à-vis the Lutheran Paul, *Perspectives Old and New on Paul: The 'Lutheran' Paul and His Critics*. Eerdmans.

A less challenging read, but a very useful one on Paul's thought and mission, is that of David G. Horrell, (2006). *An Introduction to the Study of Paul*. Second Edition. Continuum.

In light of the emphasis on 'context' in this present study, I applaud the way Jewish scholar, Mark Nanos (2002) situates Galatians in a fittingly intra-Jewish context for his reading of the text through the lens of 'Socratic irony', *The Irony of Galatians: Paul's Letter in First-Century Context*. Fortress.

I would be remiss if I did not suggest a reading of E. P. Sanders (my own valued mentor in the 1970s, and one who ignited the flame of the 'new perspective'). His little book (2001) on Paul in the Oxford Past Masters Series, *Paul: A Very Short Introduction*. Oxford University, would be a good start.

Consult also relevant commentaries as appropriate in the 'Letters of Paul' section of the Bibliography.

11 Pauline Thought in Transition: Other Letters under Paul's Name

Ancient literary convention in both formative Judaism and early Christianity found the practice of writing under the name of a past hero of faith acceptable, if not desirable. Numerous such works from the period prove the point, and have survived to this day. The crucial question for many believers today is whether such writings could have found their way into the Bible. For some modern people of faith such a practice would not square with their doctrine of Scripture, and would therefore be ruled out as a possibility, regardless of compelling evidence in favour. Faith and reason are said, by some, to cancel each other out, but that is a false dichotomy. Reason is as much a gift from God as the capacity to believe beyond reason. The two work together well. If one of the goals of reading the Scripture is to reach truth while fostering faith, then the approach to the reading of the texts should be open to making sound judgements from the data of the text before our eyes. I propose that we move together carefully and respectfully within the literary landscape of the remaining letters and epistles of the New Testament with a view to understanding their literary quality, social history and patent theology authentically and faithfully.

1. Mimèsis

One of the most difficult questions related to writing under the name of a deceased leader concerns motivation. Why would a believer – or group of believers – within a Christian community decide to write under the name of an important figure from the past? Why not simply write under their own name? The writers of such documents remain silent on the matter. We can only infer their motives from the texture of their writings.

It would be out of order to infer that their aim was to deceive. Similarly, they did not deliberately seek to defame the figure under whose name they wrote. If anything, the nameless writers – the actual authors – were humble in their undertaking. Rather than take up position on their own authority concerning this or that matter of thought and life, these 'behind-the-scenes' writers called up the more important authority to speak to the issue facing the community in their new time. Preachers, in their own way, do the same still. They will cite Jesus or Paul or John or Peter without actually using their exact words. Their own words – spoken in the voice of their source – speak more pointedly to the current issue. It is a kind of *imitation*: if Paul were here now dealing with this situation he would say this.

A telling example of a modern counterpart to the ancient practice of giving current voice to a past hero happened recently in a church service. It was the first Sunday of Advent. The sermon was on Mary, the mother of Jesus, as a model for Christian life. At one point in the service a young woman moved to the front and began to speak in Mary's name and voice. The speech *echoed* Luke's Mary, but went beyond the words of Mary in Luke. The new Mary spoke in terms of the present time and situation in life. The congregation delighted in hearing Mary's experience and words expanded into a new form. Luke's Mary was not lost altogether. But it was clear that the language and thought was that of Mary reconstituted in a twenty-first century voice and vernacular.

A number of times in his letters Paul calls upon his readers to be imitators of him. The Greek word is *mimètès-ai*, from which we derive the English 'mimic'. Imitation was part of ethical instruction. A teacher of morality at the time of Paul could not disseminate ethical philosophy without himself modelling in life what he taught in speech. Hence Paul says to his readers, 'Be imitators of me' (1 Cor. 11.1. See also 1 Cor. 4.6; Phil. 3.17; 1 Thess. 1.6; 2.14). In some respect, those who wrote under Paul's name were doing what he asked of them. They were imitating his practice of letter-writing for the purpose of bringing about appropriate thought and behaviour for their situation in life as he had done. The imitation was not, nor could it be, exact duplication of Paul's letters. As situations changed, so also the need for a Pauline word on target. For example, Paul wrote of an imminent end of the age with the return of the Christ. But Paul died. Years passed. The end did not come. The church had to find its place in the Roman world as an ongoing movement. Not surprisingly, eschatological statements about the end took on a different texture. Some parts still future in Paul – such as resurrection of believers – became more realized, while other parts became more apocalyptic. In short, the church in the world developed its theology beyond that of Paul, but in keeping with the tradition Paul set in motion. Letters written after his death, but under his name, seem to have been a valiant attempt to keep the Pauline teaching and tradition alive in the new situations facing the church in the world.

2. Beyond the seven letters of Paul

Of the six letters of questionable authenticity under Paul's name, two are somewhat less contested than the others. These are 2 Thessalonians and Colossians. To them we turn first.

a. 2 Thessalonians

Either Paul wrote 2 Thessalonians very soon after 1 Thessalonians, while the wording of the first letter was still fresh in his mind, or a later disciple wrote 2 Thessalonians using 1 Thessalonians as a template. The salutation is *virtually identical*, from the names of the three writers to the description of the recipients to the form of the greeting (1.1-3). The thanksgiving likewise is directly patterned after the thanksgiving in the first letter.

Unlike 1 Thessalonians, however, 2 Thessalonians seems to be aware of letters circulating under Paul's name that do not truly represent Paul's thought (2.2). For there to be such letters would be strange indeed, if Paul himself wrote the second letter on the heels of the first, while he was still alive and well. The closing likewise makes a *special plea* for the readers to recognize Paul's handwriting. 'I, Paul, write this greeting with my own hand. This is the mark in every letter of mine; it is the way I write' (3.17). The readers are encouraged to receive this new letter as Paul's word retold. And in many respects 2 Thessalonians adds nothing new to Paul's first letter to the Thessalonians.

But in one important respect 2 Thessalonians alters the eschatological thinking of 1 Thessalonians. Whereas 1 Thessalonians taught that the end of the age at the coming of Christ was imminent, like 'a thief in the night', this second letter has apocalyptic figures and portents appearing *before the end* comes. In this letter – and only in this letter – we meet 'the lawless one', 'the one destined for destruction', 'the one who now restrains'. The readers should not expect the coming of the Lord 'unless the rebellion comes first' (2.1-12). Beyond the twelve verses in which this apocalyptic imagery is set out, 2 Thessalonians stays close to the tone and texture of 1 Thessalonians.

What has changed from the time of 1 Thessalonians, it seems, is the situation in the Christian community. Some of the members have ceased from working for a living. Their idleness has led to the corrective measure that 2 Thessalonians calls for. Their motive for quitting their jobs seems to have arisen out of an understanding of the nearness of the end, which they could easily have picked up from 1 Thessalonians. In short, the aim of 2 Thessalonians is to issue a back-to-work order: 'Now we command you . . . to keep away from believers who are living in idleness . . .. Anyone unwilling to work should not eat' (3.6, 10). Underwriting this 'command' to work for a living, instead of being dependent on others, is the apocalyptic vision of signs before the coming of the Lord: the coming of the end is delayed. Beyond these two coordinates, (1) necessity of work while waiting for (2) apocalyptic signs, 2 Thessalonians has little theological development beyond the earlier letters. If this letter was written by someone after Paul's time, as the delay of the *parousia* (second coming of Christ) implies, the time of writing is almost impossible to fix. Inner clues are missing.

b. Colossians

The letter to the Christian community in the city of Colossae shows marked *development* of thought beyond the seven undisputed letters of Paul. If Paul wrote Colossians himself, then the change of thought must be attributed to him. In that case, some reckoning would have to be given to account for the nuanced Christology, ecclesiology, eschatology, and household ethics within a very short period, perhaps as little as two years. By comparison, the period during which the seven undisputed letters were written was about eight years. Throughout that time, with the diverse situations Paul faced in it, his major convictions about the Christ, the church, the resurrection of the dead at the coming of Christ remained dynamically consistent. The development of thought, vocabulary and style evident in Colossians has led many scholars to conclude that this letter post-dates Paul's mission in the decade of the fifties CE.

i. The Christ-hymn (Col. 1.15-20)

Among the points of development in Colossians, none is more pronounced than the Christology in the hymn of Colossians 1.15-20. Its lyric character can be detected in the following pattern:

Stanza I

15 [Christ] is the image of the invisible God,
    the firstborn of all creation;
16 for in him all things in heaven and on earth were created,
    things visible and invisible,
        whether thrones or dominions or rulers or powers—
        all things have been created through him and for him.
17 He himself is before all things, and in him all things hold together.

Stanza II

18 He is the head of the body, the church;
    he is the beginning, the firstborn from the dead,
        so that he might come to have first place in everything.
19 For in him all the fullness of God was pleased to dwell,
20   and through him God was pleased to reconcile to himself all things,
        whether on earth or in heaven,
    by making peace through the blood of his cross.

There appear to be two stanzas, the break coming between verses 17 and 18. Some similarity exists between this hymn and the one found in Philippians 2.6-11. Both poems picture Christ as having pre-temporal existence. Whereas the Philippians hymn pictures Christ 'in the form of God', the Colossians hymn describes Christ as 'the image of the invisible God, the firstborn of all creation' (1.15). But the cosmic scope of the Christ in the Colossians hymn is as vast as the infinite universe. Five times the phrase 'all things' occurs in the two stanzas. And 'all things' includes those structures that humans set up, 'thrones or dominions or rulers or powers' (v. 16). The Christ pre-dates all created things, and inhabits the created universe, sustaining it by his powerful presence.

It would be a mistake to equate the historical person of Jesus with the cosmic Christ who existed at the beginning of creation. The one from the beginning is represented in the historical person, Jesus, but the cosmic Christ of the hymn is completely unbounded by history or by individual human identity. The Christ of the hymn looks very much like the Wisdom figure in the Hebrew tradition, who was in the beginning with Father-God. (See Prov. 8.22-31). Whereas in 1 Corinthians 1.24 Paul calls 'Christ the power of God and the wisdom of God', in the Colossians hymn Christ is 'the image of the invisible God, the firstborn of all creation' (1.15).

Some scholars see an affinity between the Gnostic myth of creation and the Christ of the hymn, especially so in the phrase, 'in him all the fullness of God was pleased to dwell' (v. 19). Gnostics conceived of a sphere of 'fullness' (*plèròma*) wherein the abode of the divine secrets of creation lay. More likely, however, the Christ of the hymn is associated primarily with a Christ-Wisdom drawn from the Hebraic idea of Wisdom, and perhaps tinted with Gnostic terminology prevalent already in the latter part of the first century. Above all, the hymn is a powerful confession of the Christ as pre-eminent both in creation and redemption.

One of the most striking developments pertains to the imagery of Christ and the church. In the second stanza of the hymn, the church, reconciled to God by the 'blood of his cross', is pictured as a body belonging to Christ, the head. One might think the image is already boldly evident in the earlier Paul, yet not in exactly the same way. The specific metaphysic set forth in the hymn differs from the metaphor in the earlier letters. In 1 Corinthians 12.12-31 Paul addresses the church members as 'the body of Christ and individually members of it' (12.27). Similarly in Romans 12: 'we, who are many, are one body in Christ, and individually we are members one of another' (v. 5). By comparison, the church in the Colossians hymn is a 'body' distinguished from Christ, the head. The body imagery was probably drawn from Stoic philosophy in which the human community as a whole was pictured as a body, with all parts working in harmony. In the hymn, however, the body image is limited to the church under the rule of Christ.

Christ in the hymn is Lord of the church-body, the head to which the body responds, and from which the members receive divine direction for living. There may have been some discomfort at the time of Colossians with Paul's indistinguishable identification between Christ and the church. In Colossians the two are distinguished: Christ is Lord, or head, of the church in all its variety. The union is organic and dynamic.

ii. Realized eschatology (Col. 2–3)

There is also a shift in eschatological thinking in Colossians. Believers in Jesus Christ enter into relationship with Christ through baptism into the community of faith: 'When you were buried with him in baptism, *you were also raised with him* through faith in the power of God, who raised him from the dead' (Col. 2.12). One can hear in this text an echo of Romans 6.4: 'We have been buried with him by baptism into death, so that, just as Christ was raised from the dead by the glory of the Father, so we too might walk in newness of life.' Here in Romans, as elsewhere in the early letters, the resurrection of believers is reserved for a future time. The consequence of being united with Christ by baptism, says Paul in Romans, is a new way of living in the present time, but not resurrection-experience in the present time. In Colossians, on the other hand, there is no reservation in saying that believers baptized into Christ have been raised with Christ. In some respect, therefore, eschatology has already been realized. Chapter 3 continues the same theme: 'If you have been *raised with Christ*, seek the things that are above.. . . When Christ who is your life is revealed, then you also will be revealed with him in glory' (3.1, 4). *Revelation* of the *present* resurrected state is all that is reserved for the future, when Christ is 'revealed'. This realized eschatology is perhaps the most compelling evidence against genuine Pauline authorship of Colossians.

iii. The household code (Col. 3–4)

Another feature of Colossians not appearing in the early letters is the so-called 'household rules' in Colossians 3.18–4.1. Paul had ample opportunity to lay out in writing a structure of household rules for his newly formed churches, but he was not so inclined in his letters. In Colossians, however, the household structure is hierarchical, drawn, no doubt, from conventional thinking in the Graeco-Roman environment.

Husbands

Wives

Parents

Children

Masters

Slaves

Into this conventional household hierarchy, Colossians infuses the Christ-factor: the relationship between the persons in the household is to be 'fitting in the Lord' (3.18). The Lord had laid down his life for others, forgiving them, reconciling them to God, and loving them unconditionally. This character of Christ occupying the community should also occupy the

Christian household. With that Christian character operating in all members of the household, the hierarchical relationship remains. One cannot, in fairness to the texture of Colossians 3.18-4.1, interpret the hierarchy as 'mutual submission'. However much the modern phrase applies today, Colossians does not support it. Mutual respect based on Christian love is a possible interpretation, but the 'submission', or 'obedience', flows in a direction defined by the texture of the text: wives to husbands; children to parents; slaves to masters. The modern ideal of mutual submission/obedience would have run counter to the understanding of social order, which Colossians seems unwilling to abandon. What makes the social order of the household different in Colossians is the mind of Christ.

iv. Situation at the time of writing

Opponents of the tradition on which the church was founded are implied in the letter. They are characterized as teachers of deceitful philosophy, appealing to 'the elemental spirits of the universe, and not according to Christ' (2.8). The Christ-hymn serves to counter the opponents' claims. Readers are encouraged to content themselves with the reality of Christ occupying their lives: 'Christ in (or 'among') you, the hope of glory' (1.27).

The congregation at Colossae was almost certainly non-Jewish (2.13), founded perhaps by Epaphras initially (1.7-8; 2.1; 4.12). The letter is said to be written from prison (4.3), but the city name for the prison is not given. Most likely, the tradition of Paul's imprisonments informs the texture of this letter – as also Ephesians (cf. Phil. 1.12-14; Philemon 1, 13, 23). The date of composition cannot be determined precisely. Considerable time would have elapsed since Paul's mission in the region to allow for the rise of para-Christian 'philosophers' to challenge Pauline Christology and ecclesiology. Colossians proposes an alternate view of Christ and the church in keeping with Paul's thought, shaped in a way that will counter the opposing views. The time of writing would not have been earlier than the mid-sixties, and probably some 20 years later.

c. Ephesians

Inasmuch as 2 Thessalonians and Colossians are of doubtful Pauline authorship, Ephesians is almost certainly not from the hand of the historical Paul during his mission to the Gentiles. This does not diminish the magisterial quality of the letter. The complexity and grandeur of the language and thought of Ephesians bespeaks an author whose education and Pauline-Christian reflection are second to none in the New Testament. The Thanksgiving running from 1.3-14 is one sentence in Greek, with numerous relative clauses tying one sub-thought to the next, with ever increasing vistas about the workings of God to bring about the divine purpose for the salvation of the world.

Ephesians could be titled 'The teaching of Paul in all his letters for a new situation'. Numerous *theological and linguistic echoes* of the earlier Paul appear in Ephesians, but are deftly woven into the fabric of the letter: Paul's 'new creation' (2 Cor. 5.17; Gal. 6.15) becomes in Ephesians 'new humanity' (2.15); 'height and depth' related to the inseparable love of Christ (Rom. 8.39) becomes the 'breadth and length and height and depth' of the love of Christ that surpasses knowledge (Eph. 3.18). A catalogue of echoes and allusions would be too long to include here. Either Paul had the rare ability of retaining the patterns of speech he used in his various letters for later development in this one letter, or a disciple (or disciples) of Paul had access to a collection of letters ready for use in composing this summary letter. The latter is more probable than the former.

i. For all the faithful everywhere (Eph. 1.1)

Acknowledging the strong affinity of thought in Ephesians with the earlier thought and language of Paul in the seven letters, there is one significant difference (among others). Ephesians lacks the specificity so prominent in Paul's earlier letters. Originally Ephesians had no specific addressees or destination. The best manuscripts of this letter did not contain the phrase 'in Ephesus' at 1.1. Without this designation the text reads, 'to the saints who are faithful in Christ Jesus', making this a *general*, or *circular*, letter.

Along with this general address, Ephesians is missing personal greetings, so common in the genuine letters addressed to particular congregations known to Paul. Compounding the matter is the fact that Paul founded the church in the city of Ephesus, and had very close ties with the congregation(s) there (1 Cor. 15.32; 16.8; Acts 18.19–20.17). It would be passing strange for Paul to write to a congregation well known to him without a single mention of anyone in the congregation. Clearly, Ephesians was not intended for a specific church in a specific city. Nowhere in Ephesians does the word 'church' (*ekklesia*) refer to a local group. Always the word means the church universal, going even as far as the church cosmic (3.10). By contrast, Paul in the genuine letters uses 'church' exclusively as a local gathering of believers in Jesus as the Christ.

Table 11.1 Word for Word Parallel

Ephesians 6.21	Colossians 4.7
all things he will make known to you, Tychicus, the beloved brother and faithful minister in Lord	all things he will make known to you, Tychicus, the beloved brother and faithful minister . . . in Lord

ii. Between Colossians and Ephesians

Of all the points of affinity between Ephesians and the seven letters of Paul, none is more striking than the one between Ephesians and Colossians. Christology, ecclesiology and eschatology are a close match, all three of the categories significantly elaborated in Ephesians. The outline of the content is similar between the two, even to the placement of the 'household rules' in the ethical segment. If that were not enough, the vocabulary, grammar and syntax at one point are identical from Colossians to Ephesians. The likelihood of that happening in letters written independently of each other at different times to different congregations is very remote. The comparison in Table 11.1 is a literal rendering from Greek into English of the Greek word order in each case.

There can be little doubt that Colossians was the template for the more elaborate theologizing in Ephesians. It has been suggested that Ephesians was written as a capstone for a collection of Paul's letters that included Colossians.

iii. The sweep of Christian thought (Eph. 2–4)

Taking the letter of Ephesians on its own merit, the sweep of Christian thought and form of expression is breathtaking. Christ is truly cosmic, powerful, and 'seated . . . at [God's] right hand in the heavenly places, far above all rule and authority and power and dominion, and above every name that is named, not only in this age but also in the age to come' (2.20-21). The phrase 'heavenly places' is unique to Ephesians, occurring five times throughout the letter. Not only is Christ seated in 'heavenly places', but so also the church. Like Christ, the church has a cosmic dimension as well as being universal on earth. From its position with Christ in 'heavenly places' the church makes known 'the wisdom of God in its rich variety' to rulers and authorities who likewise exist in 'heavenly places' (3.10).

Yet the church remains still in the world, 'built upon the foundation of the apostles and [Christian] prophets, with Christ Jesus himself as the cornerstone' (2.20). This is clearly a major step forward from Paul's 'foundation' metaphor in 1 Corinthians 3.11. There Paul posits only one foundation and 'that foundation is Jesus Christ'. In Ephesians, Christ becomes 'the corner-stone' of the one church. Honouring the place of 'apostles and prophets' as the founding forebears of the universal church points to a time well beyond that of Paul. At another point in the letter the original group are called 'holy apostles and prophets', a term of reverence reflecting back. This writer in his time is not prepared to say, 'what they actually were makes no difference to me; God shows no partiality'(Gal. 2.6). That was Paul.

iv. One new order of humanity (Eph. 2.11-20; 4.1-17)

One of the outstanding passages in Ephesians reveals the mystery of God in Christ, namely the creating of *one new humanity* out of the two (2.11-20). The two are Jewish and non-Jewish people of the world. From the perspective of a Jewish person, the inhabited world consisted of those two cultures, clashing as they were for many years. The breakthrough as depicted in Ephesians is where Christ came and broke down the wall of hostility between the two groups, 'thus making peace' (2.15). This view of the church is remarkable to say the least. The targeted readers were Gentiles. But they are urged to consider themselves 'no longer strangers and aliens, but . . . citizens with the saints and also members of the household of God' (2.19).

The unity of the church is a principal theme in Ephesians. There is only one body of Christ, with Christ as its head, and only one Spirit, one Lord, one faith, one hope, one baptism, and one God and Father of all (4.4-5). This is so because there was only one humanity created by God, and only one to be saved in the end. And that new humanity, called the body of Christ, is saved already, according to Ephesians. Their being 'in Christ' means the members of the body 'grow up in every way into him who is the head, into Christ, from whom the whole body, joined and knit together by every liga-ment with which it is equipped, as each part is working properly, promotes the body's growth in building itself up in love' (4.16-17). (Speaking of com-plex sentences in Ephesians, this is a classic example!).

Eschatology in Ephesians is almost altogether *realized* and *spatial*. Christians are already seated with Christ in the heavenly places, whatever their place in the temporal social world might be. And whatever the age to come might hold, the church will still be what it is already in Christ Jesus. Members have had their trespasses forgiven; they have been made alive by the grace of Christ, 'raised . . . up with him and seated . . . with him in the heavenly places in Christ Jesus' (2.6). Resurrection is no longer future hope for the Christian, but a present reality, 'for by grace you have been saved through faith, and this is not your own doing; it is the gift of God – not the result of works, so that no one may boast even when we were dead through our trespasses' (2.8-9). In Ephesians Sin is not a tyrannical power from which human beings can be delivered by grace (cf. Rom. 3.9). Rather, individual *transgressions* of God's law are *forgiven* by the grace of Christ in Ephesians, and thus the forgiven believer in Christ stands 'saved'.

v. Ethics in Ephesians (Eph. 4.25–6.9)

Saved as it is, the church universal still requires ethical instruction. And Ephesians devotes a lengthy section of the letter to just such advice (4.25–6.9). All of it is summed up in one concise injunction: 'let all of us speak the truth to our neighbors, for we are members of one another' (4.25). Evidently the intended neighbour is a fellow member of the church. Truth really matters to the writer of Ephesians. Five times he draws attention to it (1.13; 4.15, 21, 25; 6.14). Once he qualifies it: 'speaking the truth in love' (4.15). Truth on its own can hurt a fellow member. When it is tempered with love it heals and frees.

Set at the end of the ethical advice is the 'household rules' (5.21–6.9), as we had them in Colossians. In Ephesians, however, the rules of order are elaborated significantly. Christ in relation to the church remains the centrepiece, the model for the way the household hierarchy is supposed to work.

The pericopè is introduced with a general statement in 5.21: 'Be subject to one another out of reverence for Christ'. From this statement especially, some modern interpreters, moved appropriately to promote an egalitarian attitude and practice, have coined the phrase 'mutual submission'. Mistakenly they have then applied the idea to the texture of the house rules that follow. It is possible that verse 21 was meant for members of the church universal, without specific reference to household at that point. That is, members of the church portrayed in the letter thus far should listen to one another in all matters of life and thought, and thus decide on the direction to take. Then comes verse 22 immediately, which leads directly out of the church setting into a household setting. When that happens, the notion of 'mutual submission' within the Christian household no longer fits the texture of the rest of the text, down to 6.9.

Another way of reading verse 21 could be as an introduction to what follows in the household code of order. That is, the submission to one another is specified within the social household order. Then the reading would look like this:

5.21   Submit to one another:
5.22   wives to husbands (as the church to Christ)
6.1   children to parents
6.5   slaves to masters

Mutual submission simply cannot be construed as a way of understanding the structure of this text. The earlier egalitarian perspective of Paul – 'no longer Jew or Greek, no longer slave or free, no longer male and female; for all of you are one in Christ Jesus' (Gal. 3.28; also 1 Cor. 7.3-5) – is left in the background with the passing of time and the delay of the coming of Christ and the end of the age. Society continued, and the Christian church and household with it. The social convention is here appropriated within the Christian household, but with one significant difference: the love of Christ as the dynamic centrepiece. Husbands are to love their wives, not merely in terms of a physical and emotional love, but 'as Christ loved the church and gave himself up for her' (5.25).

To argue that Christ in love submits to the church's will, just as the church submits to the will of Christ, violates the formal texture of the text. However grating the implications of the text may be to our egalitarian sensibilities, we cannot in good conscience make the text say something and mean something ('mutual submission') it refuses to say and mean. If the submitting to one another of 5.21 means mutual submission throughout the rest of the section, then the rest should read like this: wives submit to your husbands, and husbands do likewise to your wives; just as the church submits to Christ, and Christ to the church; children submit to your parents, and likewise parents to your children; slaves submit to your masters, and likewise masters to your slaves.

The qualifier permeating the order of the household is the presence and grace of the Lord Jesus Christ. Within that presence all oppressive behaviour is ruled out. In the end both master and slave alike submit to the rule of Christ, the head of the church (6.9). Similarly, in the other household relationships.

Having said all of that for the text, we in our time need to surrender that hierarchal model for a more egalitarian Christian household, one more in line with the thought of the Apostle Paul, yet beyond him too. Authenticity matters above all.

vi. Military metaphors (Eph. 6.10-20)

Ephesians ends with a metaphorical battle alert. Christians are to put on armour, not that of Rome, but that of God. The battle is not one of expanding geographical borders, of wiping out the enemy. It is a battle 'against the rulers, against the authorities, against the cosmic powers of this present darkness, against the spiritual forces of evil in the heavenly places' (6.12). While the rulers and authorities seem like an unseen group in 'heavenly places', the earthly ones may not be altogether separated from them. There seems to be an understanding in Ephesians that for every earthly reality there is a corresponding reality 'in heavenly places', e.g. the church on earth universal corresponds to the church in the 'heavenly places' (3.10). Why then should the rulers and authorities in 'heavenly places' be disconnected from their counterparts on earth? They probably are not.

When, where, why and by whom would such a letter have come into being? The 'when' is somewhat easier to ascertain. Paul's letters had been collected and were available to the writer, including also Colossians. The author used the letters of Paul, with Colossians, to bring the Apostle up to date, so to speak. If Paul's letters were not collected until after the publication of Acts, as seems likely, then the date of Ephesians would be some time in the last decade of the first century. Where it was written is unknown. Clues to its place of origin are totally absent from the letter. Mention of the prison is of little help. Imprisonment is a motif in all of the post-Pauline letters: with Paul locked away, his disciples have to speak for him. Ephesians probably originated in one of the cities of Paul's mission, possibly Colossae.

The purpose of Ephesians seems not to have arisen out of any specific occasion, but rather from observations that the church was in danger of becoming fragmented. The Gentile members had brought much of their old thought and behaviour with them into the church, and had not shed them to the satisfaction of the writer of Ephesians. Hence the extensive litany of theological and ethical advice. The more general purpose was to promote oneness among all branches of the Christian communities scattered around the Roman world. Ephesians, of all the writings in the New Testament, is the most strongly catholic: one new humanity, one body, one Lord, one baptism, one building, etc.

Some have suggested a much older Onesimus not only collected the letters of Paul – making sure the special one to Philemon was included – but also wrote Ephesians as the all round letter that would gather up Paul's multifaceted theology into one magnificent summary for the ongoing life of the church in the world. If Onesimus wrote it, he must have availed himself of a first class Graeco-Roman education along the way. Ephesians shows all the signs of erudition in keeping with a literary education of the time. In the end, though, no one really knows who wrote Ephesians, if not Paul.

d. The Pastoral letters

Called Pastorals, the letters of 1 Timothy, 2 Timothy, and Titus are concerned with proper church ministry. The two men, Timothy and Titus, were faithful friends of Paul during his mission in the fifties. Both names appear numerous times in the seven undisputed letters. The two men in the Pastorals are *paradigmatic* of church ministers everywhere. Timothy's parish is Ephesus (1 Tim. 1.3) and that of Titus the island of Crete (Tit. 1.18; 4.12). But church ministers in any other location are expected to view the instructions given to these two pastors as the pattern for their own pastoral charge.

i. Officers of the church

Ministry in the church is not merely a general notion of service in the Pastorals. It is a structured, official ministry. Leaders have *titles*, which gives them authority to safeguard the church and its doctrines against heresy. Two titles in particular come to the surface as the names of offices within the church at large: 'bishop' (*episkopos*) and 'elder' (*presbuteros*). A 'bishop' acts as an overseer, probably over more than one congregation. His character as official leader, more so than his function, is described in the Pastorals. An 'elder' is generally considered a teacher. The Greek word implies an older person, as 'elder' does today. An older person in the ancient world was considered more experienced and wiser than someone younger. Again, the function is not as important as the *character* of the designated leader (1 Tim. 3.1-2; 4.14; 5.9, 17; Tit. 1.5, 7). The two official titles may be interchangeable, each one applicable to the same official person. 'Deacons', presumably those who assist the higher officials, are likewise urged to demonstrate good character (1 Tim. 3.8-10).

Church officials are highly regarded in the Pastorals. 'Whoever aspires to the office of bishop desires a noble task' (1 Tim. 3.1). But the noble *task is left undefined* in favour of the characterization of the church official. Here is a sampling:

> A bishop must be above reproach, [husband of one wife], temperate, sensible, respectable, hospitable, an apt teacher, not a drunkard, not violent but gentle, not quarrelsome, and not a lover of money. He must manage his own

household well, keeping his children submissive and respectful in every way –
for if someone does not know how to manage his own household, how can
he take care of God's church? He must not be a recent convert, or he may be
puffed up with conceit and fall into the condemnation of the devil. Moreover,
he must be well thought of by outsiders, so that he may not fall into disgrace
and the snare of the devil. (1 Tim. 3.2-7)

ii. Appointed by laying on of hands (1 Tim. 4.14; 2 Tim. 1.6)

A church member does not simply enter into the office by consensus of a
congregation, much less by his own sense of call. The ministry requires a
gift, bestowed by the ritual of the laying on of hands. The act is evidently
that of ordination to the ministry (1 Tim. 4.14; 2 Tim. 1.6). Official leadership in the church is given this mark of distinction because of the gravity of
the task. Above all the minister is charged with the preservation of 'the faith',
to safeguard the church against any inroads of false doctrine. The stress on
the structures and offices signals a danger facing the church in the world
pictured in the Pastorals (1 Tim. 1.3-4, 19; 3.9, 15; 4.1, 6-7; 6.10-20; 2 Tim.
1.13-14; 2.15-18; 3.14-17; Tit. 1.9-13; 2.1-2).

iii. Heresy, the faith and godliness

Heresy appears to have entered the church in some quarters. 'Christian'
heresy marks a departure from the tenets of Christian tradition handed
down from the apostolic period. Perhaps the plural, *heresies*, is more appropriate for the Pastorals. Some forms may have had a Jewish connection
(1 Tim. 1.6-7; Tit. 1.10-16; 3.9), but the more pronounced heresy falls under
the rubric, 'ascetic Gnosticism'. Gnostics believed in a spiritual salvation
achieved through various rituals and practices (1 Tim. 4.1-7; 2 Tim 3.1-9;
Tit. 3.9). Not all Gnostic thought and practice was the same. The form
depicted in 1 Timothy 4.1-6 is *world-denying*. Abstinence from sexual intercourse and from certain foods is its particular feature. The faithful minister
of the true church should reject such teaching, and warn his members
against it while denouncing its perpetrators, because 'everything created by
God is good' (4.4). Similar denunciation of Gnostic teaching appears in the
Patristic writings of the second century CE, which may say something about
the date of the Pastorals.

Congregations facing these false doctrines and practices require nurture
so as to withstand the false teachers implied in the Pastorals. Congregants
should be 'nourished on the words of *the faith* and of the *sound teaching*
that you have followed' (1 Tim. 4.6). Repeated in the Pastorals, '*the faith*' is

said to be the hallmark of the true church. In an earlier time in the mission of Paul, 'faith' was the principle by which one entered into a saving relationship with Christ. In the Pastorals, Pauline 'faith' takes on a confessional structure, a body of doctrine called 'the faith' (e.g. 1 Tim. 1.2, 19; 3.9, 13; 6.10; 2 Tim. 1.13; 4.7; Tit. 1.13; 3.15). 'The faith' is closely related to 'sound teaching', which appears to be creedal, if not catechetical, in character. Here is an example of a creedal formulation from 1 Timothy 3.16 set forth with poetic rhythm:

> Without any doubt, the mystery of our religion is great:
> He was revealed in flesh,
> vindicated in spirit,
> seen by angels,
> proclaimed among Gentiles,
> believed in throughout the world,
> taken up in glory.

The theology is weighty enough, but missing two central features of Paul's theology, the death of Jesus Christ on a cross and his subsequent resurrection by the power of God. Gnostics would have very little trouble with 'the faith' expressed in this poetic dress. Perhaps the aim of the doctrinal formula was to undercut Gnostic propaganda, and assuage the pressure on members to adopt Gnostic thought and life: they already believe the six lines of the confession without going outside the established church.

One word in the creed deserves attention. '*Religion*' (*eusebeia*), sometimes translated '*godliness*' or 'piety', occurs no less than thirteen times in the Pastorals, but not once in Paul's letters. But the piety, so important in the Pastorals, bears the mark of Hellenistic piety with little Christian or Hebraic distinction. The NRSV translation, 'religion', at 1 Timothy 3.16 is perhaps more appropriate. Christianity at the time of the Pastorals was vying for recognition in the Roman world of multiple religions. Still, most of the other twelve uses of the word have to do with piety. That is, members of the true Christian community should demonstrate disciplined thought and behaviour achieved by training. Hence the injunction to the church minister: 'Train yourself in godliness, for, while physical training is of some value, godliness is valuable in every way, holding promise for both the present life and the life to come' (1 Tim. 4.7-8). In Paul's letters, the Spirit in the believing community is the guarantee of life to come after the present life. Here in the Pastorals godliness constitutes the promise.

Little is said in the Pastorals about the working of *the Spirit*. Titus 3.5 comes closest to the Pauline understanding of the saving work of the Holy Spirit. 'God . . . saved us, not because of any works of righteousness that we had done, but according to his mercy, through the water of rebirth and renewal by the Holy Spirit. This Spirit he poured out on us richly through Jesus Christ our Savior, so that, having been justified by his grace, we might become heirs according to the hope of eternal life' (Cf. 1 Tim. 4.1; 2 Tim. 1.14).

One exception to Pauline theology stands out. Whereas Paul reserves salvation for a future time, this text assumes God has 'saved' the church members already, giving them hope of eternal life. At no point in these three letters is the return of Christ imminent. Signs will precede the coming of the end. 2 Timothy 3.1-6 implies the believers are living in *the last days*, surrounded by impious people. Readers are assured that 'all who want to live a godly life in Christ Jesus will be persecuted' (2 Tim. 3.12). The matter is merely stated, not argued. Nowhere in the Pastorals do we find anything approaching a sustained argument, compared to the undisputed letters of Paul where theological argument is the fingerprint of Paul's style of letter writing.

iv. Women in leadership or not? (1 Tim. 2.8-15)

Much has been written in recent years on 1 Timothy 2.8-15 concerning the *exclusion of women* from the ministry of the church. The text reads:

8. I desire, then, that in every place the men should pray, lifting up holy hands

9. without anger or argument; also that the women should dress themselves modestly and decently in suitable clothing, not with their hair braided, or with

10. gold, pearls, or expensive clothes, but with good works, as is proper for women who profess reverence for God.

11. Let a woman learn in silence with full submission.

12. I permit no woman to teach or to have authority over a man; she is to keep

13. silent. For Adam was formed first, then Eve;

14. and Adam was not deceived, but the woman was deceived and became a

15. transgressor. Yet she will be saved through childbearing, provided they continue in faith and love and holiness, with modesty.

Noted already, the instructions for church officials in the Pastorals are addressed to men, Timothy and Titus being paradigmatic. Here in this text at verse 8 men exclusively are called upon to pray in proper order. Women, presumably wives of the praying men, are asked to present themselves modestly and decently (vv. 9-10). Verses 11 and 12 appear to bar women from the ministry of church. Is the prohibition because of the gender of the woman, making the restriction permanent? Or is the prohibition against women because women generally in the Roman world were uneducated? The single operative verb in the so-called prohibition holds out an olive leaf to women in the Christian church of the Pastorals: they are given the *opportunity to learn.* Moreover, rather than reading the text as permanently restrictive, or prohibitive, it could be read as promising. 'Let a woman learn' is positive, given the social pressure against the education of women in that world. Inspired women prophets in some churches known to the writer of the Pastorals may already have exercised leadership. Given the bent of the Pastorals towards a well trained leadership in the church to ward off heresies and false teachers, 'inspired' leadership without training would be viewed as wanting. The injunction to the women is to have them learn from the men, the ones who, like Timothy and Titus, are already instructed in 'the faith'. Can we infer from the text that when a woman learns 'the faith' from the learned men, she can then lead in prayer and teaching in the church? To the ears of educated Christian women and men of conscience in the twenty-first century, the restriction as it stands reads like finger nails scratching a black board.

Compounding the problem, the prohibition is reinforced by incorporating (strangely!) the story of Adam and Eve in Genesis 2 and 3: Adam has chronological priority in that creation story. Conversely, Eve has priority as the one first deceived; she became a transgressor, then Adam. 'Yet she will be saved through childbearing, provided they continue in faith and love and holiness, with modesty' (v. 15). Perhaps the point is that just as Adam was created first, then Eve from Adam, so now in the church the man having learned first is in a position to teach the woman. The woman in turn is urged to submit to the teaching of the man. The 'logic' of verse 15 stands undeveloped, as usual in the Pastorals. The best guess is that childbearing, like that of Mary's bearing a saviour, Jesus, constitutes a saving action. In other words, an unlearned woman should not be unduly concerned with the need to learn in order to serve alongside the men. Salvation comes to women by a means not possible for men: childbearing.

v. Points of tension

Could the earlier Paul have written these letters? Is this the same Apostle who instructs women how to pray and prophesy in the worship service (1 Cor. 11.4-6)? It is hard to fathom this creation order of Adam first then Eve coming from the same mind that says, 'In the Lord woman is not independent of man or man independent of woman. For just as woman came from man, so man comes through woman; but all things come from God' (1 Cor. 11.11-12).

Numerous other elements stand in *tension with Paul's thought* in the seven undisputed letters. Remarkably few allusions to Old Testament texts can be found in the Pastorals. In the Pastorals also, the debate about the Law is no more. The Law of the Pastorals 'is laid down not for the innocent but for the lawless and disobedient, for the godless and sinful, for the unholy and profane' (1 Tim. 1.9). 'Good works', like godliness, make Christians conspicuous to the world (1 Tim. 2.10; 5.10; 5.25; 6.18; Tit. 2.7; 3.8; 3.14). 'Good works' is one of the hallmarks of the Pastoral Epistles, as compared to the earlier letters of Paul. One or another of these items of tension by itself could be explained, but all of them together are utterly compelling against authorship by the historical Paul.

For some readers of the Pastorals, Paul's name as sender in the salutation along with the personal notes here and there constitute sufficient ground for attributing the Pastorals to the historical Paul, regardless of the un-Pauline character of the instructions, style and vocabulary. Some have accounted for the personal notes, e.g. 2 Tim. 4.13: 'When you come, bring the cloak that I left with Carpus at Troas, also the books, and above all the parchments', by positing the incorporation of fragments of genuine letters at various points in the Pastorals. However, the personal elements, whether drawn from fragments of letters or not, have the effect of sealing the *mimesis*, the imitation of Paul.

There are other matters to consider with regard to the *time and situation* of the Pastorals. The chronology implied in the Pastorals for Paul is virtually impossible (1 Tim. 3.14; 4.13; Tit. 3.12). The only way to accommodate the chronology is to propose an additional flurry of missionary travel and preaching in the east after Paul's imprisonment in Rome (Acts 28.16, 30-31). But Paul clearly intended to proceed westward to Spain after his time in Rome (Rom. 15.24, 28). Since the Pastorals are prison letters, a further positing of a second imprisonment has to be made. Such an imprisonment is unaccounted for apart from this complicated and speculative construal.

The Pastorals are not well attested among the early witnesses to the collected letters of Paul. The first list of Paul's letters came from *Marcion* in the mid-second century, but the Pastorals did not appear on his list of letters. Tertullian (160–235 CE) accused Marcion of heresy, and believed he deliberately omitted the Pastorals from his list because they criticized his brand of Christian confession. This does not hold, because Marcion's followers later added the Pastorals to the list. A more likely scenario is that Marcion in the mid-second century did not have the Pastorals at hand to put them on his list.

The best, and earliest, manuscript evidence of the Pauline letters is known as P^{46} (*c.* 175–225 CE). That codex (book form) does not contain the Pastorals. The pages could, of course, have been torn from the codex. More likely, however, P^{46} did not contain the Pastorals originally. In short, the Pastoral letters do not make a public appearance until the middle of the second century.

What situation is implied in the Pastorals? And who would have written these three letters if not Paul? The church implied in the Pastorals is an established institution in the world. Its heritage of 'the faith' is threatened by heresies from within and false teaching from without. To maintain its integrity as a church in the world following the tradition of Paul, its ministers, called bishops (overseers), presbyters (elder-teachers), and deacons (assistants), will have to practice and teach sound doctrine, live pious lives, and denounce heretics and false teachers. To do so the ministers, all male, acquire the gift of ministry by the laying on of hands. Women are barred from leadership, seemingly because they have not yet learned 'the faith' sufficiently from the male leaders.

The Pastorals open *a window* overlooking the ecclesiastical landscape of the second to third generation of the Christian church in the world. In that stage, the church had to consolidate its resources, distinguish between clergy and laity, arm itself with a sound body of doctrine to ward off false teachers and to correct heresies. One could see this as marked development of Paul's earlier, more charismatic, vision of ministry. Conversely, the Pastorals represent a circling of the wagons, so to speak, to the point of casting a shadow over the earlier dynamic missionary thought and life of the great Apostle Paul.

3. Conclusion

With the passing away of Paul in the early sixties CE, the churches he founded continued without him, under the leadership of others. As the churches grew in numbers several trajectories began to define themselves along one or another line of thought. Various Gnostic notions were attractive to some churches. Leaders within those groups promoted a Christian variety of Gnostic thinking and practice. By the last quarter of the second century, Marcionite churches were about as numerous as the 'orthodox' ones in the Roman world.

This second century phenomenon did not happen suddenly, but insipiently. As signs of aberrant Christian thought and life appeared to people devoted to Paul, they sought to counter the various 'philosophies' by bringing the renown Apostle to bear on the situation. Colossians and Ephesians put forward a concerted appeal for the church to consider itself ONE, not many. The cosmic character of the one church far outweighed the particularity of disparate groups of Christians defining themselves over against other groups of Christians.

The Pastoral letters sought the solution to diversity in the church in the world in the training of official leaders for the churches. These educated leaders, characterized by piety, were charged with teaching 'sound doctrine' for the preservation of 'the faith'. Their training also helped them denounce false teachers, while undermining the heresies that threatened the established church as it entered the second century of the Common Era. All six of the letters discussed in this chapter represent Pauline thought in transition.

Further related reading

An excellent resource for understanding the heresy-orthodoxy issue reflected already in the letters covered in this chapter is that of Walter Bauer (1972), *Orthodoxy and Heresy in Earliest Christianity*. SCM.

For those interested in pursuing a study of the Colossians hymn further, the very recent work of Matthew E. Gordley (2007), who reads it within a very wide context of hymns in Hellenism and Judaism, should prove useful, *The Colossian Hymn in Context*. Mohr Siebeck.

The ideology, mythology and cosmology of Gnosticism is explored in depth by Kurt Rudolph (1998) in *Gnosis: The Nature and History of Gnosticism*. Continuum International.

I recommend two books to help understand the theological and ethical concerns in the context of the Pastorals: Frances M. Young, (1994). *The Theology of the Pastoral Epistles*. Cambridge

University, and J. Christiaan Beker (1991). *Heirs of Paul: Paul's Legacy in the New Testament and in the Church Today*. Fortress.

Consult also commentaries as appropriate under 'Post-Pauline Letters/Epistles' in the Bibliography.

Post-Pauline Trajectories: Five Catholic Epistles ![12]

Not everyone agrees that the five catholic (general) Epistles of Hebrews, James, 1 and 2 Peter, and Jude are post-Pauline trajectories. Four of them were written under apostolic names, which, if authentic, would put these four at least as early as Paul, or earlier. At the beginning of the twentieth century Joseph B. Mayor (1913, p. cl) argued that James was written between 40 and 50 CE, and therefore before Paul launched the Gentile mission. L. T. Johnson (2004, pp. 24–25), while not subscribing to Mayor's dating, continues to place the general epistle of James in a first generation Jewish-Christian context, possibly written by James of Palestine, the brother of Jesus. At the other end of the spectrum, Gerard Sloyan is 'convinced that none of the companions of Jesus had a writing function but that the task fell to others of a later time in various churches' (1977, p. 49).

Whether the *Palestinian Apostles* had a writing function in their time or not, all the traditional evidence we have points to the *death of Peter* at about the same time as the death of Paul under Nero, between 64 and 67 CE. Josephus tells of the *death of James* the brother of Jesus after the death of Porcius Festus and before the installation of Lucceius Albinus (*Antiquities* 20. 9). That would put the death of James the brother of Jesus two years before the death of Paul. Armenian tradition puts the *martyrdom of St. Jude* at about 65 CE. The point to this exercise is simply to say one of two things: (1) that the documents, if authentically written by these apostles, were written at the same time as Paul's missionary endeavours in the north Mediterranean, or (2) that these general letters were written under the names of these apostles to churches subsequent to Paul's revolutionary preaching and letter writing in the decade of the fifties. If the second alternative is correct, as I believe, then we have in the case of the Epistles of James, 1 and 2 Peter, and Jude, imitators of the early apostles facing social and theological issues beyond those of Paul during his mission.

The Epistle to the Hebrews is anonymous. But it too, in its own way, may act as a counterbalance to Paul's Law-free gospel. Hebrews tends towards a typological fulfilment of the covenant in the person of Jesus Christ, which calls on believers to adhere to the faith that keeps them from sinning. 'Anyone who has violated the law of Moses dies without mercy "on the testimony of two or three witnesses". How much worse punishment do you think will be deserved by those who have spurned the Son of God, profaned the blood of the covenant by which they were sanctified, and outraged the Spirit of grace' (Heb. 10.28-29).

1. Epistles rather than letters?

To this point the writings under Paul's name, including the *mimetic writings*, were discussed under the genre 'letter'. Each of them carried the stamp of a real letter, one that any resident of the Roman world would recognize as such. They all opened with a recognizable salutation addressed to a specific congregation or person, followed by a body of instruction, and closing with a final greeting and benediction. By contrast, none of the five writings under investigation in this chapter measures up fully to the genre we have to this point called 'letter'. Hence the designation 'epistle' to distinguish the five documents listed above from a conventional 'letter'. These Catholic Epistles are missing one or more of the recognizable features of the letter form. All of them are addressed to a general readership. Hebrews reads more like a sermon, with no opening salutation whatever (The same holds for 1 John discussed in Chapter 7).

The function of these Epistles reflects that of the earlier real letters Paul used to guide the thought and life of his fledgling congregations. These General Epistles served more as encyclical correspondence with churches now spread over a wide area. Their aim as such seems to have been to keep the churches on the right path as they made their way in the world. Hebrews is concerned with some members 'falling away' from the church, back to the old community from whence the members came. James argues against the notion that a person is justified by faith apart from works. 1 Peter reads like a sermon to new converts on the occasion of their baptism. 2 Peter and Jude see trouble brewing for churches that fail to deal with heretical elements worming their way into the congregations.

In summary, the contours and content of the five Catholic Epistles under review point to a time and situation after the success of the Pauline mission to the Gentile world. Paul did not require of his Gentile converts the covenantal signs of circumcision, sabbath keeping and food rules. Gentiles thus incorporated into the new community of Christ could quite reasonably conclude, in Paul's absence, that other requirements of the Jewish Law were no less susceptible to being rendered inoperative. Given another generation of Christian offspring and new converts, the developing church ran the risk of losing its ethical and theological bearing in relation to its Hebraic heritage of faith. The Catholic Epistles, written under the names of key figures from the Palestinian Jewish side of primitive Christianity, had the effect of bringing the church in line with the mores of its Palestinian Jewish origin. In this regard, 2 Peter overtly refers to the teaching of Paul in his letters, which some had twisted to their own destruction (2 Pet. 3.14-16).

We shall have occasion to return to this text later. In the meantime, the point to be made is that 2 Peter implies a collection of Paul's letters already revered as Scripture at the time of writing. At the same time, some 'ignorant and unstable' people were distorting the teaching of Paul in the collected letters to their own advantage. 2 Peter calls the offenders to account, and the churches to be on guard against a distorted Paulinism.

2. Texture of the Catholic Epistles

Temporal, geographical, ideological and social contexts of the Catholic Epistles are important for their interpretation, but not apart from reading the texts themselves. By grappling with the texture of the texts we confirm context, enabling a grasp of the theology and ethics embedded therein. We turn first to the Epistle of James.

a. The Epistle of James

By exploring the text of the Epistle of James we should be able to glean insight into the character of the author, the purpose the Epistle served in the church to which it was addressed, and something of the theological ethics embedded in the texture.

i. The name 'James'

The *unusual salutation* is the first to catch the eye. 'James, a servant of God and of the Lord Jesus Christ, To the twelve tribes in the Dispersion: Greetings' (1.1). The name 'James' is a much-used name in English. But 'James' hardly does justice to the symbolic weight the original name carried in its Jewish context. The Greek name was a straight carry-over from the Hebrew name 'Jacob'. The Greek spelling is *Iakòbos.* The English translation into 'James' came via the side door of the Old French, *Jaimes,* which seems to have come from a later Latin rendering, 'Jacomus'. In any case, the spelling of the Greek name in the salutation plays a larger role than the mere identification of an individual. It connects the writing with Jacob, or Israel. Not surprisingly, then, the content of the rest of the text resonates with the name assigned to the document: the content stands in the tradition of Hellenistic Jewish wisdom.

But the name 'James' was strongly connected to the Christian, more precisely Jewish Christian, heritage as well. There was James the son of Zebedee, disciple of Jesus (Mk 1.19 par.), James the son of Alphaeus, also a disciple of Jesus (Mk 3.18 par.), James 'the younger', the son of a woman named Mary who witnessed the crucifixion (Mk 15.40 par.) and James the brother of Jesus (Mk 6.3 Par.), who became a post-resurrection believer and leader of the church in Jerusalem (1 Cor. 15.7; Gal. 1.19; 2.9; cf. Acts 15.13). The salutation gives no good clue to the identity of the particular James who wrote this treatise. He is designated simply as 'a servant of God and of the Lord Jesus Christ' (1.1), a designation that could apply to any of the believers in Jesus by the name 'James'. However, the most likely candidate is James the brother of Jesus, the one hovering in the background of Paul's mission. Paul recognized him as one of the 'pillars' in the Jerusalem church (Gal. 2.9), and the person sponsoring the Jewish-minded visitors to Antioch when Peter was there. This James of Jerusalem, brother of Jesus, later labelled 'James the just' – probably because of his efforts to ensure the churches practiced works of righteousness – is likely the one implied in the salutation. Origen of the third century was the first to cite the Epistle of James and ascribe the identity of the author to 'the brother of the Lord'. Ever since Origen that ascription has held sway.

ii. A Christian document or not

But the name of James is most likely salutary. James of Jerusalem serves as a cipher to endorse the *wisdom teaching* in which the implied churches of the Epistle are delinquent. Those churches are labelled 'the twelve tribes in the Dispersion (*diaspora*)' (1.1), an unmistakable allusion to the Israel of God scattered throughout the Hellenistic world. If this Epistle, from its salutation to its conclusion, is a genuinely Christian document, then this unique designation of the readers views them as the new manifestation of the elect people of God related to the Messiah of Israel, 'the Lord Jesus Christ' (1.1). The real author, writing under the name of James of Jerusalem, scarcely represents Hebraic style that would have been characteristic of James the brother of Jesus and head of the church in the Holy City. Rather, the Epistle of James is thoroughly Hellenistic Jewish in its socio-literary and ethical orientation. It stands in the tradition of *Sirach, Wisdom of Solomon, 1* and *2 Enoch*, and the *Testament of the Twelve Patriarchs*. The last may well have prompted the label for the readers of this Hellenistic Jewish Christian treatment of wisdom, 'the twelve tribes of the Diaspora'.

But was the document really Christian originally? On only two occasions does the title 'Christ' appear, once in the salutation, and again in a rhetorical question at the beginning of the polemic against the disparity between rich and poor (2.1). Because of the sparse Christology in James some scholars have postulated an original Jewish wisdom document that a Christian leader adapted minimally for use among churches that had begun to forget their rootedness in the ethics of Judaism. There is some warrant for this proposition judging from the Jewish character of the ethical material in 5.7-12. It is unusual also for a Christian congregation of believers to be called a 'synagogue' (*sunagògè*) rather than a 'church' (*ekkèsia*) (2.2). Even more unusual for a Christian writing, the readers are encouraged to be patient in suffering without acknowledging the suffering of Jesus Christ. They are called to remember the examples of the faithful who suffered before them. Prophets are mentioned. Job is highlighted. But the patient suffering of Jesus, so prominent in the Gospels and in Paul, does not enter the exemplary picture in James 5 at all. A Pauline Christian would surely wonder at such a massive lacuna!

Even though 'Jesus Christ' is mentioned only twice in the whole Epistle, 'the Lord' is used repeatedly, 15 times in all. It has been argued that the title 'Lord' (*kurios*) is nothing more than an echo of the title for God in the LXX.

However, at two points in James 'the Lord' seems to be defined along Christian lines. Christians had learned to expect the coming of their Lord, Jesus Christ. James picks up that theme as follows: 'Be patient, therefore, beloved, until the coming of the Lord' (5.7); 'Strengthen your hearts, for the coming of the Lord is near' (5.8). Of course, Jewish expectation of divine vindication on their behalf was also in wide circulation. In that sense 'the coming of the Lord' could just as readily be interpreted as belonging to Jewish expectation of a visitation of the Lord their God. It was this ambiguity, this lack of clear and present Christology, which led Martin Luther in his 'Preface to the New Testament' (1522) to stigmatize the Epistle of James as an 'epistle of straw'. He was likewise unimpressed (to say the least) with the Roman Catholic Church's effort to make 5.14 support the Church's doctrine of extreme unction: 'Are any among you sick? They should call for the elders of the church and have them pray over them, anointing them with oil in the name of the Lord.'

There is another way of understanding the extant James to be a Christian document originally. The more Gentile the church became, the less it made conscious connection with its Jewish heritage of faith, especially with the ethical instruction characteristic of that heritage. By the middle of the second century a large body of Christians had followed Marcion who had set the Jewish Scriptures aside altogether. The Epistle of James could to be a response to such a minimizing of the Jewish (Hebraic) parent of Christianity, which put great stock in right living under the grace of 'the Lord'. Moreover, the genre of James is more that of ethical advice (*parenesis*) than it is 'letter' or 'epistle'. Besides, James seems to be responding to the Pauline thesis, faith apart from works, to which we will turn shortly. These together – a minimizing of the connection with the ethics of Judaism and the critique of 'faith apart from works' – give credence to the view that this document represents a Christian trajectory in the post-Pauline wave of Christian history. Some scholars go further in finding echoes of the sayings of Jesus in James. But the sayings in James could just as well be traced to other sources within Hellenistic Judaism, including and especially the Greek Scriptures of Judaism.

iii. Wise counsel for the good life

At this point an exploration of the advice in the text of James would be in order. All of the advice is given in the context of Wisdom. The Epistle opens with the testing of faith (probably meant as faithfulness). Trials in life have the effect of producing endurance, a mark of maturity (1.2-4). A mature person is a wise person. If anyone lacks wisdom, God will give it generously, as long the request is made in faith, 'never doubting' (1.5-16). Wisdom, like every perfect gift, comes from God above, called 'the Father of lights' (1.17). The term is unique to James. Its background in Hellenism is well documented. Philo of Alexandria associated the transcendent God with light. Light in Philo is a symbol of the revelation of divine wisdom. In James 1.17 the 'Father of lights' seems to be related to the unchangeableness of God, echoing the tract of Philo by that name.

The way of *wisdom is religious*. But religion can become impure. On the other hand, 'religion that is pure and undefiled before God, the Father, is this: to care for orphans and widows in their distress, and to keep oneself unstained by the world' (1.27). One of the reasons there are orphans and widows in distress is because the rich hold on to their money and oppress the poor. The critique of the Epistle against the rich is sharp in the extreme. The rich folks he has in view are those in the assembly. They seek the best seats while they expect the poor to wait on them hand and foot (2.1-7). There is a call to the poor to rise up against such placating of the powerful rich in the assembly. A series of polemical questions serves the purpose: 'Is it not the rich who oppress you? Is it not they who drag you into court? Is it not they who blaspheme the excellent name that was invoked over you?' (2.6-7). A similar diatribe against the rich appears later in the Epistle as well. The problem with the very rich in James is that they oppress those who are not. The diatribe cuts to the quick:

> Come now, you rich people, weep and wail for the miseries that are coming to you. Your riches have rotted, and your clothes are moth-eaten . . . The wages of the laborers who mowed your fields, which you kept back by fraud, cry out, and the cries of the harvesters have reached the ears of the Lord of hosts. You have lived on the earth in luxury and in pleasure.. . . You have condemned and murdered the righteous one, who does not resist you (5.1-6).

The 'righteous one' may be an allusion to Jesus, although that is far from certain (cf. Acts 3.14; 7.52). There is no indication in the Passion narratives in the Gospels that rich people killed Jesus because they were rich and he was not. In James the 'righteous one' probably refers to the one who lives by the Law of God, who does not oppress fellow human beings. Transgressors of God's Law have little regard for Law-observant people without power.

The Law in James receives high praise. A low regard for the Law would leave the orphan, the widow and the poor in distress. The Law is summed up in one commandment: 'You shall love your neighbour as yourself'.

Here James is in line with Paul who makes a similar point (cf. Rom. 13.9; Gal. 5.14). Orphans and widows and poor people are neighbours. To treat them as of no consequence is to 'commit sin' and be 'convicted by the Law as transgressors' (2.9). The Law in James is neither Roman law nor strictly Christian, but Jewish law, otherwise called 'the royal law' (2.8); 'the perfect law' (1.25), and 'the law of liberty' (1.25; 2.10). This law is not a relic of the past to be admired and forgotten, but a law to be fulfilled. It tames the tongue and thus guides the whole body (3.1-12). It opens the door to pure, peaceable, gentle, merciful wisdom, resulting in righteousness (3.13-18). It dissolves conflicts, both interior and exterior, and destroys boastful pride that shatters relationships (4.1-16). The law produces an attitude of prayer to God, the healing of body and soul, because the prayer is that of a righteous person, a law-observant person (5.13-18). In sum, the law gives transient life its true meaning, which is otherwise 'a mist that appears for a little while and then vanishes' (4.14).

iv. Faith-works debate (James 2.14-26)

We turn now to the faith-works debate of 2.14-26. The form of this passage is the only one in the Epistle that could be loosely described as 'argument'. Like so many other passages, this one is polemical. By setting up a 'straw man' and asking a series of rhetorical questions to him, the debater seeks to overthrow the notion that a person is justified (put right) before God by faith apart from good deeds – the kind described above. The rhetoric of the passage brings Paul's thesis immediately into play, only to turn it on its head. Now the question is: Is the writer of James arguing directly against Paul, or is he arguing against a later Paulinism gone astray? As it stands, the text reads as though antithetical to Paul in Galatians and Romans. The figure of Abraham in James proves that a person is justified by works and faith together. James uses the same key text from the Abraham story, but to prove the opposite point from that of Paul: 'Abraham believed God and it was credited to him as righteousness' (2.23). A closer examination of the movement of the text of James will bring its structure and conclusion to light.

It starts out with one poignant question: 'Can faith save you?' In answering that lead question, the debater posits a case of a naked and hungry person who is told by the hypothetical person of faith to 'go in peace; keep warm and eat your fill'. If the bodily needs are not met what good is your faith alone? It is dead! (2.14-16). Then another hypothetical person speaks: 'You have faith and I have works.' Response: works prove faith. Faith by itself proves nothing. 'Even the demons believe – and shudder'. The preliminary conclusion remains the same as before: 'faith apart from works is barren' (2.18-20).

The rest of the argument sets out the proofs for the thesis, that good works and faith together put the person right before God. Abraham is called to testify first. Unlike Paul, the writer of James cites the act of Abraham in offering his son Isaac on the altar. Abraham's act was one of faith, not an act as a result of faith, as though the two – faith and works – operated independently of each other. The key text is then summoned to prove the point that Abraham was put right (justified) by works and faith together. The conclusion is unambiguous: 'You see that a person is justified by works and not by faith alone' (2.24). As though that were not enough, Rahab the prostitute is called to witness as well. How is a prostitute to be justified before God? Answer: she was 'justified by works when she welcomed the messengers and sent them out by another road'.

Between Paul and James on the matter of how a person is put right before God, there appear to be polar-opposite conclusions, as depicted in Table 12.1 below.

The disparity can be resolved by appealing to context. The context of Paul's conclusion is the Gentile mission. He had concluded already that Gentiles did not need to receive the covenantal mark of circumcision to be accepted into the community of Christ. Physical circumcision was the 'work' in particular against which Paul had to argue in Galatians and Romans. That context pushed him to make categorical statements that appeared to rule out all good works prescribed by the Law. But he did no such thing. Once incorporated into Christ and his community, the believer had to prove his good works in order to remain in fellowship (e.g. 1 Cor. 5.1-13). Good works—other than circumcision (and probably also dietary and Sabbath observance) – were required of members in the communities Paul established.

The *context for James* was quite different. There is not a single mention of circumcision in James. The works that concern James are the ethical manifestation of a right relationship with God, such as caring for orphans,

Table 12.1 Polar-opposite Conclusions

Paul	James
We hold that a person is justified by faith apart from works prescribed by the law. (Rom. 3.28)	You see that a person is justified by works and not by faith alone. (James 2.24)

widows, the poor and the sick. Paul would have affirmed the same. But post-Pauline congregations may have moved towards applying Paul's thesis – faith apart from works of the Law – to all aspects of Christian life. Paul also held that 'the just requirement of the law might be fulfilled in us, who walk not according to the flesh but according to the Spirit' (Rom. 8.4). The writer of James in his time and place may well have been battling, not against Paul, but against a misappropriation of his teaching. The alternative for James was a revival of the perfect, royal law of liberty that called for good works as integral to genuine faith.

b. The Epistle of 1 Peter

Unlike the Epistle of James, the Epistle of 1 Peter leaves no doubt about its Christian origin and character. It stands squarely within *the Pauline tradition*, even to the use of Paul's minted phrase, 'in Christ' (3.16; 5.10, 14). We may approach an understanding of this richly textured writing under the following headings: 'identity of author and readers'; 'occasion and purpose of writing'; 'literary character of the document'; 'exile and election'; 'suffering for and with Christ'; and 'the social code'.

i. Identity of author and readers

In the prescript there is no mistaking who is meant by 'Peter, an apostle of Jesus Christ' (1.1). For some readers today there is no need for further investigation into the author's identity. Peter is well known from the Gospels and Acts, and from the Letters of Paul. But as suggested earlier in this chapter, the practice of writing under the name of a noted leader from the past was not uncommon. The question is: Does the evidence support the surface reading of the author's identity?

If the author was Simon Peter, son of John, disciple of Jesus and complementary missionary with Paul, then he would have written this epistle no later than the early sixties when Paul was still alive, or shortly after his death. Both Peter and Paul met their death at about the same time under Nero between 64 and 67. Why Simon Peter would not make even the slightest mention of Paul in a letter addressed to the churches Paul founded is difficult to understand. More to the point, why would Peter write to Paul's churches at all with Paul still alive, or very recently deceased?

From clues throughout the Epistle it is evident that the readers are of Gentile extraction. They are instructed not to be 'conformed to the desires that you formerly had in ignorance' (1.14). This is surely an allusion to their practices as Gentiles in ignorance of the Jewish law. Similarly, the readers are told they 'have already spent enough time in doing what the Gentiles like to do' (4.3). It seems out of order for the historical Apostle Peter to be writing to Gentile churches that Paul had founded. Paul in Galatians understands the leadership of the missionary endeavour to be divided up between himself and Peter: 'I [Paul] had been entrusted with the gospel for the uncircumcised [Gentiles], just as Peter had been entrusted with the gospel for the circumcised [Judaeans]' (Gal. 2.7). It seems unlikely, therefore, that Simon Peter would instruct the Gentile churches of Paul's mission in Paul's lifetime.

The style of 1 Peter also calls the genuine Petrine authorship into question. Among the writings of the New Testament, 1 Peter stands out as one of the best in Greek vocabulary, grammar and syntax. The Apostle Peter was a Galilaean fisherman, probably more familiar with Aramaic, at least in the synagogue, than with literary Greek. The Epistle of 1 Peter has all the signs of a well educated author, familiar with writing in formal Hellenistic style. That the historical Peter would have achieved such a Hellenistic facility prior to his death is highly doubtful.

Finally, the letter purports to come from Babylon (5.13). The actual city of Babylon in the Tigris–Euphrates region is hardly the place intended. There is no record of the founding of a church in Babylon during the lifetime of Paul or Peter. Babylon is symbolic, a cryptogram for the city of Rome. But that *symbolic use of Babylon* to signal Rome did not come into use either in Judaism or Christianity until after the destruction of the Temple of Jerusalem in 70 CE, some years after the death of Peter. The book of Revelation, written late in the first century, likewise uses Babylon as a cover name for Rome (e. g. Rev. 14.8; 16.19; 18.21). Rome, like Babylon 600 years earlier, laid waste the sacred place of the Jewish people. The result was exile. Now in the aftermath of the more recent destruction of the Temple by Rome, Babylon is recalled and employed as a cover name for the present power responsible for the exile among Christians. Just as the writer and his readers would have understood the meaning of Babylon, so also they probably caught the significance of the adopted name of 'Peter' (rock) for the writer of this Epistle. That man suffered death at the hands of 'Babylon' (Rome), just as Paul did. Peter's name served the purpose of the Epistle well, as the name of one who could console the churches of the provinces of Asia Minor in their suffering.

As indicated already, the composition of the churches was almost certainly non-Jewish. Yet this Epistle assigns them all the honours and privileges traditionally at home in Judaism. They are called 'exiles of the Dispersion' (1.1) and 'aliens and exiles' (2.11). This is an unmistakable allusion to the exile of the Jewish people after they suffered the loss of their homeland and sacred place of worship and identity. The readers were Gentile to be sure, but they were also Christian. That meant they had left their former ways, such as idolatry and social conformity. Their identity as Christians meant suffering from Roman authority, just as the earlier Judaeans had suffered at the hands of the Babylonians. 'If any of you suffers as a Christian, do not consider it a disgrace, but glorify God because you bear this name [Christian]' (4.16). As Christians, the readers had become exiles and aliens in their own land, and as such suffered at the hands of the authorities operating under the orders of Rome.

ii. Occasion and purpose of writing

Having reached some understanding of the situation of the churches in which this Epistle would have been read, the occasion and purpose of writing fall into place. Members of *the new movement in Asia Minor* were being maligned and abused, having left the old religions and the old ways of living to join the new Christian way (3.16). Knowledge of the abuse suffered by the new converts touched the heart of this educated Christian writer, prompting him to write words of consolation and encouragement. It would have been easy for the persecuted Christians, recently baptized into the new community of Christ, to fall back into their former life.

The purpose of 1 Peter is to instruct the newly baptized members especially concerning the place of suffering in relation to their salvation (1.5-6, 9; 2.2). Roman socio-political order did not take kindly to new movements operating under the name of an unknown god. Such movements could become seditious and subversive. 1 Peter urges the members not to provoke the socio-political powers unnecessarily. Instead, they are to prove that they are good members of society while they live by the standard of Christ. Their defence as Christians should be 'with gentleness and reverence . . . so that, when you are maligned, those who abuse you for your good conduct in Christ may be put to shame' (3.15).

iii. Literary character of the document

Structurally 1 Peter falls into two rather distinct parts bounded by the usual epistolary prescript (1.1-2) and a closing greeting and benediction (5.12-14). The first of the two principal parts falls within 1.3 and 4.11. The second within 4.12 and 5.11.

A number of scholars believe the canonical 1 Peter evolved into its present form in two stages. The first main part (1.3–4.11) was originally *a homily aimed at newly baptized believers* in Jesus Christ. They are called 'newborn infants' in need of spiritual nurture (2.2). Their baptism incorporated them into the community of Christ, as stones into a building, with Christ being the cornerstone (2.6). It is believed that if the letter had been composed as a letter to congregations scattered across Asia Minor the address to 'newborn infants' would hardly have been appropriate. Newly baptized believers needed to learn proper Christian conduct within the church, but also within society. The homily of 1.3–4.11 appears to serve that particular purpose. Moreover, the original setting of that part of 1 Peter is said to be the baptism of new converts. They are told in the homily that 'baptism, which [the eight persons with Noah] prefigured, now saves you – not as a removal of dirt from the body, but as an appeal to God for a good conscience, through the resurrection of Jesus Christ' (3.21).

Before leaving this section of the Epistle, the difficult wording of 4.6 calls for brief comment: 'the gospel was proclaimed even to the dead, so that, though they had been judged in the flesh as everyone is judged, they might live in the spirit as God does.' The NRSV translation in the phrase, 'even to the dead', implies that Christ went to the realm of the dead to preach to spirits there. The issue hangs on the emphatic sense of the Greek connective *kai*, translated 'even' in the NRSV. But *kai* could just as readily be translated 'also' rather than 'even'. The difference is subtle but important. Beyond that, the singular aorist passive verb (*euangelisthè*) means 'he/it was proclaimed'. Moreover, a legitimate translation could read: 'he [Christ] was preached also to the dead'; that is, while they were still alive. They died in the flesh, but as a result of hearing the proclamation of Christ before they died, the physically dead Christians are alive in the spirit as God is. Recall Paul's consolation to the Thessalonian Christians who had concern about the state of the Christians who had died (1 Thess. 4.13-16). A similar concern may have prompted this complex statement at the time of 1 Peter.

The second literary part of the Epistle (4.12–5.11) is *a series of admonitions*, characteristic of the ending of the letter form. The readers, apparently, needed such words of advice and encouragement for their life in the world. 'Like a roaring lion' their adversary the devil was prowling around seeking to devour them (5.8). The stark imagery depicts, not some spiritual inner battle, but a battle in society where the Christian members were being forced to abandon their new calling 'in Christ' in support of the established

Roman gods authorized by the state. A number of Roman Emperors and governors, in an effort to keep the Roman gods appeased by sacrifices, took serious umbrage at Christians for refusing to sacrifice in honour of the given emperor. Nero's persecution of Christians (64–67 CE) is well documented. But a number of emperors after him continued the policy of having the people of the provinces honour the Roman gods by sacrifices, and thus honour the Emperor. Domitian (81–96 CE) and Trajan (98–117 CE) both persecuted Christians for their perceived anti-Roman religion. One form of persecution of Christians in Rome was to throw them to 'roaring lions' that eventually mauled them to death. In the admonition section of the Epistle, Christians are urged to resist the lion-like adversary, 'steadfast in your faith, for you know that your brothers and sisters in all the world are undergoing the same kinds of suffering' (5.9). The time could well be that of Domitian or Trajan.

Many modern interpreters of 1 Peter disavow its two-stage composition in favour of a unified single composition (e.g. Senior 2003, p. 10). The letter was composed on one occasion for a new generation of Christians facing persecution in the latter part of the first century. The persona of Peter, by this judgement, seeks to save the church for the future. Eschatology plays a fairly significant part in the letter as a whole. With the end in sight (4.7) the new members are encouraged not to give up in the face of hard times. They will see the outcome in the future only if they persevere through the 'fiery ordeal'. Either way of assessing the literary structure and history – an original baptismal homily with admonitions added later to make it a letter, or a letter written on one occasion to encourage the ongoing life of the church in Asia Minor in the midst of persecution – the Epistle of 1 Peter as we have it represents a situation in the post-Pauline church towards the end of the first century CE.

iv. Exile and election

Exile was an experience of alienation, of deracination. It was not that the members had come from some other place to reside in Pontus, Galatia, Cappadocia, Asia and Bithynia. They had probably grown up in the area, felt at home in the society, worshipped in the local shrines, and behaved according to the conventions and customs of the society. The Christian way of life was in many respects exclusive. The new religion was not another one to add to the *polytheistic mix*. Had it been so, the suffering for being Christian may not have been so severe. What the new members, 'like newborn infants', need to stay the course is nourishing spiritual milk. This Epistle is just such milk for Christian exiles, living faithfully under the banner of Christ while living in a society that maligns them.

A large part of the nourishing milk 1 Peter provides is the assurance that they are God's privileged people. They are chosen, as Israel was long before. Even when Israel was in slavery in Egypt, and later in exile, they were still chosen, belonging to God while suffering in the world. That conviction, amplified in this letter, puts the readers in the good company of *God their protector* (1.5). All the blessings and functions that once belonged to Israel exclusively are here in 1 Peter transferred to the Gentile Christians. If one were to select a theme text from 1 Peter it could well be 2.9-10:

> But you are a chosen race, a royal priesthood, a holy nation, God's own
> people, in order that you may proclaim the mighty acts of him who called you
> out of darkness into his marvellous light. Once you were not a people, but
> now you are God's people; once you had not received mercy, but now you
> have received mercy.

In these two verses are gathered up, from various parts of the Jewish Scriptures, all of the characteristics of the elect people of God. Now they characterize the persecuted Christians of Asia Minor. The adjectives are telling: 'chosen', 'royal', 'holy', 'owned'. The last one is translated in the NRSV as 'God's own people'. It is a single composite word in Greek (*peripoièsis*). Etymologically it carries the notion of 'making a circle around', a reminder of the tents of Israel encamped around the tent of the Lord in the wilderness (Num. 2.2). In that sense the word connotes ownership, possession. The suffering church can hold on to that theological image in the face of the Roman domination. Whatever the suffering, the readers can go through it confident that their destiny rests not with the power of Rome, but with the power of God. The idea of destiny ordained by God stands out in this Epistle (1.2, 11, 20; 2.8).

Destiny and divine foreknowledge were not as offensive to ancient people as they are among some modern thinkers. On the contrary, God's foreknowledge of the plan of salvation, including the election of a people, were consoling concepts. To know that the greater will of God preceded the human response was cause for rejoicing. God the Creator and Redeemer in Christ is loving, not tyrannical.

The 'royal priesthood' in 1 Peter does not signify a select group of mediators between non-priestly worshippers and God. The whole community is called, in Exodus 19.6, 'a kingdom of priests, and a holy nation' (KJV). Here in 1 Peter the honour is passed on to the Christian exiles in Asia Minor. To call the Christian exiles a 'holy nation' is in some sense subversive. To be holy is to be set apart, not merely from individual sins, but from the surrounding national, political and social milieu. For the churches in exile to take on this characteristic could mean ongoing abuse. The Jewish nation in exile in the Roman world had, by the end of the first century, gained sufficient recognition from Rome to avert serious repercussions. The new Christian movement, however, continued to be maligned and abused. Even so, says 1 Peter, your badge of honour and identity is yours by divine decree. Wear it honourably and humbly (3.8; 5.5-6).

Verse 2.10 makes clear that the *churches in exile* were once Gentile, and as such not a people of God. By God's mercy the congregations can now claim the status of God's own people with all the privileges.

v. Suffering for and with Christ

Further to the matter of suffering in exile, the members are exhorted not to bear their suffering in isolation, without purpose. The precise nature of the suffering is not given. But by the graphic description it must have been severe. It is called a 'fiery ordeal' (4.12). The victims should not be surprised. The 'fiery ordeal' tests the character of Christian life and witness. By bearing the ordeal bravely they enter into a deeper relationship with Christ. The suffering members are encouraged to 'rejoice insofar as you are sharing Christ's sufferings, so that you may also be glad and shout for joy when his glory is revealed' (4.13). One can hear an echo of the language in Philippians 3.10. Paul was glad to share in the sufferings of Christ so that he might attain to the resurrection.

Suffering is said to be the calling of the Christian, 'because Christ also suffered for you' (2.21). This sounds like the substitutionary suffering of Christ: Christ suffered 'for you'. It could be taken to mean Christ suffered so those who believe in him don't have to suffer. But given the total context of 1 Peter this notion cannot be sustained. The sense of suffering 'for you' in 1 Peter is that Christ does not ask you to suffer alone. He suffered, 'so that you should follow in his steps' (2.21). Still, the substitutionary aspect is also present, especially at 3.18: 'Christ also suffered for sins once for all, the righteous for the unrighteous, in order to bring you to God.' The point, it seems, is that the one who suffers in the flesh has overcome sin, which is the following of 'human desires' (4.2).

vi. The social code

We come now to the social code (2.13–3.7). This code is not limited to the household code, as we found in Colossians and Ephesians. In 1 Peter the Christian version of the code instructs the exiles how to behave as members of the Roman socio-political environment, including life in the household. It begins by instructing the exiles on proper Christian conduct in relation to 'every human creation, whether of the emperor as supreme, or of governors, as sent by him to punish those who do wrong and to praise those who do right. For it is God's will that by doing right you should silence the ignorance of the foolish' (2.13-15). The NRSV has 'every human institution', but the Greek word means literally 'creature/creation'. The human creation in view is the Roman socio-political system. The Emperor is said to be supreme, but only within the human creation. God is supreme over all human creation. By implication, the members are not to compromise their faith in Christ in their respect for the Emperor and his governors in the provinces. Even if it means suffering, the exiles are urged to bear the pain in honour of the higher power. Above all, Christians are to do right whatever the cost in human life. A series of proverbs conclude the first part of the Christian social code.

Slaves are addressed directly as persons in their own right, as they were in Colossians and Ephesians. In the Graeco-Roman world slaves were property. Aristotle had taught that a master could not do injustice to a slave, because as property a slave is not a person, but an instrument (e.g. *Politics* 1.4. 1-2). In 1 Peter slaves are addressed as persons, but are not told to seek freedom from slavery. Instead, they are told to accept the authority of the master, even if the master is harsh. By enduring the pain that a harsh master (non-Christian presumably) inflicts, the slave has God's approval (2.20). God's approval is for doing right, not merely for bearing the pain. But doing right and bearing pain are often intertwined. Again, Christ is the example for the slave who does right. 'He committed no sin, and no deceit was found in his mouth' (2.22). Masters are not addressed in 1 Peter.

Wives are then addressed. In accordance with the hierarchal model in society, they are counselled to 'accept the authority of [their] husbands' (3.1). Even if some of the husbands are not obedient to the word – a reference to non-Christian men – the wife still should put herself under the husband's authority. By so doing she may win the husband over to the Christian way 'without a word'. The *silence of the woman* in relation to her husband's authority is implied. A wife's decorum matters: she should wear modest clothes, and not adorn herself with fine jewellery and braided hair.

Sarah is called in as example of a wife who submitted to her husband's authority (3.6).

Husbands are addressed directly. They are to show honour to the woman 'as the weaker sex, since they too are heirs of the gracious gift of life– so that nothing may hinder your prayers' (3.7). However much the code goes against the grain of our current consciousness, it was more than one small step beyond the social norm. Women were next to slaves in Hellenistic society. Even in Judaism a woman was not given equal status with men, to the extent that a Jewish man could thank God he was not born a woman. Of course, that Jewish male prayer had to do with permission given to men to study Torah. Still, the very idea is repugnant to our present sense of good attitude and conduct. In 1 Peter women 'are also heirs of the gracious gift of life' (3.7), and as such are entitled to equal honour with the men. Even with all the Christian overlay, important as it is, the code in 1 Peter still accommodates the social convention as far as possible.

In the end, though, the writer calls for *reciprocal respect and love* among all the parties named in the code (3.8). Sayings of Jesus from the Synoptic tradition (or the Synoptic Gospels) seem to lie behind, or within, the concluding words of the code. 'Do not repay evil for evil or abuse for abuse; but, on the contrary, repay with a blessing. It is for this that you were called– that you might inherit a blessing' (cf. Mt. 5.11, 44; Lk. 6.27-29). *Suffering without retaliating* results in blessing, first to the sufferer but also to the one inflicting the suffering. The blessing holds only if the Christian suffers for 'good conduct' (3.16). One would think good conduct would not bring suffering, and 1 Peter believes as much in principle. 'Now who will harm you if you are eager to do what is good?' (3.13). But then the writer concedes that suffering for good conduct can happen. Even then, the Christian response is not to pay back in kind. By suffering abuse for good conduct the abusers 'are put to shame' (3.16). How so? If a person stands defenceless and non-violent before a powerful abuser, and the abuser inflicts pain for no good reason, then all who observe see the abuser as unjust. The abuser is shamed. At the same time, if the issue has to do with support of some imperialist policy and practice and the Christian objects on the ground of 'conscience' (3.16), such objection could be viewed as subversive, not 'good conduct'. The reference point in 1 Peter, as in Paul, is the suffering of the non-violent Christ (3.17; cf. Rom. 8.13; Phil. 3.10).

c. The Epistles of 2 Peter and Jude

A problem with the two Epistles of 2 Peter and Jude involves the *close literary relationship* between them at a number of points. So close is the relationship that a decision has to be made about literary dependence. Which writer depended on the work of the other? With the answer comes the need for a decision as to which Epistle to treat first in order to show the degree of dependence. For the moment, though, it would be worthwhile to set up the text references where close parallels occur. In some cases the wording and ideas are identical and in others similar. A preliminary check on these texts in the Bible, referenced in Table 12.2, would help with the understanding of the discussion to follow.

At least three factors suggest the *dependence of 2 Peter on Jude*, rather than the other way round. First, Jude is a general Epistle in the fullest sense of the term. The addressees are simply designated as 'those who are called' (v. 1). Nor are there any further clues as to the identity of the implied readers, or the specific issues facing them beyond the danger of having immoral heretics in their midst. The sharp censure of the intruders is generic. 2 Peter, on the other hand, is addressed to those who stand in the tradition of 'a faith as precious as ours through the righteousness of our God and saviour Jesus Christ' (1.1). Furthermore, 2 Peter specifically defends traditional

Table 12.2 Words and Ideas in Common

2 Peter	Jude
Chapter 2	
vv. 1, 3b	v. 4
vv. 4, 6	vv. 6-7
v 5	v. 5
vv. 10-11	vv. 8-9
v. 12	v. 10
vv. 13, 15	vv. 11-12
v. 17	vv. 12b-13
v.18	v. 16
Chapter 3	
vv. 1-4	vv. 17-18
10-13	vv. 14-15
vv. 14-18	vv. 20-25

Christian faith against an attack on divine theodicy responsible for judgement. Second, a writer is more likely to expand a source than to reduce it. If 2 Peter were the source for Jude, why would Jude omit so much worthy material from 2 Peter – about two-thirds missing? Third, 2 Peter does not cite *1 Enoch* and the *Assumption of Moses* found in Jude, a sign of movement towards the fixing of traditional writings for use in the churches. For these reasons Jude is considered a source for 2 Peter, and will therefore be treated first to accommodate citation in the discussion of 2 Peter.

i. Jude

The identity of the particular figure called 'Jude' (or Judas) is not immediately obvious, despite the stated sibling relation with someone called James. This Jude is said to be a 'servant of Jesus Christ', not an Apostle. That seems to eliminate the Apostle 'Judas son of James' (Lk. 6.16. Judas Iscariot is definitely ruled out). The most likely candidate is Judas son of Mary, brother of James and Jesus (Mk 6.3). One wonders why the relationship to Jesus was not invoked. Perhaps the distinctive character of Jesus as the Christ in the church precluded an appeal to the brotherly connection of Jude with Jesus. But why the claim to be 'the brother of James'? The James in view had to be one well recognized in the church at large. He is invoked as one not needing further identification. The only candidate then would be James, the brother of Jesus, who became an important figurehead in the church of Jerusalem.

But can we take this identification of Jude to be historical or mimetic? Some read it as historical, making the generic Epistle of Jude a rather early document. Many more scholars, however, treat Jude as belonging to the post-mission church encountering heresies of various sorts. One thing characterizes Jude more than any other: sharp polemic directed to every (Gnostic?) brand of *heresy* threatening the inner life-blood of the church. That situation did not reach the wide-ranging scale depicted in this general Epistle until the end of the first and into the second century of the church's history. The effect of pressing the connection to the Palestinian James tradition was to call those churches with libertine tendencies back to the tradition of righteousness that gave them birth initially. Brothers James and Jude of the primitive mission fit the profile very well (1 Cor. 9.5). The date of composition cannot be fixed definitely. The turn of the century seems likely, a few years before the writing of 2 Peter.

The literary genre of Jude is peculiar. The prescript (vv. 1-2) is recognizable as appropriate to a general letter: sender, addressees, greeting. But the ending is not that of a letter. A beautiful doxology to close, indeed (vv. 24-25), but no final greetings, encouragement, travel plans or the like. Between the prescript and the doxology lies a sustained polemic, at times invective, against those who would put in jeopardy 'the faith that was once for all entrusted to the saints' (v. 3b). Jude may be labelled a denunciation tract. Its main function was to brand the heretics, and by so doing broker a pact between the writer and the vulnerable Christian readers.

The ones reading the graphic critique are the '*beloved*', whose salvation the writer shares (v. 3a). They are the ones he seeks to protect against the incursion of heretics. It is not as though the false teachers are outside looking in on the gathered community around the communion meal. As *intruders* they 'have stolen in among you' (v. 4). That implies that they participate with the 'beloved' in their sacred meals in the name of the Lord Jesus, called 'love feasts' (v. 12a). But 'they feast with you without fear, feeding themselves' (v. 12b).

The author of Jude weaves his *polemic* around selected events and persons from Scripture, including the books of *1 Enoch* and *Assumption of Moses*, texts questioned as to their suitability for church life and worship. Jude reaches back to Genesis and Exodus, books of origin, to underwrite his invective against the heretical intruders. 'The Lord' saved a people out of Egypt, but destroyed people who did not believe (v. 5). The intruders are like the unbelievers of Egypt. Angels also, presumably the 'sons of God' of Genesis 6.2, moved out of their proper domain into the human family with the result that they were consigned to 'eternal chains' in 'deepest darkness' for the day of judgment (v. 6). Imagine what will happen to the out-of-place intruders in the church! Sodom and Gomorrah indulged in sexual immorality and incurred punishment of 'eternal fire' (v. 7b). The writer then cites a legend from the *Assumption of Moses* about a dispute between the archangel Michael and the devil concerning the body of Moses, but Michael would not dare slander Moses. Yet these misguided intruders in the churches shamelessly slander the true Christians. 'Woe to them', the writer says. The writer in turn slanders them with a whole battery of unbecoming images. They are like 'irrational animals' (v. 10); they go the 'way of Cain' (v. 11) who killed his brother; they fall into 'Balaam's error' (v. 11), understood as selling out God's people for gain; they are 'blemishes' (lit. reefs beneath the surface of the water); 'waterless clouds'; 'autumn trees without fruit, twice dead, uprooted' (v. 12a); 'wild waves of the sea', 'wandering stars' (vv. 12b-13).

What a *scandalous picture* of people! But the function of an invective tract is not to argue a case against an opponent with reasoned rhetoric, but to lambast the third party opponent to the end that the second party, the 'beloved', will shun them. The 'beloved' are implicitly urged to remove them from the communion setting to a place where God will deal with them, all in good time.

The writer then calls in antediluvian Enoch, quoting the second century BCE book of *1 Enoch* (1.9) to witness concerning the end that awaits these 'grumblers and malcontents' who wallow in their own lusts (vv. 14-16). The Lord will execute judgement on all the ungodly people, like those in the churches of Jude.

Attention then turns to the 'beloved' again before the majestic benediction. They are advised to remember what 'the apostles of our Lord Jesus Christ' had to say about the scoffers who would come (vv. 17-23). The allusion may be traced to Acts 20.29-30: wolves will attack the church 'distorting the truth in order to entice the disciples to follow them'. As fortification against the intrusion, the 'beloved' are to build themselves up in their 'most holy faith; pray in the Holy Spirit' and keep the love of God strong. By so doing they will attain eternal life (v. 21). As well, they are to snatch others 'out of the fire' ignited by lustful heretics, while avoiding the garments 'defiled by their bodies' (v. 23b). This last image is strange to modern minds. There was an ancient belief that the clothes that covered a person magically carried the good or bad contagion of the person. In Mk 5.27-30 and Acts 19.12 the clothes of Jesus and Paul respectively carried healing power to the sick.

The grand sweep of *the doxology* (vv. 24-25) recalls the polemic while holding out a hopeful word of benediction to the 'beloved' and faithful members: 'Now to him who is able to keep you from falling, and to make you stand without blemish in the presence of his glory with rejoicing, to the only God our Savior, through Jesus Christ our Lord, be glory, majesty, power, and authority, before all time and now and forever. Amen.'

ii. 2 Peter

The author of 2 Peter, even though borrowing heavily from Jude, moulded a literary-theological Epistle of distinction. Certain *phrasing and imagery* are unique to 2 Peter: e.g. 'divine nature' (1.4 *theias phuseòs*), 'Tartarus' (2.4 *tartaros*, the deepest abyss of Hades, translated 'hell' in NRSV), 'eyewitnesses' (1.16 *epoptès*). This Epistle is the product of a writer steeped in various traditions – Jewish, Hellenistic, and Christian. Of course, the writer belonged to the Christian tradition, which had grown in the soils of other traditional religions and philosophies. Moreover, the author of 2 Peter was a capable literary artist having behind him many years of development in Christian tradition, including a collection of Paul's letters regarded on par with other sacred writings (3.15-16). His reference to 'your apostles' (3.2) also distances him and his readers from the first group that started the Christian movement. He draws on a wide range of material about the Apostle Peter from various traditional sources, probably even written gospels such as the Synoptics. His more immediate source, of course, is the Epistle of Jude.

While the opening of the Epistle calls 'Simeon Peter' the writer, the internal elements of the Epistle noted above rule out that possibility. The most compelling of these elements is the high regard the author has for '*our beloved brother Paul*...in all his letters' (3.15-16). However many letters the author had in mind, 'all' surely means more than two. Galatians and Romans seem to be echoed in 2 Peter, but 'all' implies a collected body recognized as having the status of Scripture. By all accounts, that phenomenon did not exist before the end of the first century, probably sometime after the publication of Acts. Since Peter died at *c*.65 CE he could not have written this document. Instead, the *tradition* of Peter is invoked under the name of the Apostle as a way of calling the orthodox groups to continue confessing their faith about the coming of the Lord, against those who would slander them for doing so. Making the appeal to the tradition of Peter even more striking, the Epistle is said to be the testament of the Apostle written shortly before his death (1.14-15).

The '*testament*' genre was common in both Judaism and Hellenism. Its form had the effect of making the matter addressed more grave. The 'testament' had to be that of an established figure in the tradition, Moses and the Patriarchs in Judaism, Peter and other Apostles in Christianity. Peter was an important apostolic figure at the founding of the Christian movement (see Mt. 16.18; Gal. 2.9). A 'testament' in his name carried great weight. Reference to a previous letter at 3.1 is almost certainly to 1 Peter, which may or may not have been written by the same person.

The material of the Epistle is laid out in the form of *a debate*, one in which all Christian churches of the world of the time are supposed to engage. The main topic of the debate is 'theodicy', argument proving the goodness and reliability of God against those who would say otherwise. The debate concerns the coming of the Lord (*parousia*) for the salvation of the faithful and the judgement of the wicked. Repeatedly 'judgement' comes up for review (2.4, 9, 11; 3.7). Knowledge of God's coming judgement is supposed to motivate the readers to live good moral lives. The detractors claim that God is not concerned with wrongdoing. If God were concerned about the state of evil in the world, why let it continue? Because things have remained the same through aeons past (3.4), belief in a God who judges unrighteousness is ill-founded. 2 Peter defends the belief in the coming of the Lord to save the righteous and bring an end to the world of the ungodly (3.9-10).

One of the persistent themes in 2 Peter is that good theology produces a good life. Theology and ethics coexist. Because the faithful members are participants in the divine nature, they are to 'make every effort to support your faith with goodness, and goodness with knowledge, and knowledge with self-control, and self-control with endurance, and endurance with godliness, and godliness with mutual affection, and mutual affection with love' (1.5-7).

The *Transfiguration* of Jesus in the Synoptic tradition plays an important role in the debate. The ungodly detractors want evidence of God's coming day of salvation/judgement. The Apostles' experience of the 'voice from heaven' and the sheer majesty of the moment on the 'holy mountain' of transfiguration served as a precursor to the coming great and glorious day of the Lord (1.16-18). So when the scoffers ask, 'Where is the promise of his coming?', the true church can point to the event of the transfiguration of Jesus as the sign and promise that the final outcome of good and evil in the world is assured. In a sense, the reality of the transfiguration of Jesus in the memory of the church is already the beginning of the end-time experience. Remembering is very much part of the fabric of 2 Peter. Addressing his readers, the author says, 'I intend to keep on reminding you of these things' (1.12; 3.1-2). This 'reminding' is nothing less than an appeal to the Christian tradition that has shaped the church as it made its way into the world. The transfiguration was the promissory part of that tradition.

God's providence in holding back the end of the world is a gift, not slackness. It is a gift in that God waits patiently for the unrepentant to repent, 'not wanting any to perish' (3.8-9). The long wait for the Lord to come is only long from the human perspective, not by the standard of divine calculation: 1,000 years = 1 day; 1 day = 1,000 years, an allusion to Psalm 90.4.

The *apocalyptic imagery* depicting the end of the age is at least as frightening as that depicted in Revelation. Precursors exist in the long tradition of Judaism. Both Jude and 2 Peter draw on those past events of judgement on ungodliness. God judged the angels who had sinned by chaining them and casting them into Tartarus (2.4). God judged the world of Noah by a great flood, saving only eight persons (2.5). God judged the cities of Sodom and Gomorrah, reducing them to ashes and saving only righteous Lot (2.6-7; cf. Gen. 19.15-30, which includes Lot's two daughters). Given these earlier acts of divine judgement, the final judgement will surely come with even greater force, so the prophecy of 2 Peter predicts. Warning: 'the day of the Lord will come like a thief' (3.10), as Paul had prophesied earlier (1 Thess. 5.2; cf. Mt. 24.43), so keep alert. By that time, evil in the world will be so widespread that 'the heavens will pass away with a loud noise (cf. 1 Cor. 15.52), and the elements will be dissolved with fire, and the earth and everything that is done on it will be disclosed' (3.10). In light of this apocalyptic disclosure, the author asks his faithful readers: 'What sort of persons ought you to be in leading lives of holiness and godliness?' (3.11).

Again, eschatological theology grounds ethics. The scoffers of 'the last days' (3.3) have a point if the theodicy fails. If God has no plan to come in judgement, no interest in saving the world and its people, then there is no reason to live righteous lives. But the author of 2 Peter argues in favour of God and judgement. The final outcome, however, is not mass destruction by fire (3.7, 10). Rather, drawing on the prophecy of Isaiah (65.17; 66.22), 'we' the righteous ones who believe the word of God await 'new heavens and a new earth, where righteousness is at home' (3.13; cf. Rev. 21.1-2). With such a new home in view the true Christians should 'strive to be found by him at peace, without spot or blemish; and regard the patience of our Lord as salvation' (3.14).

Meanwhile, using much of the *scathing diatribe* of Jude, the scoffers are severely censured for their lack of godliness and their assault on the faithful church. They are 'like irrational animals', 'blots and blemishes', 'following the road of Balaam', 'waterless springs and mists driven by a storm'. They are committed to the lusts of the flesh rather than to God who rewards the righteous and punishes the ungodly. For them the 'deepest darkness has been reserved' (2.12-18). One has to keep in mind that 2 Peter at heart is an apology (*apologia*, 'verbal defence') for a theology of rewards and punishment, aimed at promoting ethical behaviour. The faithful members in the church are also called upon to be ready to make a similar defence to anyone who demands an accounting of the hope that is in them. It is to be done with 'gentleness and reverence' (so 1 Pet. 3.15-16). One wonders if 2 Peter is a good example of a defence made with 'gentleness and reverence'.

Two more points remain to be considered. First, this Epistle puts to rest any hint of theological-ethical differences between Paul and Peter from the past (as in Gal. 2.11; cf. 1 Cor. 1.12). Paul is now called 'our beloved brother', and 'all' his letters are regarded as authoritative even though some things in them are hard to understand (3.14-15). Implicitly, Peter of 2 Peter and Paul of 'all his letters' agree on the matters of wisdom debated in this Epistle. But the 'ignorant and unstable twist [Paul's arguments] to their own destruction' (3.16). This latter statement may signal an early stage of what was to become the Marcionite trajectory of the second century. Marcion (*c*.110–160) adopted Paul's teachings from his letters as pivotal and authoritative for his congregations. But from the orthodox perspective, Marcion had misunderstood Paul, as also some people known to the writer of 2 Peter. The Epistle of 2 Peter is probably the latest writing of the New Testament (*c*.100–115), and the closest in time to the Marcionite movement within early Christianity.

Second, the interpretation of the Scriptures is not 'a matter of one's own interpretation'. Scriptures did not come into being by human intention, but by the movement of the Holy Spirit (2.20-21). Here as nowhere else in the New Testament we find a move towards a normative interpretation of Scripture. If the Scriptures came into being by the divine Spirit resident in the church, then the interpretation should come out of that same communal environment where the Holy Spirit continues to live and move. The text seems to imply that private interpretations, as compared to churchly interpretations, lead to a twisting of theology and ethics like that of the 'ignorant and unstable' who twist Paul's statements in his letters (3.16).

b. The Epistle of Hebrews

To call Hebrews an 'epistle' is to stretch the definition of the term to its limit. The only distinctive mark of an 'epistle' in Hebrews is in the final exhortation and greeting in chapter 13. That begs the question of the literary form of this document, and what its function was in its first setting. For purposes of this inquiry, the discussion will be confined to the following: form and context of the document; rhetoric of Christocentric finality; the problem with the warnings in 2.1-4, 6.1-8 and 10.26-31; and the goal of perfection.

i. Form and context of the document

The opening to Hebrews has no sign whatsoever that it is a letter, or the imitation of a letter. There is no sender named, no recipients, and no greeting.

The thanksgiving and/or prayer, present in all of Paul's letters except Galatians, is non-existent. Nor are there any personal references until chapter 13, at which point the personal pronoun 'I' comes to the fore several times as the person writing: '**I** urge you all the more to do this, so that **I** may be restored to you very soon' (v. 19); **I** appeal to you, brothers and sisters . . .; **I** want you to know that our brother Timothy has been set free; and if he comes in time, he will be with me when **I** see you'.

The *figure of Timothy* comes into the picture at the close, along with people from Italy who send greetings. This minimal feature of a letter, occurring only in chapter 13, has led a number of scholars to treat chapter 13 either as an appendix, not integral to the consistent structure of the other 12 chapters, or as a later addition to a document that was not intended as a circular letter in its original composition. Some interpreters have suggested that the personal ending, especially the mention of Timothy, was added to give this otherwise anonymous writing a Pauline touch.

Leaving chapter 13 aside for the moment, the literary quality of chapters 1 through 12 of Hebrews is that of a well educated person acquainted with the ideological world of Hellenism, or more specifically the world of Hellenistic Judaism. A number of Greek words are *hapax legomena*, occurring only in Hebrews, e.g. *apaugasma* (1.3, 'reflection'), *charactèr* (1.3, 'exact imprint'), and *hupostasis* (11.1, 'assurance'). The style is well developed, not complex, but rich in rhetorical texture. As a document it reads more like a theological treatise than a letter. Yet one of its distinctive features is that the theological argumentation is laced with ethical instruction in the form of warnings. These are not tacked on to the end of the document, as one might expect in an epistle. They are woven into the texture of the elevated Christology that pervades the whole. The urgency that so characterizes these ethical injunctions points to a specific situation to which this subject matter is directed.

Moreover, this is not a theological treatise in abstraction. Its urgency points to *a concrete threat* to the life of the Christian community, or at least to some members in the community. If the document was not first meant as a circular letter, it became so as the sense of urgency continued to present itself. It is possible that the document contained within chapters 1 through 12 was first composed as a sermon for a worship setting. The number of times the author uses the verb 'to speak' could be construed as a clue to the original homiletical function of the material in the document (2.5; 6.9; 9.5; 11.19; 12.25). The point should not be pressed too far. After all, the author also uses the present tense of the verb 'to speak' with reference to authors of the Old Testament Scriptures. Beyond this literary convention, the document does read like a sermon laden with theological nuance for the purpose of cultivating ethical endurance in a time of trial. The thanksgiving at the end appears as an appropriate conclusion to a sermon on acceptable worship. 'Therefore, since we are receiving a kingdom that cannot be shaken, let us give thanks, by which we offer to God an acceptable worship with reverence and awe; for indeed our God is a consuming fire' (12.28-29).

Now if chapter 13 was added, either as *an appendix* by the same author, or as an addition by a later redactor, the letter had a destination and use beyond a local worship setting. From the geographical note in the final greeting – 'those from Italy send you greetings' (v. 24), some have argued that it was written from Rome by a Hellenistic Jewish Christian for like-minded Christians in the Diaspora. Others read the greeting as the author's way of connecting with the churches in the city of Rome. He was writing from some other location outside Palestine and outside Italy where he was in contact with some Italian Christians. Still some others believe Hebrews was written to Jewish Christians in Palestine, in or near Jerusalem, before the destruction of the Temple. The writer speaks in the present tense about the sacrifices that go on in the Jewish cult at Jerusalem. This is not a tenable argument. The cult is that of the wilderness, and the meeting place that of the tent of the Lord described in the book of Exodus. The character and style of the document is thoroughly Hellenistic, not likely to find an open door in Palestine during the sixties CE.

From very early times, church leaders were interested in determining the identity of authors of *anonymous* documents that became part of the Scripture of the church. Hebrews was no exception. Origen (*c.*185–254 CE) was the first to assign the name of Paul to the document, principally because of the mention of Timothy. Origen viewed the thought as Pauline, but the style as belonging to someone else, perhaps a friend of Paul who took liberties in shaping the diction of the document. In the end though, Origen was not completely convinced. Only God knows who wrote the document, he said. Other names were put forward. Tertullian (*c.*160–235 CE) suggested Barnabas. Luther (1483–1546 CE) believed Apollos. By the fifth century in the West, however, Pauline authorship was affirmed, and remained so in the church until the modern period. Today scholars treat the book as an anonymous composition, without attaching a name to it. The only author in evidence is *the one implied* in the texture of the writing itself who shall remain anonymous.

Hebrews most likely was written in the last quarter of the first century. The reference in 10.32-33 to an earlier persecution endured by Christians may be the one that Nero inflicted. If so, the present trial must be some time later. Furthermore, in the admonition at 2.3 a second generation Christian writer and readership is clearly implied. Outside of Hebrews, the first sign of an allusion to this document comes from Clement, bishop of Rome from 88–99 CE. The allusion is debatable. Beyond that possible reference to Hebrews little is known of the document until the latter part of the second century. It was not put on the Muriatorian list of churchly books (*c.*200 CE).

Given the developed Christology, the familiarity with classical Hellenistic Jewish thought, a memory of persecution past, and the experience of persecution present, Hebrews is a post-Pauline document, most likely directed to Hellenistic Jewish converts to Christ. They are under pressure to abandon their new faith and return to their less persecuted religion, probably the Diaspora synagogue setting.

ii. The rhetoric of Christocentric finality

It is now well recognized that Hebrews belongs within the Hellenistic worldview espoused by Philo of Alexandria (*c.*20 BCE–50 CE). Other traditions can be traced to the literary–theological fabric of Hebrews, but the broad pattern espoused for setting forth the person of Christ as high priest of the new covenant reflects the Platonism espoused by Philo. In particular, the idea of shadow and reality comes through in Hebrews implicitly and explicitly. The sanctuary in which the Israelites worshipped was a 'shadow' of the heavenly reality (8.5), 'a mere copy of the true one' (9.24). As shadow and copy the earthly sanctuary moves, changes, and ultimately disappears. The heavenly sanctuary, the abode of the exalted Christ at the right hand of God (1.3; 8.1), is permanent, real. Likewise, the sacrifice in the earthly tent is a 'shadow' of the '*once for all*' atoning sacrifice of Christ, which he offered in his own blood before God (7.27; 9.12, 26; 10.2, 10). Of course, the idea of the real and the shadow could have come right out of the Exodus account (Exod. 25.9-10, 40). Moses was shown the 'pattern' of the tent of meeting, which he followed in making the material tent in the wilderness.

Still, the way the thought is formulated in Hebrews is similar to the way it appears in Philo. In Hebrews the *shadow/reality* in the Christological rhetoric is that of finality, or perhaps even superiority. Numerous times the word 'better'/'superior' (*kreittòn*) comes up. Christians have a better hope (7.19), a better covenant (7.22), better promises, (8.6), a better resurrection (11.35), a better word (12.24). Christ is even superior to angels (1.4) and to Abraham (7.6-7).

The author of Hebrews masterfully connects his Christocentric vision with the history of salvation in Israel as recorded in the Scriptures of the LXX. The most important comparisons in Hebrews are between the Aaronic sacrificial system set out in the Pentateuch, and the priestly sacrifice of Christ. The 'five books of Moses' were the highest, most sacred court of appeal in every branch of Judaism. Christ is compared to the sacrificial system set out in that revered literature. Implicitly, that sacred system has run its transitory course, reaching its end in Christ's death and resurrection to 'the right hand of the throne of the Majesty in the heavens' (8.1). This majestic Christocentric exposition undergirds the interlaced warning rhetoric, to be examined shortly.

While recognizing *the context of Hebrews* within the Hellenistic Jewish milieu, exemplified in Philo's work, there is something about the theologizing in Hebrews that does not quite correspond with Philo. Philo *allegorizes* the texts of his Scripture (LXX). He associates some lofty idea with an event, person or artefact in the Scripture. For example, Philo associates the wandering of Abraham towards the Promised Land with the soul in search the true God, the Existent One. The author of Hebrews, by comparison, *theologizes using typology*. Before inquiring into that structure, which informs the shaping of the whole text from 1.4 to 12-29, we should examine the tightly woven texture of the prologue (1.1-3), in which the central theme of the book is captured succinctly. The literal translation is mine, to illustrate the grammatical and syntactical structure of this sophisticated prologue.

> At many times and in many ways God, having spoken to the fathers of old by the prophets, has spoken to us in these final days by Son, whom he has appointed heir of all things through whom also he made the ages, who being the outshining of the [God's] glory and the exact image of his reality, upholding all things by the word of his power, and having made a purification for sins, sat down at the right hand of the majesty in the highest heights (1.1-4; cf. Ps. 110.1, 5).

The 'many times' and 'many ways' relate to the multiple forms of revelation given through the Jewish ancestors of the past through the word of the prophets. God 'spoke' through them. By comparison, in these 'final days', God 'has spoken', not in many and various ways as before, but 'by Son'.

There is no definite article and no pronoun before 'Son'. The article in Greek bespeaks identity, whereas the absence of the article speaks of quality or character. Moreover, the identity of 'Son' is not the issue here, but the character of the revelation as compared to the earlier forms of revelation. Instead of multiple voices and multiple events, rituals and places, there is a singular form of divine expression: Son. This form is final, not a forerunner to some others yet to come. As the exposition that follows the prologue will confirm, this final form is not merely final, but 'better' than all that has gone before. The nature of this final form of divine revelation is further described by two terms found only here: 'outshining of the glory' and 'exact image of his reality'. The glory is that of God, and the Son is the effulgence of that glory.

The idea is traceable to Philo's notion of the relation of the *Logos* to the Existent One. The *Logos* is pictured in Philo as the light shining from the sun, properly suited to the eye that meets the light. If one were to experience the sun by itself, it would blast the observer out of existence. The *Logos* mediates the light of the sun so that it gives life and enables just judgement. Philo also calls the *Logos* 'Son of God'. The writer of Hebrews seems to be acquainted with this pattern of thinking. The outshining, or effulgence, of the glory is not different in quality from the unmediated glory. It is the same in *charactèr* ('exact image'), but the glory is tempered appropriately for reception in the human mind.

This is *the Son*, the *Logos*-Word-Power that created the world of ages, and that upholds and sustains the world. The same Son-Word has purified sins, thus completing the task of revelation and redemption. The task completed, the *Logos*-Son takes his regal seat at the highest imaginable place in the universe, yea beyond the universe in the presence of the ever-existent God. Given this character of divine sonship, as compared to all other revelations and rituals of the past, the author of Hebrews is in a position to expound the superiority of Jesus Christ over the earlier religious experiences of God. Rhetorically, the readers are urged to value their calling within this theological configuration. They should stay the course, not fall back to the old ways, endure persecution, and win the reward when 'the one who is coming will come and will not delay' (10.37).

Much of what is going on in Hebrews may be called typological theologizing. Typology is a kind of comparison. Where the allegorical comparison could be described as vertical, typological comparison is more horizontal. It takes the factors of history seriously. But the comparison is not merely between like entities. Typology compares some feature of the past record with something in the present time and experience to show that the reality of the present time has exceeded its prefiguration in the past. Everything about Christ and his work of salvation in Hebrews is so much '*better*' than the saving factors and persons of the past as to render the past factors inoperative in the present time and experience. If the 'better' revelation of salvation has come, why would anyone want to cling to the inferior revelation and ritual related to the past? That is the rhetorical question embedded in the whole typological theologizing in Hebrews, and one that the readers are strongly advised to take seriously.

First, the 'Son' is better than the *angels* (1.5–2.18). In this section the author cites a number of royal psalms, along with other Scriptures, to prove the point. In Jewish tradition angels were considered the highest form of created reality, and the mediators of the Law of Moses. But the writer of Hebrews asks: 'To which of the angels did God ever say, "You are my Son; today I have begotten you?" (1.5, Ps. 2.7). Or again, "I will be his Father, and he will be my Son?"' (1.5, 2 Sam. 7.14). Psalm 110 in particular plays an important role in the typological argumentation in support of the enthronement of the Son to the highest place, and also in establishing the better priesthood of Jesus Christ. More on that topic momentarily.

Second, the Son is better than *Moses* who gave the people the Law to guide them in right living under God (3.1-18). The people rebelled, and did not enter into God's 'rest'. The 'rest' in Hebrews is God's Sabbath-rest; it is salvation from sin, oppression, injustice, etc. 'Yet Jesus is worthy of more glory than Moses, just as the builder of a house has more honor than the house itself' (3.3). Moses is servant within the house, but Jesus is the Son who owns the house.

Third, Jesus Christ, the Son, is better than Joshua who led the people into the promised land of Canaan. There they were supposed to settle down after their wandering. There they were to find 'rest' from their enemies, but did not find it in Canaan. 'For if Joshua had given them rest, God would not speak later about another day' (4.8).

Fourth, Jesus Christ, the Son, is mediator of a better *covenant* (8.1-13). This comes from the central section of the whole treatise, which runs from 8.1–10.18. The covenant now inaugurated by the Christ event, especially in the death of Jesus in which he shed his blood, becomes a major talking point. It is called the 'new covenant' (8.8, 13; 9.15; 12.24). Jeremiah is called in as prophetic voice hailing the coming of the new. Again, the implication of a 'new' covenant seems to be that the 'old' covenant has been set aside, especially so if the new incorporates all of the essentials of the old in the covenant made by the Son, Jesus Christ.

Fifth, the *sacrifice* of Christ is also said to be 'better' than the sacrifices of the past that were set in place to take away sins (9.23–10.18). Sacrifices in Israel were repeated. The sacrifice on the Day of Atonement involved the sprinkling of blood on the mercy seat once every year. That atoning sacrifice was a 'type' of the 'once for all' sacrifice of Christ (10.2, 10). Much is made in Hebrews of the blood of the sacrifices, which prefigures the blood of Jesus Christ poured out in his death. But the sacrificial blood of Christ was not merely sprinkled on an earthly mercy seat, but became effective in the heavenly sanctuary, the true sanctuary, for the purification of sins (9.24; 10.12).

All of this Christological theologizing is carried out by an interpretive method known in Judaism as *midrash*, commenting on a Scripture text with an eye to the present situation. Psalm 110, as indicated earlier, was a key text for the author of Hebrews. That Psalm was performed at enthronement ceremonies during the monarchy in Israel. The King of Israel would rise to take his seat in the highest place in the nation. He was God's anointed leader of the people. But more than that, Psalm 110 speaks of a priesthood that implicitly surpasses the Aaronic priesthood. The latter point plays an important role in the argument of Hebrews.

The priest in whose order Jesus is said to follow is *Melchizedek* (7.1-17). The story of his priesthood appears in Genesis 14.18-20. The significance of the elements of the story for Hebrews is patent. His name means 'king of righteousness', and he is called King of Salem (peace), and 'priest of the Most High God'. This Melchizedek meets up with Abraham after a battle. The priest blesses Abraham. Abraham pays a tithe of his booty to Melchizedek. For Hebrews, that means Melchizedek was better than Abraham (7.7). The sudden appearance of Melchizedek on the scene in Genesis 14, without genealogy or record of his death, signals to the writer of Hebrews his resemblance to the eternal Son of God. If Melchizedek is a type of the priest-king character and function of Jesus Christ, then it is positive type, or type with direct correspondence. And Psalm 110 confirms the priesthood of Melchizedek as that which belongs to the king of Israel. Within Hebrews, the statement from Psalm 110 is a Christological affirmation: Melchizedek is the figure of the Christ-priest-king.

The covenanters of Qumran made something of Melchizedek as well. He became for them an eschatological figure who would come to inaugurate the true priesthood in Jerusalem, and bring peace and righteousness to bear in the land (11Q Melchizedek). The writer of Hebrews may have been aware of the discussions at Qumran, but makes his own case in keeping with his experience of Jesus Christ.

iii. The problem with the warnings in 2.1-4; 6.1-8 and 10.26-31

It remains now to examine the *severe warnings* of Hebrews against *apostasy*. Failure to heed the warnings would lead to irreparable dissociation from the church and from the God who saves the members through Jesus Christ. The first thing to remember is that, like all ancient agrarian life, the believers in Jesus Christ thought and lived by communal standards. Modern people, especially of the West, live as individuals. If a member of an ancient church chose to leave the church he/she would be obliged to join some other community, provided they qualified for membership there. There was no such thing as solitary residents in a province.

The warnings are interspersed throughout the typological theologizing that honours Jesus Christ as the final revelation of God and ultimate mediator between God and humans. Three are selected for inquiry. The first is in 2.1-4. 'if the message declared through angels was valid, and every transgression or disobedience received a just penalty, how can we escape if we neglect so great a salvation?'(vv. 2-3). The answer to the rhetorical question is not open for discussion. Such salvation as that found in the Son has to be honoured, confessed, and lived. If it is neglected, the penalty will be more severe than that meted out on those disobedient to the Law mediated by angels. The severe language in the warnings is unforgiving. Christ purified sins 'once for all' (7.27; 9.12; 10.10). The 'once for all' character of the sacrifice in the context of Hebrews implies that the believer once incorporated into Christ and his church cannot sever the relationship and then return later to be reincorporated. The warning in 2.1-4 against apostasy does not hold out the option of repentance, forgiveness and restoration. The warning against *apostasy* in 6.1-8 is even more stark and disturbing:

> For it is impossible to restore again to repentance those who have once been enlightened, and have tasted the heavenly gift, and have shared in the Holy Spirit, and have tasted the goodness of the word of God and the powers of the age to come, and then have fallen away, since on their own they are crucifying again the Son of God and are holding him up to contempt.

Again, it should be emphasized that an interpretation is not found in individualistic, existential experience. The warning is related to membership in the community of Christ. Incorporation of members happened at baptism. Christian confession was made at the time. Baptism was not then, and not now, a repeatable sacrament. It was a 'once for all' event, in the manner of the 'once for all' sacrifice of Christ. The description of the status of members of Christ leaves no room for doubt that these were fully incorporated members of the community who had confessed their faith in Jesus Christ. The falling away (*parapiptò*) is not some ethical error. The texture of this text constitutes outright denial of Christ as Son of God to the point of holding him up to contempt as the scoffers did at the crucifixion of Jesus. That kind of deviation from the faith of the church means the *disavowal of the baptism* by which the deviants were once incorporated into Christ. Given that situation, such deviants cannot come back to the church at some later date and expect to repent and be baptized into the community again. Their incorporation was 'once for all' in Hebrews.

As an aside, the Catholic Church at a later time found it difficult to accept Hebrews as canonical because of this restriction on second repentance. The Church had devised ways by which repentant ex-communicants were readmitted to communion. Hebrews seemed to go against the practice. In 367 CE Bishop Athanasius had put Hebrews on his list of books for public reading in the Church, and it has remained in the canon to the present time.

The final warning of this kind in Hebrews comes at 10.26-31. This one reads as follows: 'if we willfully persist in sin after having received the knowledge of the truth, there no longer remains a sacrifice for sins.' Instead, such recalcitrant deviants are reserved for judgement in the end, because they have 'profaned the blood of the covenant by which they were sanctified' (10.29).

Again, these severe warnings occur throughout the texture of the elaborate Christological schema. There is not the slightest segregation of ethics from theology. What one believes about Christ determines the ethics of perseverance. The book ends with an emphasis on that kind of faith. Chapter 11 cites example after example from the past to illustrate for the community how persevering faith reaps a reward. Christ himself is cited as one who set his face unflinchingly toward the goal. Members are encouraged to run the race with perseverance, 'looking to Jesus the pioneer and perfecter of our faith, who for the sake of the joy that was set before him endured the cross, disregarding its shame, and has taken his seat at the right hand of the throne of God' (12.2).

iv. The goal of perfection

With Christ as *the perfecter of faith*, it follows in Hebrews that believers in Christ should make perfection their goal. 'Let us go on toward perfection', says the author as he introduces the warning at 6.1. 'Perfection' (*teleiotès*) is goal oriented. The aim of Christian confession and life is to complete the course, to finish 'the race that is set before us' without deviating from the chosen path (12.1; cf. 2 Tim. 4.7). *Perfection* in this context is not so much about personal sinlessness as about persevering in the confession of Christ without turning to the side. In doing so the members are encouraged to maintain community life, 'not neglecting to meet together, as is the habit of some, but encouraging one another, and all the more as you see the Day approaching' (10.25). In addition, the appendix of chapter 13 requires of the members that they 'remember [their] leaders' (13.7), 'obey [their] leaders and submit to them' (13.17), and 'greet [their] leaders' (13.24). By inference, the leaders are expected to guide their members on the path of faith and truth as it is in Christ Jesus.

The *benediction* in Hebrews 13.20-21, which captures much of the theology expressed throughout the document, will serve to bring closure to the exploration:

> Now may the God of peace, who brought back from the dead our Lord Jesus, the great shepherd of the sheep, by the blood of the eternal covenant, make you complete in everything good so that you may do his will, working among us that which is pleasing in his sight, through Jesus Christ, to whom be the glory forever and ever. Amen. (13.20-21)

3. Conclusion: post-Pauline or non-Pauline?

In 1971 Robinson and Koester drew attention to ideological trajectories extending out from the missionary preaching of Paul in the decade of the fifties to become varieties of hybrid Paulinism many decades later (1971, pp. 20–70; 269–79) . Gnostic movements evidenced in the Nag Hammadi library from Egypt (discovered in 1945) were no less Christian by their self-definition than others that claimed Jesus as saviour of the world, and Paul as the great missionary of Jesus following his death and resurrection. As the churches encountered different circumstances and pressures – politically, socially, philosophically, theologically – the terms of reference by which they expressed their faith in Jesus as the Christ changed, and also the way they practised their religious convictions. The five epistles discussed in this chapter echo Paul's preaching of Jesus past, while grappling with new forces at work, including persecution for believing as Christians within the highly charged political–religious environment.

That the Catholic Epistles show signs of post-Pauline circumstances is most clearly evident in the epistles of James and 2 Peter. James deals with a situation in the church in which the 'works of the law' that Paul had set aside to allow Gentiles to come into the community of Christ were taken to mean any and all ethical behaviour. 2 Peter recognizes that some in his time and place had twisted Paul's teaching in his letters. Since Jude and 2 Peter have much in common, it follows that the two documents represent a similar set of circumstances: 'heretics' in the church whose ethical behaviour belies bad theology. Hebrews in its own way bears witness to a situation in the life of a Jewish oriented church (whether actual Judaeans or Gentiles wanting to be Jewish) in which members were under pressure to return to a religious practice less subject to persecution. From its typological, midrashic argumentation to the severe warnings against apostasy, Hebrews instructs its members to stay the Christian course in light of the 'once-for-all' work of Christ, textured in a quasi-Platonic dress.

The next generation of Christian witness in the world, after the time of the Catholic Epistles, will see even more trajectories, not the least that of Marcionism in the second half of the second century. In that community Paul continued to be honoured as the great missionary-teacher of spiritual salvation originating with Jesus. Ironically, the Jewish Scriptures from which Paul drew much of his inspiration were set aside by Marcion as antithetical to the teaching of both Jesus and Paul concerning the merciful, loving character of God. By the middle of the fourth century, after the conversion of Emperor Constantine to Christianity, the Christian church, East and West, had drawn up creeds and canons that effectively eliminated Christian offshoots in the name of Christian orthodoxy.

Further related reading

One of the insights gained from exploring the New Testament literature is that the understanding of Jesus as the Christ evolved through the phases of the church's life in the world. James D. G.

Dunn (1996) has traced the development of Christology admirably in his *Christology in the Making: A New Testament Inquiry into the Origins of the Doctrine of the Incarnation*. Second Edition. Eerdmans.

On the background and function of Christian social ethics examine the work of Gordon M. Zerbe (1993), *Non-retaliation in Early Jewish and New Testament Texts: Ethical Themes in Social Context*. Continuum.

An insightful book on Hebrews is that of Ernst Käsemann (1984), *The Wandering People of God: An Investigation of the Letter to the Hebrews*. Augsburg; add to that the research of Jonathan M. Issak (2002), *Situating the Letter to the Hebrews in Early Christian History*. Studies in Bible and Early Christianity, Vol. 53. Edwin Mellen.

A perusal of James M. Robinson and Helmut Koester (1971), *Trajectories through Early Christianity*. Fortress, would also be worthwhile.

Consult commentaries as appropriate under 'Post-Pauline Letters/Epistles' in the Bibliography.

View from an Island: The Apocalypse of John

The Revelation of John, called 'the Apocalypse', has fuelled many debates among Christians in the modern age, and generated many books and musicales. Popular apocalyptic eschatology sells well. Hal Lindsay's book, *The Late Great Planet Earth* (1970) has sold 15,000,000 copies, and the *Left Behind* series by Tim LaHaye and Jerry Jenkins more than 65,000,000. George Fredric Handel incorporated significant portions of Revelation into his oratorio, *The Messiah,* in 1741 CE. That musical masterpiece is one of the best loved oratorios to this day. In 1996 Canadian composer, Victor Davies, premiered his oratorio, *Revelation*, consisting of large portions of text from the New Testament book by the same name. Perhaps the book of Revelation is best understood when it is put to music.

On a more sombre note, Revelation has been responsible for the formation of church dogma related to eschatology. For example, in 1909 Cyrus I. Schofield published his annotated Bible (revised 1917) in which he conceived of seven dispensations between the creation of the world and the final judgement, the seventh being the 1,000-year earthly reign of Jesus Christ soon to come (cf. Rev. 20). Numerous fundamentalist Christians have bought into Schofield's premillennialist, dispensationalist eschatology. Because they find Schofield's comments 'in the Bible' – i.e. around and below the text – they are led to believe Schofield's word to be on par with the Word of God. Dispensationalist doctrine has staunch followers to this day, including those who accept the age of the universe as just over 6,000 years, which they also find in Schofield's notes.

But the book of Revelation is more dramatic than it is doctrinaire, more musical than prosaic, more visionary than programmatic. By virtue of its generic character, Revelation refuses to yield a single, simple interpretation. On the contrary, its literary structure is notoriously difficult to pin down, and its theological overtures too manifold to fit within a consistent system.

1. A post-Pauline composition?

The Apocalypse at the end of the New Testament canon was probably influenced to some degree by Paul's mission and letter-writing. It could hardly be otherwise. The seven churches addressed in Revelation are situated in a region of Paul's missionary activity, Asia Minor (2.1–3.22). Those congregations of Revelation could probably have traced their Christian heritage back to the great Apostle. The letter-form Paul used also frames Revelation (1.4; 22.21). And like Paul in his letters, the author of Revelation addressed specific situations in each of the seven churches.

Revelation is also post-Pauline chronologically. It reflects a period in the history of the seven churches in which the *members experience persecution*, if not from official Roman authorities, then from local groups participating in civil religion and/or imperialist commerce (18.9-19). Most commentators today date the composition of its present form in the second half of the reign of Domitian (81–96 CE), or even after his time. Christians in Asia Minor had to decide how they were to live and work in the society influenced by civil religion. The motivation behind the attacks on Christians in Asia Minor is not stated explicitly in Revelation. A fair inference is that it was related to Christian witness.

Early Christian self-definition was exclusive, both in its view of God and in its Christian worship and ethical behaviour. An exclusivist attitude and practice might constitute a reason for the attacks. Or it may have had something to do with commerce. Christians involved in trade throughout the Empire had to decide whether they would participate in the system, or withdraw from it. Withdrawal would have meant adverse circumstances for their personal earthly lives. Participation would probably have involved certain complicity with the Roman system. The seer of Revelation calls for a firm stand in light of the coming Day of the Lord for judgement and salvation: judgement for the beast of Babylon (Rome), and salvation for those who refused to bear the mark of the beast.

2. Entering the apocalyptic maze

For the present purpose, the discussion of the Apocalypse that follows may be divided into four parts: the author as visionary prophet in his time and place, the genre called 'apocalyptic', structure and content of the work, and the central theological rhetoric.

a. The author as visionary prophet in his time and place

God entrusted the Revelation (*apocalupsis*) of Jesus Christ to a man named John through the mediation of an angel (1.1). This John is called God's servant, nothing more. 'John' was a common name with roots in the Hebrew tradition. But when the book of Revelation began to be read in church services in the mid-to-late second century, the church leaders deemed it appropriate to define further the *identity of the author*. They construed the author to be John, son of Zebedee, disciple of the historical Jesus. That tradition about authorship has remained in the church through the centuries. More recently, scholars have found the tradition of John the Apostle untenable. The author named John does not refer to himself as an apostle who followed Jesus. Furthermore, the author points to the group of twelve apostles in the past, as though he were not one of them (21.14). The probable time of composition at the turn of the first to second century also militates against the possibility of John the Apostle as author.

John the Elder has also been proposed, the one mentioned in the Epistles of 2 and 3 John, a figure also known to Papias, bishop of the early second century (EH 3.39). But John of Revelation need not be either John the Apostle or John the Elder. He presents himself in Revelation simply as God's 'servant', and 'brother' to those envisioned as recipients of the document. Given this latter factor, John most likely hailed from some part of Asia Minor to which his Revelation was addressed. At the time of the vision and composition, John was on the island of Patmos on the south east part of the Aegean Sea, probably banished there 'because of the word of God and the testimony of Jesus' (1.9).

Implicitly, the author of this Revelation was *a prophet*. He does not so designate himself, nor does the angel call him 'prophet'. Even so, a prophet is one who 'sees' beyond the ordinary affairs of earthly life to a realm that reflects the divine intention for a people called by the name of the Lord. In that sense John is then a 'seer'. Numerous times the author, speaking in the first person, tells of what he saw in a vision (e.g. 1.2b; 12, 17; 4.4; 5.1). The vision, while prophetic, belongs not to John himself but to the angel, and ultimately to God. His mediated vision is that of Christ, his rule and his plan for the church and for the world (1.9-20). As chosen recipient of the vision and of the commission to write it, John of Revelation may justly be called 'prophet'.

In some respects John stands within the same threshold as the great prophets of the Hebrew Scriptures, such as Isaiah and Jeremiah. John, like them, sees a problem with the present situation in which the people of God live in the world, and then reveals a divine plan by which the present bad situation will be resolved. But unlike the earlier prophets, John's visions are out of this world, cosmic in scope, replacing the old world order with a new order, 'a new heaven and a new earth' (21.1). One can hear an echo of Isaiah's 'new heavens and the new earth' (Isa. 65.17; 66.22), with greater cosmic symbolism added. John also echoes the apocalyptic prophecy of Daniel 7, among other apocalyptic traditions of Judaism and Graeco-Roman mythology.

The *eschatological aspect* of John's prophecy holds out hope to his churches in Asia Minor, on the condition that they endure the present trials without adopting the unjust system of Rome. The aim of his prophecy appears to be one of encouragement and consolation for Christians under pressure from some opposing force in their setting in Asia Minor. From a very early time, the setting of Revelation was believed to be that of Emperor Domitian (81–96 CE) who purportedly sponsored official persecution of Christians in the Empire. The writings of Tacitus, Pliny the Younger and Suetonius, published after Domitian, may have exaggerated Domitian's anti-Christian harshness. According to those sources, Domitian decreed that the people proclaim him 'lord and God' and participate in his worship. Recently, however, the information about Domitian's official persecution of Christians has been found wanting. There is insufficient evidence that Domitian sanctioned an all-out persecution. The suffering of Christians in Asia Minor depicted in Revelation may have been local, perhaps terrorist attacks from various quarters. For example, John accuses Judaeans (*Ioudaioi*), not Romans, of slandering the churches of Smyrna (2.9) and Philadelphia (3.9). This is probably an allusion to the renewal of Judaism taking place at Jamnia a few decades after the destruction of Jerusalem. The slander of Christians is implied in one of the Eighteen Benedictions reconstituted at Jamnia (*c.*90 CE). On the other hand, much of the physical persecution of Christians in Asia Minor probably came from local non-Jewish residents in league with the Roman system in one way or another.

Even if Rome did not officially sponsor the persecution, Revelation paints the imperialist system of Rome as corrupt and subject to the impending judgement of God. The *grotesque beast* represents the evil system that oppresses the weak while it reaps great gain for itself from the citizenry. The teaching of the Nicolaitans, which appears to have advocated a compromise of Christ with Rome, is that which the prophet John hates (2.6, 15).

b. The genre called 'apocalyptic'

The interpretation of any literature starts with the identification of *the genre* to which a given document belongs. Recognizing Revelation as belonging to the genre 'apocalyptic' is an important step towards unravelling the mysteries wrapped up in the extraordinary visions of things to come. It is time now to unpack in more detail the definition of 'apocalyptic' given in chapter 5.

Most obvious, the book of Revelation belongs to literature that claims to *unveil* the redemptive secrets of God for the people of Christ on their way through the world. The recipient of the vision is a human being, but does not receive the unveiling directly from God. God is transcendent and infinite; humans are earthly and finite. Thus, a being from another realm mediates the disclosure from God, or Christ, to the human recipient for communication to other humans in the world system. The disclosure is not merely one that calls for a change in thinking and behaviour on the part of human beings. The message is about transcendent reality that sees the unfolding drama of human history from the vantage point of the other world of angels and God. End-time salvation comes not from revising the current system, but from overthrowing the existing system of society to provide a whole new cosmic order. In the process of saving the righteous, the wicked will be judged for their crimes against humanity. Moreover, the visionary message aims at sustaining a group, or groups, caught in a crisis situation, and this by means of exhortation and consolation authorized by the divine mind.

Much of *the exhortation* in Revelation is in code. The symbolic universe of apocalyptic does not release its interpretation to the uninitiated. Only those on the 'inside' will catch the force of the images described in apocalyptic dress. The identity of the earthly reality symbolized in the beast 'rising out of the sea, having ten horns and seven heads' (13.1-2) remains symbol. Of course, such a beast could hardly be construed as something wholesome and good. Its grotesque nature together with its origin in the sea bespeaks something like the Leviathan of the biblical books of Job, Psalms and Isaiah (Job 3.8; 41.1; Ps. 74.14; 104.26; Isa. 27.1). It is a beast to be dreaded, without mercy, and having authority. Whatever the interpretation, in whatever time, such a beast could not represent the goodness of God, but the evil character of Satan, the adversary of God.

Moreover, while the interpretation of apocalyptic literature is by definition *polyvalent*, the character of the symbolic imagery has to remain in focus for the interpretation to be valid. Apocalyptic is made up of narrative, poetry (music?) and drama. Inside these literary features *the symbolic message* of salvation and judgement live and breathe. In the case of Revelation, the 'letter' frames the whole. Following the preface (1.1-3), the author employs the letter form already recognized, since Paul, as a medium for theological and ethical exhortation. Now it is John's turn to write a letter, yet far more than a letter.

> John to the seven churches that are in Asia: Grace to you and peace from him who is and who was and who is to come, and from the seven spirits who are before his throne, and from Jesus Christ, the faithful witness, the firstborn of the dead, and the ruler of the kings of the earth. To him who loves us and freed us from our sins by his blood.

This is clearly how a letter of the time would open: the name of sender, the designation of the recipients, and a greeting. What follows in short order thereafter are reasonably straightforward exhortations to the seven churches in Asia Minor (2.1–3.22). But then these exhortations burst out into cosmic symbolism using various numbers, along with seven messages, seven seals, seven trumpets, and seven bowls with repetition and cadence quite unlike any ordinary letter or prose narrative. Then when all the extravagant visions are finished, the work closes with a usual benediction that one might find at the end of any regular letter form: 'The grace of the Lord Jesus be with all the saints. Amen' (22.21). The first person singular narrator also adds to the letter quality, but is also characteristic of apocalyptic.

The many-sided apocalyptic genre – revelatory narrative, letter, poetry, cosmic symbolism – was not written merely as a work of art. It had purpose. The apocalyptic genre projects a vision of an end time when the wrongs of society will be made right. The wicked will be judged, and the righteous saved. But the New Testament Apocalypse is not about the reward awaiting the souls of historical persons when they get to heaven. The Apocalypse envisions a change in the way things are carried out on earth. The old world order, corrupt as it is, will be replaced by a new order. Jerusalem once said to be holy, having had a temple at its centre, will be replaced at the end of days. The futuristic outlook of apocalyptic is very much part of its genius. By hearing the vision described – as in hearing the book read aloud in congregations – Christians addressed in Revelation are enabled to go through the present trials with the promise of a great new future, when tears will be wiped away, and the new heaven and new earth will come into being. A New Jerusalem also will come 'down out of heaven from God, prepared as a bride adorned for her husband' (21.2).

In short, a determination of the genre of apocalyptic should take into account the *form*, *content* and *function* of the document. In this regard, the insight of David E. Aune makes a fitting closure to this section on the genre of apocalyptic:

> [In *form*], an apocalypse is a first-person recital of revelatory visions or dreams, framed by a description of the circumstances of the revelatory experience, and structured to emphasize the central revelatory message. In *content*, an apocalypse involves the communication of a transcendent, often eschatological perspective on human experience. Finally, apocalypses typically have a threefold *function*. They legitimate the message through the appeal to transcendent authority by the author (i.e. it is from God), they create a literary surrogate of the author's revelatory experience for readers or hearers (i.e. God speaks to the modern reader just as he spoke to John), and they motivate the recipients to modify their views and behaviours in conformity with the transcendent perspectives (i.e. they demand changed behaviour). (Aune 2006, p. 2)

c. The structure of the work

The compositional structure of Revelation is difficult to nail down precisely. A glance at commentaries on Revelation will reveal at once that scholars are not agreed on the structure of the work. Some of the themes and images are repeated with *variations*, but with little logical connection between them. Of course, what appears as repetition could be recapitulation, something like the repetition of a musical theme in the course of a symphony. Perhaps this recapitulation notion is what draws composers of music to Revelation.

Yet many scholars of the twentieth century, observing the *textual seams* in the flow of thought in the literature, were led to propose the existence of sources in Revelation. In that view, the redactor failed to make coherent connection between the incorporated sources. But this author, John, who echoes Scripture randomly, is hardly likely to incorporate literary sources in a way that scholars will be able to detect them ages hence. There may indeed be sources as well as non-literary traditions embedded in Revelation, but the apparent 'seams' may not be the way to identify them. The *recapitulation* theory is more in line with the stated form of the writing. It is the product of a heavenly vision, mediated by a heavenly being. The apparent incoherence between visions coupled with repetitiveness may be nothing more than a deliberate attempt to reinforce the message of the visions.

Revelation, by its very character, refuses to be linear and logical. It could be more aptly compared to a *musical fugue*. A theme will come into the foreground only to be picked up by another and another, and return later for further variation. Revelation is dramatic, not factual description or logical argumentation. The prophet-author blesses the one who 'reads aloud' the prophecy, and also those who hear the prophecy read aloud.

More recent studies have validated an essential unity of Revelation within the generic field of literature to which it belongs. For example, the number seven occurs over and over in the main part of the book: seven churches, seven seals, seven trumpets, seven bowls, etc. The number seven used thus throughout Revelation becomes one overt principle of organization. Besides, the prevailing themes of persecution, judgement and salvation appearing in cyclical fashion contribute to the unification of Revelation.

Any attempt to reduce a complex literary work like Revelation to a simple outline runs the risk of devaluing the work. Yet a succinct analysis can provide ready access to this document which might otherwise remain obtuse to the uninitiated reader. Only one who has spent much time in research and writing on the book of Revelation would be qualified to render such an analysis. Adela Yarbro Collins qualifies, and I appeal to her structural outline provided in her commentary on Revelation (1990, p. 10).

Professor Collins believes Revelation as it stands in the canon is the product of the author's literary design, and that recapitulation and the number seven are important devices ordering the document. Narrative events do not follow one after the other. Events begin afresh, nuanced but recognizable from what went before, all of them exhibiting the same triadic theme of persecution, judgement and triumph. The book seems to fall into two major parts related to two scrolls.

> **Part I The Sealed Scroll, chapters 1–11**
>> A. Prologue, 1.1-8
>> B. John gives an account of his inaugural vision and commission to write, 1.9–3.22
>> C. John sees what is and what is to take place hereafter, 4.1–8.5
>> D. Plagues prepare the way for the kingdom of God, 8.6–11.19
>
> **Part II The Open Scroll, chapters 12–22**
>> A. The church in a cosmic conflict, 12.1–15.4
>> B. Fallen, Fallen is Babylon the Great! 15.5–19.10
>> C. The Destiny of the world, 19.11–22.5
>> D. Epilogue, 22.6-21

At the heart of these two blocks of revelatory material is found a series of sevens – in musical terms, septets. Each of the sets of seven has a recurring *triadic theme* of persecution, judgement and salvation, or triumph. Collins believes 'it is this underlying pattern of persecution, judgment, and salvation that is the real message of the Apocalypse' (1990, p. 14). Her outline of the septets is as follows:

> 1. The seven seals
>> a. persecution 6.9-11
>> b. judgment 6.12-17
>> c. triumph 7.9-17
> 2. The seven trumpets
>> a. allusion to persecutions 8.3-5
>> b. allusion to judgment 9.15
>> c. triumph 11.15-19
> 3. Seven unnumbered visions
>> a. persecution 12–13
>> b. judgment 14.14-20
>> c. triumph 15.2-4
> 4. The seven bowls
>> a. persecution 16.4-7
>> b. judgment 16.17-20
>> c. triumph 19.1-10
> 5. Seven unnumbered visions
>> a. persecution 20.9
>> b. judgment 20.10-15
>> c. triumph 21.1–22.5

The *throne scenes* of Revelation are particularly impressive. An examination of one of these will serve to illustrate. Chapter 4 narrates the transport of John, at the behest of a voice sounding like a trumpet, through an open door into the very court of heaven. 'Come up here, and I will show you what must take place after this' (4.1). Once in heaven, John saw in the spirit a throne standing, and a figure seated on it looking like jasper and carnelian (both reddish gems). An emerald-looking rainbow surrounded the throne. The description goes on and on, with twenty-four elders dressed in white, and with them four living creatures, each with six wings and full of eyes. These four sing incessantly: 'Holy, holy, holy, the Lord God the Almighty, who was and is and is to come' (4.8). The twenty-four elders prostrate themselves in worship before the one who sits on the throne. They cast their crowns before the throne and sing, 'You are worthy, our Lord and God, to receive glory and honor and power, for you created all things, and by your will they existed and were created' (4.11).

Two principal literary *antecedents* to the throne scene of Revelation 4.1-11 can be traced in the Jewish Scriptures. The first is in Isaiah 6. In that vision the Lord is seated on a throne, 'high and lofty'. But the court in Isaiah 6 seems to be the heavenly temple. Around the throne are six-winged seraphs flying: 'with two they covered their faces, and with two they covered their feet, and with two they flew' (Isa. 6.2). The seraphs call to each other in song, 'holy, holy, holy is the Lord of hosts; the whole earth is full of his glory' (Isa. 6.3). The scene is not identical to that of Revelation 4, but has similar features of apocalyptic. The vision is recorded in the first person; the imagery is majestic, and the other-worldly attendants sing the praises of the one who sits on the throne.

The second antecedent is from Ezekiel 1. The prophet Ezekiel likewise reports his visions of God in the first person. The heavens were opened to him. The imagery is grand scale. Four living creatures with human and lion features fly around under a dome. The throne scene comes into focus at the end of the narrative about the activity of the four living creatures. Ezekiel's throne-vision, like that of Revelation 4, is full of splendour, surrounded by a rainbow. All of this to express the glory of the Lord in contrast to the earthly glory of Babylon where the prophet lived in exile (Ezek. 1.1). John was likewise in exile on the island of Patmos when he saw the heavenly court.

Other sources in Jewish apocalyptic literature were doubtless known to the author of Revelation. Echoes of *1 Enoch* 14 and 71 appear also in Revelation.

The visionary Enoch is transported into the lofty heaven, there to witness the throne of the Great One. Around the throne are attendants, but in *1 Enoch* the number is 'ten thousand times ten thousand [standing] before Him, yet He needed no counsellor' (*1 Enoch* 14.22-23). Similar apocalyptic imagery appears in the *Apocalypse of Abraham* 18.1-4. The vision is also of a throne, and the throne has 'four living creatures' in attendance. In *2 Enoch* 20–22 the visionary (under the guise of Enoch of Genesis 4–5) was carried up to the seventh heaven from whence he saw God in the tenth heaven seated on the great throne surrounded by seraphim and cherubim. God sent the archangel Gabriel to escort Enoch before the face of God, 'ineffable, marvellous and very awful, and very, very terrible' (*2 Enoch* 22.2). (See additional apocalyptic imagery reported about the throne of God in 3 *Apocalypse of Baruch* 2, and *3 Maccabees* 6).

The specific *points of connection* between these sources and Revelation does suggest John's familiarity with the material. At the same time, a word of caution might be in order. All of these sources belong to the apocalyptic genre. When a seer felt the urge to report on a heavenly vision related to the situation of trial and to the end of time, certain stock images were at hand ready for use. One might say there was cross fertilization of apocalyptic seed. John, as a Christian prophet in the tradition of Judaism, had ample apocalyptic resources in his Scriptures. Isaiah and Ezekiel have been mentioned already in connection with the throne scenes in Revelation. The Apocalypse of Daniel 7 would almost certainly have informed John's vision of the beast that roams around in Revelation all the way from chapter 11 to chapter 20. The two beasts, Daniel's and John's, are not described in exactly the same way in the two books, but by the time of Revelation the multi-headed and multi-horned beast had become an apt symbol of an evil force at work in the world.

Returning to the throne scene of Revelation 4, it creates a sense of *transcendent power* and mystery and majesty belonging to the God of splendour who is on the side of the persecuted. The figure on the throne is altogether worthy, altogether holy. 'Holy, holy, holy, the Lord God the Almighty, who was and is and is to come' (4.8). Beside such a throne there is no equal in the world of humankind. There can hardly be any doubt that the glory and power of the Roman throne, surrounded by members of the senate, acted as a backdrop to this celestial vision of the throne of God and of the Lamb. By writing the vision to be read aloud in the seven congregations the author, the angel, Christ and God all aim to give heart to those who feel the oppressive power of the society in opposition to their confession of faith in the Lamb, Jesus Christ.

In a book that purports to reveal the plan of God for the just and the unjust, remarkably little comes directly from the mouth of God on the throne. Only three times does God speak directly through the seer. The *throne speeches* are short but poignant, occurring at 1.8, 21.5-8, and 22.12-13.

> **1.8**: I am the Alpha and the Omega.

> **21.5-8**: See, I am making all things new . . . Write this, for these words are trustworthy and true . . . . It is done! I am the Alpha and the Omega, the beginning and the end. To the thirsty I will give water as a gift from the spring of the water of life. Those who conquer will inherit these things, and I will be their God and they will be my children. But as for the cowardly, the faithless, the polluted, the murderers, the fornicators, the sorcerers, the idolaters, and all liars, their place will be in the lake that burns with fire and sulfur, which is the second death.

> **22.12-13**: See, I am coming soon; my reward is with me, to repay according to everyone's work. I am the Alpha and the Omega, the first and the last, the beginning and the end.

Alpha and omega, appearing in each of the three speeches, are the first and last letters of the Greek alphabet. In the mouth of God they speak of totality, completeness, inclusiveness. There is nothing in human language and life that escapes divine scrutiny. God who created the world in the first place will also bring the same world to its end to make way for the new. All things fall under the sovereign will of God, especially the will and the power to execute justice. The righteous will be rewarded and the unrighteous punished.

The Babylon visions (17.1–19.10) are vivid and shocking. They picture the downfall of 'Babylon the great, mother of whores and of earth's abominations' (17.5). Those in league with Babylon will make war with the Lamb, but the Lamb will be victorious. 'Fallen, fallen is Babylon the great! It has become a dwelling place of demons, a haunt of every foul spirit, a haunt of every foul bird, a haunt of every foul and hateful beast' (18.2). Babylon of history, still in the memory of the Judaeans as the power that destroyed their religious symbols – land and temple – and took them captive, has become in the reported vision of John a cryptogram of Rome.

The last section (19.11–22.5) envisions *judgement and salvation* meted out on humankind 'according to their works' (20.12). Those who have sold themselves to do evil will be punished according to their works. Those who opposed the Lamb (Christ) by persecuting his followers will be punished according to their works. When all the battles are fought and won by the Lamb who is worthy, then Satan will be 'thrown into the lake of fire and sulfur, where the beast and the false prophet were' (20.10). Then will come a new heaven, a new earth, and a new Jerusalem, to replace the first heaven and the first earth, and the former Jerusalem (21.1-2).

d. The central theological rhetoric

Revelation, while apocalyptic, is no less theological. Its goal at heart is to draw a compelling picture of the character of God as sole ruler of the cosmos: compelling, insofar as the author has charted an electrifying theological and ethical course for his churches in Asia Minor to follow through the trials that oppress them in the present. They are expected to pick up clues about their current earthly experiences and connect them with the transcendent and sovereign will of God that rules the whole cosmos from God's majestic throne in heaven. To lose that vision of God, so the seer implies in his imagery, is to lose heart and to lose out altogether at the end of days.

Perhaps it is this conviction about the protecting, promising power of the rule of God on behalf of the faithful people who follow *the Lamb-Christ* that led John to warn the readers not to treat his apocalypse lightly. The warning seems over the top. Yet the sense is that if they change the vision of the book they will lose the promise it contains.

> I warn everyone who hears the words of the prophecy of this book: if anyone adds to them, God will add to that person the plagues described in this book; if anyone takes away from the words of the book of this prophecy, God will take away that person's share in the tree of life and in the holy city, which are described in this book (22.18-19).

There is no question about *the life-situation* out of which the book of Revelation came to be written. Christians known to John were going through persecution of some sort from an adversarial source. The message of Revelation is not that suffering produces good character. That might come from Athens, but it is not the message of Revelation. Even Paul's understanding of suffering in the present time is not quite that of Revelation, although there is some apocalyptic visioning happening in Romans 8. In that text Paul pits the present sufferings against the eschatological outcome of the divine plan: 'The sufferings of this present time are not worth comparing with the glory about to be revealed to us. For the creation waits with eager longing for the revealing of the children of God' (Rom. 8.18-19). The Revelation of John gives a much more dramatic picture of the outworking of the plan of God on behalf of the people of faith in Christ, the Lamb of God. Pictured in highly symbolic imagery, the power-filled plan of the supreme God gives meaning to an otherwise hopeless situation of persecution.

It seems that the persecution could be avoided. If the readers, or rather hearers, of the apocalypse in Asia Minor were suffering as John himself suffered 'because of the word of God and the testimony of Jesus', then the alternative would be to renounce the word of God and the testimony of Jesus. That would likely bring the suffering of the Christians to an end. But that course would also make the ones renouncing their witness accomplices with those inflicting the persecution. The theological rhetoric of Revelation challenges the churches to endure persecution in view of the sure and certain *victory* of the sovereign God, and the equally sure and certain judgement of the persecutors. Apocalyptic ethics has more to do with outcome than with piety for the sake of piety. There is divine reward for staying the course of righteousness and faithfulness. Just as surely there is judgement and punishment for a life of injustice and self-indulgence.

There is in Revelation a theology of the Lamb that underwrites the salvation awaiting those who follow in the footsteps of the Lamb. The Lamb is introduced early in the apocalypse as 'faithful witness', 'firstborn from the dead', 'ruler of the kings of the earth', and the one 'who loves us and freed us from our sins by his blood' (1.5). There could be an echo here of the 'lamb of God' in John 1.29, 31 who takes away the sin of the world. Christians could hardly miss the identity of the Lamb in any case. They knew from the proclamation of the gospel that Jesus loved them, that he freed them from their sins by shedding his blood on the cross. The allusion is unmistakable. Later on the Lamb is pictured as one who was slaughtered. His blood 'ransomed for God saints from every tribe and language and people and nation' (5.6-9). Again, Christians would recognize the gospel of Jesus Christ crucified.

The once *slaughtered Lamb* in Revelation occupies the throne room with God. The Lamb is the one deemed worthy to open the scroll with seven seals. The twenty-four elders and the four living creatures together sing a new song to the Lamb on the occasion of the opening of the seven seals. The Lamb is 'worthy' of the 'new song', having given himself up in a bloody death to ransom the people of the world for God.

The Lamb also redeemed the 144,000 who had not 'defiled themselves with women, for they are virgins; these follow the Lamb wherever he goes' (14.3-4).

The description speaks of an *ascetic* pilgrimage. There was a notion in early Christian thought and practice that a believer in Jesus Christ could serve better unmarried. Paul states as much in 1 Corinthians 7.8, 25,32-34. Something similar appears in Matthew 19.12: 'there are eunuchs who have made themselves eunuchs for the sake of the kingdom of heaven.' There may also be an allusion to the unmarried state of Jesus. At any rate, the 144,000 are said to have followed the Lamb wherever he goes. The notion of 'following' signals *discipleship*. Followers of the Lamb learn the way of the Lamb. They become vulnerable, non-violent, victors over their persecutors. Followers of the Lamb 'did not cling to life even in the face of death' (12.11). The theology of the Lamb speaks loudly to those who might consider armed resistance against their persecutors, and also to those who might consider giving up the confession of their faith to avoid a backlash.

The Lamb remains in view to the end of the book. He will be there on judgement day, when the kings of the earth and the magistrates and the generals and the rich cry out to the mountains and rocks, 'Fall on us and hide us from the face of the one seated on the throne and from the wrath of the Lamb' (6.15-16). The Lamb will be there when the redeemed people from the nations stand before the throne singing, 'Salvation belongs to our God who is seated on the throne, and to the Lamb!' (7.10). These last will join the Lamb as his bride at the marriage feast at the end of the day when suffering is a thing of the past. 'Write this', the seer is told, 'Blessed are those who are invited to the *marriage supper of the Lamb*' (19.9).

The presence of evil in the world is not permanent in Revelation. However dualistic the theology may sound at times, the victory of God and goodness over Satan and evil is assured in Revelation. For the time being, the cosmos is caught in the grip of Satan, the dragon, the serpent, but not interminably. The angel from heaven seized the dragon, bound him with a chain, and cast him into the bottomless pit for a 1,000 years (20.2). When the thousand years were up, the Devil was released for a while, still the same deceiver and killer, but his final end was swift and certain in the vision. He was 'thrown into the lake of fire and sulfur, where the beast and the false prophet were, and they will be tormented day and night forever and ever' (20.10). The rhetorical effect of such a horrendous picture of eschatological punishment for Satan, the beast and the false prophet, is the sense of divine justice that seems so absent from the lives of the persecuted. If the persecuted saints prevail, they will participate in their own triumphant salvation, but will witness also the just punishment coming from the throne of God on the forces of evil that pollute the world.

Revelation ends on a bright note. A *new heaven and a new earth* will come down from God out of heaven, as well as a new city of Jerusalem. The promise is bright, and the prospect sure. The sovereign God rules in righteousness through the Lamb. 'The kingdom of the world has become the kingdom of our Lord and of his Messiah, and he will reign forever and ever' (11.15). He will reign, not in some transcendent throne in the tenth heaven, but on the earth *among mortals*. So the voice from the throne proclaimed: 'See, the home of God is among mortals. He will dwell with them; they will be his peoples, and God himself will be with them; he will wipe every tear from their eyes. Death will be no more; mourning and crying and pain will be no more, for the first things have passed away' (21.3-4). This is the testimony of the Lamb, the Lord Jesus. 'Surely I am coming soon.' And the people in the seven suffering churches of Asia Minor are expected to reply, 'Come, Lord Jesus!' (22.20).

Further related reading

The collected essays in the book by David. E. Aune (2006) provide different angles of vision on the role of apocalyptic in early Christianity, *Apocalypticism, Prophecy and Magic in Early Christianity: Collected Essays*. Nohr Siebeck.

Clear and to the point, the book by Adela Yarbro Collins (1984) is worth exploring, *Crisis and Catharsis: The Power of the Apocalypse*. Westminster/John Knox.

Loren L. Johns (2003) investigates the use of 'the Lamb' as a nuanced Christology, *The Lamb Christology of the Apocalypse of John*. Mohr Siebeck.

Another special study of revelation is that of Nelson Kraybill (1996), *Imperial Cult and John's Apocalypse*. Sheffield Academic.

Perceptive also is the work of Elizabeth Schüssler Fiorenza. (1991), which focuses the justice/injustice motif in *Revelation: Vision of a Just World*. Proclamation Commentaries. Fortress.

Consult commentaries as appropriate under 'Revelation' in the Bibliography.

APPENDIX I
Emperors from Augustus Octavian to Hadrian

The Outside Edges of the Period of the New Testament

Emperor's Name	Period of Rule
Augustus Octavian (Caesar)	31 BCE–14 CE
Tiberius	14–37
Gaius, also known as Caligula	37–41
Claudius	41–54
Nero	54–68
Julius Vindex	68
Clodius Macer	68
Galba	68–69
Otho	69
Vitellius	69
Vespasian	69–79
Titus	79–81
Domitian	81–96
[Antonius Saturninus]	[89]
Nerva	96–98
Trajan	98–117
Hadrian	117–138

APPENDIX II
The Rise and Fall of the Herodian Dynasty

Antipater: From Idumea (ancient Edom), was appointed Governor of Judaea, 47–43 BCE.

Herod I: ('song of a hero', 37–4 BCE): son of Antipater, was appointed by his father as governor of Galilee in 48 CE; affirmed as Tetrarch of Galilee by the Roman Mark Anthony and Augustus Octavian in 42; adopted the Jewish religion. Fled to Rome, and convinced the Senate to elect him 'King of Judaea'. Herod I, called 'the Great', ruled the region of Judea, Perea (east of Jordan), Samaria and Galilee, from 37 BCE until his death in 4 BCE.

Achievements of Herod I (The Great): Rebuilt the Second Temple of Jerusalem in a 'magnificent scale' (20–19 BCE); the harbour city of Caesarea (25–13 BCE); aqueducts to supply water to Jerusalem and Caesarea, fortresses including Masada and Herodium. He is also noted for his wanton cruelty, even killing members of his own family. The Gospel of Matthew also gives this side of Herod's character (Mt. 2.16).

Herod Antipas: son of Herod I to his fourth wife Malthace. Ruled as Tetrarch of Galilee and Perea (4 BCE–39 CE). He divorced his first wife to marry Herodias, wife of his brother Philip. Herod Antipas had John the Baptist beheaded (Mk 6.27-28). Herod Antipas was responsible for the building of Tiberias and Sepphoris, 'ornament of all Galilee' (Josephus). The Romans exiled Antipas to Gaul.

Herod Archelaus: son of Herod I, full brother of Antipas. At his father's death (4 BCE) Rome appointed him 'ethnarch' of Samaria, Judea and Idumea. He ruled until 6 CE when Rome deposed him. Judea was thereafter ruled by Roman governors, such as Pontius Pilate (26–36 CE). According to the Gospel of Matthew, Archelaus was the 'king' that Joseph feared upon his return from Egypt with the infant Jesus (Mt. 2.13-23).

Herod Philip I: son of Herod I, to his third wife Mariamne II. Philip's wife was Herodius. Their daughter was Salome. Herodias divorced Philip and married his half brother Antipas. John the Baptist considered this marriage immoral by Jewish Law, and challenged Antipas on this point. Antipas thereupon beheaded John (Mt. 14.3-11).

Herod Philip II: son of Herod I to his fifth wife Cleopatra of Jerusalem. Philip, called the Tetrarch, ruled the north-eastern part of the kingdom of his father, Herod I, from 4 BCE until 34 CE. The Gospel of Luke refers to the territory as 'the region of Ituraea and Trachonitis' (Lk. 3.1). This Philip married his niece, Salome (see Herod Philip I above). Philip II rebuilt the old city of Paneas at the head waters of the Jordan and called it Caesarea Philippi in honour of the Emperor and himself, and presumably also to distinguish it from the Caesarea built by his father. Jesus elicits a confession from his disciples at the site of Caesarea Philippi (Mk 8.27; Mt. 16.13).

Herod Agrippa I: grandson of Herod I, son of Aristobulus IV and Berenice. Agrippa found favour with Rome. He was instrumental in the accession of Claudius to the throne in 41 CE, and in the banishment of his uncle, Herod Antipas, from Galilee. Emperor Claudius granted Agrippa I the province of Judea, a territory as extensive as that of his grandfather, Herod I. Agrippa I ruled until 44 CE. He died after celebrating Passover in Caesarea, possibly from a heart attack. He killed James the disciple of Jesus, and imprisoned Peter. Acts 12 says he was struck down suddenly and eaten by worms. Another account says he was assassinated by the Romans who resented his growing power and popularity. After Agrippa's death the province reverted to the rule of Roman governors, called procurators.

Herod Agrippa II: son of Agrippa I, and great grandson of Herod I. Claudius granted the young Agrippa II oversight of the Temple of Jerusalem; he was empowered to appoint the Jewish High Priest. After the death of his uncle, Herod of Chalcis, in 48, Rome appointed Agrippa II in his uncle's place. Chalcis was an independent city in Syria, north of Palestine. Emperor Claudius added the territories of Philip the Tetrarch (see above), but also appointed a strong procurator (Felix of Acts 25) over Samaria and Judea to keep Agrippa II under control. Nero added to the realm of Agrippa II the city of Tiberias of Galilee, and parts of Perea. Agrippa II resided in Jerusalem and Caesarea. In Caesarea Agrippa II met the Apostle Paul and listened to his defence. Agrippa II probably witnessed the destruction of the Temple in 70 CE under the order of General Titus, the same Temple his great grandfather had built, and he himself had renovated only seven years earlier.

With the fall of Jerusalem, and the ravaging of the surrounding country, Agrippa II lost his right to rule over the Jewish inhabitants in the Roman province of Palestine. Thus ended the Herodian dynasty of kingship of the Judaeans.

Agrippa II was permitted to rule Tiberias in Galilee and some surrounding territory for many years after the fall of Jerusalem in 70. He died at the end of the first century, in the reign of Trajan (*c.*100 CE).

APPENDIX III
Glimpses at Ancient Philosophers (Viewed Chronologically)

Thales of Miletus: early sixth century BCE. His record is mixed with legend. He is said to have predicted the solar eclipse of May 28, 585. His hypothesis about the origin of the universe was that it came from one first principle called an *archê*, 'cause'. He identified this first principle with water. Thales continued to hold a religious belief that deities populate the universe.

Pythagoras of Samos: *c.*570–480 BCE. Believed, like Thales, in a single first cause. He believed the harmony of the universe could be understood in terms of *numbers*. Hence his reputation as the father of mathematics. Towards the end of his life he founded a school in Italy. His earlier contact with Brahmans may have led him to a belief in reincarnation.

Heraclitus of Ephesus: *c.*500 BCE. Much of his written work is lost. From what remains it seems he proposed the *logos* as the essential principle of the cosmos. Because human beings can understand the universe by rational thinking, it follows that the universe must run by the same principle. The perfect logos principle expresses itself in the material world in the form of fire.

Parmenides of Elea in Italy: *c.*500 BCE. He opposed 'being' to 'non-being', maintaining that being cannot come from non-being. The only way to grasp the order in the universe is through the exercise of the intellect, as opposed to experience through the senses. Thus began the notion that has influenced western culture to this day: that there are *two realms*. One we experience through the senses, which is illusionary, and the other which we grasp in understanding, which is the real realm of being.

Democritus of Abdera in Thrace: fifth century BCE. In answer to the problem that Parmenides raised, Democritus proposed that matter is made up from *atoms*. Atoms were constantly in motion, combining variously and then changing. Still, being does not come from non-being. Democritus trusted both the senses and the intellect.

Socrates of Athens: 469–399 BCE. While the forerunners of Socrates tried to solve the riddle of the universe with its diversity, Socrates probed the nature of human being and acting: ethics. He believed it to be axiomatic that a person would not knowingly commit a bad act. Consequently, *knowledge* is important because it leads to *good conduct*. One of his students committed treason, which challenged his idea about knowledge leading to good action. Socrates in the end was forced to drink the poisonous hemlock when he was charged with corrupting young people. The well known Plato was one of his notable students.

Antisthenes of Athens: *c*.445–365 BCE. A student of Socrates, Antisthenes gained great respect as a philosopher in the years following the death of his mentor. He continued to think about the meaning of *words*, and how words (logoi) related to reality. He viewed words as fluid in meaning, beyond definition. Antisthenes noted that a person has not only to know but also to be strong in character to do good. He encouraged physical exercise and refraining from opulence and pleasure.

Plato of Athens: *c*.427–347 BCE. He was a student of Socrates, but he drank from other philosophical wells. His philosophy has in it strong echoes of the ideas of Parmenides. He viewed the phenomenal world as shadow of the real world of *ideas*. This desk is recognized as such because the idea, 'desk', is prior to the material object in our consciousness. Plato's Republic argues that only the wise persons in the polis, who understand the dual nature of the cosmos, are capable of ruling the republic. Plato postulated that the human soul had prior existence in a better realm beyond the fallen world of the physical. Salvation involves the return of the human soul to that higher, better place. Christianity adapted aspects of Plato's thought to its theology. The notion and practice of Platonic love had, and has, its critics. Platonic love was homosexual, between teacher and student, purportedly for pedagogical purposes.

Diogenes of Sinope, modern Sinop in Turkey: *c*.412–323 BCE. A student of Antisthenes, Diogenes developed a philosophy known as *cynicism*. Cynicism espouses the simple life. Too much high culture robs the human spirit of true happiness. Nature provides the human person with the necessary qualities of the good life. Animals adhere to this by instinct. Humans should do so by reason. Things that prevent human happiness are the result of human structures, such as money, luxury and the like, and should be abandoned. The Cynics had a following, but their criticism of the state, such as that of Plato's Republic, could not prevail. They were seen as harmless, but not socially and politically realistic.

Aristotle of Stagira in Macedonia: *c.*384–322 BCE. Student of Plato and teacher of Alexander the Great, Aristotle was a scientist in his own right. Many of his writings are fragmentary. His lecture notes have survived. Investigations of Aristotle's extant writings indicate that he reworked his teacher's speculations into a more practical philosophy of reality. He is famous for defining the rules of logic, in his Prior Analytics. But his other works include Physics, Animal History, Rhetoric, Poetics, Metaphysics, Politics, and above all his Nicomachean *ethics*. It has become a truism to say that Aristotle is the most influential philosopher to the present time. To him may be ascribed the honour of founder of modern science.

Pyrrho of Elis, in Southern Greece: *c.*360–270 BCE. Pyrrho was not so confident that rational thinking led to truth. Knowledge could never be certain. Statements cannot be judged as absolutely true or false. This being so, an ethical system such as that of Aristotle is not possible. People would find greater fulfilment in giving up intellectual pursuits and postponing judgements. What he did not seem to recognize in his hypotheses was that he was using reason and knowledge to make the very judgements he claimed should be postponed. If certainty is impossible, how could he be so certain about uncertainty? Pyrrho is the founder of *scepticism*, and is sometimes called the prototype of postmodern thinking that came into the limelight in the 1980s.

Epicurus of Samos (island in the Aegean Sea): *c.*342–271 BCE. His is a happiness philosophy. Happiness is the greatest good of the human experience. Humans are happiest when they are free from suffering, much of which they bring on themselves. To obtain the goal of true happiness one should pursue the virtuous life. He had little space in his philosophy for the deities. He thought they were not interested in the wellbeing of humans. He would not speculate on life after death, since it was beyond his, or anyone else's grasp. Like the gods, life after death is an unknown. His philosophy was very popular, especially among the ordinary people. They understood it. Christian thinkers criticized *epicurism*, especially the scepticism about the afterlife.

Zeno of Citium, in Cyprus: *c.*336–264 BCE. Zeno put no stock in honour and status, common in the city states. He focused on personal peace, which came with letting go of striving for status. The theory was the espousal of apathia. The world for Zeno was ordered by the power of logos. The human mind should therefore order the emotions and the senses, as the logos harmonizes the universe. The philosophy is called *stoicism*.

Chrysippus of Soli, in Cilicia *c.*279–206 BCE. He became head of the school of Stoicism in Athens. He continued the study of logic with a particular focus on paradox, and on the proper construction of an argument. He proposed the allegorical reading of texts, such as those of Homer, maintaining that texts contain hidden meanings. Thus, the Iliad and the Odyssey became sources of philosophy. The allegorical method of reading flourished in Neo-Platonic Alexandria of Egypt in the centuries following Chrysippus. Witness the Jewish philosopher, Philo, of the first century CE, and the Christian theologian, Origen, of the third century CE. Chrysippus expanded the notion of the logos inhabiting the universe. If the universal logos could be construed as divine, then the cosmos must be a revelation of God. This doctrine entered Christianity, especially in the Johannine writings of the New Testament.

Posidonius of Apamea, in Syria: *c.*135–51 BCE: This man, few of whose works have survived, was often quoted by other writers. If there was such a thing as applied philosophy, this man was such. Head of the school of the Stoics in his time, he had read the science and theory of his predecessors and tried to put them to use. He wrote history, for example, in accordance with the rules of logic and investigation. He applied Stoic philosophy to human existence: emotions, ethics and peace. He was an educator of the many, applying the best from other philosophers. His successors in philosophy followed his example of blending ideas they judged to be good and true.

Apollonius of Tyana, in Cappadocia: first century CE. He has been called a 'charismatic teacher and miracle worker'. He put his own stamp on the earlier Pythagoreanism, combining it more or less with mysticism. He wrote books on astrology and on sacrifices. He did not believe in blood sacrifices, common in the ancient world. God was one, and required nothing from humans to sustain the divine being. Religious leaders took issue with Apollonius on this point. In the centuries following Apollonius was recognized as a great philosopher and teacher. Philostratus of Athens wrote a biography of the man. He has been compared to Jesus of Galilee who was also charismatic and performed miracles. Apollonius echoes some of the Psalms and Prophets of the Jewish Bible (Ps. 51.17; Micah 6.8).

Plutarch of Chaeronea, in Greece: *c.*46–122 CE. He was a priest at Delphi, but also a practical philosopher. He explained philosophical arguments and theories to a wide audience. He wrote on such moral issues as anger, the art of listening, virtue, advice to a bride and groom, among others. Plutarch wrote biographies of important, comparing one with the other. He explored the characters of the figures of history who made an impact on society and world. Readers were expected to reflect on the characters of the historical figures for their own moral benefit.

Epictetus of Phrygia: *c.*50–125 CE. In his younger life he became a slave in Nero's court, serving one Epaphroditus. When he was old he was set free, but without means of support. To make a living he taught the Stoic philosophy in Rome until Domitian had all philosophers expelled in 89. Thereafter he taught in Nicopolis, a city in western Greece. Epictetus explained Stoicism systematically and practically, and had many students, some from the rich, political sector of society. One of his students was Hadrian who later became emperor (117–138). Epictetus wrote a Handbook of philosophy, one of the most popular books of its time, or any time, on the subjects of philosophy.

Plotinus of Egypt: *c.*205–270 CE. Not much is known of his place of origin, but some accounts have him born in Lyco in Egypt. He studied and taught in Alexandria in Egypt, where attempts at a synthesis were already well under way. The writings of the Jewish Philo are a prime example. Moreover, the claim that Plotinus was the founder of Neo-Platonism needs some qualification. He did systematize a synthesis of the philosophies, but the practice was already happening before his time. Following Plato, Plotinus accepted that the created world is the product of a transcendent One; that the material part of the universe is a shadow of the realm of Ideas. That realm was another shadow of yet another higher world, which was a shadow of the transcendent Being. Altogether, then, there are four levels of reality in Plotinus' schema, with one God being the highest, then the intellect, then the soul and finally matter. In this schema the knowledgeable person would seek by ascetic, mystical practice to unite with the uppermost level, and thus find salvation. (It could be argued that Gnosticism found support for its doctrine in Plotinus). Christian thinkers, especially Ambrose and Augustine, adapted the philosophy of Plotinus to their understanding of the Christ and the Church. The school of Plotinus continued to be widely accepted until the twelfth and thirteenth centuries when the work of Aristotle was re-evaluated positively, as in the influential writings of St. Thomas Aquinas (*c.*1225–1274 CE).

Examples of Variants in the KJV that Lack Support

The following is taken from V. George Shillington, *Reading the Sacred Text*. (T & T Clark International, 2002), pp. 161–163:

Listed below are some well-known texts in the King James Version (KJV) New Testament that lack support in the better manuscripts now available. The newer versions in English have the emended text, or the KJV text set off in a footnote or a square bracket.

John 7.53–8.11, the text about the adulterous woman and Jesus writing in the sand, appears in the KJV. The pericopé seems to have existed in the early Jesus tradition, but was probably not published in the earliest text of the Fourth Gospel. It is missing from such important MSS as $P^{66, 75}$ ℵ B L N T W X Y Δ Θ Ψ 0141 0211 22 33 and many others. In deference to the possibility that this is a likely story from the tradition of Jesus, the UBS Greek New Testament has included it inside square brackets.

Mark 16.9-20 appears in the KJV, but is missing from the oldest and best manuscripts, ℵ and B, and from the writings of Clement and Origen, both of Alexandria. Eusebius and Jerome say that the passage is missing from the Greek MSS known to them. Some MSS include some words after verse 8, while others include other words. The most likely ending of Mark when it first circulated came at verse 8. Because of the rather negative tone of verse 8, and lack of a commission from the resurrected Jesus, copyists were inclined to bring the ending of Mark in line with the positive endings in other gospels. Mark 16.8 reads: *So they went out and fled from the tomb, for terror and amazement had seized them; and they said nothing to anyone, for they were afraid.*

1 John 5.7-8 contains the Trinitarian insert in the KJV: *in heaven, the Father, the Word, and the Holy Ghost: and these three are one. And there are three that bear witness in earth.* This insertion comes from a few late sources. It appears in some later copies of the Latin Vulgate and in a few Greek MSS that are translations out of late copies of the Latin Vulgate. It is certain that these Trinitarian words were not in the earliest text of 1 John.

Luke 2.14 has 'Glory to God in the highest, and on earth peace, good will toward men' in KJV. The NRSV has 'Glory to God in the highest heaven, and on earth peace among those whom he favors!' The difference comes from the ending of one Greek word, *eudokias*, rather than *eudokia*. The first is a genitive ending (NRSV) and the second a nominative (KJV). The genitive (NRSV) means that the peace comes to people of good will, or *those whom God favors*. The nominative means that peace and good will comes to everyone, good and bad. The genitive is supported by the oldest Greek MSS. The change may have happened as a result of oversight on the part of some copyists. In the days of uncial writing style, missing one letter, such as 'ς', at the end of a word was easy to do, especially so if the meaning made sense without the final letter.

Col. 1.14 in the KJV reads: In whom we have redemption *through his blood*, even the forgiveness of sins. The NRSV omits the phrase, *through his blood*, simply because it is not in the oldest and best MSS, such as ℵ and **P**⁴⁶. The omission is not (as some would have us believe) from a theological bent of the modern versions, but from lack of textual warrant. A later scribe may have inserted the phrase as a parallel to the same phrase in verse 20, attested in the most trustworthy MSS.

The Doxology of Romans is the last, and rather complicated, example of a difference between the KJV and the recent translations. The KJV has a benediction at Romans 16.24 followed by a doxology and second benediction (25-27), whereas the NRSV does not have verse 24, but does have verses 25-27. Some MSS have a benediction at the end of chapter 14 in addition to 16.24-27, and still others have a doxology at the end of chapter 15 but not after 16.23.

The variants in the MSS related to the ending of Romans can be grouped into five categories as follows:

(1) 1.1–16.23 + doxology (24-27)	**P**⁶¹ ℵ B C 81 1739, and some copies of the Vulgate, a Syriac and Coptic version.
(2) 1.1–14.23 + doxology + 15.1–16.23 + doxology	A P 5 33 104
(3) 1.1–14.23 + doxology + 15.1–16.24	L Ψ 0209 181 326 330 614 1175 and some translations.

(4) 1.1–16.24	F G 629
(5) 1.1–15.33 + doxology + 16.1-23	P[46]
(6) 1.1–14.23 +16.24 + doxology	Vulgate MSS, An Old Latin version.

In light of these variant endings to Romans, and in the knowledge that Marcion's Romans (*c.*150–175) did not have chapters 15 and 16, some scholars have judged that Paul wrote Romans (1) in two versions, a long one and a short one, (2) that chapter 16 was originally part of another letter, which was later attached to the ending of Romans. Whatever the literary argument, clearly there was some confusion on the part of the various copyists as to the placement of the doxology and benediction.

Bibliography

1. Commentaries

i. Gospels

Allison, Dale C. (2004). *Matthew: A Shorter Commentary*. Continuum International.

Barrett, C. K. (1955). *The Gospel According to St. John*. Westminster.

Barrett, C. K. (1978). *The Gospel According to St. John: An Introduction with Commentary and Notes*. Westminster/John Knox.

Beasley-Murray, G. R. (1987). *John*. Word Biblical Commentary. Word Books.

Boring, M. Eugene. (2006). *Mark: A Commentary*. Westminster/John Knox.

Bovon, François.(2002). *Luke 1: A Commentary on the Gospel of Luke 1:1–9:50*. Translated by Christine M. Thomas. Hermeneia. Fortress.

Brown, Raymond Edward. (1988). *The Gospel and Epistles of John: A Concise Commentary*. Liturgical.

Bruce, F. F. (1983). *The Gospel of John*. Eerdmans.

Bruner, Frederick Dale. (2004). *Matthew: A Commentary*. Eerdmans.

Bultmann, Rudolf Karl. (1971). *The Gospel of John: A Commentary*. Translated by George Raymond Beasley-Murray. Blackwell.

Cole, Robert Alan (1971). *Mark: An Introduction and Commentary*. Tyndale.

Collins, Adela Yarbro. (2007). *Mark: A Commentary*. Hermeneia. Fortress.

Davies, William David and Allison, Dale C. (1997). *A Critical and Exegetical Commentary on the Gospel According to Saint Matthew*. Continuum International.

Davies, William David and Allison, Dale C. (2004a). *A Critical and Exegetical Commentary on the Gospel According to Saint Matthew: 1–7*. Continuum International.

Davies, William David and Allison, Dale C. (2004b). *A Critical and Exegetical Commentary on the Gospel According to Saint Matthew: 19–28*. Continuum International.

Donahue, John R. and Harrington, Daniel J. (2005). *The Gospel of Mark*. Liturgical.

Edwards, James R. (2002). *The Gospel According to Mark*. Eerdmans.

Ellis, E. Earle (1981). *The Gospel of Luke*. Eerdmans.

Fowler, Robert M. (2001). *Let the Reader Understand: Reader–Response Criticism and the Gospel of Mark*. Continuum International.

France, R. T. (1985). *The Gospel According to Matthew: An Introduction and Commentary*. Eerdmans.

Gardner, Richard B. (1991). *Matthew*. Believers Church Bible Commentary. BCBC. Herald.

Geddert, Timothy J. (2001). *Mark*. BCBC. Herald.

Grayston, Kenneth. (1990). *The Gospel of John*. Narrative Commentaries. Trinity Press International.

Green, Joel B. (1997). *The Gospel of Luke*. Eerdmans.

Gundry, Robert H. (1994). *Matthew: A Commentary on his Handbook for a Mixed Church under Persecution*. Eerdmans.

Haenchen, Ernst. (1980). *John 1*. Hermeneia. Translated by Robert W. Funk. Fortress.

Haenchen, Ernst. (1984). *John 2*. Hermeneia. Translated by Robert W. Funk. Fortress.

Howcroft, Kenneth G. (2003). *The Gospel of Mark*. Epworth.

Johnson, Luke Timothy. (1991). *The Gospel of Luke*. Liturgical.

Keener, Craig S. (2003). *The Gospel of John: A Commentary*. Hendrickson.

Lincoln, Andrew T. (2005). *The Gospel According to Saint John*. Continuum International.

Long, Thomas G. (1997). *Matthew*. Westminster/John Knox.

Luz, Ulrich and Koester, Helmut. (1992). *Matthew 1–7*. Vol. 1. Hermeneia. Fortress.

Luz, Ulrich. (2001) *Matthew 8–20*. Translated by James E. Crouch, Vol. 2. Hermeneia. Fortress.

Luz, Ulrich. (2005). *Matthew 21–28*. Translated by James E. Crouch, Vol. 3. Hermeneia. Fortress.

Malina, Bruce J. and Rohrbaugh, Richard L. (1992). *Social-science Commentary on the Synoptic Gospels*. Fortress.

Malina, Bruce J. and Rohrbaugh, Richard L. (1998). *Social-science Commentary on the Gospel of John*. Fortress.

Marshall, Ian Howard. (1978). *The Gospel of Luke: A Commentary on the Greek Text*. Eerdmans.

Neyrey, Jerome H., ed. (2006). *The Gospel of John*. Cambridge University.

Patella, Michael. (2005). *The Gospel According to Luke*. Liturgical.

Raymond E. Brown. (1966–70). *The Gospel According to John: Introduction, Translation and Notes*. Anchor Bible. Doubleday.

Reicke, Bo Ivar. (1964). *The Gospel of Luke*. John Knox.

Reid, Barbara E. (2005).*The Gospel According to Matthew*. Liturgical.

Rhoads, David M. (2004). *Reading Mark, Engaging the Gospel*. Fortress.

Schnackenburg, Rudolf. (2002). *The Gospel of Matthew*. Translated by Robert R. Barr. Eerdmans.

Sloyan, Gerard. (1988). *John*. Interpretation. John Knox.

Talbert, Charles H. (1994). *Reading John: A Literary and Theological Commentary on the Fourth Gospel and the Johannine Epistles*. Crossroad.

Witherington, Ben. (2001). *The Gospel of Mark: A Socio-rhetorical Commentary*. Eerdmans.

ii. Acts

Bruce, F. F. (1988). *The Book of the Acts*. Eerdmans.

Fitzmyer, Joseph A. (1998). *The Acts of the Apostles*. Doubleday.

Gaventa, Beverley Roberts. (2003). *The Acts of the Apostles*. Abingdon.

Hamm, M. Dennis. (2005). *The Acts of the Apostles*. New Collegeville Bible Commentary. Liturgical.

Johnson, Luke Timothy. (1992). *The Acts of the Apostles*. Sacra Pagina.Vol. 1. Liturgical.

Johnson, Luke Timothy. (2006). *The Acts of the Apostles*. Sacra Pagina.Vol. 2. Liturgical.

Luedemann, Gerd. (1989). *Early Christianity According to the Traditions in Acts: A Commentary*. Translated by John Bowden. Fortress.

Marshall, I. Howard. (1980). *The Acts of the Apostles: An Introduction and Commentary*. Eerdmans.

Talbert, Charles H. (1997). *Reading Acts: A Literary and Theological Commentary on the Acts of the Apostles*. Crossroad Herder.

Tannehill, Robert C. (1994). *The Narrative Unity of Luke-Acts: A Literary Interpretation. Volume Two: The Acts of the Apostles*. Fortress.

Walaskay, Paul W. (1998). *Acts*. Westminster Bible Companion. Westminster/John Knox.

Willimon, William H. (1988). *Acts*. Interpretation. John Knox.

Witherington III, Ben. (1998). *The Acts of the Apostles: A Socio-rhetorical Commentary*. Eerdmans.

iii. The letters of Paul

Achtemeier, Paul J. (1985). *Romans*. Interpretation. Westminster/John Knox.

Barnett, Paul. (1997). *The Second Epistle to the Corinthians*. Eerdmans.

Barnett, Paul William. (1997). *2 Corinthians*. The New International Commentary on the New Testament. Eerdmans.

Barrett, C. K. (1968). *A Commentary on the First Epistle to the Corinthians*. Adam & Charles Black.

Barth, Karl. (1968). *The Epistle to the Romans*. Oxford.

Barth, Karl. (2002). *Epistle to the Philippians*. Translated by James W. Leitch. Westminster/John Knox.

Barton, Bruce B. (1995). *Philippians, Colossians, Philemon*. Tyndale House.

Belleville, Linda L. (1996). *2 Corinthians*. InterVarsity.

Betz, Hans Dieter. (1979). *Galatians*. Hermeneia. Fortress.

Betz, Hans Dieter. (1985). *2 Corinthians 8 and 9: A Commentary on Two Administrative Letters of the Apostle Paul*. Hermeneia. Fortress.

Bruce, F. F. (2007). *Romans*. Tyndale Commentaries. Eerdmans.

Carson, D. A. (1984). *From Triumphalism to Maturity: An Exposition of 2 Corinthians 10–13*. Baker Book House.

Cole, R. A. (1989). *The Letter of Paul to the Galatians: An Introduction and Commentary*. Eerdmans.

Collins, Raymond F. (1999). *First Corinthians*. Liturgical.

Conzelmann, Hans. (1975). *1 Corinthians*. Hermeneia. Fortress.

Cousar, Charles B. (2001). *Reading Galatians, Philippians, and 1 Thessalonians*. Smyth & Helwys.

Craddock, Fred B. (1985). *Philippians*. John Knox.

Danker, Frederick W. (1989). *II Corinthians*. Augsburg.

Dunn, James D. G. (1993). *The Epistle to the Galatians*. Hendrickson.

Esler, Philip F. (1998). *Galatians*. New Testament Readings. Routledge.

Fallon, Francis T. (1980). *2 Corinthians*. Michael Glazier.

Fee, Gordon D. (1987). *The First Epistle to the Corinthians*. Eerdmans.

Fee, Gordon D. (1999). *Philippians*. InterVarsity.

Fitzmyer, Joseph A. (1993). *Romans: A New Translation with Introduction and Commentary*. Anchor Bible. Doubleday.

Fowl, Stephen E. (2000). *Philippians*. Eerdmans.

Furnish, Victor Paul. (1984). *II Corinthians: Translated with Introduction, Notes, and Commentary*. Anchor. Doubleday.

Gaventa, Beverly Roberts. (1998). *First and Second Thessalonians*. John Knox.

Hays, Richard B. (1997). *First Corinthians*. Interpretation. John Knox.

Jewett, Robert. (2006). *Romans: A Commentary*. Hermeneia. Fortress.

Käsemann, Ernst. (1980). *Commentary on Romans*. Translated by Geoffrey W. Bromily. Eerdmans.

Keck. Leander E. (2005). *Romans*. Abingdon New Testament Commentary. Abingdon.

Lohse, Eduard. (1971). *Colossians and Philemon*. Translated by William R. Poehlmann and Robert J. Karris. Hermeneia. Fortress.

Martin, Ralph P. (2007). *Philippians*. InterVarsity.

Martyn, J. Louis. (1997). *Galatians: A New Translation with Introduction and Commentary*. Anchor. Doubleday.

McCant, Jerry W. (1999). *2 Corinthians*. Sheffield Academic.

Richard, Earl. (1995). *First and Second Thessalonians*. Liturgical.

Saunders, Ernest W. (1981). *1 Thessalonians, 2 Thessalonians, Philippians, Philemon*. John Knox.

Shillington, V. George. (1998). *2 Corinthians*. BCBC. Herald.

Stuhlmacher, Peter. (1994). *Paul's Letter to the Romans: A Commentary*. Translated by S. J. Hafemann. Westminster/John Knox.

Thiselton, Anthony C. (2000). *The First Epistle to the Corinthians: A Commentary on the Greek Text*. Eerdmans.

Toews, John E. (2004). *Romans*. BCBC. Herald.

Witherington, Ben. (1995). *Conflict and Community in Corinth: A Socio-rhetorical Commentary on 1 and 2 Corinthians*. Eerdmans.

Wright, N. T. (1988). *The Epistles of Paul to the Colossians and to Philemon*. Eerdmans.

Wright, N. T. (2004). *Paul for Everyone: The Prison Letters: Ephesians, Philippians, Colossians*. Westminster/John Knox.

iv. Post-Pauline letters/epistles

Achtemeier, Paul J. (1996). *1 Peter: A Commentary on First Peter*. Hermeneia. Fortress.

Bauckham, Richard. (1983). *Jude, 2 Peter*. Word Biblical Commentary. Word Books.

Best, Ernest, (1993). *Ephesians*. Continuum International.

Bruce, F. F. (1964). *The Epistle to the Hebrews*. NICNT (The New International Commmentary on the New Testament). Eerdmans.

Collins, Raymond F. (2002). *1 & 2 Timothy and Titus: A Commentary*. Westminster/John Knox.

Davids, Peter H. (1982). *The Epistle of James: A Commentary on the Greek Text*. Eerdmans.

Debelius, Martin. (1975). *James*. Revised by H. Greeven. Translated by M. Williams. Hermeneia. Fortress.

Debelius, Martin and Conzelmann, Hans. (1972). *Pastoral Epistles*. Hermeneia. Fortress.

Dodd, C. H. (1966). *The Johannine Epistles*. Hodder and Stoughton.

Elliott, John Hall. (2000). *1 Peter: A New Translation with Introduction and Commentary.* Anchor. Doubleday.

Green, Michael. (1987). *Second Peter and Jude.* Tyndale Commentaries. Eerdmans.

Hagner, Donald A. (1995). *Hebrews.* New International Biblical Commentary. Paternoster.

Hanson, Anthony Tyrrell. (1990). *The Pastoral Epistles.* HarperCollins.

Hanson, Anthony Tyrrell. (1996). *The Pastoral Epistles.* Eerdmans.

Hartin, Patrick J. (2003). *A Commentary on the Epistle of James.* Liturgical.

Hiebert, David Edmond. (1962). *An Introduction to the Non-Pauline Epistles.* Moody.

Johnson, Luke Timothy. (2006). *Hebrews: A Commentary.* Westminster/John Knox.

Kelly, J. N. D. (1993). *The Pastoral Epistles.* Black's New Testament Commentaries. Hendrickson.

Knight, Jonathan. (1995). *2 Peter and Jude.* Continuum International.

Krodel, Gerhard, ed. (1977). *Hebrews, James, 1 and 2 Peter, Jude, Revelation.* Proclamation Commentaries. Fortress.

Lane, William L. (1991). *Hebrews.* Word Biblical Commentary. Word Books.

Laws, Sophie. (1993). *The Epistle of James.* Black's New Testament Commentaries. Hendrickson.

Lock, Walter. (2000). *A Critical and Exegetical Commentary on the Pastoral Epistles: I & II Timothy and Titus.* Continuum International.

Long, Thomas G. (1997). *Hebrews.* Interpretation. John Knox.

MacDonald, Margaret Y. (2000). *Colossians and Ephesians.* Liturgical.

Marshall, I. Howard. (2004). *A Critical and Exegetical Commentary on the Pastoral Epistles.* Continuum International.

Mayor, Joseph B. (1913/1954). *The Epistle of St James : The Greek Text with Introduction, Notes and Comments, and Further Studies in the Epistle of St. James.* Zondervan.

Mills, Watson E. (2000). *General Epistles and Revelation.* Mercer Commentary on the Bible. Mercer University.

Mitton, C. Leslie. (1966). *The Epistle of James.* Marshall, Morgan & Scott.

Mitton, C. Leslie. (1989). *Ephesians: Based on the Revised Standard Version* Eerdmans.

Moffatt, James. (1942). *The General Epistles: James, Peter, and Judas.* Hodder and Stoughton.

Neufeld, Thomas R. (2002). *Ephesians.* BCBC. Herald.

O'Brien, Peter Thomas. (1994). *The Letter to the Ephesians.* Eerdmans.

Painter, John. (2002). *1, 2, and 3 John.* Liturgical.

Perkins, Pheme. (1995). *First and Second Peter, James and Jude.* Interpretation. John Knox.

Plummer, Alfred. (1894). *The Pastoral Epistles.* Hodder & Stoughton.

Rensberger, David. (2001). *The Epistles of John.* Westminster/John Knox.

Senior, Donald. (2003). *1 Peter.* Sacra Pagina. Liturgical.

Thurston, Bonnie Bowman. (1995). *Reading Colossians, Ephesians, and 2 Thessalonians: A Literary and Theological Commentary.* Crossroad.

v. Revelation

Boring, M. Eugene. (1989). *Revelation.* Interpretation. Westminster/John Knox.

Collins, Adela Yarbro. (1990). *The Apocalypse: A Biblical and Theological Commentary.* Liturgical.

Cory, Catherine A. (2006). *The Book of Revelation*. New Collegeville Bible Commentary. Liturgical.

Mounce, Robert H. (1997). *The Book of Revelation*. Eerdmans.

Schüssler Fiorenza, Elizabeth. (1991). *Revelation: Vision of a Just World*. Proclamation Commentaries. Fortress.

Talbert, Charles H. (1994). *The Apocalypse: A Reading of the Revelation of John*. Westminster/ John Knox.

Witherington, Ben. (2003). *Revelation*. The New Cambridge Bible Commentary. Cambridge University.

2. One volume commentaries

Brown, Raymond E., Fitzmyer, Joseph A. and Murphy, Roland E., eds (1990). *The New Jerome Biblical Commentary*. Prentice Hall.

Newsom, Carol Ann and Ringe, Sharon H. (1998). *Women's Bible Commentary*. Westminster/John Knox.

Radmacher, Earl, Allen, Ronald and House, Wayne, eds (1999). *Nelson's New Illustrated Bible Commentary*. Thomas Nelson.

3. Dictionaries, encyclopaedias and atlases

Achtemeier, Paul, ed. (1996). *HarperCollins Bible Dictionary*. Revised Edition. HarperSanFrancisco.

Ben-Dov, Meir. (2002). *Historical Atlas of Jerusalem*. Continuum International.

Bromiley, Geoffrey, ed. (1979–1988). *The International Standard Bible Encyclopaedia*. Revised Edition. 4 vols. Eerdmans.

Buttrick, George. (1962). *The Interpreter's Dictionary of the Bible: An Illustrated Encyclopaedia*. 4 vols. Abingdon.

Freedman, David, ed. (1992). *Anchor Bible Dictionary*. 6 vols. Doubleday.

Freedman, David, ed. (2000). *The Eerdmans Dictionary of the Bible*. Eerdmans.

Marshall, I. Howard, ed. (1996). *New Bible Dictionary*. Third Edition. Intervarsity.

May, Herbert. (1984). *Oxford Bible Atlas*. Third Edition. Oxford University.

Metzger, Bruce M. and Coogan, Michael, eds (1993). *The Oxford Companion to the Bible*. Oxford University.

Prichard, James. (1987). *The Harper Atlas of the Bible*. Harper.

Roth, Cecil and Wigoder, Geoffrey, eds (1970). *The New Standard Jewish Encyclopaedia*. Doubleday.

Sakenfeld, Katherine Doob, ed. (2006). *The New Interpreter's Dictionary of the Bible*. Vol. 1: A–C. Abingdon.

Skolnik, Fred, ed. (2006). *Encyclopaedia Judaica*. 22 vols. MacMillan.

Soulen, Richard N. (2001). *Handbook of Biblical Criticism*. Westminster/John Knox.

4. Journal articles

Aune, David E. (2006). 'The apocalypse of John and Palestinian Jewish apocalyptic'. *Neotestamentica*, 40 no. 1, 1–33.

Best, Thomas F. (1982). 'The Apostle Paul and E. P. Sanders: the significance of Paul and Palestinian Judaism'. *Restoration Quarterly*, 25 no. 2, 65–74.

Bruce, F. F. (1983). 'Some thoughts on the beginning of the New Testament canon'. *Bulletin of the John Rylands University Library of Manchester*, 65 no. 2, 37–60.

Burge, Gary M. (1984). 'A specific problem in the New Testament text and canon: the woman caught in adultery'. *Journal of the Evangelical Theological Society*, 27 no. 2, 141–148.

Chancey, Mark A. (2006). 'Paul and the Law: E P Sanders's retrieval of Judaism'. *Christian Century*, 123 no. 12, 20–23.

Chilton, Bruce D. (1988). 'Jesus and the repentance of E P Sanders'. *Tyndale Bulletin*, 39, 1–18.

Coggins, Richard J. (1982). 'The Samaritans and Acts'. *New Testament Studies*, 28 no. 3, 423–434.

Cohen, Shaye J. D. (1984). 'The significance of Yavneh: Pharisees, Rabbis, and the end of Jewish sectarianism'. *Hebrew Union College Annual*, 55, 27–53.

Cook, Michael J. (2006). 'Paul's argument in Romans 9–11'. *Review & Expositor*, 103 no. 1, 91–111.

Crossan, John Dominic. (2002). 'The parables of Jesus'. *Interpretation*, 56 no. 3, 247–259.

Dewey, Joanna. (1997). 'Women in the Synoptic Gospels: Seen but not Heard?'. *Biblical Theology Bulletin*, 27, 53–60.

Donfried, Karl P. (2007). 'Paul and the revisionists: did Luther really get it all wrong?' *Dialog*, 46 no. 1, 31–40.

Dunn, James D. G. (1982a). 'The relationship between Paul and Jerusalem according to Galatians 1 and 2'. *New Testament Studies*, 28 no. 4, 461–478.

Dunn, James D. G. (1982b). 'The authority of Scripture according to Scripture'. *Churchman*, 96 no. 2, 104–122.

Dunn, James D. G. (1983). 'The new perspective on Paul'. *Bulletin of the John Rylands University Library of Manchester*, 65 no. 2, 95–122.

Ellis, E. Earle. (1980). 'Dating the New Testament'. *New Testament Studies*, 26 no. 4, 487–502.

Espy, John M. (1985). 'Paul's "robust conscience" re-examined'. *New Testament Studies*, 31 no. 2, 161–188.

Fasching, Darrell J. (1985). 'Can Christian faith survive Auschwitz'. *Horizons*, 12 no. 1, 7–26.

Fowl, Stephen E. (1985). 'The canonical approach of Brevard Childs'. *Expository Times*, 96 no. 6, 173–176.

Freyne, Sean. (2001). 'The Geography of Restoration: Galilee–Jerusalem Relations in Early Jewish and Christian Experience'. *New Testament Studies* 47, 289–311.

Golb, Norman. (1985). 'Who hid the Dead Sea Scrolls'. *Biblical Archaeologist*, 48 no. 2, 68–82.

Grant, Robert M. (1982). 'Literary criticism and the New Testament canon'. *Journal for the Study of the New Testament*, no. 16, 24–44.

Gundry, Robert H. (1985). 'Grace, works, and staying saved in Paul'. *Biblica*, 66 no. 1, 1–38.

Hanhart, Karel. (1981). 'The four beasts of Daniel's vision in the night in the light of Rev 13:2'. *New Testament Studies*, 27 no. 4, 576–583.

Hickling, Colin J. A. (1983) 'John and Hebrews: the background of Hebrews 2:10–18'. *New Testament Studies*, 29 no. 1, 112–116.

Hock, Ronald F. (2002). 'Romancing the parables of Jesus'. *Perspectives in Religious Studies*, 29 no. 1, 11–37.

Hollenbach, Paul W. (1985) 'Liberating Jesus for social involvement'. *Biblical Theology Bulletin*, 15, 151–157.

Hooker, Morna D. (1981). 'Beyond the things that are written: St Paul's use of scripture'. *New Testament Studies*, 27 no. 3, 295–309.

Horrell, David. (2007). 'The label Christianos: 1 Peter 4:16 and the formation of Christian identity'. *Journal of Biblical Literature*, 126 no. 2, 361–381.

Howard, John M. (2006). 'The significance of minor characters in the Gospel of John'. *Bibliotheca Sacra*, 163 no. 649, 63–78.

Hultgren, Arland J. (1982). 'The Johannine footwashing (Jn 13:1–11) as symbol of eschatological hospitality'. *New Testament Studies*, 28 no. 4, 539–546.

John, V. J. (2000). 'Ecology in the parables: the use of nature language in the parables of the Synoptic Gospels'. *Asia Journal of Theology*, 14 no. 2, 304–327.

Johnson, E. S. (1979). 'Mark 8:22–26: the blind man from Bethsaida'. *New Testament Studies*, 25 no. 3, 370–383.

Kuhn, Karl A. (2006). '2 Peter 3:1–3'. *Interpretation*, 60 no. 3, 310–312.

Lea, Thomas D. (1984). 'The early Christian view of pseudepigraphic writings'. *Journal of the Evangelical Theological Society*, 27 no. 1, 65–75.

Lindars, Barnabas. (1981). 'John and the synoptic gospels: a test case'. *New Testament Studies*, 27 no. 3, 287–294.

Lowe, Malcolm. (1987). 'Real and imagined anti-Jewish elements in the Synoptic Gospels and Acts'. *Journal of Ecumenical Studies*, 24 no. 2, 267–284.

Lowe, Malcolm F. and Flusser, David (1983). 'Evidence corroborating a modified proto-Matthean synoptic theory'. *New Testament Studies*, 29 no. 1, 25–47.

Meyer, Ben F. (1983). 'The pre-Pauline formula in Rom 3:25–26a'. *New Testament Studies*, 29 no. 2, 198–208.

Miller, James C. (2007). 'The Jewish context of Paul's Gentile mission'. *Tyndale Bulletin*, 58 no. 1, 101–115.

Moloney, Francis J. (2005). 'The Gospel of John as scripture'. *Catholic Biblical Quarterly*, 67 no. 3, 454–468.

Morrison, Craig E. (2005). 'The "hour of distress" in Targum Neofiti and the "hour" in the Gospel of John'. *Catholic Biblical Quarterly*, 67 no. 4, 590–603.

Nolland, John. (1980). 'A fresh look at Acts 15:10'. *New Testament Studies*, 27 no. 1, 105–115.

Oakman, Douglas E. (1985). 'Jesus and agrarian Palestine: the factor of debt'. *Society of Biblical Literature Seminar Papers*, no. 24, 57–73.

Oropeza, B. J. (2007). 'Paul and theodicy: intertextual thoughts on God's justice and faithfulness to Israel in Romans 9–11'. *New Testament Studies*, 53 no. 1, 57–80.

Pamment, Margaret. (1983). 'The Son of Man in the First Gospel'. *New Testament Studies*, 29 no. 1, 116–129.

Phipps, William E. (1982). 'Is Paul's attitude toward sexual relations contained in 1 Cor. 7:1?' *New Testament Studies*, 28 no. 1, 125–131.

Reinhartz, Adele. (1999a). 'Introduction: "father" as metaphor in the fourth gospel'. *Semeia*, no. 85, 1–10.

Reinhartz, Adele. (1999b). ' "And the word was begotten": divine epigenesis in the Gospel of John'. *Semeia*, no. 85, 83–103.

Reinhartz, Adele. (2007). 'Why comment? Reflections on Bible commentaries in general and Andrew Lincoln's The Gospel according to Saint John in particular'. *Journal for the Study of the New Testament*, 29 no. 3, 333–342.

Ringe, Sharon H. (1999). 'Reading back, reading forward'. *Semeia*, no. 85, 189–194.

Shillington, V George. (1991). 'Paul's success in the conversion of gentiles: dynamic center in cultural diversity'. *Direction*, 20 no. 2, 125–134.

Shillington, V. George. (1998a). 'Atonement Texture in 1 Corinthians 5.5'. *Journal for the Study of the New Testament*, no. 71, 29–50.

Shillington, V. George. (1998b). 'The Lord's Supper: Believers Church perspectives '. *Journal of Mennonite Studies*, 16, 273–275.

Shillington, V. George. (2004). 'Significant Translation: exchange as literary–theological pattern in the Fourth Gospel'. *Direction*, 33 no. 2, 158–170.

Skaggs, Rebecca and Doyle, Thomas. (2007). 'Violence in the Apocalypse of John'. *Currents in Biblical Research*, 5 no. 2, 220–234.

Spencer, F Scott. (2005). ' "Follow me": the imperious call of Jesus in the Synoptic Gospels'. *Interpretation*, 59 no. 2, 142–153.

Stanton, Graham N. (1985). 'Aspects of early Christian–Jewish polemic and apologetic'. *New Testament Studies*, 31 no. 3, 377–392.

Stein, Robert H. (2000). ' "Saved by faith [alone]" in Paul versus "not saved by faith alone" in James'. *Southern Baptist Journal of Theology*, 4 no. 3, 4–19.

Theissen, Gerd. (2007). 'The new perspective on Paul and its limits: some psychological considerations'. *Princeton Seminary Bulletin*, 28 no. 1, 64–85.

Thiering, Barbara E. (1981). 'Qumran initiation and New Testament baptism'. *New Testament Studies*, 27 no. 5, 615–631.

Thiering, Barbara E. (1980). 'Inner and outer cleansing at Qumran as a background to New Testament baptism'. *New Testament Studies*, 26 no. 2, 266–277.

Tracy, Steven R. (2006). 'Domestic violence in the church and redemptive suffering in 1 Peter'. *Calvin Theological Journal*, 41 no. 2, 279–296.

Von Wahlde, Urban C. (1982). 'The Johannine "Jews": a critical survey'. *New Testament Studies*, 28 no. 1, 33–60.

Walker, William O. (1982). 'The Lord's Prayer in Matthew and in John'. *New Testament Studies*, 28 no. 2, 237–256.

Weiss, Herold. (1990). 'The Sabbath in the Synoptic Gospels'. *Journal for the Study of the New Testament*, no. 38, 13–27.

Wenham, John William. (1981). 'Synoptic independence and the origin of Luke's travel narrative'. *New Testament Studies*, 27 no. 4, 507–515.

Wilson, Todd A. (2006). 'The law of Christ and the law of Moses: reflections on a recent trend in interpretation'. *Currents in Biblical Research*, 5 no. 1, 123–144.

Ziesler, John A. (1979). 'Luke and the Pharisees'. *New Testament Studies*, 25 no. 2, 146–157.

5. General

Abegg, Martin, Flint, Peter and Ulrich, Eugene, eds (2002). *The Dead Sea Scrolls Bible*. HarperSanFrancisco.

Achtemeier, Paul J., Green, Joel B. and Thompson, Marianne Meye. (2001). *Introducing the New Testament: Its Literature and Theology*. Eerdmans.

Akurgal, Ekrem. (1967). *Treasures of Turkey*. Skira.

Annas, Julia. (2000). *Ancient Philosophy: A Very Short Introduction*. Oxford University.

Aristotle. (2000). *Politics*. Translated by Benjamin Jowett. Courier Dover Publications.

Atkins, E. Margaret and Osborne, Robin, eds (2006). *Poverty in the Roman World*. Cambridge University.

Aune, David E. (2006). *Apocalypticism, Prophecy and Magic in Early Christianity: Collected Essays*. Nohr Siebeck.

Aune, David E., ed. (2006). *Rereading Paul Together: Protestant and Catholic Perspectives on Justification*. Baker.

Badenas, Robert. (1985). *Christ the End of the Law: Romans 10:4 in Pauline Perspective*. JSNT Supplement Series 10. Sheffield University.

Barrett, C. K. (1995). *New Testament Background: Writings from Ancient Greece and the Roman Empire*. HarperSanFrancisco.

Bauer, Walter. (1972). *Orthodoxy and Heresy in Earliest Christianity*. SCM.

Baumgarten, Albert I., ed. (2000). *Apocalyptic Time*. Brill.

Beasley-Murray, G. R. (1991). *Gospel of Life: Theology in the Fourth Gospel*. Hendrickson

Beker, J. Christiaan. (1980). *The Apostle Paul: The Triumph of God in Life and Thought*. Fortress.

Beker, J. Christiaan. (1991). *Heirs of Paul: Paul's Legacy in the New Testament and in the Church Today*. Fortress.

Blessing, Charles A. (1973). *The Form of Cities in Perspective. The Graeco-Roman World – 500 B.C. to A. D. 200*. Center for Coördination of Ancient and Modern Studies. University of Michigan.

Boccaccini, Gabrielle. (1998). *Beyond the Essene Hypothesis*. Eerdmans.

Bornkamm, Günther. (1995). *Paul*. Translated by D. M. G. Stalker. Fortress.

Boyarin, Daniel. (2006). *Border Lines: The Partition of Judaeo-Christianity*. University of Pennsylvania.

Branick, Vincent P. (1998). *Understanding the New Testament and its Message: An Introduction.* Paulist.

Brown, Raymond E. (1979). *The Community of the Beloved Disciple.* Paulist.

Brown, Raymond E. (1986). *A Crucified Christ in Holy Week: Essays on the Four Gospel Passion Narratives.* Liturgical.

Brown, Raymond E. (1997). *An Introduction to the New Testament.* Doubleday.

Brown Raymond E. (2003). *An Introduction to the Gospel of John.* Yale University.

Brown, Raymond E. and Meier, John P. (1983). *Antioch and Rome: New Testament Cradles of Catholic Christianity.* Paulist.

Brueggemann, Walter. (2002). *The Land: Place as Gift, Promise, and Challenge in Biblical Faith.* Second Edition. Augsburg Fortress.

Campbell, W. S., Hawkins, P. and Schildgen, B. D., eds (2007). *Medieval Readings of Romans.* Series: Romans Through History and Cultures. T&T Clark International.

Carson, D. A., Moo, Douglas J. and Morris, Leon. (1992). *An Introduction to the New Testament.* Zondervan.

Casey, Maurice. (1991). *From Jewish Prophet to Gentile God: The Origins and Development of New Testament Christology.* Westminster/John Knox.

Charlesworth, James, ed. (1990). *John and the Dead Sea Scrolls.* Crossroad.

Charlesworth, James, ed. (1992). *Jesus and the Dead Sea Scrolls.* Doubleday.

Childs, Brevard S. (1984). *The New Testament as Canon: An Introduction.* Fortress.

Chilton, Bruce. (1986). *Beginning New Testament Study.* Eerdmans.

Chilton, Bruce. (1996). *Pure Kingdom: Jesus' Vision of God.* Eerdmans.

Chilton, Bruce and Evans, Craig A., eds (2002). *Authenticating the Words of Jesus.* Brill.

Cohen, Jeffrey. (1996). *Blessed are You.* Jason Aronson

Collins, Adela Yarbro. (1984). *Crisis and Catharsis: The Power of the Apocalypse.* Westminster/John Knox.

Collins, John Joseph. (1979). *Apocalypse: The Morphology of a Genre.* Scholars.

Collins, John Joseph. (1998). *The Apocalyptic Imagination: An Introduction to Jewish Apocalyptic Literature.* Eerdmans.

Collins, Raymond F. (1987). *Introduction to the New Testament.* Doubleday.

Cox, Stephen. (2005). *The New Testament and Literature: A Guide to Literary Patterns.* Open Court.

Crosby, Michael H. (2004). *House of Disciples: Church Economics and Justice in Matthew.* Wipf & Stock.

Cross, Frank. (1995). *The Ancient Library of Qumran and Modern Biblical Studies.* Third Edition. Fortress.

Crossan, John Dominic. (1991). *The Historical Jesus: The Life of a Mediterranean Jewish Peasant.* HarperSanFrancisco.

Crossan, John Dominic. (1992). *In Parables.* Polebridge.

Crossan, John Dominic and Reed, Jonathan L. (2002). *Excavating Jesus,* Revised and Updated. Harper Collins.

Culpepper, R. Alan. (1983). *Anatomy of the Fourth Gospel: A Study in Literary Design*. Fortress.

Davies, W. D. (1974). *The Gospel and the Land: Early Christianity and Jewish Territorial Doctrine*. University of California.

Davies, W. D. (1989). *The Setting of the Sermon on the Mount*. (186 Brown Judaic Studies). Scholars.

Dix, Gregory. (1953). *Jew and Greek: A Study in the Primitive Church*. Dacre.

Dodd, C. H. (1953). *The Interpretation of the Fourth Gospel*. Cambridge University.

Dodd, C. H. (1961). *The Parables of Jesus*. Charles Scribner's Sons.

Donaldson, Terrance L. (1997). *Paul and the Gentiles: Remapping the Apostle's Convictional World*. Fortress.

Donfried, Karl P., ed. (1991). *The Romans Debate*. Hendrickson.

Drane, John. (2001). *Introducing the New Testament*. Fortress.

Duke, Paul. (1985). *Irony in the Fourth Gospel*. John Knox.

Dungan, David L. (1999). *A History of the Synoptic Problem*. Doubleday.

Dunn, James D. G. (1992). *The Partings of the Ways: Between Christianity and Judaism and Their Significance for the Character of Christianity*. Continuum International.

Dunn, James D. G. (1996). *Christology in the Making: A New Testament Inquiry into the Origins of the Doctrine of the Incarnation*. Eerdmans.

Dunn, James D. G., ed. (1999). *Jews and Christians: The Parting of the Ways A. D. 70 to 135*. Eerdmans.

Eakin, Frank. (2005). *Getting Acquainted with the New Testament*. Kessinger.

Efird, James M. (1980). *The New Testament Writings*. Westminster/John Knox.

Ehrensperger, Kathy. (2007). *Paul and the Dynamics of Power: Communication and Interaction in the Early Christ-Movement*. T&T Clark International.

Ehrman, Bart D. (2007). *The New Testament: A Historical Introduction to the Early Christian Writings*. Oxford University.

Elliott, James Keith. (2005). *The Apocryphal New Testament: A Collection of Apocryphal Christian Literature in an English Translation*. Oxford University.

Elliott, Neil. (1994). *Liberating Paul: The Justice of God and the Politics of the Apostle*. Orbis.

Engberg-Pederson, Troels, ed. (1994). *Paul in his Hellenistic Context*. T & T Clark.

Esler, Philip Francis. (1987). *Community and Gospel in Luke-Acts. The Social and Political Motivations of Lukan Theology*. Cambridge University.

Esler, Philip Francis. (2003). *Conflict and Identity in Romans: The Social Setting of Paul's Letter*. Fortress.

Eusebius. (1998). *Ecclesiastical History: Complete and Unabridged*. Translated and edited by Christian F. Cruse. Hendrickson.

Evans, Craig A. and Porter, Stanley E., eds (1995). <u>*The Synoptic Gospels: A Sheffield Reader*</u>. Sheffield Academic.

Farmer, William R. (1976). *The Synoptic Problem: A Critical Analysis*. Mercer University.

Finley, Moses. (1983). *Politics in the Ancient World*. Cambridge University.

Fiorenza, Elizabeth Schüssler. (1998). *In Memory of Her: A Feminist Theological Reconstruction of Christian Origins*. Crossroad.

Fortna, Robert T. and Gaventa, Beverly R., eds (1990). *The Conversation Continues: Studies in Paul and John.* Abingdon.

Fowl, Stephen. (1998). *Engaging Scripture.* Blackwell.

Fredriksen, Paula. (1988). *From Jesus to Christ.* Yale University.

Frend, W. H. C. (1965). *The Early Church.* Fortress.

Freyne, Sean. (1998). *Galilee: From Alexander the Great to Hadrian 323 BCE to 135 CE: A Study of Second Temple Judaism.* Continuum International.

Freyne, Sean. (2002). *Texts, Contexts and Cultures.* Veritas.

Freyne, Sean. (2005). *Jesus, a Jewish Galilean.* London: T & T Clark International.

Funk, Robert W. (1985). *New Gospel Parallels.* Fortress.

Furnish, Victor Paul. (1993). *Jesus According to Paul.* Cambridge.

Gager, John G. (2000). *Reinventing Paul.* Oxford University.

Glancy, Jennifer A. (2002). *Slavery in Early Christianity.* Oxford University.

Goehring, James E., Hedrick, Charles W., Sanders, Jack T. and Betz, Hans Dieter, eds (1990). *Gospel Origins & Christian Beginnings.* Polebridge.

Goodacre, Mark S. (2002). *The Case against Q: Studies in Markan Priority and the Synoptic Problem.* Trinity Press International.

Goppelt, Leonhard. (1982). *Typos: The Typological Interpretation of the Old Testament in the New.* Translated by Donald H. Madvig. Eerdmans.

Gordley, Matthew E. (2007). *The Colossian Hymn in Context.* Mohr Siebeck.

Gorman, Michael J. (2007). *Reading Paul.* Wipf & Stock.

Grant, Robert M. (2001). *Paul in the Roman World.* Westminster/John Knox.

Hanson, Paul D. (1979). *The Dawn of Apocalyptic.* Fortress.

Harding, Mark, ed. (2003). *Early Christian Life and Thought in Social Context: A Reader.* Continuum International.

Harrison, Everett F. (1964). *Introduction to the New Testament.* Eerdmans.

Hay, David M. and Johnson, E. Elizabeth, eds (1995). *Pauline Theology: Romans.* Vol. III. Fortress.

Hayes, John H. and Carl R. Holladay. (2007). *Biblical Exegesis: A Beginner's Handbook.* Third Edition. Westminster/John Knox.

Hellholm, David, ed. (1989). *Apocalypticism in the Mediterranean World and the Near East.* Mohr Siebeck.

Hengel, Martin. (1977). *Crucifixion.* Translated by John Bowden. Fortress.

Hengel, Martin. (1979). *Acts and the History of Earliest Christianity.* Translated by John Bowden. SCM

Hengel, Martin. (1983). *Between Jesus and Paul.* Translated by John Bowden. Fortress.

Herzog II, William R. (1994). *Parables as Subversive Speech: Jesus as Pedagogue of the Oppressed.* Westminster/John Knox.

Hiebert, D. Edmond. (1962). *An Introduction to the Non-Pauline Epistles.* Moody.

Hooker, Morna. (1986). *Continuity and Discontinuity: Early Christianity in its Jewish Setting.* Epworth.

Horrell, David G. (2006). *An Introduction to the Study of Paul.* Second Edition. Continuum International.

Horsley, Richard A. (1996). *Archaeology, History and Society in Galilee: The Social Context of Jesus and the Rabbis.* Trinity Press International.

Horsley, Richard A., ed. (1997). *Paul and Empire: Religion and Power in Roman Imperial Society.* Trinity International.

Horsley, Richard A. and Silberman, Neil Asher. (2002). *The Message and the Kingdom: How Jesus and Paul Ignited a Revolution and Transformed the Ancient World.* Fortress.

Horsley, Richard A., Draper, Jonathan A., Foley, John Miles and Kelber, Werner H. (2006). *Performing the Gospel: Orality, Memory, and Mark.* Fortress.

Hübner, Hans. (1984). *Law in Paul's Thought.* T & T Clark.

Irwin, Terence. (1989). *Classical Thought.* Oxford University.

Issak, Jonathan M. (2002). *Situating the Letter to the Hebrews in Early Christian History.* Studies in Bible and Early Christianity, Vol. 53. Edwin Mellen.

Jeremias, Joachim. (1966). *The Eucharistic Words of Jesus.* Translated by Norman Perrin. SCM.

Jeremias, Joachim. (1972). *The Parables of Jesus.* Translated by S. H. Hooke. Charles Scribner's Sons.

Jeremias, Joachim. (1982). *Jesus' Promise to the Nations.* Translated by S. H. Hooke. Fortress.

Johns, Loren L. (2003). *The Lamb Christology of the Apocalypse of John.* Mohr Siebeck.

Johnson, Luke Timothy. (1986). *The Writings of the New Testament: An Interpretation.* Fortress.

Johnson, Luke Timothy. (2004). *Brother of Jesus, Friend of God: Studies in the Letter of James.* Eerdmans.

Jones, Arnold H. (1971). *The Cities of the Eastern Roman Provinces.* Clarendon.

Josephus, Flavius. (1999). *The New Complete Works of Josephus.* Translated by William Whiston. Kregel Publications.

Käsemann, Ernst. (1969). *New Testament Questions for Today.* SCM.

Käsemann, Ernst. (1971). *Perspectives on Paul.* Translated by Margaret Kohl. Fortress.

Käsemann, Ernst. (1984). *The Wandering People of God: An Investigation of the Letter to the Hebrews.* Augsburg.

Keck, Leander E. and Martyn, J. Louis, eds (1966). *Studies in Luke-Acts.* Abingdon.

Keefer, Kyle, ed. (2007). *The New Testament As Literature: A Very Short Introduction.* Oxford University.

Kingsbury, Jack Dean. (1975). *Matthew: Structure, Christology, Kingdom.* Fortress.

Kloppenborg, John S. (2006). *The Tenants in the Vineyard: Ideology, Economics, and Agrarian Conflict in Jewish Palestine.* Mohr Siebeck.

Knox, John. (1959). *Philemon Among the Letters of Paul: A New View of Its Place and Importance.* Abingdon.

Koester, Helmut. (1995). *Introduction to the New Testament.* Walter de Gruyter.

Kraybill, J. Nelson. (1996). *Imperial Cult and John's Apocalypse.* Sheffield Academic.

Kümmel, Werner G. (1975). *Introduction to the New Testament.* Translated by Howard Clark Kee. Abingdon.

Kysar, Robert. (1984). *John's Story of Jesus.* Fortress,

Levick, Barbara. (2000). *The Government of the Roman Empire: A Sourcebook.* Routledge.

Levine, Amy-Jill. (2006). *The Misunderstood Jew: The Church and the Scandal of the Jewish Jesus.* HarperSanFrancisco.

Levine, Amy-Jill, ed. (2002). *A Feminist Companion to Luke.* Continuum International.

Levine, Amy-Jill, ed. (2003). *A Feminist Companion to John,* Vol. II. Continuum International.

Lincoln, Andrew T. and Wedderburn, A. J. M. (1993). *The Theology of the Later Pauline Letters.* Cambridge University.

Lindars, Barnabas. (1991). *The Theology of the Letter to the Hebrews.* Cambridge University.

Lindsey, Hal with Carlson, Carole C. (1970). *The Late Great Planet Earth.* Zondervan.

Lonergan, Berrnard J. F. (1972). *Method in Theology.* Herder and Herder.

Luedemann, Gerd. (1984). *Paul, Apostle to the Gentiles: Studies in Chronology.* Translated by F. Stanley Jones. Fortress.

Luz, Ulrich. (1995). *The Theology of the Gospel of Matthew.* Translated by Bradford Robinson. Cambridge University.

Malina, Bruce J. (1993a). *The New Testament World: Insights from Cultural Anthropology.* Revised Edition. Westminster/John Knox.

Malina, Bruce J. (1993b). *Windows on the World of Jesus: Time Travel to Ancient Judea.* Westminster/John Knox.

Malina, Bruce J. and Neyrey, Jerome H. (1996). *Portraits of Paul: An Archaeology of Ancient Personality.* Westminster/John Knox.

Martinez, Florentino Garcia. (1996). *The Dead Sea Scrolls Translated: The Qumran Texts in English.* Translated by W. G. Watson. Eerdmans.

Martyn, J. Louis. (1997). *Theological Issues in the Letters of Paul.* Continuum International.

Martyn, J. Louis. (2003). *History and Theology in the Fourth Gospel.* Westminster/John Knox.

Mazzaferri, Frederick David (1989). *The Genre of the Book of Revelation from a Source–Critical Perspective.* Walter de Gruyter.

McGinn, Sheila E. (2005). *Celebrating Romans: Template for Pauline Theology.* Eerdmans.

Meeks, Wayne A. (2003). *The First Urban Christians.* Revised. Yale University.

Metzger, Bruce M. (1965). *The New Testament: Its Background, Growth and Content.* Abingdon.

Meyer, Ben F. (1986). *The Early Christians: Their World Mission and Self-discovery.* Michael Glazier.

Meyer, Ben F. (1994). *Reality and Illusion in New Testament Scholarship: A Primer in Critical Realist Hermeneutics.* Liturgical.

Miller, Robert J., ed. (1994). *The Complete Gospels.* Polebridge.

Mitchell, Margaret M. (1991). *Paul and the Rhetoric of Reconciliation: An Exegetical Investigation of the Language and Composition of 1 Corinthians.* Westminster/John Knox.

Moyise, Steve. (2004). *Introduction to Biblical Studies.* Second Edition. T & T Clark International.

Murphy-O'Connor, Jerome. (1983). *St. Paul's Corinth: Texts and Archaeology.* Michael Glazier.

Nanos, Mark D. (1996). *The Mystery of Romans: The Jewish Context of Paul's Letter.* Fortress.

Nanos, Mark D. (2002a). *The Irony of Galatians: Paul's Letter in first Century Context.* Fortress.

Nanos, Mark D., ed. (2002b). *The Galatians Debate: Contemporary Issues in Rhetorical and Historical Interpretation.* Hendrickson.

Neusner, Jacob. (1986). *Judaism in the Matrix of Christianity.* Fortress.

Neusner , Jacob. (1994). *Rabbinic Literature and the New Testament.* Trinity Press International.

Neusner, Jacob. (trans.1988). *The Mishnah: A New Translation.* Yale University.

Neyrey, Jerome H. (1990). *Reading Paul in Other Words: A Culture Reading of His Letters.* Westminster/John Knox.

Neyrey, Jerome, ed. (1991). *The Social World of Luke-Acts: Models for Interpretation.* Hendrickson.

Nickle, Keith F. (2001). *The Synoptic Gospels: An Introduction.* Revised and Expanded. John Knox.

Perrin, Norman and Duling, Dennis C. (1982). *The New Testament: An Introduction.* Second Edition. Harcourt Brace Jovanovich.

Petersen, Norman R. (1993). *The Gospel of John and the Sociology of Light.* Trinity Press International.

Porter, Stanley E., ed. (2007). *The Messiah in the Old and New Testaments.* Eerdmans.

Ramsay, William Mitchell. (1908). *The Cities of St. Paul: Their Influence on His Life and Thought.* A. C. Armstrong.

Reed, Jonathan L. (2000). *Archaeology and the Galilean Jesus: A Re-examination of the Evidence.* Continuum.

Reicke, Bo. (1968). *The New Testament Era: The World of the Bible from 500 B. C. to A. D. 100.* Translated by David E. Green. Fortress.

Reinhartz, Adele. (2001). *Befriending the Beloved Disciple: A Jewish Reading of the Gospel of John.* Continuum International.

Rensberger, David. (1996). *Johannine Faith and Liberating Community.* Westminster/John Knox.

Richard B. Hays. (1989). *Echoes of Scripture in the Letters of Paul.* Yale University.

Richardson, Peter and Hurd, John C., eds (1984). *From Jesus to Paul.* Wilfrid Laurier University.

Richardson, Peter, Granskou, David M. and Wilson, Stephen G. (1986). *Anti-Judaism in Early Christianity.* Wilfrid Laurier University.

Riches, John K., Telford, William, Tuckett, C. M and McKnight, Scot. (2001). *The Synoptic Gospels.* Sheffield Academic.

Rives, James. (2006). *Religion in the Roman Empire.* Blackwell.

Rivkin, Ellis. (1984). *What Crucified Jesus?* SCM.

Robbins, Vernon K. (1996a). *Exploring the Texture of Texts.* Trinity Press International.

Robbins, Vernon K. (1996b). *The Tapestry of Early Christian Discourse: Rhetoric, Society and Ideology.* Routledge.

Robinson, James M. (2002). *The Sayings of Jesus: The Sayings Gospel Q in English.* Fortress.

Robinson, James M. (2005). *The Sayings Gospel Q.* Peeters.

Robinson, James M., ed. (1984). *The Nag Hammadi Library in English.* Brill.

Robinson, James M. and Koester, Helmut. (1971). *Trajectories through Early Christianity.* Fortress.

Roetzel, Calvin J. (1998). *The Letters of Paul: Conversations in Context.* Westminster/John Knox.

Roetzel, Calvin J. (2003). *Paul, a Jew on the Margins.* Westminster/John Knox.

Rousseau, John J. and Arav, Rami. (1995). *Jesus and His World: An Archaeological and Cultural Dictionary.* Augsburg Fortress.

Rudolph, Kurt. (1998). *Gnosis: The Nature and History of Gnosticism.* Continuum International.

Salmon, Edward Togo. (1968). *A History of the Roman World from 30 B. C. to A. D. 138.* Routledge.

Sanders, E. P. (1977). *Paul and Palestinian Judaism.* Fortress.

Sanders, E. P. (1983). *Paul, the Law and the Jewish People*. Fortress.

Sanders, E. P. (1985). *Jesus and Judaism*. Fortress.

Sanders, E. P. (2001). *Paul: A Very Short Introduction*. Oxford University.

Sanders, E. P. and Davies, Margaret. (1989). *Studying the Synoptic Gospels*. Trinity Press International.

Sandmel, Samuel. (1978). *Anti-Semitism in the New Testament?* Fortress.

Sandmel, Samuel. (1979). *The Genius of Paul*. Fortress.

Sanneh, Lamin. (1989). *Translating the Message: The Missionary Impact on Culture*. Orbis.

Santos, Narry F. (2003). *Slave of All: The Paradox of Authority and Servanthood in the Gospel of Mark*. Continuum International.

Scholz, Susanne, ed. (2003). *Biblical Studies Alternatively: An Introductory Reader*. Prentice Hall.

Schweitzer, Albert. (1912). *Paul and His Interpreters: A Critical History*. Translated by William Montgomery. A. and C. Black.

Schweitzer, Albert. (2001). *The Quest of the Historical Jesus. The First Complete Edition*. Edited by John Bowden. Fortress.

Schweizer, Eduard. (1991). *A Theological Introduction to the New Testament*. Translated by O. C. Dean. Abingdon.

Shillington, V. George. (2002). *Reading the Sacred Text: An Introduction to Biblical Studies*. Continuum International.

Shillington, V. George. (2007). *An Introduction to the Study of Luke-Acts*. Continuum International.

Shillington, V. George, ed. (1997). *Jesus and His Parables*. Edinburgh: T & T Clark.

Siker, Jeffrey S. (1991). *Disinheriting the Jews: Abraham in Early Christian Controversy*. Westminster/John Knox.

Stemberger, Günter. (1995). *Jewish Contemporaries of Jesus: Pharisees, Sadducees, Essenes*. Fortress.

Stendahl, Krister. (1976). *Paul among Jews and Gentiles*. Fortress.

Strabo. (1917–1932). *Geography*. Loeb Classical Library, 8 vols. Translated by Horace L. Jones. Harvard University.

Suetonius. (2000). *Lives of the Caesars*. Translated by Catharine Edwards. Oxford University.

Tacitus, P. Cornelius. (2004). *The Annals*. Translated by Alfred J. Church and William J. Broadribb. Kessinger.

Tannehill, Robert C. (1994). *The Narrative Unity of Luke-Acts: a Literary Interpretation*. Fortress.

Tarazi, Paul Nadim. (1999). *The New Testament: An Introduction, Luke and Acts*. St Vladimir's Seminary.

Theissen, Gerd. (1978). *Sociology of Early Palestinian Christianity*. Translated by John Bowden. Fortress.

Theissen, Gerd. (1982). *The Social Setting of Pauline Christianity*. Translated by John H. Schütz. Fortress.

Theissen, Gerd. (2003). *Fortress Introduction to the New Testament*. Translated by John Bowden. Fortress.

Thiessen, Henry C. (1947). *Introduction to the New Testament*. Eerdmans.

Thompson, Marianne Meye. (1988). *The Humanity of Jesus in the Fourth Gospel*. Fortress.

Throckmorton, Burton H. (1992). *Gospel Parallels*, NRSV Edition. Nelson.

Toews, John E., Rempel, Valerie and Wiebe, Kate Funk, eds (1992). *Your Daughters Shall Prophesy: Women in Ministry in the Church.* Kindred Productions.

Toombs, Lawrence E. (1960). *The Threshold of Christianity: Between the Testaments.* Westminster.

Vermes, Geza. (1983). *Jesus and the World of Judaism.* Fortress.

Vermes, Geza. (2000). *An Introduction to the Complete Dead Sea Scrolls.* Third Edition. Fortress.

Watson, Duane Frederick. (2002). *The Intertexture of Apocalyptic Discourse in the New Testament.* Brill.

Westerholm, Stephen. (1988). *Israel's Law and the Church's Faith: Paul and His Recent Interpreters.* Eerdmans.

Westerholm, Stephen. (2004). *Perspectives Old and New on Paul: The 'Lutheran' Paul and His Critics.* Eerdmans.

White, L. Michae. (2004). *From Jesus to Christianity.* HarperSanFrancisco.

Wire, Antoinette Clark. (1995). *The Corinthian Women Prophets: A Reconstruction through Paul's Rhetoric.* Fortress.

Wright, N. T. (1996). *Jesus and the Victory of God.* Fortress.

Young, Frances Margaret. (1994). *The Theology of the Pastoral Epistles.* Cambridge University.

Zerbe, Gordon M. (1993). *Non-retaliation in Early Jewish and New Testament Texts: Ethical Themes in Social Context.* Continuum International.

Ziesler, J. A. (1983). *Pauline Christianity.* Revised Edition. Oxford University.

Index of Biblical References

Index of Subjects and Authors